Bread and Autocracy

Bread and Autocracy

Food, Politics, and Security in Putin's Russia

JANETTA AZARIEVA, YITZHAK M. BRUDNY,
AND EUGENE FINKEL

OXFORD
UNIVERSITY PRESS

Oxford University Press is a department of the University of Oxford. It furthers
the University's objective of excellence in research, scholarship, and education
by publishing worldwide. Oxford is a registered trade mark of Oxford University
Press in the UK and certain other countries.

Published in the United States of America by Oxford University Press
198 Madison Avenue, New York, NY 10016, United States of America.

© Oxford University Press 2023

All rights reserved. No part of this publication may be reproduced, stored in
a retrieval system, or transmitted, in any form or by any means, without the
prior permission in writing of Oxford University Press, or as expressly permitted
by law, by license, or under terms agreed with the appropriate reproduction
rights organization. Inquiries concerning reproduction outside the scope of the
above should be sent to the Rights Department, Oxford University Press, at the
address above.

You must not circulate this work in any other form
and you must impose this same condition on any acquirer.

Library of Congress Control Number: 2023940948

ISBN 978-0-19-768437-5 (pbk.)
ISBN 978-0-19-768436-8 (hbk.)

DOI: 10.1093/oso/9780197684368.001.0001

Paperback printed by Marquis Book Printing, Canada
Hardback printed by Bridgeport National Bindery, Inc., United States of America

To Leon J.A.

To Noa and Ethan Y.B

Contents

Acknowledgments ix

    Introduction: Russia's Nutritional Autocracy   1

1. The Starving Empire: Food and Politics in the USSR   19
2. Food and Market: The Hungry, 1991–1993   36
3. Farmers Will Not Feed Russia: The Failure of Yeltsin's Agrarian Reforms   49
4. The Rise of Grain, 2000–2010   64
5. Food, Security, and Food Security   85
6. Sanctions and Countersanctions   101
7. Top Feeders: The Government and Russia's Agro-Capitalism   115
8. The COVID-19 Food Crisis, 2020–2021   131
9. The War in Ukraine and Russia's Food Politics   147
10. Conclusion   160

Notes 169
Bibliography 209
Index 235

Acknowledgments

This project has its origins in Janetta Azarieva's doctoral thesis "Grain and Power in Russia, 2001–2011" (The Hebrew University of Jerusalem, 2015), co-supervised by Yitzhak Brudny and Zvi Lerman. In the following years, the scope of the research was greatly expanded. The ongoing war in Ukraine has shown the great relevance of our project for understanding the nature of Russian authoritarianism.

Writing a book during the COVID-19 pandemic became a solitary experience, punctuated by Zoom meetings, conducted mostly from our attics and basements. Yet even during a global pandemic one does not write a book alone. In the process of research and writing this book we greatly benefited from advice of our colleagues in Israel, United States, Russia, and Ukraine. We thank them for all their time and knowledge helping us to advance the project. We are grateful to Susan Wengle who shared parts of her most recent research on Russia's food production and to Jessica Fanzo, Jeff Kopstein, Dan Miodownik, Eitan Alimi, and Gulnaz Sharafutdinova for their support, advice, and comments on various parts of the projects. Peter Rutland took the time to read the entire manuscript and offered many helpful suggestions. Our special thanks to Connie Hachbarth and Amina Frassl who selflessly edited many chapters of this book. David McBride at Oxford University Press was an enthusiastic believer in this project from its early stages. We also thank the anonymous reviewers for their comments and critiques.

Parts of this manuscript and our arguments about the general connection between food and autocracy have been published in several outlets. We thank Tarek Masoud and Will Dobson for inviting us to contribute to the *Journal of Democracy* and their comments on our paper "Bread and Autocracy in Russia," *Journal of Democracy* 33, no. 3 (2022): 100–14. We also thank Christian Caryl for his support for our op-ed "Kazakhstan Reminds Putin What He Really Needs to Fear," *Washington Post*, January 6, 2022; and Marlene Laruelle, Henry Hale, and PONARS Eurasia for *Pasta and Sugar, Not Navalny, Are Putin's Main Worries* (PONARS Policy Memo 689, 2021).

We also want to thank our spouses, Constantine, Catherine, and Julie. This book was written during a global pandemic and a war in a region we were born in and study. We can only hope that future generations enjoy a world that is peaceful, democratic, and nutritionally secure.

Introduction: Russia's Nutritional Autocracy

On October 21, 2021, Russian president Vladimir Putin addressed a select group of domestic and foreign experts at the annual meeting of the Valdai Discussion Club. As expected, Putin railed against Western policies and values, touted Russia's achievements, and snapped at even mild critiques of his government's actions. Putin also framed food as an emerging global concern. "Russia is making a significant contribution to food security today . . . we are exporting over US$25 billion worth of foodstuffs," the Russian president boasted. According to him, the country owed this to domestic food producers as well as the hostile West and the sanctions it introduced in the wake of Russia's annexation of Crimea in 2014. "Now we must thank the Europeans for their agricultural sanctions. Well done. Thank you for all your sanctions. We have introduced countermeasures in agriculture and invested appropriate resources. By the way, we have boosted the so-called import substitution in industry, not only in agriculture. And I must say, the effect has been good."[1]

Leaders rarely thank adversaries for sanctions. Yet Putin's sarcasm and inaccuracies aside—the European Union (EU) did not sanction Russia's agriculture—the Russian president was correct in linking sanctions, import substitution policies, and the country's booming agricultural sectors. Russia, until early 2000s a major importer of grain, now is not only self-sufficient, but is the world's largest exporter. Beyond grain, the country is quickly establishing itself as a key exporter of meat. The value of Russia's agricultural exports is larger than that of weapons, an industry for which it is globally renowned.[2] And as Putin indicated, even before the massive sanctions imposed on Russia in the wake of its invasion of Ukraine in February 2022, the country was striving to achieve self-sufficiency through import substitution in multiple sectors of the economy. Agriculture led the way; other industries followed.

Bread and Autocracy. Janetta Azarieva, Yitzhak M. Brudny, and Eugene Finkel, Oxford University Press.
© Oxford University Press 2023. DOI: 10.1093/oso/9780197684368.003.0001

Food is also Putin's potent weapon. After Russia invaded Ukraine on February 24, 2022, it blockaded Ukrainian ports to limit the country's grain exports, disrupted the harvest, and stole gargantuan amounts of Ukraine's wheat, thus threatening a global famine.[3] This was not an unintended consequence of warfare but a deliberate strategy. Dmitry Medvedev, Russia's ex-president and current deputy chairman of the country's Security Council, explicitly argued on his Telegram channel that Russia should supply food only to "friendly countries" and deny it to the unfriendly ones. Weeks later, an article published by the state-owned *RIA Novosti* news agency echoed the warning: Russia's food weapon, it said, is more potent than its missiles, for Russia controls almost a quarter of the global wheat market and nearly half of the sunflower oil market. After all, "one can survive without [mobile] phones and the internet, but not without bread, even if it is baked from totalitarian Russian wheat," the article boasted.[4]

At the same time, food prices in Russia have been rising rapidly since early 2020. Paradoxically, while Russia's agriculture is thriving, ordinary Russians are hurting. In fact, just the day after Putin's jubilant remarks at the Valdai, Russia's Ministry of Agriculture intervened in the food market to stem the skyrocketing prices of meat and sausages. In 2020 alone the cost of pasta increased by 10 percent, sunflower oil by 24 percent, and sugar by more than 70 percent.[5] Such price increases are a politically sensitive issue, for in Russia people spend a high share—between 30 and 40 percent—of their income on food.

To address the growing food affordability crisis, since December 2020 the Kremlin introduced, by fiat, price caps on several staple foods, tariffs, and export bans. In the Russian food sector, the market economy was effectively replaced by a system better described as "command capitalism." Yet despite the government's efforts, the prices kept rising. One solution that the government never considered was reversing food import substitution and reopening the Russian market to Western food imports, banned since 2014. For Putin, food is not an economic issue. It is a political concern and a key pillar of regime survival.

Why should students of contemporary autocracies such as Russia care about food, and what does it say about the survival strategies of nondemocratic leaders and regimes? What is the role of food in contemporary Russian politics? Why and how did Russia so quickly transform from a country recently plagued by severe food shortages to an agricultural powerhouse? What are the political and social causes and implications of such a major yet mostly overlooked shift, and what can Russia's experience teach us about autocratic politics more broadly? These are the questions we address in this book.

Food and Politics from Early States to the 2022 War in Ukraine

Food and food security, which the 1996 World Food Summit defined as peoples' "physical and economic access to sufficient, safe and nutritious food that meets their dietary needs,"[6] are now key issues on international and domestic political agendas. Until recently, these topics have primarily been the focus of scholars of the developing world, agricultural systems, welfare, public health, and nutrition. Developed countries, the assumption went, no longer needed to worry about feeding their citizens; outside small pockets of extreme poverty, this problem is a thing of the past. An overabundance of (often highly processed) food and the social and public health ills associated with it were perceived as a far more pressing problem in rich and middle-income states.[7] The COVID-19 pandemic challenged these assumptions as severe food insecurity became more widespread in rich regions such as North America and Western Europe.[8]

Russia, some analysts predicted, was better positioned to weather the COVID-19 crisis than the West. The reason was neither superior governance nor a more efficient aid and welfare distribution system; the country is not a paragon of either. Rather, it was Russia's earlier push to ensure self-sufficiency in response to Western sanctions imposed in 2014.[9] While the rest of the world believed in and relied on global trade, Putin opted for self-sufficiency. Food became central to the president's strategy of building Fortress Russia, retaining his hold on power and subjugating opponents.

The re-emergence of access to food as a key social and political concern is just the latest manifestation of food's crucial role throughout human history. Nutrition is the most basic human need, and therefore, food politics—production, control, and distribution of food—has shaped history since the emergence of early communities. We often view food as something that binds and brings people together in a shared experience of a meal. But when unequally distributed and not universally accessible, it is a potent tool of domination and social control.[10] Food *is* and *has always been* power, from the early states to the twenty-first century.

According to James Scott, the birth, expansion, and collapse of early states was directly linked to the cultivation and storage of grain, an easily accessed and taxed product. Access to food, primarily bread, impacted state-building, social stability, the nature, and survival of political regimes. Thus, in the second century BCE, Roman statesman Gaius Gracchus pioneered the introduction of the Grain Law, one of many social laws popular among the Romans. Under it, poor citizens could obtain grain below the market price from the state-run grain magazines. In the same period, ancient Rome's famous culture of "bread and circuses" emerged, which alludes to the political use of food and entertainment to appease the masses. Later Roman leaders expanded the practice. Grain distribution and subsidies functioned as an essential tool allowing Roman emperors to maintain popular support. At some point, up to 200,000 received food subsidies and rations from the state.[11]

The political significance of access to food has not diminished since. Food insecurity remains a major, potentially disastrous source of political and social vulnerability. As Jean-Jacques Rousseau famously argued: "The only way to maintain a state in independence from others is agriculture. Should you have all the riches of the world, if you do not have the wherewithal to feed yourself you depend on others."[12] "If only I have bread, it will be child's play to beat the Russians," quipped Napoleon.[13] But the Russians did have bread, and Napoleon was defeated.

An important but largely overlooked argument attributes the rise of Nazism to Germany's grain sector. *Bread and Democracy in Germany*, published by the prominent economic historian Alexander Gerschenkron in 1943, accuses the Junkers, the large landowners of Prussia, of derailing the country's democracy and creating fertile grounds for Hitler's rise to power.[14] According to Gerschenkron, in the early twentieth century, Junkers used their political status and connections to stymie agricultural reforms and protect Germany's domestic grain market from external competition. This, in turn, precluded the emergence of a countryside based on small and medium-sized farms and kept power in the hands of a small, nationalist, and militaristic rural elite. The flawed reconstruction of Germany after World War I failed to transform the country's agricultural landscape, thus undermining democratic institutions and enabling Hitler's rise. Barrington Moore's seminal *Social Origins of Dictatorship and Democracy* also emphasized the importance of commercial agriculture and the relationship between food-producing and urban elites, presenting it as the key factor explaining the emergence of democratic, authoritarian, and communist regimes.[15]

After World War II, the analysis of the political role of food shifted almost exclusively to the Global South. This focus on the developing countries was understandable. In the second half of the twentieth century, the importance of food decreased significantly in developed countries but remained salient in the Global South. There, food allowed leaders to wield political power while political power ensured access to food. Thus, as the economist Amartya Sen famously argued, famines were first and foremost outcomes of political decisions and preferences of the ruling elites.[16]

Supplying politically active and better-educated cities with cheap food became the paramount concern of politicians in rapidly urbanizing developing countries. This food-driven "urban bias," as Robert H. Bates described it, benefits city dwellers at the expense of peasants and continues to define state-society relations in many developing states.[17] According to Bates, the government regulates relationships between farmers in rural areas, who produce food, and the urban elites interested in keeping food prices low to ensure social stability. When conflicts of interests between the farmers and the urbanites arise, the authorities invariably take the latter's side. However, in studying developing countries, most of which were authoritarian, Bates and other earlier scholars of food and politics in the Global South assumed that the nature of the regime is not a critical factor.

The political importance of food in the Global South is not limited to its provision. An equally potent strategy is withholding food from one's opponents. For instance, in the impoverished Zimbabwe the dictator Robert Mugabe allegedly distributed food in opposition strongholds only to those who agreed to give up identification papers required to vote.[18]

The salience of food may have diminished in developed countries, but it never really disappeared. Even in the prosperous United States, the poverty line is still calculated relative to the cost of a minimum food diet.[19] Leaders fully understand food as a tool of social domination; food is always political. A famous quote attributed to Henry Kissinger maintains, "if you *control* the *oil* you *control* the country; if you *control* food, you *control* the people."[20]

And when governments cannot ensure citizens' access to food, they are in peril. In 2008, citizens of at least forty-eight countries across the globe, from Indonesia to Morocco and from Argentina to Yemen, took to the streets to protest against a sharp spike in food prices. The protests turned violent in several places, with riots toppling the governments of Haiti and Madagascar.[21] Moreover, a severe drought in Russia sparked protests in Egypt, the country's primary grain importer. Thousands demanded "bread, freedom, and social justice" in a wave of social mobilization that contributed to the Arab Spring and eventually led to the fall of President Hosni Mubarak.[22] Admittedly, the relationship between food prices and political stability is not linear, but a growing number of studies do observe a clear correlation between access to food, political violence, and mass protests.[23]

Food, History, and Politics in Russia and the USSR: A Brief Overview

Only in a few countries is the connection between food and politics as pronounced as it is in Russia. Virtually every major development in Russian and Soviet history since the 1917 Revolution has either been driven by or closely associated with the question of food and access to it. The country's ability to feed itself should not be taken for granted. Despite possessing rich and abundant agricultural land, food was the Achilles heel of both the Romanov Empire and the USSR. In the early eighteenth century, Peter the Great proposed establishing state-run grain magazines throughout the country to protect it from bad harvests and hunger. Empress Catherine II implemented the plan in 1761, declaring the price of bread "ought to always be in my hands."[24]

Yet despite the government's efforts, bread triggered the downfall of the Romanov Empire. In February 1917, bread shortages, skyrocketing food prices, and subsequent food riots in the capital Petrograd sparked a revolution that abolished the monarchy, replacing it with the Provisional Government. But when it too failed to improve the food supply, the new regime also lost popular support. Vladimir Lenin and his Bolshevik faction of the Communist Party came to power following a coup in October 1917. Visionary though he was, Lenin was also pragmatic and shrewd enough to understand that the fate of the Communist Revolution primarily relied on his government's ability to feed the cities. The communists declared a "food supply dictatorship" and initiated a statewide grain expropriation program, carried out by the dedicated Food Supply Army (*Prodarmiia*), created specifically for the task.[25] A massive famine, in which millions in Ukraine and Russia's Volga region died, followed. Only an international relief operation, spearheaded by the American Relief Agency (ARA), saved the nascent communist state from collapse.

War Communism, as Lenin's measures became known, was replaced by the market-oriented New Economic Policy (NEP), the central components of which were the end of expropriations and free trade in food. NEP effectively meant that the regime lost control over food production, procurement, and distribution. Joseph Stalin, who became the Soviet leader in 1924, saw this as a threat to the communists' hold on power. In the late 1920s and early 1930s, the regime brutally collectivized the countryside by forcing peasants into large state and collective farms. Another famine, even deadlier than that of the early 1920s, broke out.[26]

World War II devastated the country's agriculture and created further food shortages. In the besieged Leningrad alone up to a million people died from starvation and related diseases. Hitler's plans for the region, dubbed the "Hunger Plan," envisioned man-made starvation of a hundred million Slavs to make space for German colonization. After the war, food supplies improved, particularly in major cities, but food insecurity never disappeared entirely.

A combination of chronic food shortages and a painful spike in prices triggered the largest popular protest prior to Gorbachev's reforms, the Novocherkassk Massacre of June 2, 1962. Troops killed more than twenty Soviet citizens when firing on a crowd demanding milk and meat. Spooked by Novocherkassk, Soviet authorities refrained from raising the prices of staple foods for the next twenty-nine years, the ballooning expenses of inefficient collective agriculture be damned. As the Soviet population grew, the USSR shifted from a modest exporter of grain to a fast-growing importer, soon to be the world's largest. The cost of subsidies to the failing domestic agriculture, coupled with the need to buy massive amounts of food abroad, became a heavy burden on the Soviet budget and prevented much-needed investments in other sectors.[27]

The reliance on foreign food suppliers also signaled geopolitical vulnerability. When the United States imposed sanctions on the USSR following its invasion of Afghanistan in 1979, a grain embargo was paramount to American efforts, precisely because the Soviet Union depended on US grain to feed its citizens. Even though the sanctions failed to change Soviet behavior and were quietly scrapped by President Reagan, they forced the Kremlin to hastily find alternative suppliers to prevent Soviet citizens from going hungry.

The country's already severe food problems peaked during the *perestroika*. In the late 1980s, long breadlines and rationing of staple foods, personally experienced by the authors, doomed Gorbachev's plans to revitalize communism. Following the dissolution of the USSR in December 1991, supermarkets throughout Russia lacked essential products, causing the government to fear widespread famine. Feeding the country became the new rulers' top priority; restocking grocery stores was the primary aim of the painful market reforms in the early 1990s.

Economic reforms, especially the 1992 liberalization of food prices and fully opening the Russian market to imports, filled the shelves but also made many food products inaccessible to the average Russian. However, in the minds of the reformers, limited domestic food production and reliance on food imports were not problems but natural outcomes of the country's integration into the global market economy. This changed with Putin's rise to power. Unexpectedly and largely ignored by many Russia experts, domestic food production expanded rapidly. In the early 2000s, the world's recent largest importer of grain became a modest exporter and then a global powerhouse. Abandoned ports on the Volga-Don canal flourished, and Glencore, Cargill, and Louis Dreyfus—the world's main grain trading companies—became familiar names throughout large parts of Russia. Grain led the way; milk and meat, whose production depends on feed grains, followed.

The shift from a vulnerable importer to the world's largest exporter of grain had profound political and security implications. A regime that is unable to feed its subjects is a very different beast from one that is nutritionally secure and controls the bread pantries of most of its neighbors and of major regional powers, such as Egypt. In 2010, a major drought hit Russia. Instead of scrambling for external supplies, begging for international help, or potentially facing famine, as the Soviet Union did, Putin's government secured food by restricting grain exports. When the United States, the EU, and several additional countries sanctioned Russia for its annexation of Crimea and unleashing the war in Donbas in 2014, Putin retaliated by banning food imports from those states (dubbed in Russia as "countersanctions"). The contrast to 1979–1980 could not have been starker.

Yet, as the 2020–2021 food prices crisis demonstrates, Russia's food supplies are still at risk. Once again, access to food has emerged as a political and social problem, reviving fears and painful memories of Soviet-era food shortages.

What explains Russia's transformation from a major food importer to an agricultural superpower? And why, despite such spectacular successes, do many Russians lack access to affordable food? Finally, what can the focus on food tell us about the nature of Putin's regime, state-society relations, and politics more broadly in Russia and beyond?

Bread and Modern Autocracy

In this book, we put forward several arguments. Food, we maintain, offers an important but often ignored lens to understanding autocracy in Russia. The basic insight that food is a powerful tool of social control allows us to move beyond the currently dominant focus on authoritarian institutions or repression to the broader framework of government-society relations.[28] Studying how autocrats ensure food supplies shifts the focus from sources, causes, and mechanisms of regime transition to better grasping the fundamentals of authoritarian stability.[29]

Recently, scholars have begun explicitly analyzing the relationship between food production and autocratic politics. Supplying cities with cheap food at the expense of the countryside, argues Jeremy Wallace, benefits the more politically active urban constituencies in the short term. But over a more extended period, urban bias is a source of political instability. It drives heavily taxed farmers out of the countryside into the sprawling, impoverished, and politically volatile urban slums. In China, the communist government practiced urban bias but escaped its long-term dangers. A mix of repression, heavy restrictions on internal migration, and more recently, growing investment in the countryside and small and medium-sized towns have allowed the Chinese authorities to feed the cities without undermining social stability and endangering the regime.[30]

The nature of the regime can also help explain whether a regime practices urban bias. Henry Thomson maintains that agricultural policies pursued by nondemocratic rulers primarily depend on the threat the government faces. According to his "conflict theory of authoritarianism," autocratic regimes adopt urban bias when faced with urban unrest. On the other hand, rural bias policies follow when a coup led by landed elites threatens an autocrat's survival. Authoritarian rulers who confront both threats often establish a military dictatorship because the military is an actor that is not entirely beholden to either urban or rural interests.[31] Our analysis builds on but also differs from these explanations. In Russia, we argue, Putin's policies constitute a different model that is explicitly dependent on nutritional self-sufficiency.

Similar to the developing countries of the Global South, Soviet food supply policies exhibited strong urban bias. As in China, these policies contributed to the mass migration to the big cities and the adoption of severe restrictions on internal mobility, including a highly restrictive residency registration (*propiska*) system. Putin's Russia, however, differs significantly from the USSR. After Stalin's brutal collectivization devastated the Russian countryside and the Kremlin executed, starved, and exiled millions, the government no longer needed to fear rural mobilization from below. Soviet rural elites—chairmen of collective and state farms and directors of state-owned agro-industrial enterprises—did represent an influential lobbying group in the Soviet era. However, violence, let alone a coup led by the rural elites, was never a serious threat to regime stability. The years of market reforms in the 1990s further undermined the power of old agricultural elites and their control of the countryside.

By the early 2000s, Russia's rural elites were politically weak, the peasantry compliant, and the threat of rural insurrection nonexistent. President Putin thus could reshape rural society and the economy by creating a new class of politically loyal and economically reliable agrarian elites. These profit-seeking, but regime-dependent actors would then prop the regime up domestically by supplying abundant food to the cities and preventing food shortages similar to those that destroyed the Romanov Empire and crippled the USSR. By investing in regime-dependent large food producers, the Kremlin would extend urban bias policies without having to worry about elite opposition or rural mobilization. The rise of large producers would also limit the numbers and the influence of small and medium farmers, typically the most pro-democratic segment of rural population.[32] Internationally, the policy would protect the regime by reducing the dependence on food imports. Food is security in Putin's Russia, and well-stocked shelves are key to regime stability.

Having created these new food-producing elites, Putin then moved to protect them by imposing policies of food import substitution and self-reliance. Kremlin stuck to these policies even when domestic food producers failed to stem sharp price increases during the COVID-19 pandemic. While self-sufficiency and protectionism only recently became fashionable again in the West, a consequence of the populist tide and the COVID-19 pandemic, in the food sphere Russia has been trying to achieve these objectives since the early 2000s. Numerous autocratic states have previously adopted import substitution policies in the industrial sphere. Putin's Russia is arguably the first modern autocracy to explicitly consider import substitution in food production fundamental to regime survival.[33]

Putin's policies in food production thus deepen our understanding of contemporary authoritarian regimes, their priorities, threat perceptions, and especially their capacity to innovate and take policy risks. Authoritarian regimes and Putin's Russia, in particular, are often perceived as deeply conservative.[34] We show that behind such a façade, one can find radical initiatives to reshape the nature of state-society and its economic priorities.

This book further demonstrates the dangers of such bold policies and efforts to overcome the basic principles of the market economy. Paradoxically, the Kremlin's spectacular success in nurturing and protecting domestic food producers caused Russia's current food prices crisis. By subordinating the market to political needs, the government eliminated competition, concentrated production in the hands of a few well-connected mammoth companies, and forced the citizens to pay increasingly higher prices for lower-quality food products. Yet as long as Putin believes that nutritional autarky, rather than economic efficiency, is vital to regime survival, the government can only proceed by increasing state intervention in the economy.

Understanding Russia through Food

Studying food supply and availability is crucial to understanding politics and society in Russia. As Putin's remarks at the Valdai demonstrated, food policies often indicate where the country is headed. Food is the proverbial canary in the Russian history coal mine, a harbinger of future policies, reforms, and crises. Because it is such a fundamental need and a critical political concern, food tends to be the starting point of big changes. The food supply question either triggered or steered the 1917 Revolution, the New Economic Policy of the 1920s, the collectivization, the collapse of the USSR, and the market reforms of the 1990s. If history is any guide, Putin's heavy-handed efforts to decrease food prices by fiat signal the dawn of command capitalism, a new form of state-business relations in the country.

Yet despite its significance, food is rarely discussed as a principal political issue and only a few scholars of the region take food seriously.[35] We can only speculate why this is the case. In part, this oversight might be attributed to the broader tendency to fail to view food and access to it as significant political factors outside the Global South. In an oil-rich, advanced, and culturally sophisticated nuclear power, such as Russia, other topics might be more exciting to study. Additionally, this may be an inevitable outcome of the production of knowledge and expertise. English-language research on Russia is produced predominantly by scholars trained and based in the West, mostly (though not exclusively) urbanites who tend not to view food in macropolitical terms. Most of them are well aware of food shortages in the late USSR; some undoubtedly encountered empty shelves during their work in Russia. But by having access to hard currency, foreign scholars experienced food insecurity very differently than did the locals. For those born and raised in the USSR, like us, food insecurity was a formative, persistent, deeply felt, and profoundly political experience. Scholars who entered the field only after the Soviet collapse found well-stocked groceries; poverty rather than empty shelves made food inaccessible. Whatever the reason, in the voluminous academic studies and policy analyses of Russian politics, food is at best a marginal topic and most often nonexistent.

Food and Security

What explains the meteoric rise of Russian food production? How did the country reinvent itself as an agricultural powerhouse after decades of heavy reliance on imported grain? Several factors have contributed to this transformation. The transition to a market economy replaced the inefficient collective agriculture, putting farms that did survive the 1990s in a better position to bounce back. Putin's early reforms modernized the Land and Labor Codes and promoted stability, with climate change opening new lands for cultivation and new technologies spurring productivity. The industry leaders we interviewed predictably waxed poetic about the role of big agribusiness.

In this book we zoom in on a different story, one that puts politics front and center and combines contingency and strategic planning, bureaucratic ambition, and deeply held ideological convictions. We do not argue that politics and ideological visions are the only factors that mattered, but we are convinced that they are the most crucial ones.

Russia's food production began recovering from the wreckage of the Soviet collapse in the late 1990s. The 1998 financial crisis devastated the ruble and made domestic products more appealing to Russian customers simply because imported ones suddenly became out of reach for many. In 2000, when Putin became president, the future already looked modestly promising for the industry.

There is no indication that Putin, born and raised in Leningrad, the country's second-largest city, initially cared much about agriculture and food production. Yet he must have understood the importance of food shortages. Putin's parents starved and barely survived the siege of Leningrad during World War II. Putin's own experience with food shortages was much milder, but his ex-wife Lyudmila does recall the shock of seeing empty shelves and spending hours waiting in lines after the family's return to the USSR from East Germany, where the future president served as a KGB officer. As a senior official in the St. Petersburg city council, Putin was deeply involved in desperate efforts of bringing food into the city. The first evidence of the president's large-scale corruption dates to these events. During the 1998 financial crisis, Putin, then head of the FSB, Russia's main internal security service, undoubtedly monitored the food situation in the country when fears of massive shortages became widespread.

Putin cares deeply about staying in power, state security, and shielding Russia and his own rule from domestic and foreign threats. In early 2000s, these priorities created an opening which Aleksei Gordeev, then minister of agriculture, skillfully exploited. Gordeev, a clever and competent bureaucrat, made his career in various Soviet agricultural agencies and was appointed the minister of agriculture in 1999. Politically conservative, he was a firm believer in Russia's need to achieve self-sufficiency in food production. Reframing self-sufficiency as a national security issue thus allowed Gordeev to latch his agenda onto Putin's desires, increase his political clout, and promote the industry he headed.

The securitization of food and increasing attention from the president endowed food production with prominence, prestige, and funding it has not enjoyed in many decades. Economists Aldo Musacchio and Sergio Lazzarini define state capitalism as "widespread influence of the government in the economy, either by owning majority or minority equity positions in companies or by providing subsidized credit and/or other privileges to private companies."[36] Russian food production in 2000s fits this definition. In

2000, the government created the state-owned *Rosselkhozbank* (Russian Agricultural Bank) tasked with providing credit to agricultural producers. The Kremlin set up the state-owned *Rosagroleasing* a year later to provide domestic producers with modern technologies and equipment. Both the Rosselkhozbank and Rosagroleasing were established during a period that many consider the high-point of Putin's economic liberalism and free-market approach.[37] Shifting the focus to agriculture thus challenges the common perception of Putin as the champion of free market during the early years of his rule. The state also subsidized railroad transportation of grain and invested in storage facilities and shipping terminals. Since 2002, hardly a year has gone buy without the Russian government directly intervening in the grain market, including outright export bans during droughts. Historically, most countries have intervened in food markets. A small number desire nutritional self-sufficiency,[38] yet few do so as intensively as Russia; almost none went as far in securing nutritional autarky.

Buoyed by the rapid growth of domestic agriculture, in 2008, the Kremlin began developing a dedicated Food Security Doctrine, which was formally adopted in 2010. According to President Dmitry Medvedev (2008–2012), it reflected the Kremlin's belief that food security is essential for Russia's national security and domestic social stability.[39] In a government saturated with security services alumni,[40] food security has lost its original meaning and morphed into a national defense strategy. In Russia, food security is no longer individuals' access to "sufficient, safe and nutritious food that meets their dietary needs," as defined by the UN Food and Agriculture Organization. Instead, food security in Russia means domestic production of at least 95 percent consumed grains and potatoes, 90 percent milk and dairy products, and 85 percent of meat.

It seems that the state's investments paid off. Putin would not have been able to use food as his weapon of choice to retaliate against Western sanctions in 2014 or to blackmail the world during the war in Ukraine without having confidence in Russia's ability to feed itself. This demonstrates the extent to which the Kremlin perceives food as yet another political tool. In 2018, the subordination of food supplies to state security became complete with the appointment of a new minister of agriculture, Dmitry Patrushev. A graduate of the FSB service academy, he had little experience in agriculture but hails from a prominent *siloviki* family. His father, Nikolai Patrushev, is the head of Russia's Security Council, a former director of the FSB, and a member of

Putin's innermost circle. The elder Patrushev, who "makes Putin look like a moderate,"[41] is also on the US sanctions list.

The foundations of Russia's agricultural success existed even before the government began heavily investing in food production. But the state fueled agriculture's rapid growth by credit, subsidies, investments in infrastructure, and access to new technologies. We argue that such a remarkable transformation of Russian agriculture would not have occurred without the explicit securitization of food and efforts to make domestic production a key pillar of national defense and regime survival.

The Seeds of Crisis: Food, the Present and the Future of Putin's Model

In the past, scholars explained the Russians' acquiescence to Putin's autocracy by alluding to an informal "social pact" between the Kremlin and the population. Russians, the argument went, refrain from political activism and voicing demands in exchange for economic growth and rising living standards. This explanation no longer holds. The country's economy has been largely stagnant since the 2008 financial crisis. Combined effects of Western sanctions imposed in the wake of the annexation of Crimea and decreasing oil prices made Russians economically worse off with time. Russians are hurting, but only a few are taking to the streets.

Various analyses attribute this lack of popular mobilization to a number of factors, such as state repression and manipulation of the media, propaganda, territorial expansion and geopolitical resurgence, cooptation of key social groups, psychological and ideological congruence between Putin and the majority of the Russian population, corruption, and macroeconomic stability.[42] These explanations have merits, but as we maintain, the Russian elite increasingly considers abundant and affordable food critical to social stability. Thus, when food prices started to rise sharply, the president leaped into action. But why would a country with such productive agriculture face a severe food crisis in the first place?

We argue that the Russian government's efforts to ensure nutritional self-sufficiency are also the root causes of the food affordability crisis. The Kremlin originally designed these measures to shield the country from food shortages during turbulent times. The Russian government likely did not consider the possibility of a global pandemic when they formulated the Food Security Doctrine, but was the system Putin built resilient enough to cope with such a crisis? The evidence is mixed. Yes, the country did not run out of supplies and Russians, unlike some Italians, did not depend on the mafia to put food on the table. But the government achieved this at the cost of direct and unprecedented intervention that exposed the system's inherent flaws and vulnerabilities.

Any long-term state intervention eventually distorts market mechanisms. The Kremlin set the stage for rapidly rising food costs by heavily favoring major agricultural companies and shielding domestic producers from Western competition by food countersanctions. When the Russians' incomes took a nosedive due to the COVID-19 pandemic and domestic consumption plummeted, agricultural producers simply switched to exporting more of their products, mostly to China. Lack of alternative sources of food supply and falling demand incentivized Russian retailers to raise prices to compensate for decreasing profits. As costs rose, an increasing number of Russians could no longer afford the products, in turn leading to even sharper price hikes.

Reopening the Russian food market to competition could have broken this feedback loop of food insecurity and skyrocketing prices. But because food is subordinated to politics in Putin's mind, he opted for brute coercion. If the market, however distorted, cannot provide Russians with affordable staple foods on its own, then the Kremlin will. The government, after all, did not spend so much on domestic producers just to sit back and allow them to reap profits. What Putin gave, he decisively took back by imposing export bans and price caps on staple foods. Executive action has the allure of offering easy solutions and immediate results. The compliance of state-dependent food producers is all but certain. In the long run, however, this solution is unsustainable. If the prices set by the government do not ensure profits, producers will not fight back but will simply stop growing wheat or raising cows, and food shortages will inevitably return to Russia and threaten the regime.

Book Structure

This book is not an in-depth study of Russian agriculture and food productions. Neither is it a comprehensive historical analysis of Russian food industry. Readers interested in these topics should turn to excellent studies produced by scholars such as Stephen Wegren, Grigory Ioffe,

Tatyana Nefedova, Natalya Shagaida, Vasily Uzun, and Susanne Wengle.[43] Our goal is to focus on the connection between regime, politics, and food in Putin's Russia. We also want to show the ideas, perceptions, and fears that center on the political role of food and their impact on regime's stability and survival.

We proceed as follows. The next chapter surveys the link between food and politics in Russia from the 1917 Revolution until the dissolution of the USSR in December 1991. Chapters 2 and 3 focus on President Yeltsin's years from the country's independence to Putin's rise to power in 2000. This period began with acute food shortages and fear of widespread famine. Yeltsin's rule ended in the aftermath of the 1998 economic crisis that revived fears of hunger. Luckily, Russia did not experience famine in 1992 and 1998, but the post-Soviet economic reforms plunged millions of Russians into poverty and endemic food insecurity. This period also witnessed a bold yet ultimately failed attempt to solve the country's food supply problems by embracing the free market, fully integrating the country into the global economy, and establishing agriculture based on small and medium-sized farms.

The following chapters focus on the Putin era. Chapter 4 describes the political and ideological factors that drove the transformation of Russia's food production and transformation, the actors that spearheaded these changes, and the main mechanisms that supported Russia's grain expansion from importer to a global leader. Chapter 5 centers on the Food Security Doctrine, the main document that links food to Russia's national security and sets the goal of food independence.

Chapter 6 zooms in on the regime's attempt to secure food independence after 2014, under conditions of an emerging geopolitical confrontation, Western sanctions, and Russia's countersanctions that focused on food. Chapter 7 discusses the business aspects of the transformation of food production in Russia. More specifically, we focus on the country's top feeders, the agro-holdings, major conglomerates that dominate the industry and operate in a symbiotic relationship with the central and regional governments.

Chapter 8 centers on 2020–2021, the years of the COVID-19 pandemic and the food prices crisis. It shows how the short-term success of Russia's drive to achieve nutritional self-sufficiency planted the seeds of the later food crisis. Chapter 9 presents the role of food during the early stages of the war in Ukraine and, especially, the ability of Putin's regime to avoid a severe crisis of food supply despite harsh Western sanctions. Chapter 10 concludes the book by discussing the broader implications of the country's attempts to solve food supply problems through self-sufficiency.

As food re-emerges as a key global issue and nations increasingly turn inward, Russia's experience in building nutritionally autarkic dictatorship is especially illuminating. It offers important lessons and warning signs for the contemporary world. Autocracy, governments' control of food, and self-sufficiency might be where other states are also headed. Russia has gone down this road before. Those who want to understand autocracy beyond repression, populism, or misinformation should take a serious look at food politics in the country.

1

The Starving Empire

Food and Politics in the USSR

Popular perceptions of the USSR typically center on symbols of industrial prowess and technological sophistication: the *Stakhanovites*, the T-34 tank, the MiG jet, *Sputnik*, and Chernobyl. Yet, at its core, the Soviet state was dominated by a primal and decidedly premodern quest to feed the growing and increasingly urban population. Soviet history was a constant and ultimately failed struggle to overcome, adapt to, and survive the chronic and often acute food shortages that more than once escalated into widespread famines. In 1917, food shortages sparked a revolution that ushered in seven decades of communist rule. During the 1980s, they sealed communism's fate and facilitated Soviet collapse.

In this chapter, we discuss the political role of food and food supply in the USSR. Our goal is not to provide a comprehensive overview of the Soviet agriculture and food distribution system. Rather, we demonstrate how food was inherently and closely linked to, or essentially the catalyst of, key events of Soviet history, from the state's birth to its demise.

Lenin: Bread and Revolution

Low levels of industrialization, underdeveloped transportation networks, inadequate training, and inept leadership all contributed to the Russian Imperial army's catastrophic performance against Germany on the Eastern Front during World War I.[1] Yet defeats on the battlefield did not bring down the Romanov dynasty. Food riots at home did.

When World War I broke out in July 1914, few Russians could have imagined food shortages, let alone food-induced riots in the country. The Russian Empire was a major exporter of grain; provisioning the army and the home front was not a major concern. Very quickly, however, food supplies "came to be seen as a problem, then as a crisis, and finally as a catastrophe" that preoccupied the Tsarist government until hungry crowds swept it out of power.[2]

A sharp decline in food production was an inevitable outcome of the long war. Large numbers of Russian peasants and draft horses were sent to the front, and the shrinking rural population was unable to compensate for these losses. The army consumed a disproportionately large share of agricultural output. For instance, in 1916, half of the marketable grain went to the military. Several essential food-growing and processing regions were now under foreign occupation.[3] Still, the crux of the problem was not production but storage, transportation, and distribution of food,[4] weaknesses that would also occur repeatedly throughout Soviet and the immediate post-Soviet history.

Falling food supply inevitably meant shortages and substantially higher prices in the empire's fast-growing industrial centers. During the first two years of the war, prices increased by more than 150 percent in Petrograd and roughly 130 percent in Moscow.[5] By October 1915, three quarters of Russia's cities experienced food shortages, and at the end of the year, women of Petrograd had to "stand in line for hours in subzero weather to buy pitifully small quantities of sugar and flour."[6] In 1916, the government introduced rationing and food coupons for key food items, most notably sugar. Popular discontent exploded into open clashes on numerous occasions, and a wave of what the media and official reports described as "bazaar disorders," "hunger riots," "pogroms," and "women's riots" occurred throughout the country. As the war progressed and shortages became more acute, subsistence riots increasingly assumed political dimensions. Citizens tore down a Tsar's portrait while ransacking of a shop in Southern Russia, and in the Moscow region, the shortage of bread turned people against the war.[7]

Unsurprisingly, by the end of 1916, provisioning the home front became the central political question. Food shortages, troubling though they were for the hungry urbanites, also indicated the empire's much larger structural problems and governance failures. The government's inability to feed Russia triggered a period of social instability, breakdown of authority, state collapse, revolution, and civil war.[8]

On February 23, 1917, an angry, mostly female crowd of Petrograd residents took to the streets protesting bread shortages, long queues, and high food prices. Slogans such as "Down with high prices!" quickly transformed into "Down with the Tsar!" On the next day, the city's workers went on strike. The soldiers of the Petrograd garrison refused to put down the rebellion and defected to the protestors' side. In a matter of days, the 300-year-old Romanov dynasty was deposed, and the Russian Empire ceased to exist.

The Provisional Government that replaced the tsarist rule was equally unable to solve the food crisis. The general collapse of political authority following the February Revolution only exacerbated the existing problems. Currency, issued by the Provisional Government, was worthless, and peasants refused to sell their produce.[9] Bereft of supplies, the army disintegrated. In October 1917, Petrograd was on the verge of running out of flour. Other major cities fared no better. The communists, led by Vladimir Lenin, skillfully leveraged the popular anger over the worsening food shortages. After the government reduced the rations of the Petrograd garrison, discontent soldiers actively supported Lenin's violent takeover of power in November 1917.[10]

Lenin had no doubt that the fate of communist rule depended first and foremost on its ability to feed the cities. Communist authorities spared no effort to procure food for the urban proletariat. The government also "capitalized on food shortages to promote their vision of ideal socialist society"[11] through introduction of communal kitchens and dining halls that were meant to replace home cooking and eating. Another feature was the state's ability to use food allocation as a powerful weapon of social control.[12] Even though communal dining never became as widespread as the communists hoped, the use of food distribution as a powerful instrument of domination became an important component of Soviet politics.

By the end of 1917, the food situation improved somewhat, mainly due to the confiscation of grain from private traders, but severe shortages returned in early 1918. The government declared a "food supply dictatorship," the guiding principle of which was "organized revolutionary violence." In practical terms this meant that food for the urban centers and the Red Army would be procured by using extreme coercion rather than incentivizing peasants to produce or sell grain. The food supply dictatorship also meant the creation of armed and overzealous Food Detachments and then the Food Supply Army (*Prodarmiia*), tasked with forceful requisitioning of surplus grain and other produce from farmers, especially the most affluent ones. At its peak, the Food Supply Army consisted of about 77,000 servicemen and more than 150,000 people served in its ranks throughout the revolution and the civil war. The regular military was also tasked with grain procurement. Lenin even went as far as suggesting to reform the War Commissariat into the War-Food Supply Commissariat. Leon Trotsky shared this sentiment when he stated in April 1918 that "civil war is the struggle for bread."[13] "[U]se all energy and all revolutionary measures to send grain, grain and more grain!!!" implored Lenin of the communist authorities in Ukraine.[14]

The essence of War Communism, the name given to the procurement system, was extreme violence that produced grain for the regime in the short term at the cost of the peasants' unspeakable suffering. The policy deliberately targeted the most successful (and hence, most affluent) farmers and eliminated the peasants' incentives to produce beyond subsistence levels. War Communism devastated the countryside, caused strikes and peasants revolts, and, as Lenin grudgingly realized, endangered the government's very survival. In 1921, Lenin introduced the New Economic Policy (NEP). War Communism was abolished, a tax in kind replaced food requisitions, and the government rescinded its grain monopoly and legalized free food trade.[15]

But it was already too late to prevent a catastrophe. Before the revolution, the provinces of the Volga region, Southern Russia, and Ukraine produced about 20 million tons of cereal a year. Their combined yield declined to 8.45 million tons in 1920. It seemed that the fate of the revolution depended on the 1921 harvest. "If there is a harvest, then everybody will hunger a little, and the government will be saved. Otherwise... the government will perish," predicted Lenin in March 1921.[16] Unfortunately, it turned out to be a drought year in central Russia and Ukraine. A widespread famine followed since neither the peasants nor the state had grain reserves to fall back on.

According to the *Pravda* newspaper, the regime's mouthpiece, about 25 million people suffered from malnutrition during the famine.[17] The dead were too numerous to be buried, and cases of cannibalism were recorded widely. Yet despite Lenin's fears, the government survived, though just barely. The United States saved it. When the Russian writer Maxim Gorky appealed for international help to combat the famine, American Relief Administration (ARA), a humanitarian organization established and led by future US president Herbert Hoover, offered assistance. The communist leadership was suspicious—"food iz a veppon," the Soviet deputy commissar of foreign affairs Maxim Litvinov explained to ARA representatives in a heavy accent—but also desperate.[18] The Soviets permitted ARA to enter the USSR. For two years, the Americans fed up to 11 million Soviet citizens, saving countless lives. Other foreign humanitarian organizations also provided aid, though on a much smaller scale. Yet, even with this gargantuan help effort, up to 5 million people, most of them peasants, perished during the famine.

Stalin: Making a Hungry Superpower

The food supply question was no less crucial for Stalin, Lenin's successor. The regime's "collectivization" policy that brutally forced individual farmers into collective (*kolkhoz*) and state (*sovkhoz*) farms was driven by the state's desire to ratchet up food production to supply the growing cities and increase grain exports to fund breakneck industrialization. Mechanized, large farms, the argument went, would produce more than individual farmers ever could. Another important aspect of collective farming was improving state monitoring of and control over production and procurement.[19]

The crisis that led to collectivization began in 1927 and was an outcome of unexpectedly small grain procurement levels. To a larger extent, this was due to the cash-strapped government that focused on industrialization and set prices too low. Alarmed and well aware of the potential dangers of widespread food shortages—the 1917 Revolution was just a short decade prior—the government resorted to large-scale expropriations.[20] Next, it replaced recalcitrant and socially threatening individual farmers, especially the wealthier ones (*kulak*s), with collective producers. Extreme levels of coercion accompanied collectivization. State agents threatened, arrested, exiled, beat, and killed those deemed socially alien or unwilling to join collective farms. The peasants resisted, mostly passively, occasionally violently.[21] Unwilling to transfer livestock to collective ownership, farmers resorted to mass slaughter. Twenty-five million cattle, over 10 million pigs, and 17.7 million horses were slaughtered to avoid collectivization. Levels of pre-collectivization livestock would only be reached again in the late 1950s.[22] Collective ownership also removed any individual incentives to work hard and produce more.

The loss of livestock and incentives to produce decimated agriculture exactly when the state was hell-bent on squeezing the countryside to feed the urban proletariat and finance industrialization through grain exports. The government set unrealistically high quotas and expected local representatives to meet them at any cost. Peasants' failure to meet state quotas was met with forced requisitions, repression, and use of force. A massive famine erupted between 1932 and 1933.[23] This time, however, there were neither pleas for humanitarian assistance nor external help. Stalin's food procurement policies killed at least 5 million people, the majority of whom were peasants in Ukraine, Kazakhstan, and Southern Russia.[24] In contrast, urban workers received food coupons. The regime was determined to supply the cities at any cost. The urban residents' dependence on state food distribution was so high that when Sergei Kirov, the Communist Party leader in Leningrad, was murdered in December 1934, many believed his killer was driven by anger of the government's plan to abolish bread rationing.[25]

World War II and the occupation of most agriculturally productive regions by Nazi Germany led to yet another food crisis; the state simply was unable to feed everyone. In 1943, writes Donald Filtzer, hunger erupted in the Soviet rear. The main victims were "males between the ages of thirty and fifty-nine. For this group, the main cause of death was either starvation or starvation in conjunction with other, often preexisting, malnutrition-sensitive diseases and conditions."[26] Yet even though food shortages were more severe than in World War I, there were no food riots or mass protests against the government. The government's knack for repression is only one part of the explanation. The other is that the regime, capitalizing on its previous experience, proved to be effective in organizing the distribution of the little that was available and managing subsistence farming.[27]

Pure coercion and total mobilization could not continue forever. Even though food supplies were still inadequate to meet the existing demand, in 1947 the government abolished food rationing. Any meaningful reform of failing collective farming was ideologically unthinkable, and Stalin therefore had no choice but to normalize and control inevitable food shortages. Moscow and Leningrad received plentiful supplies. Key urban centers got somewhat less. Most cities found themselves in the third, least privileged category and "were supplied with bread, potatoes, and some cereals; but meat, milk, and other high-quality products rarely reached them."[28]

Khrushchev: From Virgin Lands to Bloody Saturday

Stalin's death in March 1953 ended heavy investment in the industry at the expense of agriculture. Food supply policies that relied on repression and use of force were replaced by those centered on increasing incentives for production. By September of that year, procurement prices of meat had already risen by 550 percent and milk by 220 percent. Subsequent increases in procurement prices for various food products also took place in 1962, 1963, and 1964.[29] Khrushchev's years were a period of promises and bold experimentation. He assured Soviet citizens that the USSR would soon catch up with and subsequently overtake the United States, opened vast amounts of land in Western Siberia and Kazakhstan to cultivation, and invested in corn as a magic crop, destined to solve the country's food problems once and for all. Despite several short-term successes, both the Virgin Lands and especially the corn programs turned out to be expensive failures while plans to overtake America had to be unceremoniously shelved. In 1962, the government was forced to raise retail prices of several staple foods. This decision sparked protests throughout the USSR. The largest of these food protests, the Bloody Saturday in Novocherkassk, became the most important popular mobilization in the post-Stalin USSR. Fearing future unrest and being incapable of feeding the population on its own, the USSR began importing grain from the West.

Khrushchev's boldest and most extensive attempt to overcome the country's food supply woes was the Virgin Lands program. The plan called for a massive expansion of grain production to previously uncultivated areas of Western Siberia, Kazakhstan, and the Urals. A firm believer in the unstoppable power of socialist popular mobilization, Khrushchev envisioned throngs of young communist volunteers descending on the area and quickly transforming it beyond recognition. Boundless and previously unutilized steppe would be covered by a dense network of large grain-producing state farms. While the USSR had 188 million hectares under cultivation in 1953, by 1960 the area increased to 220 million.[30]

The initial results were encouraging indeed. The 1956 harvest was bountiful and surpassed even the most optimistic projections. The 1958 harvest was even better, about 70 percent above the 1949–1953 figures.[31] Buoyed by the early successes of the Virgin Lands program, in 1957 Khrushchev openly declared that in a few short years, the USSR would catch up with and overtake the United States in terms of per capita meat, butter, and milk production. Yet even several short years of extensive cultivation exhausted the Virgin Lands soil. Harvests plummeted, and in the long run, the massive start-up costs of cultivation could not be compensated for. Worse still, instead of feeding the country, the newly established farms became a massive financial burden on the state and could be sustained only with the help of generous subsidies.

Corn was another magic cure. Khrushchev's infatuation with the crop, which he called "The Queen of the Fields," knew no boundaries. In 1955, Khrushchev made a case for an "Iowa-style corn belt" in the USSR.[32] Soon, in true Soviet fashion local leaders began outcompeting each other in planting corn virtually everywhere, including in areas that were unsuitable for the crop. As cultivated land was a finite resource, corn inevitably had to be planted at the expense of other, more suitable, time-tested, and better-yielding grains. Predictably, harvests plummeted and by 1962, even Khrushchev himself understood the folly of overreliance on corn. In 1963, the state began limiting the areas devoted to corn cultivation, but the damage had already been done.

The plans to catch up with and overtake the United States had, therefore, to wait until better times. The promise also turned out to be a costly strategic misstep. As Khrushchev's biographer William Taubman points out, "whereas traditional Bolshevik boasting constituted a generalized sort of bravado, Khrushchev made a concrete pledge that proved impossible to fulfill."[33] For Soviet citizens, this promise became a reference point against which they evaluated the food supply situation in the country.[34] What mattered the most was not whether the food situation improved in absolute terms but rather whether it corresponded to what the citizens now came to believe they deserved but did not have, namely parity with the United States.

The Soviet citizens not only failed to see the promised affluence, but in the early 1960s, the country once again experienced shortages. On May 17, 1962, the government raised retail prices of milk and butter by 25 percent and meat by 35 percent. Higher retail prices, the argument went, would allow the government to raise procurement prices, which would benefit producers. But for many Soviet citizens, the new prices, which went into effect on June 1, 1962, were the last straw. A wave of protests erupted throughout the USSR. Most were small—angry missives, verbal complaints, threats of strike, or leaflets—and thus did not constitute a real threat to social stability.[35] But the situation in Novocherkassk was different.

In 1962, Novocherkassk, the Tsarist-era administrative center of the Don Cossack Host, was a rapidly industrializing, middle-sized provincial town. Housing conditions in the city were harsh, food shortages not uncommon, and communal services limited. The protest started at the Budennyi Electric Locomotive Works (NEVZ), located just outside the city. The countrywide rise of prices coincided with the local decision to increase production norms, thus adding insult to injury and substantially reducing the employees' real income. When the aggrieved workers confronted the factory's director, he responded with a dismissive suggestion that if the workers do not have or cannot afford meat, they should "eat pasties with liver" instead.[36] Enraged, the NEVZ workers went on strike.[37] Some began chanting what would become the strike's slogan: "Meat, milk, pay raise!" Soon, the protesters blocked the nearby railway, stopped a train, and wrote "Make meat out of Khrushchev" on its engine. They vandalized several factory offices and tore apart portraits of Soviet leaders. Employees of neighboring enterprises joined the growing crowds. The city's law enforcement and troops of the local garrison failed to disperse the protest.

Khrushchev and the rest of the communist top leadership were clearly alarmed. Soon, key members of the Soviet government, including Frol Kozlov, second in the country's hierarchy, Deputy Prime Minister Anastas Mikoyan, and Aleksandr Shelepin, until recently the KGB chief, arrived to the city. Large numbers of troops and KGB operatives were called in to quiet the protest. When the next day, June 2, 1962, the NEVZ workers discovered that army troops occupied their plant, they began marching toward the city center. The crowds eventually stopped on the square in front of the city's party offices. A group of protesters attempted to storm a police station, ostensibly to free fellow strikers held there. In the ensuing skirmish, someone tried to steal a firearm from a soldier guarding the station. His comrades opened fire, killing five protestors. Shortly after, the soldiers or the KGB operatives—even now it is unclear who exactly did what—shot at the crowd assembled on the main square. At least twenty-three civilians were killed and many more wounded. In a series of trials that followed the Bloody Saturday, seven Novocherkassk residents received death sentences, and over a hundred were sent to jail.[38]

In his monumental *The Gulag Archipelago*, Aleksandr Solzhenitsyn described the events in Novocherkassk as "a turning point in the modern history of Russia" because for the first time, "the people have spoken out."[39] Solzhenitsyn was correct about the impact of the Novocherkassk protest, though he misidentified the mechanism. The bloodshed stunned the Soviet leadership even though they themselves almost certainly ordered the use of force. While repressing socially suspicious peasants was acceptable for the regime, massacring urban proletariat was not, for it contradicted everything the Soviet "workers' paradise" presumably stood for. In short order, the food supplies situation improved dramatically, and raising retail prices became an anathema no matter the financial cost. "The collapse of the USSR is very much linked to the food crisis. And the basis of the food crisis is Novocherkassk," summarized a leading Russian agricultural economist Evgenia Serova.[40]

Until the late 1980s, the authorities also suppressed any memory of and references to the tragedy. In 1989, several pro-democracy politicians set out to restore the memory of the Bloody Saturday and rehabilitate its victims. A key member of this group was Anatoly Sobchak, a member of the Soviet parliament and the mayor of St. Petersburg. As part of his electoral

28   BREAD AND AUTOCRACY

campaign, Sobchak visited Novocherkassk in June 1991. A photo taken during the visit shows Sobchak speaking to local leaders. Standing right behind him, jacketless but with a colored tie, is Sobchak's recently appointed aide, Vladimir Putin.

A year after Novocherkassk, in 1963, Khrushchev was forced to confront yet another food crisis. In 1963 the USSR suffered a drought and thus Soviet agriculture, still not fully recovered from the corn disaster, simply could not feed the country. The only alternative to famine was importing grain from the capitalist West. This decision turned out to be yet another watershed moment. The USSR, until recently a grain exporter, became reliant on imports to feed itself.[41]

In October 1964, Khrushchev was vacationing on the Black Sea and brainstorming plans for future agricultural reforms, such as creating special government agencies responsible for particular crops. On October 12, Khrushchev's Politburo colleagues summoned the Soviet leader to return to Moscow for an urgent meeting. The topic, they said, was agriculture. Grudgingly, Khrushchev returned to the capital.[42] The meeting, it turned out, was not about agriculture. Khrushchev was subject to a barrage of attacks, then effectively sacked and replaced by Leonid Brezhnev.

Brezhnev: Stable Shortages

Starting in the 1970s, Western scholars of communism faced a puzzling new reality. Even though the Soviet security apparatus became substantially less repressive and rarely used deadly violence, there were no mass protests in the country. In fact, the regime seemed to be safer than ever. Compliance without massive coercion led to the formation of an influential "social contract" explanation of state-society relations in the USSR. Soviet citizens, it maintained, consented to being ruled by people they did not elect in exchange for social benefits, such as full employment, housing, and affordable consumer goods.[43] Food played a central role in this list of goods. Granted, the notion of a social contract was somewhat misleading; after all, Soviet citizens had no say over the content of the "contract" that governed their political behavior.[44] Yet, the basic premise of compliance in exchange for secure and rising living standards helped explain the Soviet realities and the extent to which Brezhnev viewed food supplies as crucial for regime stability.

The Soviet leadership's perennial problem was that the country's inefficient collective agriculture could not meet the rising demands of the increasingly urban and better-educated society. Buoyed by high oil prices, the Soviet Union spent prodigious amounts of hard currency on purchasing foreign, predominantly American grain. In several short years, the USSR became the world's largest grain importer.

In 1972, Iurii Zhukov, the *Pravda* political commentator, launched a TV program in which he answered questions sent by ordinary Soviet citizens. Many of the letters Zhukov received were not suitable for open discussion on state TV. However, they landed on Brezhnev's desk so that the Soviet leader could better familiarize himself with problems faced by the population. Many of the complaints centered on food. "We ought to help developing states, but not at the expense of the [Soviet] worker's stomach," wrote a person from Shil'da township in Orenburg. "Butter, groats, pasta—we have already forgotten to even want them," complained one Isaev from the Moscow region. "We haven't seen herring for three years now.... Today is November 1. People heard a rumor that there is flour in our stores. Standing in line since midnight and will be standing for hours under snow and rain," reported Kolesnikov from Novosibirsk. According to Mamedova from Sumgait in Azerbaijan, "people say that soon there will be war and that's why there is nothing in the stores."[45]

Such letters and the general attitudes they conveyed did not necessarily mean that the Soviet population rejected the social contract the government offered. Rather, it resented the raw deal it received and expected the state to fulfill its side of the bargain it imposed. As structural reforms of collective agriculture appeared unthinkable, the government's efforts thus constituted an alternative three-pronged approach.

First, terrified by the prospect of another Novocherkassk, Brezhnev was determined to keep staple food prices fixed, low, and decoupled from the quickly rising wages. Throughout the entirety of Brezhnev's reign (1964–1982), the retail price of bread remained exactly as it was in 1954. Meat prices, whose increase in 1962 sparked the Novocherkassk protests, were not changed during his rule.[46] Retail prices of other staple foods were equally frozen for decades. Inevitably, Soviet citizens now had more money but little to spend it on.

Second, the government tried to improve domestic production by lavishing ever-increasing budgets and subsidies on agriculture. To incentivize collective and state farms to increase production, the government raised procurement prices in 1965, 1970, and 1982. And because procurement prices grew while retail prices remained unchanged, the state budget inevitably absorbed the difference. Eventually, "the retail price covered only 37 percent of the state's cost for beef, 57 percent for milk, and 41 percent for butter. . . . [Food] subsidies [constituted] 11 percent of total budget expenditures in 1979 and more than 13.3 percent in 1985."[47]

Third, since the increasingly urbanized and better-educated Soviet population sought to consume more and more meat, even increased domestic grain harvests still fell below the needed volumes and thus the Kremlin reluctantly resorted to purchasing growing amounts of grain abroad. For instance, in 1970, Soviet agriculture produced a record-breaking 186.8 million tons of grain, but even that was lower than what the country needed.[48] In normal, let alone bad harvest years, the situation was substantially worse. Initially, the volume of imported marketable grain was modest, 3.9 million tons in 1966, 1.2 million in 1968, and 1.3 million in 1969. Yet as the 1970s progressed, imports increased steadily. The Soviet Union had imported an eye-popping figure of 46 million tons in 1981 and 37 million in 1982. Soviet grain purchases accounted for roughly 20 percent of the global grain trade. During the so-called Great Grain Robbery (1972–1973), a meager domestic harvest forced the Soviet government to embark on a grain-buying spree abroad, sending global prices sky-high and hurting numerous developing states as a result.[49]

But no matter how hard the Soviet government tried and regardless of how much money it spent, feeding the Soviet public became increasingly challenging. In the second half of the 1970s, painful food shortages grew common throughout the USSR. Anatolii Chernyaev, a high-ranking official and Gorbachev's future foreign policy aide, was shocked by the situation in Kostroma, a regional center about 400 kilometers (250 miles) from Moscow after his secretary had visited family there in 1976. "Nothing in the stores. . . . No sausage, absolutely nothing meat based. When there is meat in the stores, a commotion [ensues]."[50] Even in Moscow, which was supplied far better than the rest of the country in 1976, restaurants and cafeterias had to introduce "meatless days."[51]

The strategy also carried considerable geopolitical risks. Since only the United States produced enough to satisfy Soviet import demands, Americans soon became their rivals' main suppliers. Realizing that the Soviet Union was unlikely to regain self-sufficiency in the foreseeable future, in 1976 the USSR signed a five-year agreement to purchase 6 million tons of US grain and corn annually.[52] The security and ideological implications of food dependency on its Cold War rival were swept under the rug by the Kremlin in exchange for political stability. Yet, these eventually came to the forefront of both domestic and foreign politics following the Soviet invasion of Afghanistan in 1979.

In the West, the USSR's war in Afghanistan is primarily remembered as the "Soviet Vietnam," a conflict that demonstrated the limits of Red Army's military prowess, introduced Osama bin Laden to violent politics, and caused the United States and a host of other countries to boycott the 1980 Olympic Games, held in Moscow. An important yet now largely forgotten component of the US response to the Soviet invasion was a grain embargo, introduced by President Carter in January 1980. Cognizant of the Soviet vulnerability to food shortages, the Central Intelligence Agency (CIA) concluded that, "[a]cting alone, the United States can hurt the USSR appreciably only by its grain export embargo.... The effect of even a one-year denial of grain on Moscow's consumer programs will be marked. A longer-term curb on US grain would be even more effective if other producing countries cooperated."[53] The decision was controversial; Vice President Walter Mondale opposed it, and even the CIA's earlier analysis indicated that the impact of sanctions might be minimal, as the USSR would switch suppliers.[54]

The effects of the grain embargo were indeed not nearly as crippling as the US policymakers had hoped, but painful nonetheless. The USSR managed to compensate for the bulk of the lost American grain by turning to other suppliers, most notably Brazil and Canada, but still failed to acquire the volumes it needed. The results were felt immediately. "Carter denied us seventeen million tons of grain (in Moscow flour and pasta immediately disappeared)," Chernyaev noted in his diary. In another entry, he admitted that "Carter's measures turned out to be quite impactful (*chustvitel'ny*). Regional Party branches are forbidden to allow slaughter of cattle.... Norms of consumption are made laughable: for 1981 in [the city of] Rostov-on-Don the [annual meat] consumption plan is 2 kg [4.4lb] meat per person."[55] In the industrial city of Sverdlovsk, the party boss Boris Yeltsin was forced to ration food at 400 grams (0.9 lb.) of butter, 800 grams (1.8 lb.) of boiled sausage per person per month, and one kilogram (2.2 lb.) of meat twice a year during the May 1 and November 7 holidays.[56]

Even though President Reagan abolished the embargo in 1981, it forced the Soviet Union to confront its vulnerability to food imports. It also made even the most liberal of Brezhnev's advisors advocate for the need to ratchet up domestic food production.[57] This was not an easy task and Brezhnev himself admitted that "the food problem is the central problem of the [1981–1985] five year plan," both economically and politically, especially given that increasing funding for agriculture by raising retail prices was unthinkable as this might lead to strikes and unrest.[58]

To cope with this "central problem," the Soviet leadership eventually introduced a dedicated Food Program. The Politburo member tasked with writing and implementing the Food Program was the energetic, up-and-coming Mikhail Gorbachev. The program, presented in 1982, was explicitly designed to make the USSR nutritionally less dependent on Western food imports. Expansive, costly, yet at the same time exceptionally unoriginal, the Food Program intended to "intensify agriculture" by creating additional incentives, raising, once again, procurement prices and improving management through the introduction of additional layers of bureaucracy.[59] Western observers were unimpressed. The program, one particularly biting assessment maintained, is "likely to have little or no effect on the output performance of the food economy. One can only express surprise that a program to address such an important problem . . . was so unimaginative."[60]

The critics turned out to be correct.[61] By Brezhnev's death in November 1982, Soviet food production was embroiled in deep crisis. Agriculture began to consume 27 to 30 percent of the entire state budget and, coupled with the enormous expenses on defense, prevented meaningful investment in and spending on other needs. Gorbachev, who rose to power in 1985, had to find a way to make the system work or face potential ruin.

Gorbachev: The Hungry End of a Hungry State

Avos' means "maybe" in Russia. The word gave rise to *avos'ka*, a durable, easily folding net bag. Few Soviet citizens left their homes without an *avos'ka* during the Gorbachev years. For maybe, just maybe, there would be something, anything useful in the store, and one had to be constantly ready. The shopping vocabulary also changed. Purchasing was no longer referred to as "buying" but instead became "obtaining" (*dostat'*), for it required substantially more effort, skill, and connections than just entering a store and paying for the product.[62] When rationing became the norm, Soviet citizens started joking, tongue only partly in cheek, about "waiting in long queues to get coupons for the [food] coupons."

When Gorbachev assumed leadership of the USSR, the system was already in deep trouble. The 1982 Food Program—Gorbachev's brainchild—struggled to deliver the promised products, despite the state's substantial efforts. Worse still, it was unclear to domestic and foreign experts how to fix food supply problems without violating the regime's core commitment to both collective farming and low food prices. This conundrum, however, did not prevent Gorbachev from making bold projections. He assured the Soviet public that real incomes would increase by more than half and the output of consumer goods would double in the next fifteen years. The agricultural output, he maintained, would double even sooner, by 1990.[63]

Gorbachev's reforms, which became known as *perestroika*, transformed the Soviet state. Yet, due to preexisting constraints, their agricultural component was quite modest. The agricultural reforms, writes Stephen Wegren, moved on three fronts: liberalization of personal plot operations, legalization of land leasing, and establishment of independent peasant farms.[64] Additionally, under Gorbachev, farms received a greater autonomy to manage their affairs and contract labor and services. Simply giving enterprises and workers more freedom and encouraging initiative, Gorbachev believed, would suffice. "The Chinese managed to feed a billion people in two years. But we are scared [to take the initiative]. We have said: do what you wish, just make sure there is produce . . . need to give people the ability to act," he implored colleagues in 1987.[65] But doing more of the same, just faster and better, could not overcome structural problems. By 1990, only the policies related to liberalizing private plot operations had a noticeable impact on food production.

When the situation failed to improve quickly, Gorbachev grew concerned but remained confident and self-assured. When prominent Soviet intellectuals complained that food shortages might negate all of *perestroika*'s achievements, Gorbachev retorted that he "won't believe that the Soviet people will turn their back on *perestroika* just because there wasn't this or that in stores."[66] In fact, he misread the popular mood entirely. "The grey mass rejects the domestic, especially economic policies [of Gorbachev] because of empty shelves," Chernyaev noted.[67]

Food shortages became even more widespread without the needed structural changes and with the state's hard currency reserves dwindling due to the sharp decrease of global oil prices in the mid-1980s. Even Moscow, traditionally supplied better than the rest of the Union, was not spared. Potatoes and vegetables grew increasingly rare in city stores, and meat turned into a luxury item.[68] If anything, the reforms made food shortages even more acute.

Enterprises, given more freedom, switched to producing what was most profitable for them rather than what society needed the most. They then used the extra income to benefit employees. While salaries grew, items that could be purchased with the available money became increasingly unavailable.

The country's growing openness to the world also allowed an increasing number of Soviet politicians and even some ordinary citizens to witness Soviet failure firsthand. When Boris Yeltsin visited the United States in 1988, one of the things that shocked him the most were the cheap and plentiful grocery stores. "'What have [the communists] done to our poor people,' he agonized."[69] Of course, the vast majority of Soviet citizens could not go abroad, but they could still see Western abundance on TV.

Eventually, even Gorbachev came to recognize the scope of the problem. "The whole country is standing in lines.... The lines are tormenting people," he complained to the Politburo in 1988. Furthermore, he stated that unless agricultural output starts growing rapidly next year, "nothing can save us."[70] In 1990, only 23 of 211 essential food items were available in stores on any given day, while 73 percent of Soviet citizens reported shortages of staple foods either quite often or constantly.[71] "We have no grain, and we have no foreign currency. The situation is hopeless," admitted Soviet prime minister Nikolay Ryzhkov.[72]

In hindsight, ignoring agriculture in 1985–1986 may have doomed the entire *perestroika* enterprise. Some observers and even Gorbachev's aides argued that the reform program should have started with agriculture because early on, Gorbachev still had the legitimacy and time to implement painful but necessary changes.[73] However, at the same time, Gorbachev's situation represented a classical Catch-22 scenario. Saving the Soviet system was impossible without slashing food subsidies and raising retail prices. But doing so would have destroyed popular support for *perestroika*. Even when the government realized that raising retail prices was necessary, Novocherkassk was explicitly on their minds, stymying action. Soviet leaders went out of their way to avoid popular mobilization caused by high food prices until the very end.[74]

The catastrophe that everyone expected eventually arrived between late 1990 and early 1991. The government believed some regions were on the brink of famine, stores were empty, and only Ukraine and Kazakhstan could barely feed themselves. "Moscow likely haven't seen [anything like that] even in the hungriest years of its history," stated Chernyaev in March 1991.[75] In the Siberian city of Tyumen, authorities introduced rationing coupons for the fifteen most basic food items, including sugar, flour, eggs, and pasta. Bread lines were miles long, and since loaves were allocated per person, entire families waited for hours.[76]

On April 1, 1991, the government finally raised retail prices of staple foods, consumer goods, and services. The official retail price of bread increased threefold, and the cost of beef nearly quadrupled. Milk now cost 3.5 times more. But it was already too late to make a difference. Firstly, the Soviet citizens' nominal income rose so rapidly that the effect of increased prices was minimal. Secondly, the change in retail prices was meaningless because the stores remained as empty after April 1 as they were before.[77] And as the government feared, the price increase led to strikes throughout the country. The Soviet social contract, to the extent it still existed by spring 1991, was officially defunct. The only food source Soviet citizens could now count on were household plots, which, being merely 2 percent of the cultivated land, produced as much as one-quarter of the country's agricultural output.[78]

On August 18, 1991, when Gorbachev was vacationing in Crimea, a group of hardliners in the Politburo and the security services launched a coup. The attempt failed after three short days of turmoil. The Soviet Union limped along until its ultimate disintegration on December 26, 1991. In practice, however, following the August coup attempt, the task of feeding Russia was handed to Boris Yeltsin's government of the Russian Federation. The communist regime, whose sudden rise to power had begun with food riots, ultimately collapsed in large part due to its inability to feed the country.

2
Food and Market
The Hungry, 1991–1993

Food is key to understanding Russia's market reforms of the early 1990s. The Soviet Union entered the decade in a severe economic crisis and growing food shortages. Both reached a climax in the second half of 1991 and early 1992 when the economy stopped functioning, the government's food procurement system collapsed, the ruble lost whatever value it still had, and the state itself disintegrated. Nascent independent Russia faced potential famine, and feeding citizens became Kremlin's top priority. The country's rulers feared that food shortage would cause not just misery and unrest, but complete state collapse. At this critical juncture, food determined Russia's future and the transformation it would undergo.

What role did the food crisis play in Russia's economic transition? How and why did the newly independent state attempt to overcome food shortages that had so greatly contributed to the demise of communism? And what were the effects of these new policies on food production and provisioning? This chapter focuses on the rise of a radically new solution to the problem of feeding Russia: a free, open market. Sandwiched between the Soviet planned economy and Putin's state capitalism, this approach centered on an open and internationally integrated market economy and aimed to create a new class of individual small and middle-sized farmers. Privatization, deregulation, and decentralization of food procurement and production, this view maintained, would form the cornerstones of Russia's food security. Some elements of this approach were products of ideological convictions, while others emerged out of necessity.

The shock therapy approach adopted by liberal market reformers filled the previously empty shelves but carried a staggering social cost. Decentralization and deregulation threatened to tear the country apart and provided ample opportunities for corruption. Imported foods were abundant yet costly and out of reach for large portions of the Russian population. As Russians increasingly turned to subsistence farming and the state's agricultural subsidies largely disappeared, the country's food production rapidly contracted. The reforms' architects believed these were regrettable but inevitable and short-term consequences of the transition to a market economy. The realities of Soviet collapse, they believed, simply left them no other choice; the country was either to transform or to starve. They were confident that Russia's long-term future was bright. To get there, however, the state needed food, and since socialism repeatedly failed to keep Russians satiated, they believed that only capitalism could.

The Specter of Hunger

"The Moscow of December 1991 is one of my heaviest memories," wrote Yegor Gaidar, the architect of Russia's economic reforms and the state's de facto prime minister. "Virginally empty stores. Women, thrashing about in search for any products.... A uniform expectation of a catastrophe."[1] Soviet citizens who resided in previously better-provisioned cities, such as Moscow and Leningrad, were especially hard-hit by the growing food insecurity, and the situation came as a total shock to those few who experienced life abroad. In 1990, Vladimir Putin, a KGB officer stationed in East Germany, returned to his native Leningrad. His wife, Lyudmila, recalls the period with horror and admits that she was simply too scared to go shopping and could not bring herself to stand in the long lines.[2]

The situation was even worse in the provinces. For instance, in the Perm region in the Urals, vegetable oil was completely out of stock in stores because suppliers from other regions refused delivery. Sugar was also absent from the shelves, while bread was sold intermittently and led to the formation of long queues. The region was also dangerously short on flour. In the northern city of Arkhangel'sk, milk was available in stores for just one hour, sugar was rationed at one kilogram (2.2 lb.), and meat at half a kilogram per person each month. Bread was sold only rarely, while flour was permanently missing from the shelves. Other parts of Russia reported similar, and occasionally even more severe shortages of bread, milk, oil, and other staple foods. Russia, lamented Gaidar, was on the verge of a very real famine (*samyi nastoiashchii golod*). By late November 1991, the country possessed enough grain for just two months, and the city of Moscow had flour reserves for just ten days. The next harvest was seven long months away.[3]

In a hungry state, power is not property, money, or guns, but access to food and the ability to distribute it.[4] Food availability and the fear of starvation thus emerged as the top priority for the nascent Russian government. When Gaidar described the period from August 1991 to October 1993—from the failed GKChP coup attempt to the violent showdown between President Yeltsin and his opponents in the parliament—he put deterring a "provisioning catastrophe" first on his list of concerns. Keeping Russians fed was crucial for avoiding a civil war, staving off social and state collapse, and was a precondition to establishing functioning economic institutions.[5]

The catastrophe was long in the making, caused by the chronic inefficiencies of the Soviet agriculture and food provisioning system. In the wake of the 1991 coup, the disintegration of the Soviet Union entered its final phase and the mechanisms that kept Russian cities supplied and their residents fed disappeared almost overnight. The harvest of 1991 was poorer than the bumper crop of the previous year, yet the main reasons for food shortages were political and psychological; the real Achilles heel of Soviet food provisioning was distribution and logistics, not production.[6] Faced with an increasingly uncertain future, the collapsing value of the ruble, and "disgusted at the state's failure to deliver promised consumer goods and agricultural equipment"[7] to the countryside, farms simply ceased selling their produce to the state at a fixed price (no market prices existed).[8] Instead, agricultural producers began hoarding and independently bartering food. The Soviet government could previously requisition food by brute force, but in late 1991, the state's repressive capacity was gone, and shelves in city stores began to empty at a terrifyingly fast pace. Small towns could sustain themselves by relying on local farmers' markets and thus avoided acute food shortages. However, the medium and large cities depended on the central government's procurement and distribution and were thus facing potential famine. Even the Soviet Army relied on humanitarian food aid from the German *Bundeswehr*.[9]

Especially troubling was the situation with grain, without which one could not bake bread or feed the livestock that provided meat and dairy products. Domestic procurement could meet only half of Russia's demand, thus necessitating massive imports.[10] As we discussed in the previous chapter, reliance on grain imports was not new for the government; the difference was that, unlike in previous years, the state's income was collapsing, foreign debt ballooning, currency and gold reserves empty, and creditworthiness in tatters.[11]

To Gaidar and his team of reformers, a swift, radical even if painful transition to a market economy was the only policy that could stave off the looming collapse. The deregulation of prices, scheduled to take effect on January 2, 1992, was designed to fix the failed Soviet prices system, jump-start a functioning market, and incentivize domestic food producers to stock empty stores. "Free prices will awaken production from its sleep and will compel production of goods and services to increase, while competition, for its part, will restrain the growth of prices," declared Yeltsin.[12] Food shortages, the argument went, precluded any alternative course of reforms. Slow-paced structural changes were simply untenable against the background of empty shelves. "The gradual, Chinese-style reforms were absolutely possible in the 1960s.... Maybe it was even still possible in the early Gorbachev period, before [19]87 or so. But we [in the Gaidar government] were handed an economy that absolutely went to pieces," argued Andrey Nechaev, Gaidar's deputy minister of economics and finance and, since February 1992, the minister of economics.[13] Russia would either starve or be administered shock therapy.

Not all prices were liberalized immediately. In fact, energy prices were not liberalized and remained an important state subsidy channel. Thus, in the early 1990s, Russians were worried about going hungry but not about freezing. The cost of staple foods such as bread, milk, salt, and sugar increased threefold but remained under state control for an additional period. Later, however, even these price controls were abolished, and by the summer of 1992, the prices of only very few products were not yet fully liberalized.[14] Regional authorities also had the right to establish price caps for staple foods, thus paving the way for a patchwork of local food policies that created substantial disparities and made future centralized decision-making nearly impossible.[15] The government also did not privatize bread factories, which continued to be run by local authorities.[16] Additionally, to attract foreign food and consumer goods producers, the government lifted restrictions on imports. During the first half of 1992, notes Åslund, Russia had no import tariffs and quotas whatsoever.[17]

The policy was deeply unpopular and risky. According to public opinion polls, in 1991, only 26 percent of Soviet citizens supported the liberalization of prices.[18] Thus, Russia's leaders anticipated widespread unrest as the free prices were assumed to immediately, even if only temporarily, skyrocket.[19] The government established a special committee to monitor the situation in the regions based on the law enforcement and KGB reports and "brought in extra police on the day of price liberalization"[20] to confront the expected unrest. Yet, the reformers believed that the policy, despite all its potential dangers and hardships, was necessary. Nechaev recalled that the only alternative to the liberalization of prices was "a second edition of War Communism," including food rationing, coupons, and forced expropriation of food from peasants. Several Yeltsin aides, most notably the conservative Yuri Skokov,[21] promoted this course of action but ultimately failed, not least because, unlike in 1918, the Russian Army refused to use force against compatriots.[22]

In addition to deregulating the prices, the government needed to import food from abroad, an effort that became intertwined with the broader issues of obtaining new credit and servicing existing (Soviet) debts. The United States was crucial for both, and the Russian leaders quickly discovered that food insecurity means foreign policy weakness, indeed humiliation. According to Gaidar, in November 1991, he began participating in the debt servicing negotiations between the Paris Club and the disintegrating Soviet government. By then, the Soviet negotiators had generally agreed to the foreign creditors' terms. The US negotiator, Under Secretary of the Treasury David Mulford,[23] threatened that if the new Russian government did not immediately sign the agreement negotiated by the USSR, he would stop delivering American grain to the country. Gaidar had no choice but to accept the American terms. Thus, the direct consequence of food shortages was debt-servicing obligations that were, from Gaidar's perspective, "inflated and knowingly unrealistic."[24] But what mattered the most was that shiploads of grain were crossing the ocean. Russia could only take a firmer stand in debt negotiations once the food supply crisis subsided.[25]

The liberalization of prices and food imports eventually stocked grocery stores. Even previously rare foreign items, such as bananas or kiwis, found their way onto the shelves. Yet, the prices dumbfounded Russians and made even the staple foods inaccessible for many. "In Georgia they celebrated the New Year with a civil war, whereas we had a giant—as earlier for vodka— queue in the vegetables store. Here, the price tags have not been replaced yet. But in other stores, [these are] not price tags, but numbers from an astronomy textbook. The faces of store employees are confused and resigned. Nobody bothers them. The patrons stare at price tags and leave without asking questions. The holidays are over. The hangover has begun," wrote conservative writer Nikolai Koniaev in his diary on January 4, 1992.[26] "Some products do appear. . . . But the prices! They make my head spin," lamented the Muscovite historian Genrikh Ioffe on January 7, 1992.[27] Other diaries and reports from early 1992 also project the combined sense of despair, confusion, and only very rare cautious hope for a better, more affluent future.

Yet despite the government's fears, Russians did not rebel. No food riots, widespread social unrest, or mass protests similar to the 1962 Novocherkassk occurred. "People grumble, but don't plan on rioting. Because what would a riot accomplish? [We] will smash several dozens of front windows—that won't bring food. Will have to endure," Lev Osterman summarized the social mood.[28] The government's unrest monitoring committee only convened once. Notwithstanding the economic hardship, the lack of protest mobilization from below would become an essential feature of Russia's economic and social transition.[29] Instead of collective mobilization, Russians opted for personal, often very creative, and at times desperate survival strategies.[30] Furthermore, because high prices immediately depressed demand, the long queues that characterized the last months of Soviet existence disappeared as well. Food products remained on the shelves creating an outward appearance of affluence and abundance.[31]

Regional Responses to Shortages

While Russians did not riot between late 1991 and early 1992, they still had to get by. When food became first unavailable and then unaffordable, and the state's social safety net disappeared, the task of keeping the population fed put severe pressure on local and regional authorities, not just the central government.

Some local leaders desperately tried to appeal to the central government for assistance. Andrey Nechaev described one memorable episode. In early December 1991, the leaders of St. Petersburg, including then–vice mayor Vladimir Putin, approached him with an urgent cry for help. The city, they claimed, was running out of grain. In two to three days, the chicken in poultry enterprises that supplied the city would start dying because of the shortage of feed grain. In a week, the residents of Russia's second-largest city would become protein-deficient. This danger was especially horrifying for St. Petersburg, in which hundreds of thousands starved to death during a brutal German siege in 1941–1944. "The story ended with me, an academic just two weeks prior, urgently redirecting the last two ships with grain that were headed to Murmansk towards St. Petersburg, and opening up strategic reserves," recalled Nechaev.[32]

However, most regional authorities lacked the influence that St. Petersburg leaders had. Left to their own devices, local bosses needed to find individual strategies to weather the crisis. Bartering was one. Against the backdrop of the collapse of the ruble and the USSR's increasingly inevitable dissolution in the second half of 1991, barter became the regions' preferred strategy in their quest for food and other necessities Regional authorities

> [a]lready cannot get, say, meat, by decree (*po prikazu*) but cannot yet get it for money. What can a regional leader do? Suppose he has nails, refrigerators and bearings. He forbids the export of these items [out of the region] and says: if anyone needs these, please kindly give us meat in exchange. Oh, don't have [meat]? Well, we will take cars, then. And exchange them for meat ourselves.[33]

These interregional barter arrangements might have provided short-term local solutions but, in addition to increasing transaction costs, also kept the central government weak, sidelined, and often in the dark about the conditions on the ground. They also turned out to be especially harmful to places like Moscow, St. Petersburg, and other major government, research, and defense production hubs that only possessed a small number of valuable products to barter. The agricultural regions of Southern Russia, which had little use for military technologies or culture produced in Moscow or the Urals, simply refused to supply these regions, and no government's argument—its only tool in late 1991—could have persuaded them otherwise.[34]

To address the growing food shortages, the government also granted some regional authorities permission to export abroad valuable materials, such as oil or rare metals, in exchange for food. In St. Petersburg, Putin, the vice mayor in charge of the city's foreign relations, quickly emerged as the key participant in what was meant to be an extraordinary effort to feed the city. It turned out to be a sham, a corruption bonanza that enriched many of Putin's future key cronies but failed to provide food relief. The ensuing scandal also nearly ended Putin's career just as it was taking off.

After intensive lobbying by the St. Petersburg City Hall, on January 28, 1992, Gaidar permitted Putin to "set quotas, issue licenses, and work with suppliers directly, without having to pay export duties . . . for the sale or barter of natural resources in exchange for food."[35] Putin reportedly started engaging in these activities already in December 1991 even though he had zero legal authority to do so; Gaidar's nod simply gave a stamp of approval to what was already an established and sprawling operation. A large number of companies licensed by Putin's office quickly emerged in St. Petersburg. Their ostensible goal was to export natural resources out of Russia, sell them, use the profits to purchase food abroad, and bring it back to feed St. Petersburg. The commissions received by these entities stood at an exorbitant 25–50 percent of the deal instead of the standard 3–4 percent. In one remarkable arrangement, Dzhikop, a company established just two months earlier, was allowed to buy almost 14,000 kilograms (about 31,000 lbs.) of rare metals for a price two thousand times lower than that on the global market, thus leading to hefty profits after selling the metals abroad.[36]

Export was impossible without using the city's seaport, which was controlled by organized crime. This led to numerous speculations about the city hall and the security services' connections to Russia's underworld. Putin was believed to be the liaison between the mafia, the ex-KGB, and the mayor's office. Mobsters or not, many of the companies that received exports licenses from Putin were owned by his acquaintances or former members of the security services. For instance, Dzhikop was "co-run by the brother of one of Putin's university classmates who shared Putin's love for martial arts."[37] For some of Russia's future oligarchs, most notably Gennady Timchenko, this was their first major enrichment opportunity. The program also allowed Putin to promote and shape his public persona. When he became president, Putin's PR image centered on embodiments of masculinity and military prowess, such as riding shirtless, visiting troops in Chechnya, or sedating a tiger. February 1992 was different. A documentary he commissioned then presented Putin as an efficient administrator and centered on his efforts to secure provisions for the city.[38]

But the promised food never arrived. When the city legislature got wind of Putin's activities, it launched an investigation commission led by Marina Salye. The Salye commission discovered that the central government's $122 million export quotas to St. Petersburg provided just two tankers of cooking oil that arrived on February 3, 1992. Many of the companies ordered to bring food in exchange for natural resources simply disappeared after taking valuable materials out of Russia, selling them abroad, and depositing the money in offshore bank accounts.[39] While the investigators found no direct evidence of conspiracy, they strongly suspected that contracts signed by Putin's office were never intended to be fulfilled. The penalties for nondelivery of food were inexplicably low, ranging between 1 and 5 percent.

A handful of the contracts were also incomplete, with key signatures, stamps, and legal details missing, and thus unenforceable in court. It is unclear what became of the money made out of this scheme. Most likely Putin used, or permitted, such tactics in order to enrich associates and himself. A different version suggests that the money gained from these activities functioned as an unofficial slush fund for the city hall.[40] Either way, it was clearly not used to provide St. Petersburg with the food it so desperately needed.

The Salye commission report directly blamed Putin for the lack of promised food deliveries. It recommended his removal from office and turned the documents to the Prosecutor General Office for potential criminal investigation. Putin, protected by the mayor and his allies in law enforcement, survived the scandal, but just barely. When asked about the episode years later, Putin evaded, lied, and claimed that the investigation was just a smear campaign that targeted him because of his KGB background.[41]

In most accounts, the affair is simply treated as the first documented evidence of Putin's corruption and possible connections with organized crime. While this is certainly true, it misses the *food* aspect of the story. Corruption aside, in early 1992, Putin could not have overlooked the political importance of food and the broader social and economic implications of food scarcity on both the macro and micro levels.

The leaders of St. Petersburg were not alone in frantically trying to secure food and protect the population from its shortages. The liberalization of prices policy allowed regional authorities to establish price caps, subsidized from local budgets. This permitted regional leaders to ease the economic hardships experienced by their constituencies. Yet, it also increased centrifugal, separatist tendencies by creating a patchwork of local trade and price regimes. While wealthier regions were preoccupied with protecting their food from poorer neighbors, the have-nots resented the more affluent parts of Russia and felt increasingly abandoned and betrayed by the central government.

The relatively well-off Tatarstan had to balance the desire to keep prices low against the need to keep this cheaper food on the shelves. The solution was to issue the republic's residents tokens that entitled them to purchase ten loaves of bread per person each month.[42] In Tyumen, the regional authorities introduced two types of bread. The product itself was identical, what differed was the price. The "expensive" bread was sold freely in stores and priced at 4.5 rubles, whereas the "cheap" bread, available only to locals, cost 1.92 rubles. Tyumen residents received coupons that authorized them to buy a certain amount of "cheap" bread but also required waiting in long queues.[43] Some regions even issued regional currencies, such as the "Ural francs." Still others tried to recycle the old Soviet-era command methods. Thus, in 1993, the governor of the Orel region ordered private commercial banks to issue agricultural enterprises credits at a certain rate and struggled to understand why he had no authority to do so.[44] In Sverdlovsk, the media complained that the region is "given the role of supplier of food and means for the well-to-do existence of others" without receiving much in return.[45]

Outside the government distribution networks, individual companies established direct relations with large farms. According to these informal arrangements, large urban enterprises provided farms with labor and materials for food products. Others simply paid salaries in kind, be it shoes or condensed milk, instead of money.[46] Local authorities also utilized whatever manpower they could find come harvest time. In the Moscow region alone, about 20,000 Russian Army soldiers were engaged in agricultural labor in summer 1992.[47]

Individual Responses to Shortages

Individual Russians also adjusted the best they could, often adopting small-scale subsistence agriculture as an alternative to purchasing expensive food in stores. Most households reduced food consumption during the period. In 1990–2000, the per capita milk consumption dropped by 44 percent and meat by 45 percent.[48] According to a survey conducted in the Novgorod region, the reform also forced rural and urban residents to substantially limit their consumption of fish, fruit, and vegetables. Many picked mushrooms and berries, and "[n]early 20% of both the urban and the rural households fished all the fish they needed."[49] A study conducted in 1995 among women in Moscow revealed that 62 percent of respondents preserved food. Of those who preserved food, almost half kept over fifty jars per year.[50] Even as late as 1999, Russians on average consumed less food than in 1985.[51]

The most common survival strategy adopted by Russians in response to increasing food prices was simply growing their own food, mostly potatoes and vegetables on dachas, suburban garden plots. Even during the Soviet times, the dacha, originally a rustic summer retreat venue, gradually transformed into "an ersatz homestead for under-provisioned urbanites." Market reforms finalized this transition to the dacha's functioning as the subsistence-focused "mini farm."[52] During the 1990s, the number of household plots mushroomed throughout Russia. Thirty million such plots, occupying about 28 million hectares of land (territory larger than the state of Colorado or the United Kingdom) were registered in the country in 2002.[53] Their actual number and size were likely even larger. In 1992, 31.8 percent of Russia's total agricultural output was produced by such "mini farms." The number increased substantially to 47.9 percent in 1995, and by the early 2000s, it accounted for more than 55 percent.[54]

Yet reliance on suburban small-scale farming and gardening was not a viable long-term solution. Small garden plots were unsuitable for grains and could support only limited livestock, leading to a steep decline in Russians' meat and milk consumption. Thus, despite the skyrocketing prices, Russians still had to spend money on food purchases in stores. And spend they did; by 1995, an average family devoted almost half of its budget to food.[55] A large portion of the food Russians bought in stores was foreign. On aggregate, by early 1996, Russia was spending about $1 billion a month on food imports.[56]

Effects on Agriculture

The combined effect of open markets, decreasing demand, and removal of state subsidies on Russia's already struggling agriculture was immediate and devastating. Soviet-era farms were simply in no position to compete with Western, more efficient, and heavily subsidized agriculture, and their outputs collapsed as a result. Russia's liberal reformers saw it as an inevitable yet temporary outcome of capitalism's "creative destruction." Removal of subsidies, the argument went, would force large farms to become efficient and profitable. If they fail or fire workers, their former employees would then take up private farming instead. As a result, "[private] farmers will feed Russia."[57] The resulting slump, however, was deeper than anyone could have anticipated.

Scholars are still debating the exact scope of Russia's agricultural collapse, yet the numbers are staggering no matter which estimate or indicator is used. According to one approximation, Russia's agricultural output had declined by 60 percent by 1998.[58] Between 1992 and 1995, the average annual decline of cereals production was 11 percent.[59] The percentage of loss-making farms skyrocketed from 3 percent in 1990 to 57 percent in 1995.[60] If in 1990 agriculture accounted for 15 percent of Russia's gross domestic product (GDP), by 1994, it was just 6.5 percent.[61]

The number of cattle declined by 55 percent and pigs by 48 percent throughout the 1990s. The rate of livestock loss was even higher than during Stalin's collectivization and comparable to World War II losses. To reduce costs, some peasants replaced tractors with horses or even pulled the plows themselves.[62] The exact amount of cropland abandoned due to the market reforms is unclear, but even the lower estimates stand at 20 million hectares (77,200 sq. miles).[63] High-end estimates are twice as large, an astonishing 38–40 million hectares, about a third of all 1990 cropland (roughly 147,000–154,000 sq. miles, just slightly smaller than California).[64] However, some viewed this contraction as a "blessing in disguise."[65] A sizable portion of the abandoned cropland was of poor quality and could be cultivated only because of enormous and economically nonsensical Soviet-era subsidies. Yet even this silver lining could not mask the grim reality of agricultural tailspin. Under such conditions, the country was bound to keep relying on imports. Indeed, by 1997, 50 percent of food consumed by Russians came from abroad.[66]

Concluding Remarks

This chapter focused on a brief but dramatic period in Russia's modern history: the transition to market economy in the early 1990s. As authors argue throughout the book, food offers a unique vision of Russian politics and society. Few critical junctures demonstrate the crucial role of food more clearly than this period. Food provisioning did not only reflect the ongoing political and economic processes but arguably became the driver of the most radical transformation the country experienced since the 1917 Revolution.

The period 1991–1992 was a window of opportunity for Russia's liberal markets reformers. They leveraged the country's food shortages to promote their political vision and ideals. The reformists repeatedly claimed that the situation left them no other choice. This is not true. Other options, such as more gradual economic liberalization, did exist, though they were incompatible with the governments' moral beliefs and ideological convictions. The Soviet government tolerated and occasionally provoked massive famines within its borders. It requisitioned food, raided villages, and used deadly violence. In 1990s, the government's capacity for violent action was indeed low, but this is beside the point. Even if Gaidar and his team could pursue massive "war communism," they had zero desire to do so. Thus, Russia of the early 1990s fully confirmed Amartya Sen's famous argument that famine is an outcome of politics, not agriculture, and democratic states are spared this plague.[67] Yet, in Russia's case, the democratizing leaders did not simply deter famine. They also leveraged the threat to initiate a broader social transformation. Such an overhaul was impossible without reforming the countryside to prevent future food shortages once and for all. The next chapter focuses on these efforts and their outcomes.

3
Farmers Will Not Feed Russia

The Failure of Yeltsin's Agrarian Reforms

What could replace the Soviet-era collective and state farms? During the 1990s, Yeltsin and market reformers constantly told Russians that private farming would emerge and feed the country. Peasants who work, own, and freely buy and sell land will succeed where the old *kolkhoz* and *sovkhoz* failed. But how and why would these farmers appear in such substantial numbers? This chapter documents the Yeltsin-era liberal attempts to reform Russia's food production and transform large agricultural enterprises into small and medium-sized private farms, the Jeffersonian cornerstone of food security and democracy. Unfortunately, the vision of the yeoman-centered Russian agriculture (and by extension, democracy) failed to emerge. By the end of the 1990s, small farmers represented just a tiny segment of rural Russia and played a minuscule role in the country's food production. The Soviet Union collapsed, but its agriculture persisted.

As we documented in the previous chapter, food shortages led to "shock therapy" market reforms in the early 1990s. The reforms, their architects contended, would be painful and traumatic in the short term. However, in the long term, Russia would never again need to worry about large-scale hunger. But when Vladimir Putin replaced Boris Yeltsin—the impulsive, heavy drinking, and increasingly unpopular president who had led the country throughout this tumultuous period—at the end of the decade, the country was recovering from yet another crisis. In 1998, a combination of a financial crash, low oil prices, and a heavy drought once again sent Russian officials scrambling for emergency food aid, a déjà vu of the hungry winter of 1991–1992.[1] The financial crash and the drought wrecked the economy, plunged millions into poverty, and emptied grocery stores.

Whereas the previous chapter outlined the rise of the open market, private farming-centered solution to Russia's food provisioning problems, this chapter analyzes its demise and the persistence of Soviet-era large state and collective farms throughout the reform years.

The Attempts to Reform Russian Agriculture

When the danger of widespread famine subsided and subsequently disappeared in 1992–1993, the Russian government shifted its focus from short-term food procurement to more fundamental, structural reforms of the country's collapsing agriculture. The idea that agriculture needed to be reformed was widely accepted, even among the more conservative parts of the political spectrum. The question was the exact nature of the reform and the state's role in agricultural production and the countryside writ large. The government eventually developed several overlapping and at times contradictory and competing reform programs, but neither produced the desired long-term results.[2]

The reform program that outpaced the rest was favored by the liberal pro-market economists of the Gaidar government. Their vision of Russia's agricultural transformation rested on several key assumptions. Firstly, they believed that in the post-communist era, Russia was neither engaged in nor preparing for a confrontation with other countries and therefore did not require self-sufficiency in food production for geopolitical and national security reasons. Russian farmers thus would produce what is economically profitable, not what the state needs for self-defense. Imports would provide the country with everything else it needed. Secondly, the liberals maintained that the government does not need a designated food policy in a functioning market economy.[3] Instead, it simply had to establish a proper open market and ensure the existence of fundamental economic institutions and mechanisms, first and foremost, secured property rights.[4] A comprehensive land reform that would convert Russian peasants into small and medium-sized farmers would ensure the prosperity of the countryside and reverse the failed Soviet legacy of collective and state farms-based agriculture.[5] And thirdly, the central government's weakness necessitated giving more freedom and power to regional and local authorities, in line with Yeltsin's offer to the regions to take as much sovereignty as they can swallow.[6]

A competing vision of agrarian reforms was promulgated by Vice President Aleksandr Rutskoi, a Soviet Air Force pilot and a hero of the country's war in Afghanistan, and his conservative and nationalist allies. Even though Rutskoi was entrusted by the government to lead the agrarian reform efforts, he was anything but a natural candidate for the task. In 1993, he published a book on the topic, opening with "I have never dealt with agriculture and haven't intended to."[7] The mastermind behind Rutskoi's assignment to lead the agrarian reform was Gennady Burbulis, Gaidar's close ally in the government. The move, hatched in early 1992 following a confrontation between Rutskoi and the liberal reformers, was explicitly designed to set the vice president up for failure.[8] In the Soviet times, being in charge of the chronically underperforming and ostensibly hopeless agricultural sector could easily end an aspiring politician's career, though Gorbachev was a notable exception to this rule. Gaidar, however, quickly came to regret the decision and even asked Andrei Kozyrev, Russia's minister of foreign affairs, to arrange for the energetic but incompetent Rutskoi to be sent on government business abroad at the height of the harvest season.

Rutskoi's plan, almost certainly written by his nationalist advisor and ghostwriter Aleksei Podberezkin, opposed agriculture dominated by small landowning farmers and a food provisioning system that relied on foreign producers. "Not even one prosperous state subjects the agriculture, which is the foundation of the society's existence to the elemental forces of the market (*stikhiia rynka*).... The society itself protects this sphere with all available means," the plan argued.[9] Such an assessment would hardly surprise anyone familiar with agricultural subsidies and protectionist policies of developed market economies. However, to Russia's zealous free-market reformers, this line of thinking was an anathema.[10]

Instead of disbanding the existing state and collective farms and creating a new class of private farmers, Rutskoi's plan vied for the large farms' reconstitution as cooperatives that would serve as the backbone of the agricultural sector.[11] The changes advocated by Rutskoi and set to unfold in several stages over three years (1993–1995) were devised to be more slow-paced than the liberals' shock therapy.[12] Ivan Starikov, deputy chairman of the Agrarian Committee of the State Duma (the Russian parliament's lower house) in 1993–1995, believed Rutskoi's ideas were sensible but also mostly dominated by Soviet stereotypes.[13] Rutskoi, he recalled, simply could not comprehend the notion of private land ownership and favored long-term rentals instead. Nechaev offered an even less favorable assessment of the vice president. Rutskoi's involvement in agriculture, he argued, consisted of lobbying the interests of specific enterprises by which either Rutskoi or his entourage, "fantastic punks, swindlers all around," were presumably paid. Once, Rutskoi even threatened to have Nechaev executed for refusing preferential treatment to a certain plant. The government, however, has never discussed Rutskoi's reform plan in any detail.[14] In 1993, the vice president joined forces with anti-reform members of the parliament to oust Yeltsin. The ensuing violent confrontation cost Rutskoi his position and briefly landed him in prison. A long shot even prior to these events, his reform plan vanished from the public sphere altogether.

The measures that the government ultimately adopted reflected the liberal reformers' vision. The first and key component of the reforms was what Stephen Wegren describes as "de-collectivization" of the Soviet-era farms and land distribution to peasants willing to take it. On December 29, 1991, Yeltsin declared that farms would need to undergo re-registration as open or closed joint-stock companies, production cooperatives, or disband and distribute assets to workers. The plurality of farms became joint-stock companies, and just a meager 4 percent disbanded.[15] On March 2, 1992, Yeltsin signed a decree "On the Procedure for Establishing Norms for the Free Transfer of Land Plots to Citizens." This document declared that

> farm workers, farm pensioners, and persons who worked in the "social sphere" in the countryside were eligible to receive free plots of land for private farming or land shares if the person remained a member of a large farm. The size of the land allocation was to be determined by the total amount of agricultural land held by the farm, divided by the number of persons who had a right to a land share. The decree gave rural (village) administrations the right to set the norms governing land share size. Norms could vary from area to area within a *raion* [an administrative unit equivalent to county in the United States], depending on the density of the population.[16]

Even though the decree entitled peasants to receive and own land, it failed to establish a functioning statewide land market, as the land the peasants received could not be sold.

Private ownership of land and a functioning land market were popular ideas. In 1991, 54 percent of Russians supported the unrestricted purchase and sale of land, and just 30 percent opposed.[17] Yeltsin was committed to the idea and believed that Russian citizens should have the right to acquire and "dispose of their land in any way they saw fit, not least mortgaging and leasing it." Property rights to land and meaningful land reform, notes Åslund, "became pet issues for the democrats."[18]

In early 1992, the government proposed a law on the privatization of agricultural land. It was voted down by the Russian parliament (elected during Soviet times), in April of that year.[19] In response, the Democratic Russia movement began collecting signatures to push a referendum on the issue.

One million signatures were required to force a referendum. Although almost twice as many were collected, no referendum was held.[20] Yeltsin launched a renewed attempt at establishing an agricultural land market and instituting private ownership on land by decree in October 1993. Still, even as late as 1995, some regions did not recognize private land ownership.[21] Another legislative initiative in 1997–1998 fell by just a single vote short of the majority required for the bill's adoption.[22] Thus, despite all Yeltsin's efforts, a functioning land market in Russia would not fully emerge until Putin's presidency.

Another set of policies focused on liberalizing the grain market. The December 1993 decree "On the Liberalization of Grain Market in Russia" stipulated a free trade in grain, mandated free transportation of grain across Russia's regions (which the government failed to achieve in late 1991), shifted the burden of grain provisioning from the central government to the regional authorities, and ordered the privatization of grain processing and storage facilities (though the state retained 51 percent of shares in some enterprises).

In parallel, the government also sought to dismantle the Soviet-era agricultural subsidies regime. According to Gaidar and his pro-reform allies, given the disastrous state of the country's coffers, underperforming agricultural enterprises needed to be allowed to fail rather than becoming a financial drain on the government.[23] When large farms fail, they will disband, and their former employees would take up private farming instead. To encourage private farming, the state would provide farmers with financial and tax incentives such as freedom from land taxes and subsidized credit instead of wasting money on inefficient and underperforming large farms.

Political Backlash against the Reforms

The steep decline in domestic agricultural production made Russia's almost total dependence on food imports inevitable, at least in the short term. However, this did not trouble the free market liberals in the slightest. Despite the severe crisis, liberal reformers perceived early 1992 as a window of unconstrained opportunity to promote their vision of a new, free market and democratic post-Soviet Russia.[24] They did so by liberalizing most (and later, all) prices, opening the domestic market to imports, and establishing a legal path to splitting large agricultural enterprises into small private farms. The reformers, by and large, forgot about food altogether once the danger of large-scale famine disappeared.[25] In Gaidar's memoirs, food provisioning was not discussed at all after the winter of 1992–1993. Other issues became more prominent, with pro-market, liberal parties essentially scratching agriculture off their agenda (with the exception of the land ownership issue). And, in retrospect, many regarded their actions in that period as an unqualified success.

When in February 1996 Yeltsin declared his intent to run for re-election, he explicitly praised the government's policies in the food sphere.

> "Remember the huge queues for bread and sugar in 1991?" Yeltsin asked. . . . Remember how people stood in queues even at night and warmed themselves besides bonfires? All gone. The stores were full, and their children and grandchildren would never know what shortages and ration coupons were. What had brought about this plenty? Free-market prices introduced in 1992.[26]

The opponents of democracy and free market—the communists, the nationalists, and the representatives of Soviet-era collective and state farms—viewed things differently. In 1991–1992, many Russians protested government policies, throwing away the "food aid they received from the United States because they did not appreciate the political symbolism embodied by the food [aid]."[27] Anti-reform forces within the parliament did all they could to obstruct the government's reform efforts. During the standoff between Yeltsin and the parliament, Rutskoi, whom the parliament elected as "acting president," promised to reduce administratively fixed food prices by at least a half, compensate producers for the difference between the market and the fixed prices, and introduce steep fines to punish over-chargers.[28] Rutskoi and the parliament lost the confrontation, and food prices remained untouched. As long as Yeltsin was in power the success or the failure of the agrarian reform was in the hands of the reformers.

The parliamentary elections of December 1993 came as a painful blow to the pro-market, liberal forces. The nationalist Liberal Democratic Party (LDPR) came in first, winning 23 percent of the vote. The Communist Party of the Russian Federation (KPRF) finished third with 12.4 percent. Their rural allies, the Agrarian Party (AP), received 8 percent. Its representative, Ivan Rybkin, became the speaker of the Duma. The AP did not fundamentally oppose private farming and land ownership, yet their primary goal was to promote the interests and well-being of large agricultural enterprises.

Unsurprisingly, out of 219 participants in the party's constituting assembly, 167 were directors and chairmen of the Soviet state and collective farms. The party's main efforts concentrated on bringing the Russian state back to the agrarian sphere, either directly (through investment and subsidies) or indirectly (by protecting Russian agricultural producers from external competition). According to the party's platform, its main goal in parliament was "to ensure healthy state protectionism of the agriculture to secure its development and establishment on a modern civilized basis."[29] And because the AP was as much a lobbying group as a party, it also sought to establish working relations with the government, despite Yeltsin's unwillingness to accommodate their priorities. This approach cost the party dearly. In the December 1995 elections, the AP's vote share fell to 3.78 percent, less than half of the 1993 level.

The AP and its allies lobbied the government to introduce significant new tariffs on food imports. In March 1994, they seemingly scored a major victory when the government announced tariffs on imported meat, fish, grain, and other products. Yet, just two months after the import duties went into effect, they were substantially reversed.[30]

In 1995, agrarians and communists embarked on a flurry of legislative initiatives, which ended with little to show for their efforts. First, the Russian parliament began debating a draft law on food security devised to ensure that the state could provide food regardless of external or internal threats. However, the effort was destined to fail without the government's support, and the discussion itself was quite superficial. The parliamentarians "did not want to think about the [real] problems of the moment, [but instead] talked about some mythical food security which they did not understand," observed Evgenia Serova, an agricultural economist who testified before the parliament on the topic.[31] According to Serova, the principal food-related issue facing the country in 1995 was not food security but food safety. Yet, Duma deputies were not interested in her arguments and had other things in mind.

A more serious legislative effort took place in November 1995, with the introduction of the draft law "On the Program of Stabilization and Development of Agroindustrial Production in the Russian Federation in 1996–2000." A key provision of the program stipulated that in 1996–2000, at least 20 percent of the government's spending would be devoted to the agricultural sector. But the program that was eventually approved by Yeltsin lacked such massive financial commitments[32] and failed to allocate the budget funds needed to implement other provisions of the plan. Also, in

November 1995, the parliament approved the draft law "On State Regulation of the Agroindustrial Complex," but Yeltsin vetoed the legislation. He also overruled the revised law in 1996. "Unfortunately, now among those surrounding the President there are people who simply dislike the words 'state regulation of the economy,'" lamented Aleksei Chernyshev (KPRF/Agrarian Deputies Group), the chairman of the Duma Committee on Agriculture.[33] The law that Yeltsin eventually signed in July 1997 was a broad and toothless framework document that neither addressed financial issues nor set specific targets or quotas. After these defeats, the agrarians' legislative zeal subsided dramatically.

The Reforms Failure on the Ground

The emergence of private farming was the cornerstone of Yeltsin-era attempts to reform Russia's agriculture. The country's market reformers of the early 1990s were smart, well-educated, and deeply committed, but their efforts failed to transform the countryside quickly. Predominantly urbanities with academic backgrounds, Gaidar and his team had limited understanding of rural realities and political dynamics. Their naïve, even if sincere belief in the absolute power of property rights and market forces was simply no match to the complex social and bureaucratic realities they were up against.

In 1994, two years after the reform's enactment, private farmers worked just 6 percent of the country's cultivated land and produced a meager 2 percent of its agricultural output.[34] Individual farms controlled only about 8 percent of the country's arable land by 1998.[35] These measures alone indicate that efforts to de-collectivize Russian agriculture have failed. Furthermore, Yeltsin's reforms arguably exacerbated the issue they sought to reverse. Instead of fragmenting into smaller units, post-Soviet farms eventually transformed into even larger structures, the agroholdings, which we discuss in the following chapters.

The communists, the nationalists, and the Agrarian Party actively tried to derail the reform, but ultimately it was not their obstruction that marred the effort. The reform was nonviable from the start. It was "based on an ideal-type conception of the Western farm and lacked understanding of Soviet property relations."[36] Therefore, it simply could not succeed in this form during the timeframe its proponents sought.

More specifically, several reasons explain the non-emergence of a substantial private farmers' class in Russia. Limited land ownership and property rights certainly did contribute to the problem. But even had ideal property right existed, peasants could not become farmers overnight. First, establishing a private farm involved inevitable yet still considerable startup costs, not just financial. Second, as the reform's opponents pointed out, during the early 1990s the country's rural workers simply did not possess the entire skill set needed to engage in this enterprise. Some, the argument went, knew how to plan and organize agricultural labor but couldn't plant or harvest themselves. Others knew how to grow food but lacked any understanding of economics, finances, and marketing.[37] This assessment turned out to be closer to reality than the more naïve projections of liberal reformers who believed that land ownership would inevitably lead to the emergence of private farming.

Operating in a planned economy for decades made the transition to market relations psychologically challenging. In a telling anecdote, a chairman of a successful farm recounted spending considerable time lobbying the Ministry of Agriculture "to allocate him feed for the coming winter" during the summer of 1992. When asked why he didn't just use some of the farm's readily available cash to buy feed grain one of the new Moscow-area commodity exchanges the chairman simply shrugged his shoulders.[38]

Finally, large farms in Russia's countryside typically provided a wide range of vital social services. Abandoning the large farm and striking out on one's own meant losing access to these services when few state or local government alternatives existed.[39] Private farms could also be easily vandalized or put on fire by vengeful neighbors and thus dangerous to maintain, especially when rural law enforcement was woefully inadequate.[40] Unsurprisingly, among the few early private farmers that did appear, about 75 percent were ex-urbanites, and only 5–7 percent were peasants who left their collective and state farms.[41] The reluctance to become private farmers was thus not an outcome of a traditionally conservative and anti-market Russian peasant mentality, as some liberal critics contended, but rather a rational response to the existing socioeconomic realities.[42]

The inevitable difficulties of the fast transition were vastly exacerbated by the dogged resistance of those implementing the reform. As documented in Jessica Allina-Pisano's ethnographic work in the southern Russian region of Voronezh, despite the reform's intent, "liberal economic policies and local politics combined to produce a facade of rural ownership—a modern

Potemkin village."[43] Farm managers and rural officials who would lose the most from land redistribution and the rise of private farming could utilize their authority and influence to water down the reform. As a result, instead of benefiting the peasants, the reform often hurt them. Eventually, it even became a "mechanism by which rural people were dispossessed of property they had built or maintained under socialism."[44] The implementation of the land reform in the early 1990s was almost a mirror image of the land reform that accompanied Russia's abolition of serfdom in 1861. Then, state weakness forced the government to allocate the implementation of the land reform to local nobility, who used their power to gerrymander land allotments at the expense of the liberated serfs.[45]

Not infrequently, the local officials' resistance to reform stemmed from a strong ideological conviction that small farming is a technologically backward and inefficient mode of agricultural production. On the other hand, large agricultural enterprises were believed to enjoy a comparative advantage, and only this type of producers was viewed as capable of feeding the country.[46] This was not necessarily a retrograde view; even a liberal intellectual such as Zhores Medvedev, the author of an important history of Soviet agriculture, argued that it "would be dangerous to believe private farmers could feed the country more cheaply and more quickly than former state and collective farms."[47] And even when the land was distributed, de jure property rights did not necessarily mean de facto secure land tenure for Russia's rural dwellers.[48]

The Persistence of Soviet Farms

As private farmers failed to emerge as a class, Soviet-era farms kept limping along throughout the 1990s, though in a new form and often substantially reduced in size. Even though the market reformers sought to remove state subsidies and support for Soviet-era large farms, the deep-seated fear of food shortages simultaneously pushed the government in the opposite direction. On January 4, 1992, just two days after the liberalization of prices, the government issued a decree on compulsory food delivery to the state. Thirty-five percent of the average volume of 1986–1990 harvests were to be bought by the government. The need to procure grain to feed the population forced the state to pay as much as the farms requested, thus continuing the subsidies de facto, if not de jure. In the spring of 1992, the government once again signaled that "it placed priority on food supplies over farm efficiency"[49] and promised large farms credits and subsidies. In reality, the government's subsidies and credits were limited.[50] Still, when designated support for private farming mostly disappeared by 1994, the credits and subsidies that remained favored large farms.[51]

Even by Russian standards, the life of (and on) large farms was harsh, precarious, and often miserable. The quality of life in the countryside, considerably lower than in the urban centers even during the Soviet times, deteriorated even further following the removal of state subsidies and investment. Many collective and state farms reconstituted themselves as production cooperatives. In 1995, almost 8,000 such cooperatives, characterized by low wages and limited investments, existed throughout Russia.[52] Even though the services provided by cooperatives and the general sense of community within the village somewhat compensated for the low wages,[53] under such conditions their output was inevitably bound to decline over time. Lacking "the skills to evaluate real costs of depreciation and purchases,"[54] farm managers made bad investment and purchase decisions, resulting in further losses and shrinking output.

Social problems that plagued Soviet agriculture, such as low skills, lack of motivation, drunkenness, and endemic theft from the workplace, persisted as well. Some managers and observers simply accepted this as an inevitable, even if a regrettable feature of rural life and focused instead on ensuring that "theft does not reach the level where it is critical for business," as one agribusiness journal stated.[55] Others tried to combat the problems by measures ranging from mildly restrictive, such as paying workers in vouchers during harvest and cashing them only after the harvest is over, to violently repressive, such as making employees get implants that cause a violent physiological reaction to alcohol.[56]

But even without state subsidies and despite all the problems, many farms, especially those located in high-quality soil areas, kept functioning and producing. Their outputs might have been of inferior quality to those imported from abroad, but the demand for such products still existed in the impoverished country. After all, even during Soviet times, the central problem of the agricultural sector was distribution and not so much production.[57] Furthermore, the massive reduction in livestock also meant a substantial decline in the amount of (feed) grain the country's agriculture required. The abandonment of unproductive cropland could increase productivity, reduce waste, and lead to more efficient use of the existing resources.[58]

The social chaos that marked the early 1990s and the demise of traditional Soviet industries, culture, and research also forced numerous well-educated urbanites to switch jobs and go into private business. Some of these people ended up in the agricultural sector, often as distributors, traders, or intermediaries. Quite a few hailed from ethnic minority groups, such as the Jews or the Armenians. These people might have known little about agriculture, at least initially, but they understood the market better than the Soviet-era farm managers did, and had connections, money, and energy. For instance, Arkadii Zlochevskii, who later became the chairman of Russia's Grain Union, was a trained musician. Pre-1990s, he directed a choir and claimed to have authored the second Soviet rock opera. Zlochevskii's entry into the grain trade was due to coincidence, not a choice. Sergei Iushin, the CEO of Russia's Meat Association, had a background in foreign languages, specialized in international relations, and managed a Rotary Club before entering the meat business. "There is nothing unusual about such a trajectory," he claimed. "The majority of successful agricultural leaders in Russia have no formal education in this sphere. [They] were historians, nuclear physicists, engineers, who received general Soviet education and did whichever business they could."[59] Such people helped solve the distribution and marketing problems that agriculture faced and ensured a smoother and more reliable supply of domestic production to the stores, which the USSR had failed to achieve during the final years of its existence.

The 1998 Crises and the Origins of Agricultural Rebound

The 1997 grain harvest—88.5 million tons—was one of Russia's best since the country's independence.[60] It was still substantially lower than during the Soviet years, but given the sharp contraction of feed grain consumption, even such a harvest was capable of meeting domestic demand. And it was also much higher than the harvests of years prior, 69.2 tons in 1996 and 63.4 in 1995. Even though the government's agrarian reforms fell short of their goals, the future looked cautiously promising for the post-Soviet farms that survived the tumultuous early 1990s.

The year 1998 would become a watershed moment for Russian agriculture. Most scholars of post-Soviet Russia focus on the economic crisis of that year and the resulting political cascades that brought Vladimir Putin to power, first as prime minister (August 1999) and then as president (2000).

But in addition to the financial crash, Russia also experienced a simultaneous agricultural crisis. A severe drought knocked the 1998 harvest down to a meager 47.8 million tons, reviving fears of hunger and forcing the country to scramble for food imports without the resources to pay for them.

The financial crisis broke out in the summer of 1998. Russia's government was "debt-ridden and nearly bankrupt, reliant on short-term loans to pay pensions and fund basic public services," writes Miller.[61] When several Southeast Asian currencies fell in early 1997 and 1998, many investors and analysts predicted that Russia would be next. In August 1998, a market panic began, the ruble collapsed, and the government defaulted on its debt payments. Prices of consumer goods skyrocketed. By the end of the year, the ruble was worth just a third of its pre-crisis value, and inflation increased dramatically, wiping out savings and significantly reducing the Russians' purchasing power.[62]

Simultaneously, a drought devastated the country's agriculture. Increased imports could have compensated for the declining domestic supply, but amid financial collapse neither the government nor the citizens had the means to pay for foreign products. In the summer of 1992, Russia's market reformers believed that the danger of famine would never threaten Russia again due to the country's transformation into a market economy. Yet they were wrong. The belief that openness to foreign trade and integration into the global economy would solve Russia's food woes proved premature.

The similarities to the food crisis of 1991–1992 were impossible to miss. Images of Russia's long food queues and empty shelves appeared on Western television, and *USA Today* printed an assessment that 14 million children in Russia were "literally starving."[63] In some regions, authorities took over food distribution. In others, local leadership opted for price controls.[64] Moscow stores limited the number of loaves that could be purchased.[65] Some grain producing regions concentrated all efforts on filling out local "food funds" (*prodovol'stvennyi fond*) and simply restricted and occasionally even outright banned the transportation of grain to other parts of the country.[66] This situation persisted well into 1999, threatening intra-state trade wars.[67] Individual responses also closely resembled the early 1990s. According to anthropologist Melissa Caldwell, Russians claimed that they had experienced similar situations before and endured this crisis like previous ones. As citizens feverishly bought up the affordable food that still remained on the shelves, dachas and garden plots became once again the bedrock of subsistence.[68]

As a senior official with wealthy friends who profited handsomely from the corrupt food deals of 1992, Putin and his family were shielded from the shortages of the period. But as a newly appointed head of the Federal Security Service (FSB),[69] the successor of the Soviet-era KGB, he must have been well aware of the unfolding crisis. Even though we are not familiar with any government's assessment of or preparation for potential food riots in 1998, it is hard to believe that the connection between food and political stability was not on Putin's agenda during these days.

Just as in 1991–1992, the cash-strapped Russian government was forced to ask for foreign humanitarian food relief and credit.[70] On November 14, 1998, the government's official newspaper *Rossiiskaia gazeta* reported that the United States would provide Russia with 3.1 million tons of food. Some would be humanitarian aid, but 100,000 tons would be purchased with a $600 million credit, issued for a twenty-year term. The European Commission intended to supply the country with a million tons of grain and 250,000 tons of meat.[71] Yet, according to Zlochevskii, this was unnecessary. He believed that the state had enough grain to meet citizens' needs, despite the historically low harvest. Furthermore, the massive humanitarian aid and government's food purchases abroad devastated Russian and boosted Western producers. Russia's grain problem, Zlochevskii argued, could be solved once and for all only when the government turned its attention inward and started trusting domestic producers.

Despite Zlochevskii's fears, Western food aid and increased imports during the 1998 crisis did not put Russian producers out of business. In fact, the opposite happened. As the ruble lost its value, imported food became increasingly out of reach for the nascent but growing Russian middle class. Willy-nilly, many customers were forced to switch to much cheaper domestic food products. The financial crash, a disaster for the country, turned out to be an unexpected boon for Russian agriculture. Slowly but steadily, Russian food production bounced back.

Concluding Remarks

The liberalization of prices in January 1992 and the shock therapy market reforms were just the first steps toward transforming Russian society and the economy. Next on the government's agenda was a more fundamental restructuring of the country's agriculture. This was an audacious attempt to demolish Soviet institutions that failed to feed the country and replace them with a new model based on open markets, imports, and private ownership and production.

The reformers' vision had to compete with other ideas, some simply less radical, others outright reactionary. But as long as Yeltsin remained in power, the basic direction of change remained the same, a move toward private ownership, largely open markets, and withdrawal of the state from the countryside. Yet the expected rise of private farming in Russia never materialized. This chapter documented the reformers' vision and the reasons for their failure. Arguably, the reform was doomed from the very beginning because it failed to fully appreciate Soviet legacies, post-Soviet realities, and the historically well-documented backlash that land redistributions tend to generate.

Russian peasants refused to leave large farms, and thus these enterprises persisted, sustained by inertia, the state's need to procure food and the tacit but often effective support of rural bureaucrats. The 1998 financial crisis made the cheaper, domestically produced food more attractive for many Russians and demonstrated that the agricultural status quo of the mid-1990s was volatile, precarious, and incapable of solving the food provisioning problem. At the end of the 1990s, Russia was still vulnerable to food shortages, though at a lesser scale than in 1991–1992. Yet, new approaches to agriculture were needed.

Arkadii Zlochevskii's wish for a Russian government that believes in and supports domestic food producers finally materialized in 1999. When Putin became prime minister in August 1999, he appointed Aleksei Gordeev, a capable Soviet-era bureaucrat and the deputy chairman of the Agrarian Party, as the minister of agriculture. Under their leadership, the government continued playing a key role in the agrarian sector, and the country experienced what observers, scholars, and businesspeople often refer to as "Russia's agricultural miracle."

4
The Rise of Grain, 2000–2010

The Russian Federation entered the twenty-first century with an agricultural sector still reeling from the collapse of the 1990s and dependence on Western food aid still fresh in everyone's memory. During the fall of 1998, the Russian government needed to publicly reassure the population that, despite the financial crisis, the country was not facing potential famine.[1] Ten years later, the picture could not have been more different. Russian agriculture had rapidly recovered, the country had become a major exporter of grain, and the Kremlin was busy designing ambitious plans for full self-sufficiency in food. No longer a major social and political problem, domestic food production quickly became a point of pride and a key pillar of the regime's survival strategies.

What triggered this remarkable and astonishingly fast transformation? In this chapter, we present the fundamental reasons for the rapid growth of Russian food production, not just as an industry, but also as a political and security ideal during the first decade of Putin's leadership. We show that the securitization of food and the emergence of nutritional self-sufficiency as a key political goal resulted from both objective economic reasons and clever ideological and bureaucratic entrepreneurship. Purely economic factors, such as the sharp devaluation of the ruble and growing international demand for grain, propelled the growth of domestic food production and steadily increased output. Yet it was the ideological vision, commitment, and skills of the deeply conservative Ministry of Agriculture bureaucracy and its leader, Aleksei Gordeev, that turned food production into a central pillar of Putin's emerging statist, nationalist, and increasing authoritarian political order.

Economic Drivers of Recovery

Several reasons led to the spectacular recovery of Russia's agriculture post-2000. The first was the economic crisis of 1998. The financial crash devastated the economy and wiped out the savings of millions of ordinary Russians, but was a blessing in disguise for the country's beleaguered agriculture. When Russia defaulted on its debt, the ruble declined by 350 percent between August 1998 and January 1999.[2] As a result, Russia's emerging middle class could no longer afford many imported food products. They switched to cheaper, often even lower quality domestic alternatives. Investors, seeing profits to be made, also turned their attention to agriculture. "Oil's annual profit is at best 80%, of grain is 400%," summarized Evgenia Serova.[3]

Additionally, in 2001 Russia adopted a new Land Code and, in 2002, a Law on Turnover of Agricultural Land that that gave companies and individuals the right to own, lease, purchase, and sell commercial and agricultural land. While ownership of agricultural land was restricted to Russian citizens and entities only, foreigners still had the right to lease agricultural land. These pieces of legislation settled the thorny question of agricultural land ownership and transactions that had bedeviled Yeltsin government's reform efforts and allowed the emergence of a functioning land market and rapid development of Russia's agriculture.[4]

The international situation also favored Russia's food producers. Precisely when Russians willy-nilly warmed up to buying local, the increasing global demand for new grain suppliers provided Russian producers with an additional growth opportunity. In the first decade of the twenty-first century, increasing wheat consumption, production, and prices were the main trends on the global grain market. According to the UN Food and Agriculture Organization (FAO), between 2002 and 2011, global wheat production increased from 574 to 655.3 million tons. As wheat consumption soared, global prices jumped after a period of steep decline. Between 2003 and 2011, the average annual price of wheat rose from 160 USD to 316 USD per ton.[5]

Russia was well positioned to gain from this global dynamic. First, huge swaths of arable land that were abandoned during the 1990s could be brought back under cultivation. Second, the country's often antiquated and inefficient agricultural machinery could be updated; investment in new technologies and machinery allowed for a substantial increase in output. The world needed grain, and Russia could produce it. As a result, in the early 2000s, Russia aggressively entered the global grain trade. The country's market niche was low-quality, cheap grain, which was in high demand due to consumer needs in developing countries, particularly Egypt, Turkey, India, Jordan, Libya, and Tunisia. Russia's geographic proximity to the Middle East and North Africa also facilitated grain exports.

Whereas developed countries steadily reduced wheat exports and shifted their focus to high-value-added products, Russia's wheat export has grown steadily since 2001, becoming a dominant item among the country's agricultural export commodities (Figure 4.1) within a single decade. By 2018, Russia had become the largest wheat exporter in the world, controlling 25 percent of world exports.[6]

Russian grain expansion indeed had to be export-oriented. Despite the growing attractiveness of domestic food products, Russia's demographic decline and the low purchasing power of its population meant that domestic demand could not keep up with expanding production. Whereas the grain sector rapidly recovered, Russia's meat and dairy production bounced back much slower from the disastrous 1990s, resulting in low domestic demand for grain-based animal feed. The volume of grain utilized for industrial purposes, that is, the production of starch, alcohol, yeast, biofuels, and protein-vitamin-mineral concentrates, was also small. An increase in grain consumption for industrial purposes required large financial investments in the construction of new manufacturing facilities. Local investors were not yet ready to invest such large sums, nor were local consumers able to buy expensive products resulting from grain processing. Finally, Russia possessed one of the world's largest grain infrastructures of elevators, railroads, and ports, a legacy of Soviet reliance on imports to feed the population. Although these facilities had largely become technologically and technically antiquated by 2000, they could still be used to supply grain to local and foreign consumers. Export thus became the natural focus of Russian grain producers.

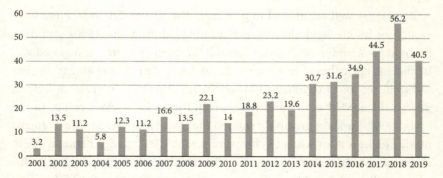

Figure 4.1. Grain exports from the Russian Federation, 2001–2019
Source: https://ab-centre.ru/news/eksport-zerna-iz-rossii-itogi-za-2019-god

International opportunities and domestic constraints created a favorable business environment for investments in Russia's export-oriented grain cultivation. Yet reliance on exports also made Russian producers vulnerable. Under conditions of laissez-faire capitalism, market fluctuations, changes in global demand, and even a good harvest could spell ruin for producers.

Thus, in 1997 a better than usual harvest coupled with constant domestic demand and the inability to export led to a sharp decrease in wheat prices and massive losses for producers.[7] In 2001 and even more so, in 2002, Russia got "catastrophically lucky with the weather." Harvests broke previous records while export opportunities were still limited. Prices took a nosedive, numerous producers were facing bankruptcy, and the government scrambled to find durable solutions to protect the industry.[8] Long-term stability thus required a growing state involvement in the market, but this was an uneasy task in a country whose leaders had little knowledge of or interest in food production and in which economic liberals still dominated economic policymaking.[9] The task of rebuilding and protecting Russian food production fell to the recently appointed minister of agriculture Aleksei Gordeev.

The Midwife of Russian Grain Boom

Aleksei Gordeev (b. 1955) was appointed Russia's minister of agriculture on August 19, 1999, and remained in control of the ministry until March 2009, making him the longest-serving person in this position during the postcommunist period. On May 19, 2000, Gordeev was also named deputy prime minister, a position he held until March 9, 2004.

Gordeev's background and professional experience were closely linked to agriculture, though not food production as such. An engineer by training, Gordeev started his government career in railway transportation and agricultural logistics, and during 1992–1997, he served as the deputy head of the Lyubertsy district near Moscow. He first joined Russia's Ministry of Agriculture in 1997 as the head of its Economics Department and was promoted to first deputy minister in May 1998. In early 1999, Gordeev was elected deputy chairman of Russia's Agrarian Party. The Agrarians called for prioritizing the Russian food industry and its backbone, the large ex-collective and state farms, in state budget allocations. Gordeev continued in this position while still minister of agriculture, leaving it only in 2003 upon joining the Putin-affiliated United Russia party.

A capable and experienced bureaucrat without major political ambitions, Gordeev managed to stay out of the Kremlin's political battles, thus ensuring the uninterrupted implementation of his priorities. Gordeev's deeply conservative, nationalistic, and borderline xenophobic views centered on the revival of Russian agriculture as the cornerstone of national security, identity, and traditional values.

In 1999, Gordeev published a 226-page book titled *Russia's Food Supply: Problems of Theory and Practice*.[10] In March 2000, the minister defended a doctoral dissertation with a virtually identical title "Russia's Food Supply: Problems and Solutions' Mechanisms."[11] Russian politicians rarely if ever produce their own doctoral dissertations and prefer to outsource the task to academic ghostwriters. Dissertations that do get published under their names, including Putin's own thesis, often contain blatant and widespread plagiarism.[12] Yet, even though we cannot be certain of the exact extent of Gordeev's authorship, the thesis closely aligns with the minister's general ideological approach and subsequent policies.[13]

The dissertation and book clearly articulate Gordeev's vision, which considers food supply to be vital to Russia's national security. According to Gordeev, the Russian government should strive to achieve food independence and needs to use the levers of state power to obtain this goal. According to the minister, the minimum threshold for food independence is for domestic production to account for at least 80 percent of the consumed food.

Gordeev also harshly criticized the Yeltsin-era market-driven food and agricultural policies. These, Gordeev argued, had led to a steep decline of Russia's agro-industrial complex and made the country dependent on food imports, draining its foreign currency reserves. Furthermore, he noted that imported food, which constituted roughly 40 percent of the retail food market in the late 1990s, was expensive, and out of reach for millions of Russians. The underlying assumption of Gordeev's argument was that local food production would thus also solve the problem of food affordability and promote the internal political stability of the regime. As we shall see, Russia's agricultural policy in 2000–2010 reflected Gordeev's ideas.

Gordeev's conservative views extended well beyond food supplies. The minister was deeply committed to reinvigorating the country's decaying countryside, which he perceived to be the key source of Russia's traditional values. These, he argued, served as the bedrock of Russia's identity, political, and military strength and were threatened by globalization.[14] For Gordeev, agriculture was thus not only an economic activity and a way of life, but crucial to "preserving [Russia's] genotype, culture, social control over territory, securing its territorial integrity and independence."[15] The decline of the countryside, he warned, would open up Russian territories in Siberia and the Far East to migration from China and threaten the country, because "in ten to fifteen years other states will lay claims on these territories."[16]

The economic model Gordeev envisioned for Russia was explicitly protectionist and aimed to defend the local producer. Liberal economic development, he lamented, was "western 'clothes' that stifle Russia, fit neither her size nor soul and appearance."[17] Instead, for the minister the market economy should boil down to "first of all adequately resisting the expansion of foreign producers supported by their governments."[18] He called the World Trade Organization (WTO) a "hypocritical body [that is] somewhat harmful for [the] global economy," and resisted Russia's membership in the organization.[19] In the early 2000s, this socially and especially economically conservative outlook differentiated Gordeev from most other Russian government members that were busy implementing liberal economic reforms, including, in 2003, the legal right to sell and purchase agricultural land.[20]

Gordeev's ability to promote his vision of Russia's agriculture was a consequence of not only his bureaucratic talents but his support of the Russian business community, especially grain growers and traders who favored the state's growing involvement in regulating agricultural markets. Indeed, it was highly symbolic that Arkadii Zlochevskii, the head of the Russian Grain Union, an industry group representing growers and traders of grain, in 2000–2002 moved to the government to lead the Ministry of Agriculture's Market Regulation Department. In his official capacity, Zlochevskii, who had a direct personal interest in the industry's growth, became the chief architect of Russia's grain intervention policies. And as we show below, grain interventions were highly beneficial to both the business community and the state.

On July 27, 2000, at the first government meeting dedicated to the topic of Russian agriculture, Gordeev presented a bleak overview of the state of Russian agriculture and food industry, while outlining the new government strategy for agrarian sector development. He initially stressed the importance of agriculture to the Russian economy: at that time, it provided 6 percent of the country's GDP, while 14 percent of Russia's workforce lived in the countryside. Gordeev continued by describing the negative trends of the Yeltsin era. Russian government investments in agriculture decreased significantly in the 1990s, which led to a sharp decline in the agro-industrial sector and a substantial increase in food imports, especially meat and dairy products. Moreover, food consumption per capita substantially diminished in the 1990s.

The solution to these problems, the minister of agriculture argued, was stronger governmental regulations and heavy government investment in the industry. To provide the population with affordable food products and increase local production, Putin's new government had to resolve two practical problems: first, it had to ensure sufficient amounts of grain on the domestic market. Second, it had to protect the Russian market from grain surplus to maintain profitability and prevent local producers from going bankrupt.[21] In other words, in 2000, Gordeev set out to solve the very problems that had almost led to the collapse of the country's grain market three years earlier.

The program for this new agricultural policy, unveiled at the July 27, 2000, government meeting, closely followed Gordeev's arguments. It called for declaring agriculture as one of the state's top priorities and a primary contributor to Russia's food security. While the program emphasized the importance of the market economy principles, it also asserted the key role of state regulation of the food market. This was supposed to allow Russia to create an economically competitive agrarian sector while integrating the country into international agricultural markets.

The government's specific goal, according to the program, was to help local producers saturate the market with domestically-produced grain (both for human consumption and animal feed), chicken, meat, eggs, vegetables, potatoes, and dairy products by the end of the decade. It also intended to institute "reasonable protectionism" in support of local food producers against foreign importers. One of the main tools in achieving this was state financing of Russian agriculture through the newly created (March 2000) state-owned Russian Agricultural Bank (*Rosselkhozbank*), discussed in more detail below. This institution, rather than private commercial banks such as the SBS Agro of the 1990s, would become the basis for financing the Russian agricultural sector. The program introduced two key innovations. First, it established grain as the leader and the engine of Russia's agricultural growth. Second, it opened the door to the government's increasingly deeper involvement, and eventually key role in the food supply sector.[22]

The Return of the State

During the Yeltsin era, the presidential decree "On the Liberalization of the Grain Market in Russia," dated December 24, 1993 (*O liberalizatsii zernovogo rynka v Rossii*), formed the legal basis of Russia's grain trade. The decree introduced a complete liberalization of the domestic grain market: Soviet-era state grain procurements were stopped, all administrative restrictions on grain transportation within the country canceled, and the responsibility for the grain supply shifted from the federal government to the regions. In the 1990s, the federal government's influence on the grain market gradually dwindled to close to zero, and numerous laws and decrees subsequently enacted during the Yeltsin period were primarily aimed at adjusting legislation to the rapid changes in the country's grain market.

In practice, however, the picture was more complicated. At times of crisis, most notably in 1998–1999, several grain-producing regions restricted and even outright banned the transport of grain outside their borders.[23] The state also "retained a monopoly on bread production through the mid-1990s."[24]

After Putin came to power, the government's approach changed dramatically. It adopted a flurry of legislative acts regulating the country's grain market from the early days of Putin's rule. The key difference between Yeltsin and Putin's regulatory approaches was a shift in the government's role from correction and supervision to direct control.

On August 3, 2001, the government issued the first regulation indicating a change in its approach to the grain market.[25] This resolution gave the authorities the power to become the main regulators of the domestic grain market through grain interventions, a mechanism that we discuss below. The government's new status was further strengthened by a series of additional legislative acts enacted in the 2000s that allowed the authorities to tighten their control of the grain market.

Generally, legislative acts issued in the early 2000s had two practical purposes. The first was to create a legal foundation for grain interventions, the main tool for market control. By adopting these acts, the government thus gained legal rights to buy and sell grain on the domestic market, becoming its most influential player. The second purpose was to create the legal foundations for financing the further development of the industry through state loans and credits.

Having acquired these new legal tools, in 2001 the government moved to establish direct state intervention in the grain market. Russia was not a pioneer in using the grain intervention mechanism. In fact, grain interventions were the most widely used regulatory instrument on the grain markets worldwide. The Russian government merely adapted this measure to the conditions of its own market. Initially, by implementing grain interventions, the government planned to achieve the relatively modest goal of keeping the grain market saturated and preventing a collapse of domestic production due to extreme price fluctuations. The longer-term implications of grain interventions were substantially more far-reaching.

The intervention mechanism was straightforward. For procurement interventions, the government established a minimum price and purchased grain once the market prices dropped to or below the declared threshold to prevent further price drops and protect the producers. Furthermore, the government fixed the maximum price for commodity interventions: when the market price rose to a fixed maximum level, the state would start selling the grain it kept in specially designated funds to keep the market saturated. The Ministry of Agriculture was tasked with fixing the maximum and minimum prices, selecting elevators for grain storage, and appointing the agents that would carry out the interventions. The state agents assigned to carry out the grain interventions were the Federal Agency for Food Market Regulation, which operated under the auspices of the Ministry of Agriculture (until 2009), and the United Grain Company (UGC), which was given authority to carry out grain interventions after 2009. Funding was provided by loans from the state-owned Rossselkhozbank. Thus, the model that granted the government the rights to buy and sell grain on the domestic market inevitably allowed the state to control the two main parameters of the grain market: the volume and the prices.

In the early 2000s, due to the systematic overproduction of grain, the state performed mainly procurement interventions. It bought grain, thus "removing" surplus grain from the domestic market. Authorities initially described the procurement interventions in 2001 as unsuccessful. Five billion rubles were allocated from the state budget, but only 675 million were spent. Most of the grain came from a single seller (a trader, not producer), and grain producers themselves did not participate. The trades conducted during the intervention's first two days were canceled because the government had purchased grain at the highest price of 2,700 rubles per ton even though the average market price was 2,400 rubles. Yet despite the cancellation, the grain from these annulled sales was resold to the state at 2,699 rubles per ton.[26]

Starting with the second intervention during the 2002-2003 season, purchases were conducted on the principle of exchange trading on the National Mercantile Exchange (NAMEX), which is part of the Moscow Interbank Currency Exchange (MICEX). Six billion rubles from the state budget had been allocated for the intervention, of which 4,459 billion rubles were spent. State intervention via NAMEX constituted a government project of unprecedented magnitude in Russia's commodity market. Using remote access systems, the interventions were carried out simultaneously in several regional centers of the country: Moscow, St. Petersburg, Nizhny Novgorod, Samara, Rostov-on-Don, Yekaterinburg, and Novosibirsk. Producers from any of the above stock exchange centers could participate in the biddings, which expanded the producers' access to trading.

Despite all the changes, the procurement intervention of the 2002-2003 season was also mired by problems. Grain is harvested in August, and thus grain prices on the domestic market are usually lowest in August and September. Small and medium-sized producers typically do not have the necessary storage facilities or infrastructure; therefore they could not wait for later procurement interventions. Yet, the state intervention of the 2002-2003 season only started in November, and by that time, most of the grain was already in the hands of grain traders when prices were at their highest. To sum up, the first interventions occurred later than needed, did little to support the producers, and were wasteful. It is unclear whether this was an outcome of corruption, incompetence, or a mix of both, but, according to Zlochevskii, the Ministry of Agriculture officials initially had little understanding of how grain interventions are supposed to be carried out, and representatives of other government bodies opposed the scheme.[27] The government only began to avoid these major blunders, even if only partially, by 2005-2006.

Equally important, interventions required significant government expenditure. Storing one ton of grain in the state grain fund cost the government an average of 1,000 rubles per year: 60 percent of it was paid to storage elevators, 27-29 percent was interest on the loan paid to Rosselkhozbank, and 10-12 percent was agent fees for conducting interventions and arranging for storage.

The grain procurement interventions implemented in the first half of the 2000s were not extensive, but, due to the rapidly growing production, they continuously increased over the years; Russia's grain market was characterized by overproduction throughout the 2000s. The state needed more and larger elevators, the number of producers selling to the state was on the rise, and procurement expanded to new regions of the country. The grain infrastructure inherited from the USSR could cope with the volumes of the early 2000s but became increasingly inadequate as production soared. All this necessitated increasingly higher (and more expensive) levels of state involvement and investment.

United Grain Company

Prior to the establishment of the United Grain Company (UGC) in 2007, nine companies accounted for 60 percent of Russian grain exports. Half of this was exported by foreign grain traders whose share in the Russian grain trade was steadily growing. The Russian government was concerned that, if this trend continued, foreign traders would come to dictate purchasing prices. Thus, three main factors prompted the government to boost the regulation of the grain market and establish a state-owned company: the failure of procurement interventions in the face of chronic overproduction of grain, the 2008 financial crisis and its negative economic and social effects, and the expanding share of foreign grain traders in the export of Russian grain.

Before the establishment of UGC, the federal government had full or partial ownership of forty-five companies engaged in storing and processing grain, including grain elevators, plant bakeries, and grain terminals. The government was the main shareholder in sixteen of these; in twenty others, it owned between 25.5 and 50 percent of the shares; in the remaining seven, it owned just a small percentage of the shares. These businesses were located in the major grain-producing and consuming regions and had significant elevator reserves for storing grain, part of which were used for the intervention fund.

The state's interests in the above companies were represented by officials from the Ministry of Agriculture and the Federal Agency for State Property Management (*Rosimushchestvo*), as well as by members of the various executive bodies of the Russian Federation. However, their activities were uncoordinated, and the government was unable to use this large but fragmented system in the interest of the state. The objective of the new state enterprise was to merge the major companies acting as instruments for the involvement of the state in the grain market into a single system, thereby creating a major player in the Russian grain market to represent the interests of the state.

The March 20, 2009, presidential decree authorized the United Grain Company to acquire the shares of thirty-one companies, eight of which were considered strategically important. The Novorossiysk Grain Plant (*Novorossiyskii kombinat khleboproduktov*)—the largest grain terminal on the Black Sea used for exporting grain out of Russia—was one of the most important enterprises that became the property of the UGC.

In establishing this new enterprise, the government pursued three main goals: to develop grain infrastructure, increase purchases of grain on the domestic market, and, crucially, implement the state policy in the grain market. The creation of the UGC, therefore, allowed the state to become not only a major regulator of the internal market but also its biggest active player, equipped with the largest and most extensive infrastructure network. According to Sergey Levin, the UGC general director, the company was simultaneously "a government agent and a market player."[28] Notably, already from the start, UGC inherited the government's intervention fund. According to Levin, in December 2010, the UGC possessed more than 9.6 million tons of grain, stored in 464 elevators across the country. "No other market actor had so much grain," he boasted.[29] During its first year, the company exported roughly 600 thousand tons of grain (11 percent of the export volume), thus establishing itself as the leading exporter of Russian grain. The company also relied on extensive state and private funding to invest in, modernize, and expand Russia's grain export infrastructure.

No less important, by creating this massive grain market enterprise and achieving dominance over the industry, the Russian government also ensured that foreign traders could not occupy a predominant position in the export of Russian grain. From that point onward, multinational companies could only play a limited role in the strategically important Russian grain market.

The Impact of New Approach

Two years—the plentiful 2008 and the catastrophic 2010—demonstrate the extent to which the government became involved in the grain market over several short years. In 2008, Russia had a record harvest—more than 108 million tons of grain. Yet, as a Russian proverb dryly observes, while a low harvest might be a problem, a bumper crop is a much bigger worry. With the annual domestic grain consumption at 70 million tons and export capacities still limited to no more than 2–2.5 million tons of grain per month due to the bottleneck at the Novorossiysk port, the government was forced to intervene to prevent the collapse of grain prices. During that season, the state had to purchase 9.6 million tons of grain, about 9 percent of the total harvest, at the massive cost of 46 billion rubles.[30]

In 2010, Russia faced the opposite problem: a severe drought had decimated the harvest. Grain prices rose dramatically and threatened higher food prices on the domestic market. To cope with the problem, the government decided to bypass interventions altogether and took its involvement in the market a step further by setting up a centralized system of grain distribution to milling plants and livestock farmers at subsidized prices. Authorities only reverted to the intervention policy and resumed selling grain from the intervention fund in February 2011.

The growing role of the state allowed the government to redefine the goals of its involvement. If originally the motivation was to protect the vulnerable and struggling producers, by the end of the decade, the focus shifted to using food as an instrument of regime stability. When the government embarked on direct distribution of grain in 2010, flour producers in Moscow, St. Petersburg, the adjacent Moscow, and Leningrad Oblast were the first to receive it from the state. Ensuring social stability by curbing the growth of bread prices in the capital and the major urban areas was now the government's main priority. This made sense. The countryside, with its lack of powerful landholding elites, coopted and weak civil society, and widespread, Putin-centered "native monarchism," was not a serious threat to regime survival.[31] On the other hand, cities, especially the capitals, were, or at the very least, were expected to be.[32]

Thus, the bread riots that had led to the 1917 Revolutions had to be prevented, and unlike in the 1980s, 1992, or even 1998, the Kremlin now had enough grain to feed the politically important urban centers without resorting to humiliating Western food aid. Despite the chronic inefficiency and possible corruption, the interventions of previous years paid off, at least politically. Supporting overproduction but purchasing surplus grain meant massive costs to the state budget, but at times of need, the government had its own grain to distribute. The key goals of Gordeev's ambitious plan had been achieved and secured. Russian grain production was thriving, the domestic grain market saturated, and prices guaranteed. Indeed, by the second half of the decade, the time had come for the government to expand its makeover of Russia's food production beyond grain.

From Grain to Meat

Grain production is necessary to ensure the bare minimum required for survival. Bread is the key, yet meat has historically marked successful production and consumption. As noted by Liefert and Liefert, the main objective of Soviet agricultural policy during the USSR's final two decades was to expand the livestock sector, to improve the population's standard of living by increasing their consumption of meat and dairy products.... By 1990, Soviet per capita consumption of meat and other livestock products was close in volume to that of many rich developed countries, despite Soviet per capita GDP being at most half of developed countries' levels.[33]

The need to provide a massive amount of animal feed required by the meat and dairy industries also converted the USSR into the world's largest grain importer. The striking workers in 1962 Novocherkassk had demanded "meat and milk," which made the communist leadership realize that it would not survive without providing those items.

In the second half of the 2000s, the government initiated several key laws and programs. In 2006, Russia adopted the law "On the Development of Agriculture" (*O razvitii sel'skogo khozyaistva*) and initiated a massive State Priority Project "Development of the Agroindustrial Complex." In the following year, the "State Program for the Development of Agriculture for the Period of 2008-2012" was adopted. The 2006 law explicitly prioritized the meat-producing sector over grain, and essentially ended the debate between the two sectors regarding the government's investment priorities.

Champions of the grain sector argued that government support should be given primarily to this industry, as it was the most advanced sector of Russian agriculture and the main generator of foreign currency. By contrast, supporters of the livestock sector contended that the government ought to support the weaker industries rather than the most developed ones. Beyond the philosophical argument over the appropriate nature of state support, the livestock industry enjoyed several political advantages. Livestock production was more geographically dispersed than grain and, thus, enjoyed more political allies. Moreover, the livestock and dairy industries provided a greater number of permanent jobs than did grain production, which was highly dependent on seasonal labor. Therefore, these sectors were better aligned with the conservative dreams of reviving traditional rural life and reversing the rapid decline of Russia's countryside. Unsurprisingly, the arguments in favor of investment in livestock typically went hand in hand with plans for social housing for young professionals in rural areas.[34] And most crucially, with bread secured, meat was now politically more important for Putin's aspiring, ambitious, but also increasingly autocratic regime. Russia's growing middle class, a popular argument went, was willing to tolerate losing political freedoms in exchange for material goods and growing standards of living.[35] More and cheaper meat fit these growing expectations, while something as basic and proletarian as bread no longer did. And even though urban centers were the regime's key focus, the government's new investment in the countryside was also designed to benefit the rural dwellers, the majority of whom (56 percent) lived below the poverty line.[36]

The 2006 federal law was thus explicitly aimed at moving beyond grain to support the development of the livestock industry. Yet investment in livestock also directly affected grain producers, as livestock farmers are major consumers of grain, the main component of animal feed. The law consisted of three main parts. The first accelerated the development of the livestock sector by subsidizing the interest payments on loans for construction, reconstruction, and modernization of existing livestock farms (6.63 billion rubles); purchasing and leasing pedigree cattle (6.0 billion rubles); and purchasing and leasing machinery and equipment (2.0 billion rubles). The second part focused on promoting the development of livestock farms by subsidizing interest rates on loans for the development of production, developing a network of consumer cooperatives, and establishing a system of land mortgage loans. The third part of the law envisioned the creation of urgently needed housing for young professionals in rural areas. The construction was supposed to be implemented through co-financing from federal, regional, and extra-budgetary sources.

Moreover, the law defined the concept of "the state agricultural policy," thereby declaring the state as the main force guiding and shaping Russian agriculture. It outlined the main directions for Russia's food policy: maintaining the stability of domestic food supply; forming and regulating agricultural markets, raw materials, and food product markets and developing their infrastructure; state support to agricultural producers; and protection of the economic interests of Russia's agricultural producers on the domestic and world markets.

The government's 2008–2012 state program for agricultural development was a natural continuation of its earlier initiatives, and cemented the state's leading role in agriculture and food provision. Central to the program was support for local food producers, which could eventually lead to import reductions, and a continuation of government's central role in the grain market through state interventions.

The government's investment in the meat sector facilitated its growth. If in 2001 Russia's total domestic meat production stood at 7 million tons, by 2012 it increased to 11.6 million.[37] Yet from the government's perspective, this was just the first step. Buoyed by the success of the grain sector, which made Russia first self-sufficient and a major exporter, the Kremlin sought to replicate its achievements in other areas. Their new, substantially more ambitious goal was nutritional independence. Russia's transformation since 1998–1999, both in production and in government's approach to food supply, was truly remarkable.

Instruments of State Support

But how was this remarkable growth stimulated and achieved in practice? Legislation, political will, and favorable macroeconomic conditions might be the necessary conditions for such an expansion, but they are hardly sufficient on their own. As the political scientist Vladimir Gel'man points out, in Russia "bad governance" is the normal state of affairs, and meaningful changes and reforms are unlikely to succeed without exceptionally strong incentives among officials, high levels of bureaucratic professionalization, and a very specific and narrow nature of the reform itself.[38] Then how did Russia do it?

The first and the most important instrument was the government's financial support. As we document in previous chapters, in the wake of the collapse of the USSR, the Soviet-era gargantuan levels of direct and indirect support for agriculture by and large collapsed, leading to the industry's decline throughout the 1990s. The state no longer had the resources to prop up the struggling and inefficient domestic agricultural production. In the eyes of the liberal economic reformers that dominated the government, direct subsidies went hand in hand with inefficiency and low productivity.

Yet government support did not cease altogether, though some of its focus shifted from support for the industry to specific producers. Initially, the Russian government adopted a system of loans, granted to agricultural producers from a special federal budget fund for concessional lending. The SBS Agro Bank received financial tranches from the state budget and used them to issue loans to producers.[39] Thus, as the money was given on credit from the state budget, neither the bank nor loan recipients were concerned that the loan should be repaid. This naturally led to a highly inefficient management of the state funds and subsequently to the closure of the concession fund.

Therefore, the Russian government invested in a new model of state support for agricultural producers in the early 2000s: subsidized lending. According to this model, grain producers could take out loans from any private bank, and the government committed to reimbursing parts of their substantial interest payments. This was more economically efficient and less costly for the state: private banks issued loans from their own funds and were thus fully responsible for ensuring repayment.

The introduction of subsidized loans allowed the government to reduce its budget allocations for agricultural development, shifted the responsibility for the loans to private banks, and, most important, significantly expanded lending by using the funds of private financial institutions.

In parallel, the government also embarked on direct involvement in financial and technical support for agriculture by establishing Rosselkhozbank and the Rosagroleasing Company. These institutions provided loans to producers and lent out agricultural technology and equipment. Subsidized credit, according to Sergei Iushin, the CEO of Russia's meat producers' organization, has become the most important instrument of state's involvement in the industry.[40] Rosselkhozbank was founded in March 2000, and in the first decade of its existence established seventy-eight large and over 1,500 small branches in main Russian agrarian regions, with a credit portfolio of 594 billion rubles ($22.8 billion).[41] In 2006, the bank's lending accounted for 70 percent of all loans for the development of small farms. Apart from the mammoth Sberbank, Rosselkhozbank is also the country's only financial institution with an extensive presence in the countryside and the second-largest provider of loans to the agricultural sector.[42] Scholars who studied the loans provided to agricultural producers also note the heavy influence on authorities, especially the regional governments, on who gets the lion's share of subsidized credit.[43]

Due to this generous lending scheme, the country's grain sector, as well as agriculture as a whole, received significant impetus for development. The loans were especially beneficial for large-scale grain producers, which possessed sufficient property for collateral and could thus take out significant loans. This flow of financial assets led to a rapid increase in grain production that extended beyond the domestic consumption level and necessitated state interventions and investment in export capacities.

The Russian Ministry of Agriculture founded the Rosagroleasing Company in February 2001 with the explicit aim of using state funds to facilitate the cheap leasing of agricultural machinery to the agrarian sector. In 2002–2003 alone, the company secured 1,000 contracts worth 15 billion rubles ($50.7 million) to lease agricultural machinery to Russian agribusinesses. In the subsequent years, Rosagroleasing also played a key role in a variety of governmental programs aimed at the boosting of Russian agriculture. The Russian government was clearly satisfied with Rosagroleasing's performance. In 2009, Elena Skynnik, the head of Rosagroleasing since its founding, replaced Gordeev, who had been appointed as the governor of Voronezh Oblast as the minister of agriculture.

Yet, in Russia, success and expansion inevitably coincide with bad governance and outright corruption. Thus, Skynnik's tenure as minister of agriculture, which began with an explicit endorsement by President Medvedev, abruptly ended in 2012 in a major corruption scandal. Russian state media outlets accused Skynnik of channeling 39 billion rubles ($1.26 billion) of government funds to private businesses under her family's control during her tenure as the head of Rosagroleasing. The government, however, was apparently uninterested in investigating Skynnik, and as a result, she was sacked but never criminally charged. During the period 2014–2017, the law enforcement of Switzerland, where Skynnik comfortably retired in 2012, initiated a money-laundering investigation and even temporarily froze over $71 million of her assets. The investigation was eventually discontinued because of an alleged lack of cooperation by the Russian authorities.[44]

Putin's Role

This chapter documents two interrelated transformations in Russia's agricultural performance and food supply policies. When Putin rose to power, Russia was heavily dependent on food imports. In 2008, by the end of Putin's second term, Russia had established itself as an important exporter of grain and was making significant progress in other food sectors, such as meat and dairy. The government's role and involvement in food supply and agriculture shifted from modest regulation and support to massive interventions, national priority projects, and dreams of total nutritional self-sufficiency.

What was Putin's role in this monumental transition? Was there a strategic master plan to protect the regime by preventing the food shortages that had destroyed the Romanov Empire and the USSR? The answer is no, at least not initially. Industry leaders, experts, politicians, and state officials that we interviewed all agree that Gordeev, rather than Putin, is the true midwife of Russia's agricultural miracle and that initially Putin paid very little attention to food production. Interventions started with and because of Gordeev; "the desire [to intervene] came with him," confirmed Zlochevskii, who nonetheless credited himself with designing the exact mechanism of this policy tool.[45] According to Anatolii Altukhov, a prominent scholar of Soviet and Russian agriculture with close ties to the government, Gordeev was *the* driving force behind the government's key initiatives such as the National Priority Project and the Food Security Doctrine (described in subsequent chapters)[46] and the change in state's approach to the question of food supply more broadly.

At the same time, could such a profound change have been achieved without Putin's approval, especially given that Gordeev's economic worldview openly clashed with that of the government's then more powerful economic liberals, such as Minister of Finance Aleksei Kudrin and the Minister of Economic Development German Gref?[47]

Several factors explain Gordeev's success. First, the minister was not simply a skillful politician but also a committed, knowledgeable, and capable bureaucrat with a deep understanding of the industry. Among the experts we interviewed, even those who opposed him politically recognized Gordeev's professional competence and experience. Second, even though many liberals scorned Gordeev's conservative ideals, few took agriculture seriously enough to actively fight his designs. For most Soviet and post-Soviet politicians, especially the city-born and raised liberals, food and agriculture were marginal and unimportant policy areas not worthy of their time and attention.

Finally, and most important, even though Putin was initially uninterested in agriculture and the question of food supply, he recognized the political importance of food for regime stability. In Gordeev's savvy rhetoric, agricultural production and state investment in and regulation of the industry were not the end goal but rather means to promote state strength, social stability, and independence from foreign pressure and interference. These were things that Putin cared deeply about; indeed, the main ideological construct of Putin's second term was "sovereign democracy." This ideological concept was most closely associated with Putin's aide Vladislav Surkov and defined sovereignty, the key pillar of Russia's existence, predominantly as freedom from foreign interference and Western meddling.[48]

A Russia dependent on others for food could never be truly sovereign, but investment in the domestic food supply advocated by Gordeev offered a solution. And once it became clear that, with sufficient state support, Russian agriculture could produce food in substantial quantities, Putin's benign indifference turned into enthusiastic political backing. Almost overnight, food independence became a key pillar of the regime's policies, a truly national agenda rather than one minister's crusade.[49]

The transformation of Russia's food supply in 2000–2010 thus offers an interesting perspective on the nature of Putin's regime. According to a view popular among some Western Kremlinologists, politicians, and security experts, Putin is (or at least was until the invasion of Ukraine in February 2022) a master strategist, an expert in multidimensional chess who predicts moves and meticulously and skillfully manipulates domestic and international affairs. An opposing view is Putin "the *adhocrat*,"[50] a purely opportunistic, swift but reactive, and not always coherent tactician who lacks a grand vision but exploits his opponents' mistakes.

What emerges from this chapter, however, is a picture that is more complex and in line with those arguments that view Putin as neither too strategic nor purely opportunistic, but rather an autocrat who enjoys only limited control over his country's affairs, a strongman that is rather weak,[51] but nonetheless has enough powers to lead the transformation of entire industries if and when he chooses. Gordeev, not Putin, was the mastermind of Russia's agricultural boom and the key person behind the securitization of nutrition. Yet it was Putin who allowed such plans to become a reality. Without his approval, such a transformation could not have been possible. When he came to power, Putin did not know much about food supply or agriculture but clearly grasped food's political importance. He was and still is driven by several fundamental principles and fears that Brian Taylor views as the "code of Putinism."[52] Presenting agricultural protectionism and nutritional self-sufficiency in ideological terms consistent with the statist core tenets of this code was precisely the magic sauce that allowed Gordeev to turn a previously neglected issue and a controversial governance approach into a cornerstone of regime security.

Concluding Remarks

This chapter focused on 2000–2010, the key period for understanding the transformation of Russia's agriculture and food supply. As we show, the change originally stemmed from the combination of economic demands outside of Russia and the ideological vision of the country's minister of agriculture Aleksei Gordeev. Food became a truly national idea only at a much later stage, supported and embraced by Putin and the security elites, the *siloviki*. Yet, once the government entered this policy area, its prominence and ambitions only grew with time. "With food comes the appetite," says a Russian proverb, and as more domestically produced food started to appear, the Kremlin's appetite grew accordingly.

Furthermore, this chapter discussed the early stages of Russia's economic transformation away from the liberal, market-oriented economy. Scholars often view the early 2000s as the heydays of Putin's economic liberalism. Indeed, this period witnessed several important liberal economic changes in areas such as taxation and land ownership.[53] But as we document in this chapter, these years also saw the emergence of the government's heavy involvement in the grain sector and then in agriculture as a whole. Gradually, through the regime's direct participation in the market, investment, state financial support, and subsidized credit, the grain sector moved firmly toward the state capitalist economic model.[54] As in many other episodes throughout Russian history, food led the way and other sectors followed suit.

5
Food, Security, and Food Security

The previous chapter analyzed the rapid transformation of Russian agriculture, specifically grain production from 2000 to 2010. We centered on the domestic and international factors that fueled the agricultural sector, the ideologically conservative and statist foundations of the government's renewed interest in domestic food production, and the instruments—financing, credit, investment in infrastructure and machinery—it used to support domestic producers. Unlike in 1917 or 1991, self-sufficiency in grain ensured that the Kremlin had enough bread to distribute in the case of major political or security upheaval. Yet, bread alone was insufficient to fully shield Russia from dependence on the West, which, Russia's political elites believed, was actively scheming to undermine and depose Putin. The success of grain was just the first step, and the Kremlin sought to replicate it in other crucial sectors, primarily meat and dairy.

On January 30, 2010, Dmitry Medvedev, who replaced Putin as Russia's president in 2008,[1] signed Presidential Decree 120, titled "The Food Security Doctrine of the Russian Federation (*Doktrina prodovol'stvennoi bezopasnosti Rossiiskoi Federatsii*)".[2] At the time, it represented the most important development in Kremlin's food policies. The decree, prepared by Russia's Security Council and signed by the president, turned food provision into a key security concern and endowed it with the elevated status of "Doctrine." The labeling was important; currently, only seven documents in the Russian Federation are defined as Doctrines, all adopted after 2000. These are not legal but, rather, ideological frameworks that cover military, energy, information security, environment, and climate issues that the Kremlin considers crucial. Together, these Doctrines roughly summarize the state's official ideology.[3]

The Doctrine suggests food security is integral to the Russian Federation's national security and vital for the preservation of Russia's sovereignty. The document asserts that Russian national interests require a "necessary" minimum level of domestic food production. It set clear goals for self-sufficiency in grain (at least 95 percent of domestic consumption), milk and dairy products (85 percent), fish, meat, sugar, and vegetable oil (all 80 percent), potatoes (95 percent), and other items.

This chapter analyzes the Food Security Doctrine, its goals, ideological foundations, the reasons for its adoption, and its wider significance for Russian politics. In the second half, we discuss the practical consequences of the Doctrine's adoption and how the regime prioritized self-sufficiency in food during the 2010 drought year.

The Road to the Doctrine

By the late 2000s, food security was not a novel concept within Russia's political debate. The idea of legislating food security originated in the mid-1990s as part of the discussion on the direction of Russia's economy between the Yeltsin administration and its leading political opponent, the Communist Party of the Russian Federation (KPRF). For the KPRF, food security signified independence from Western food imports. The party presented the reliance on Western food as part and parcel of the West's larger effort to subjugate Russia and turn it into a dumping ground for its inferior products. Prioritizing domestic food production over imports also meant investment in and subsidies for the post-Soviet large-scale agricultural enterprises, a key constituency for the communists and their Agrarian Party allies. Increased food production at home also served the interests of impoverished Russians who were unable to afford imported food products, another KPRF support group.[4]

For Yeltsin and economic liberals, on the other hand, food security meant primarily the presence of food in stores, a key social concern of the early 1990s resolved by the market reforms. Thus, the liberals justified the reliance on food imports and did not necessarily consider it a problem. What mattered was the availability (and to a lesser degree, affordability) of food, less so its geographic origin.[5]

Ironically, in this debate, neither the government nor the KPRF aimed to promote the standard understanding of food security used by the UN Food and Agriculture Organization (FAO); "everyone heard something somewhere [about food security] but nobody understood a thing about it," Evgenia Serova summarized the debate.[6] The 1996 World Food Summit stipulated that "Food security exists when all people, at all times, have physical and economic access to sufficient, safe and nutritious food that meets their dietary needs and food preferences for an active and healthy life."[7] The economic liberals of the Yeltsin government were concerned with ensuring the presence of food in stores but less so about its affordability and the citizens' access. The KPRF's focus on domestic production also sharply diverged from the traditional view of food security.[8] Ideologically, prioritizing domestic production and non-reliance on imports are closely linked to the ideas of state sovereignty, yet in the literature "food sovereignty" has become associated with critical and activist approaches that put emphasis on local practices and cultures of food production and consumption.[9] The KPRF's goal, therefore, was more in line with what Wegren and Elvestad, building on Jennifer Clapp's seminal work, view as food self-sufficiency.[10] And indeed, in Russian official discourse "food security" and self-sufficiency (*samoobespechenie*) are often used interchangeably.[11] Yet the food security that the KPRF sought was not simply self-sufficiency, but explicit protection from potential external interference, and therefore, we take a step further and view their end goal as food or nutritional independence. In fact, Food Independence Doctrine is precisely how several of the industry leaders and experts we interviewed described the Food Security Doctrine.[12]

In December 1997, the KPRF and their allies in the Agrarian Party advanced a draft law on food security in which food independence was the key component. However, both this draft and its amended version, tabled in 1999, never became law because the Yeltsin administration opposed it.[13] Despite the Kremlin's effort to adopt a Food Security Doctrine that shared numerous similarities with that of the KPRF, the communists doggedly continued to promote their own legislative initiatives and ideological visions. Thus, in 2008, when the Ministry of Agriculture was finalizing its draft of the Food Security Doctrine, the KPRF attempted to discredit this government initiative by passing its own law on food security in the State Duma. Similarly to the KPRF efforts in the 1990s, it was ultimately unsuccessful.[14] As we demonstrate below, Putin's administration essentially resolved the debate about the meaning of food security by merging two different concepts into one, thus reconciling the availability of affordable food with food independence, but also clearly prioritizing the latter over the former.

To the regime, the adoption of the Food Security Doctrine marked the culmination of food's increased political importance and the government's ever-growing involvement in the agrarian sector, as described in Chapter 5. This was also the logical outcome of Minister of Agriculture Aleksei Gordeev's relentless and skillful efforts to promote his conservative ideological vision and elevate the importance of his bureaucratic fiefdom, turning it into one of Russia's leading economic ministries. The Doctrine was the natural continuation of the law "On the Development of Russian Agriculture" (2006), the National Project "On Development of Agro-Industrial Complex" (2006–2007), and the "State Program for the Development of Agricultural Sector for the Years 2008–2012."

Finally, the adoption of the Food Security Doctrine was a response to rising world food prices during and in the aftermath of the 2007–2009 Great Recession. Russia was especially vulnerable to the price spike, due to its substantial food imports and the sharp devaluation of the ruble.[15] In just eighteen months (January 2007–June 2008), Russian food prices rose by 35 percent. In St. Petersburg, the spike was much higher, namely 120 percent, and as a result, the Kremlin feared potential social unrest.[16] This rise in prices forced the government to coerce local food producers and supermarket chains to agree to price freezes on some basic food staples from October 2007 through January 2008. Even though the liberal minister of finance Aleksei Kudrin opposed this policy and argued that it made little economic sense, it was eventually extended through April 2008.[17]

The sharp price increases thus forced the government to consider an additional set of policies to prevent similar crises in the future. On May 19, 2008, Putin, now the country's prime minister, convened a high-level meeting to address this issue. At the meeting, held in the town of Essentuki, in the southern agrarian region of Stavropol, Putin blamed the food price increases on global prices and admitted they negatively affected pensioners and other vulnerable members of Russian society. The government then moved to declare its commitment to guaranteeing the affordability of food and the stability of food prices. To achieve this goal, the government had to increase its support for domestic producers and reduce Russia's dependence on food imports. At the meeting, Putin announced an additional $1.7 billion in support of local food producers, most of it ($1.1 billion) given to Rosselkhozbank to strengthen its lending capacity. Additionally, Putin ordered government ministries to review all Russian international agreements that dealt with food imports and exports.[18]

Gordeev, speaking immediately after Putin, highlighted the danger of Russia's dependency on food imports. Citing UN World Food Programme data, Gordeev claimed that in 2007 food prices increased by 40 percent worldwide, noting that high prices would persist in the long term. These developments, he maintained, demonstrated that food imports have a high social cost and, therefore, could cause social upheaval. For Gordeev, the link between food and political stability was obvious and explicit. Shifting to Russia, Gordeev noted that in 2007 the country imported food and agricultural raw materials worth $27.6 billion, up 28 percent from 2006. In 2008, the trend of growing food imports continued unabated. Given these conditions, he warned, Russia could not create a stable market in food staples. Gordeev focused on tightening tariffs and customs to protect domestic producers. In other words, while official rhetoric continued to emphasize the importance of food affordability, Gordeev suggested that, at least in the short run, the defense of domestic production should be a higher priority than the availability of affordable food.[19]

At this meeting, Putin also likely gave Gordeev the green light to present the draft of a major document on food security to the government for approval. In fact, just two days after the discussion in Essentuki, Deputy Minister of Agriculture Aleksandr Petrikov announced that a law focused on food security was being drafted at the meeting of the Agrarian Committee of the State Duma. Yet, instead of the food security law, the Ministry of Agriculture unveiled a different document on October 31, 2008, titled the "Food Security Doctrine."[20]

What Is Russia's Food Security?

According to Arkadii Zlochevskii, the initiative to create a framework document with a Doctrine status came from Boris Chernyakov (1937–2013), a leading specialist on American agriculture, at the US-Canada Institute of the Russian Academy of Sciences. Chernyakov had direct access to Gordeev, with whom he coauthored several texts in 2006 and 2007.[21] Chernyakov believed Russia could greatly benefit from studying the US regulatory efforts in agriculture. He held American farming in high regard and viewed the state of Iowa as the agricultural capital of the world. His academic writings, among other things, focused on food security in the West and analyzed the US Food Security Act (1985) and other legislative documents.[22] Thus, Chernyakov may have likened Russia's Food Security Doctrine to the US legislation. Chernyakov never publicly discussed his role in formulating the Food Security Doctrine, but in an interview he gave shortly before his death in 2013, he came close to revealing the motivation behind it. The main mistake of the economic reformers in the 1990s, he argued, was their failure to develop a legal, financial, and organizational framework that enabled a viable domestic agricultural economy.[23] The adoption of a Food Security Doctrine, in his view, was a necessary foundation for the future success of Russian agriculture, similarly to how US legislative and regulatory acts ensure continuous prosperity of the US agricultural sector. Yet, while Chernyakov strongly believed in the state's involvement in and support of agriculture, the Doctrine's nutritional independence component most likely came from a different source.

Once Gordeev endorsed Chernyakov's Doctrine, he tasked the Ministry of Agriculture's research arm, the All-Russian Research Institute of Agricultural Economics (*Vserossiiskii NII Ekonomiki Sel'skogo Khoziiaistva*), headed by Ivan Ushachev, a prominent expert in agricultural management and a member of Russia's Academy of Sciences, to draft the Doctrine's text. Ushachev, an old-school Soviet agricultural economist and deputy minister of agriculture from 1994 to 1996, whom one of the experts we interviewed described as a "man of a very distant past," shared Gordeev's conservative convictions that food security signaled Russian independence from food imports, making it the core idea of the document.[24]

We do not know when exactly the drafting process began, but the chairman of the State Duma Agrarian Committee claimed in May 2008 that by then, the Ministry of Agriculture had already been developing the blueprint for Russia's food security for several years.

The Food Security Doctrine

The Ministry of Agriculture draft of the Food Security Doctrine was published in late October 2008, while President Medvedev signed the Doctrine on January 30, 2010.[25] The Doctrine underwent substantial changes between these two dates, highlighting Gordeev's waning influence in the Medvedev administration.[26] In fact, by its official publication date, Gordeev was no longer the minister of agriculture and vice prime minister, but the governor of the agricultural Voronezh Oblast and, thus, had substantially less political influence in Moscow.[27]

A comparison of the original draft, produced by the Ministry of Agriculture, and the final text that eventually emerged from Russia's Security Council and was signed by Medvedev also demonstrates Russia's shifting approach to food supply. Food security became state security.

The 2008 draft states from the very beginning that "food independence is a necessary condition for food security of the Russian Federation." The same section also asserts that Russian national interests require a "necessary" level of domestic food production, detailed in Sections 2 and 6. To the draft authors, true independence will only be achieved if Russia can produce 80 percent of its annual food consumption should food imports suddenly cease entirely. Section 6 repeats the possibility of food import cessation and establishes clear goals for self-sufficiency in grain (90 percent), milk and dairy products (85 percent), and sugar, vegetable oil, meat, and fish (all 80 percent). The text, however, remains silent on why and when Russia should experience a complete stoppage of food imports to the country.

The final version of the Doctrine goes even further by increasing the self-sufficiency threshold for grain from 90 to 95 percent and adding two additional food categories—potatoes (95 percent) and edible salts (85 percent). Yet, curiously, the Security Council version conspicuously dropped all references to the potential stoppage of food imports; some things are probably better left unsaid.

Section 3 of the 2008 draft contains an extended and biting criticism of Russia's dependence on food imports, which goes even beyond the figures noted in Gordeev's speech at the Essentuki meeting. Food imports, the draft asserts, undermine Russia's economic security and national interests. According to the draft, Russia's major cities import 50 to 70 percent of their food consumption. Moreover, the Doctrine draft notes that food imports grow faster than domestic food production, effectively suppressing it.

The international dimension of food imports doesn't escape the attention of the Ministry of Agriculture draft authors. They discuss the growing pressure of food-exporting countries to lower Russia's state support for its own agriculture and to further open Russia's market to their products. The authors warn that this pressure is only going to grow when Russia joins the WTO. These attacks on food imports and the WTO did not make it to the final text. Moreover, the Doctrine mentions Russia's entry into WTO in an exclusively positive light, characterizing it as step toward strengthening the country's food security. Whereas Gordeev and his conservative allies were known for their ideological objection to free trade, the Security Council officials that revised the draft were careful enough not to include such blatantly political views into an official Doctrine.

The 2008 draft also touches on the social dimensions of food, especially its affordability, the growing social gaps between the rich and the poor, and the declining ability of the most vulnerable members of Russian society to afford many food products. This focus on inequality and the welfare of the poorest members of the Russian society aligns with Gordeev and Ushachev's anti-liberal market and conservative outlook, yet this was not a concern for the more national and regime security-oriented staffers of the Security Council. The final text, predictably, remains silent on the growing inequality, social gaps, and consumption patterns of the poorest members of Russian society.

The Security Council's lack of interest in Gordeev and the conservatives' social activism is clearly visible in the Doctrine's final text. It views price stabilization—the preferred choice of economic liberals such as Kudrin—as the solution to rising food prices and does not even mention price freezes, which Gordeev strongly supported and considered central to the market economy.[28] Instead of warning that unrestrained food imports are a threat to Russian national security, the Doctrine calls the existing policy of customs and tariff regulations the best defense of domestic food producers against foreign companies (which are subsidized by their states and engage in unfair practices). Finally, the Doctrine treats the dependency of major urban centers on food imports as a given and merely highlights that the state ought to guarantee the stability of food supplies to these cities (Paragraphs 15, 21).

The Doctrine's final text, therefore, downplays social conservatism and welfare components of state policy and, instead, focuses on state security, sovereignty, and implicit external threats. At the same time, the final document is more economically liberal than that envisioned by Gordeev, his conservative allies, and the KPRF. Its aims are to achieve nutritional independence and shield Russia from dependence on external actors in the case of a major security or an economic crisis, rather than championing a crusade to eliminate food imports altogether or increase social equality. The Doctrine's final text does play lip service to food affordability, but the goal is clearly nutritional independence.

The 2010 Food Security Doctrine cemented the (re)emergence of food as a major pillar of state and regime security. In that, it built upon, but also diverged from, previous efforts. The basic impetus to protect the regime from external pressure by increasing self-sufficiency in food was similar to the Soviet reaction to the US grain embargo in the wake of the invasion of Afghanistan. Indeed, some experts involved in the Soviet 1982 Food Program, which outlined the efforts to decrease the USSR's dependence on food imports, participated in drafting the Food Security Doctrine.[29] Yet the Food Security Doctrine was also substantially more ambitious than

Brezhnev-era efforts and aimed at achieving almost complete nutritional independence, something the 1980s USSR could have never dreamt of. And most important, unlike the Soviet Food Program, the Doctrine was not an exercise in wishful thinking detached from reality but was built upon very real successes. It had a fighting chance of achieving at least some of its ambitious goals.

Which actors and forces benefited from a designated Food Security Doctrine that established nutritional independence as the government's goal and linked food supply and state security? The liberal media ridiculed the document as an empty public relations stunt. Some pro–free market agrarian experts and politicians opposed it fearing that the focus on domestic production would reduce the availability and the affordability of food and harm, not promote food security. However, a much large portion of economic and political elites welcomed the document.[30]

As any foundational document, the Doctrine emerged out of a collective effort of a coalition of forces promoting their own separate goals. And while an aspirational framework statement, the Doctrine also had a real meaning and impact. The term "Doctrine" has a distinct military connotation. In Putin's Russia, no state official or ministry could (at least publicly) ignore, let alone be seen as undermining an effort endowed with a special Doctrine, especially one with "security" in its title. The Doctrine elevated the status of the Ministry of Agriculture, endowed it with budgets, prestige, and influence in intra-governmental bureaucratic battles, and effectively put it in charge of a government-wide effort that involved multiple ministries and state bodies.[31] Indeed, just prior to the Doctrine's final approval, Minister of Agriculture Elena Skynnik claimed that food security is "one of the central and prioritized problems in the system of national security."[32] By linking food and security, the Doctrine catered to the interests of the Security Council and the *siloviki*, the representatives of the security services. It allowed them to take over yet another important economic sector, a process that culminated with the appointment of Dmitry Patrushev, a scion of a key *siloviki* family, as the minister of agriculture in 2018. Simultaneously, the Doctrine, which clearly reoriented Russian agriculture in an anti-liberal market direction, also weakened the government's economic liberals, most notably German Gref who actively tried to prevent its adoption.[33]

Furthermore, the Doctrine fit the interests of Russia's political leadership that understood the significance of domestic food supply for regime stability and survival. According to President Medvedev, food supplies were "one of the cornerstones of security in general."[34] Documents with a status of a national Doctrine outlined goals and expectations and served as important signaling and commitment devices for both the state and the producers. To Sergei Iushin, the head of Russia's National Meat Association, the Doctrine is "an insurance policy of sorts" and the government's assurance that the sector will be taken care of.[35] Additionally, producers could now use the numerical thresholds outlined in the Doctrine to request resources and funding from the state to meet these thresholds. "We need the continuation of state support . . . and [for us] the Doctrine is an instrument of cooperation with the state . . . that sets these goals," explained Artiom Belov, the CEO of *Soyuzmoloko*, Russia's dairy producers' organization.[36] Moreover, the Doctrine centralized the politically crucial issue of food supply and halted the attempts of various regional leaders to develop their own independent approaches to the topic.[37] It is doubtful that all these outcomes could have been achieved had food security been legislated as a law, rather than presented as a Doctrine. Finally, the Doctrine also reassured the Russian population that the government is laser-focused on the issue of food supply and is determined to prevent food shortages.[38]

Despite its political significance, the Food Security Doctrine was still mainly a declarative document that outlined ambitious goals but was silent on the ways of achieving them. Thus, in April 2012, the Russian government issued a "Strategy for the Development of the Food and Food Processing Industry of the Russian Federation until 2020," which effectively provided a roadmap to various state agencies for realization of the Food Security Doctrine goals. The Strategy established specific aims and benchmarks to substantially reduce Russian dependence on imported food staples by 2020. Domestic food production was projected to increase 1.4 times by 2020, with an average annual growth of 3 to 5 percent. The targets were set very high: grain production was to reach 125 million tons, milk 38.2 million tons, sugar beets 42 million tons, potatoes 34 million tons, meat (including beef, chicken, and pork) 14.1 million tons, vegetables 17.9 million tons, fruits and berries 4.13 million tons, fish and fish products 5.2 million tons, and sunflower seeds 7.5 million tons.[39]

Achieving these goals would effectively ensure that, by 2020, domestic production could supply 96 percent of Russia's sugar consumption, 88 percent of needed meat and meat products, and 85 percent of milk and dairy products. The 2016 update of the Strategy added a projected decline of imports of key food staples. Meat imports were due to decline by 67.8 percent, milk and dairy products by 30 percent, vegetables by 70.3 percent, and fruit and berries by 20 percent. The 2016 Strategy update also noted (without providing figures) that food independence thresholds set in the 2010 Doctrine had been achieved in grain, potatoes, vegetable oil, and sugar.[40]

The 2010 Drought and Its Consequences

To understand the consequences of the Russian government's shift to prioritizing domestic food supply, one needs to look no further than the 2010 drought and the Kremlin's reaction. The Food Security Doctrine was just six months old when Russia faced the first major food-related crisis of the Putin era, the 2010 drought, which severely affected Russia's grain reserves and forced the government to deal with potential food shortages. Summer 2010 in Russia was the hottest in over 130 years. The second half of July and August were marked by excessively hot and dry weather. It was clear the grain yield would be damaged. The drought affected all major grain-producing regions and "destroyed more than 13.3 million hectares of grain crops, a number that represented 17 percent of the total sown area" in the country.[41] In the Volga federal district, two-thirds of the crop harvest was destroyed. In total, the total grain harvest was one-third less than in 2009 and amounted to only 60.9 million tons.[42] The significant crop damage thus led to a sharp rise in wheat prices on the local market.

The government's initial response was a mixture of reassuring statements by senior officials that Russia has sufficient food supply to avoid any food shortages, coupled with threats that price increases had no basis in economic reality and must be dealt with by Russia's regulatory bodies and law enforcement as speculative price gouging.[43] This government rhetoric, however, could not change the reality of fast-rising food prices. In July 2010, the government was forced to sell 3 million tons of grain from its reserve funds on the domestic market in the hopes of stabilizing prices. But despite the intervention, grain prices continued to increase (Figure 5.1).

Unlike during previous food crises, despite the low yield, in 2010 Russia had enough grain for domestic consumption; years of government procurement intervention and purchase of excess grain filled up the state's storage facilities. Yet, on August 15, 2010, Prime Minister Putin imposed a ban on wheat, rye, barley, corn, and flour exports from Russia. The ban was originally only supposed to last until December 31, 2010, but it was ultimately

96 BREAD AND AUTOCRACY

Figure 5.1. Price per metric ton of wheat (rubles)
Source: FAOSTAT Statistical Database (2013)

extended to July 1, 2011. Officially, Putin justified the measure as a means to keep domestic food prices down. "True, we have enough reserves—9.5 million tons," he conceded. "However, we need to prevent the growth of domestic food prices in the Russian Federation, to retain livestock and to create reserves for next year."[44] The ban represented unprecedented state intervention, the first since Russia became a market economy in the 1990s.

The grain export ban was radical. By stopping exports, Russia voluntarily removed itself from the global international grain market, despite attempting to become a prominent global player for years. This harmed its reputation as a reliable supplier and deprived the state of hard currency revenue. Geopolitically, the ban led to food riots and destabilized Middle Eastern countries reliant on Russian grain.[45] Some analysts even view the food supply problems as one of the drivers of the Arab Spring and the downfall of the Mubarak regime in Egypt.[46] Given Russia's proximity to the region, Putin's decision undermined Russia's foreign relations and geopolitical ambitions.

In fact, it remains unclear whether the ban managed to prevent a rise in domestic prices. Figure 5.1 shows that prices continued to climb even after the ban was announced; at best, the measure slowed their growth.[47] Equally important, the Russian government could use other policies to either bring the prices down or to compensate the population for their growth. The ban, therefore, was Putin's choice. The grain export embargo, argues Welton, almost certainly increased poverty in Russia and, thus, actually reduced food security in the traditional understanding of the term.[48] Yet domestic politics and short-term regime stability, rather than economic or social, or foreign policy considerations, drove the Kremlin's decision-making.

Putin's main concern and preference were physically possessing domestically produced bread and avoiding any potential shortages. Second, the government was committed to protecting the domestic meat and dairy industries. The biggest beneficiaries of Putin's decision were Russia's meat producers because the ban aimed to assure reasonable prices of animal feed, of which grain was a major ingredient. The biggest losers were Russian grain exporters deprived of hard currency revenue. These were forced to deal with the negative impact of unfulfilled contracts on their business reputation and future opportunities. Prioritizing the producers of meat over those of grain may have been economically questionable, but it made perfect political sense beyond economics. By 2010, Russia had already achieved self-sufficiency in grain, but was still dependent on imported meat, a dynamic that the Food Security Doctrine clearly sought to reverse.[49] Food independence trumped other considerations, be it geopolitical stability, the basic principles of market economy, or the reputation and future business opportunities of Russia's grain exporters.

WTO Accession and Russia's Food Politics (2012)

The 2010 Food Security Doctrine and the export ban of 2010 highlighted the Kremlin's strategic investment in promoting and defending domestic food production. In 2012, Russia joined the World Trade Organization (WTO) following eighteen years of negotiations. This effectively ended the enforcement of the 1974 Jackson-Vanik amendment to the US Trade Act, which severely restricted US trade with the USSR, and later, post-Soviet Russia. The amendment's abolishment was a high priority for all Russian post-Soviet administrations.[50] At the same time, joining the WTO affected the Kremlin's commitment to food independence. As discussed above, the authors of the 2008 Food Security Doctrine draft perceived WTO membership as a grave danger, since it would further open the Russian domestic market to imported food products. The fears of the conservative Ministry of Agriculture bureaucrats were well founded; despite the Doctrine, food imports continued to steadily increase and reached an all-time high of $43 billion in 2013.[51] The Kremlin had to balance its commitment to food independence with the opening up of the domestic market required by the WTO accession.

According to an analysis by a team led by the Russian economist Sergey F. Sutyrin, meat and meat products, which were at the core of Russia's drive for food independence and enjoyed "the highest protection through tariff customs regulations[, were likely to] suffer the most from the liberalization of trade rules under the WTO accession."[52] To protect the industry, Russia retained the same quotas for poultry and beef. Moreover, it maintained control over the import of poultry and beef for an indefinite period and of pork until 2020. Still, the Kremlin had to slash its agricultural subsidies to domestic producers by more than half, from $9 billion in 2012–2013 to $4.4 billion in 2018. Tariffs on imported food products were set to decline from 13.2 percent to 10.8 percent within an eight-year timeframe. In addition, subsidies for dairy products were projected to decrease from 19.8 percent to 14.9 percent, for cereals from 15.1 percent to 10 percent, and for oilseeds, fats, and oils from 9 percent to 7.1 percent.[53]

The 2010 Food Security Doctrine downplayed the dangers of WTO accession for domestic food producers, and eventually, WTO membership and food independence were bound to clash. In 2012, the Kremlin had to compromise on food independence in order to join the WTO. Yet, the ideological commitment to food independence did not go away, and after Putin returned to presidency in 2012, the government's policies took an increasingly conservative and aggressive shape. A serious confrontation with the West, which threatened to cut Russia off its major food import sources, was no longer a purely theoretical possibility.

In this geopolitical environment, food independence envisioned by the 2010 Food Security Doctrine had to be achieved at all cost, the WTO accession restrictions notwithstanding. Indeed, the Medvedev-era Food Security Doctrine was no longer ambitious enough to meet the regime's needs.

In February 2014, the Revolution of Dignity—violent mass protests in Kyiv, the capital of Ukraine—toppled pro-Russian president Viktor Yanukovych. Russian soldiers without insignia appeared in Ukraine's Crimean Peninsula and a motley assortment of nationalists, adventurers, mercenaries, and Russian security services officers descended on Eastern Ukraine to foment anti-government mobilization and violence. By March 2014, Crimea had been annexed and the Donbas region was engulfed by an all-out war. The West responded to the Kremlin's aggression and territorial expansion by imposing sanctions. For Putin, this was an opportunity to break loose of any constraints on his quest to achieve food independence, protect domestic producers, and insulate the regime from food-related threats. Under the guise of a response to Western sanctions, the Russian government adopted the most radical of potential paths to food independence: it effectively banned a significant share of food imports into Russia. This marked a decisive shift in favor of domestic food producers. The era of the so-called countersanctions had begun. In essence, this move shelved the 2010 Food Security Doctrine and effectively adopted its more ambitious, radical, and conservative 2008 vision, advocated by Gordeev and Ushachev. The sanctions, which sought to promote an almost autarkic version of food import substitution, were therefore not a tactical ad hoc improvisation, but a strategic adoption of ideas and policies discussed for years that were up until then too radical to implement.

Concluding Remarks

This chapter focuses on Russia's Food Security Doctrine, a major document that cemented the link between food and national and regime security and declared Russia's goal to achieve food independence and shield itself from the external influence that stemmed from reliance on imported food. Beyond being an ideological statement, the Doctrine also established ambitious numerical goals—expected to be achieved in the near to medium term—that were required to achieve food independence.

We show that the Food Security Doctrine was a blend of two goals: the nationalists' aggressively protectionist and politically conservative desire to protect Russia's domestic food production, spearheaded by Gordeev and the Ministry of Agriculture, and the Security Council's focus on viewing and articulating policies through the security lens. The result was a securitization of food supply and the prioritization of the Kremlin's drive to achieve food independence, which became a key pillar of regime stability. In the Doctrine, food independence is couched in the language of security and state sovereignty, which in practice were tools of regime survival. Food independence, notes Wengle, is driven by Putin's own political desires[54] and fears, rather than national security concerns. According to Medvedev, social stability in Russia directly depended on food security (understood as food independence).[55]

The need to feed Russia's population without relying on food imports was preconditioned on a conflict in which such imports might be withheld or used as a weapon. Indeed, despite heavily relying on food imports and occasionally food aid, Yeltsin's government did not feel threatened or the need to prioritize domestic production, because it did not prepare for a geopolitical confrontation. Putin, however, actively did. He was confident that the West, especially the United States, was determined to bring him down.[56] Therefore, domestic food supply should ensure that food riots and shortages, which destroyed Russia's previous two political systems, do not endanger his as well.

6
Sanctions and Countersanctions

On March 18, 2014, President Putin signed a law that annexed Ukraine's Crimean Peninsula to Russia. Putin justified this audacious move by invoking the central role that Crimea had played in Russia's history and national identity in a speech to Russia's political elites. Later, Putin went as far as calling Crimea Russia's Temple Mount.[1] As Putin spoke, a motley crew of Russian nationalists, security services officers, veterans, mercenaries, and adventurers were busy trying to violently destroy the Ukrainian government's control over the eastern and southern parts of the country. These were extraordinary developments that aimed to redraw national borders and fundamentally violated the post-1991 security border in Europe. Russia's major confrontation with Ukraine but also the United States and the West more generally had officially begun.

Though bold, Putin's moves were reactive; Russia was serendipitously exploiting the window of opportunity that surfaced after violent mass protests in Kyiv, Ukraine's capital, removed the corrupt pro-Russian president Viktor Yanukovych from power, leaving the country in upheaval. The Kremlin believed it had to pounce, but as far as food independence was concerned, Russia was not yet ready for a protracted confrontation and was still heavily dependent on imports. That had to be fixed, fast.

This chapter centers on Putin's dramatic attempt to achieve food independence in the wake of the annexation of the Crimea and the final transformation of food supply into a state security domain.

The Empire Bites Back

In response to the Russian invasion and annexation of Crimea and the ensuing war in the Donbas region of Ukraine, the United States, EU, and other Western governments introduced numerous sanctions on major Russian state-owned firms and Russian politicians, media personalities, military commanders, and oligarchs close to Putin between late March and

September 2014. These sanctions ranged from travel bans and asset freezes to restricting access to capital markets and Russian state banks, bans on sales of advanced oil and gas drilling technologies, as well as dual use technologies to Russia.[2]

Russia retaliated on August 6, 2014. Putin signed decree N560 titled "On the use of separate special economic measures to protect the security of the Russian Federation" (*O priminenii otdel'nykh spetsial'nykh ekonomicheskikh mer v tseliakh obespecheniia bezopasnosti Rossiiskoi Federatsii*) ordering a one-year embargo on the import of agricultural products, raw materials, and food from countries that had imposed sanctions on Russian individuals or companies. The following day, the Russian government issued another decree that banned the EU, United States, Australia, Canada, and Norway from importing into Russia. It also supplied a list of banned products (meat, milk, fish, fruits, and vegetables) from these countries. In 2015–2016, Russia added Ukraine, Iceland, Liechtenstein, Albania, Turkey, and Montenegro to the list. The Russian government renewed the food import ban annually from 2017 to 2021, with the list of banned products remaining largely intact.[3] Moreover, on July 29, 2015, Putin ordered authorities to seize and destroy banned food imports smuggled into Russia (often via Belarus or Kazakhstan). In 2015–2020, the Federal Service for Veterinary and Phytosanitary Surveillance (*Rosselkhoznadzor*), the government agency in charge of enforcing the ban, reported that it destroyed 37,170 tons of smuggled food.[4] The food destruction was widely shown on Russian television and evoked substantial public disapproval, for the government was seen wasting products that could have been distributed to the needy. Even the Russian Orthodox Church, traditionally compliant and loyal to the regime, expressed criticism.[5] Some even compared it to book burnings of the past.

The food import ban became widely known as "countersanctions" (*kontrasanktsii*). The 2013 value of products covered by the countersanctions was estimated at roughly $9.1 billion, most of which (72.4 percent) were food imports from the EU. The banned products comprised 21 percent of Russia's imported food.[6] While this radical and historically unprecedented form of import substitution was framed as a temporary retaliatory measure that Russia was forced to adopt, in reality, it was a well-thought-out policy that had previously been advocated by nationalist and conservative agricultural actors but was considered too radical to be implemented during normal times. Geopolitical confrontation with the West finally provided an opening for drastic measures.

Neither the Western sanctions nor the Russian response was an unusual instrument of international conflict. In the post–World War I era, international economic sanctions emerged as an important tool of international politics. These measures, writes Mulder, were envisioned and codified as an "economic weapon," a peaceful, yet very potent, alternative to active warfare. A nation subject to comprehensive international sanctions was presumed to be "on the road to social collapse," and hence, likely to change its behavior.[7] This assumption and the relatively easy availability of sanctions made them a preferred policy tool for many a leader. Yet, in practice, the economic weapon was less effective than its advocates hoped for, and target states found ways to live under and subvert even the harshest sanctions. For instance, similar to Russia in the wake of Crimea, when Fascist Italy invaded Ethiopia in 1935, "three-quarters of the world's states severed most of their commercial links with Italy." In response, Mussolini launched a "campaign for comprehensive anti-sanctions autarky (*autarchia*) to survive financial attrition." Sanctions harmed Italy, but failed to save Ethiopia.[8] Other studies also note the limited effectiveness of sanctions, especially against determined and centralized autocracies.[9]

The Food Import Embargo

Food import bans to protect domestic industry were not new in Russia. The prospect of banning or severely limiting food imports was already mentioned in the 2008 draft of the Food Security Doctrine, and its origins are even deeper. The communists and their Agrarian Party allies strongly advocated for import restrictions and protectionist agrarian policies in the 1990s. Moreover, Gordeev explicitly linked the growth of Russian meat, especially poultry production, to the introduction of import quotas as minister of agriculture. Attempts to legislatively limit food, such as meat imports, were also occasionally undertaken by the Duma, though without much success.[10] According to Sergey Sobyanin, Putin's influential chief of staff and later mayor of Moscow, Russia could never establish domestic meat production without limiting exports.[11] Indeed, between 2000 and 2013, Russian imports of beef doubled, pork almost tripled, and cheese increased sevenfold.

Yet why, of all possible countermeasures and policies, did the Kremlin center its response to Western sanctions on a food import ban? There are several reasons. Russia was in no position to retaliate against the West by adopting strictly tit-for-tat measures and target US or EU countries' citizens by issuing asset freezes or visa bans. After all, few powerful Westerners had Moscow as their favorite getaway destination, held large assets in Russia, or owned mansions on the Black Sea. Second, the policy aligned well with Kremlin's broader push for import substitution.[12] An oil or gas embargo would have seriously harmed the West but would have also been too painful for Russia itself. And among other retaliation measures, food had a distinct appeal, as the import ban was perceived both as a painful blow against the West *and* as an opportunity to turn Putin's nutritional self-sufficiency goal into a reality exactly when it was needed the most.

The type of products covered by the ban and their countries of origin also indicate the highly calculated nature of the food countersanctions. As Masha Hedberg notes, the list of sanctioned products was highly selective and did not include popular food items, such as chocolate, ice cream, pasta, pickles, jam, bread, mineral water, fruit and vegetable juices, baby food, and beer.[13] Hedberg's quantitative analysis led her to conclude that

> imports of sizeable commercial value to Russia's nearest neighbors, as well as the U.S. and its non-European allies—that is, the countries the Kremlin most frequently depicts as the mainstays of anti-Russian policies—were far more likely to have been included in the embargo. By contrast, the probability of an import being banned declines significantly as the commercial value to Germany, France, Italy, and the U.K. (the so-called "Big 4" of Europe) rises.[14]

Yet despite the political attractiveness of the ban, it was also a major gamble that local producers, now shielded from Western competition, could, in a relatively short time, replace the banned imported food staples with local products. Moreover, it was also not obvious that food importers from the countries not under sanctions could quickly fill the shelves of Russian supermarkets with products of equal price and quality.[15] Yet the development of Russian agriculture in the previous fifteen years, characterized by the grain miracle and the growth of meat production, made this a possible, even if risky strategy. If the gamble succeeded, Russia would become nutritionally independent from the hostile West, thus depriving Washington and Brussels of potentially powerful weapons in the ongoing confrontation. A variation of the US grain embargo in the wake of the Soviet invasion of Afghanistan would be unfeasible after the annexation of Crimea because Russia preempted any possible Western action related to food.[16] Even if the gamble failed, Russia would still have more than enough grain to feed its citizens.

In 2014–2015, the government openly marked food independence by means of import substitution a major policy goal that needed to be achieved in the shortest possible timeframe. This was a significant escalation from the Food Security Doctrine that called for food independence, but not here and now, and not necessarily (or at the very least not explicitly) by removing Western food products from the domestic market entirely. Thus, to achieve the new goal in October 2014, Prime Minister Medvedev signed " 'A Road Map' to facilitate policies of import substitution," while in his annual address to the Russian Federal Assembly in December 2015, Putin set 2020 as the deadline for the country to be fully supplied by domestically produced food.[17]

Did the 2014 food import ban achieve its goals, and to what extent were these policies beneficial to Russian consumers? The Russian media crowed about the financial losses the West presumably suffered as a result of countersanctions. The numbers they presented were substantial, though not always consistent. The EU, United States, Australia, Norway, and Canada presumably lost up to $8.6 billion a year because they were barred from the Russian food market, reported *Rossiiskaia gazeta*. The countersanctions "had a serious negative impact on Finland's meat and dairy exports industry," wrote Regnum.ru. In 2019, five years after the countersanctions policies were adopted, Putin boasted that the cumulative fallout for the EU amounted to $240 billion, almost five times more than for Russia.[18] Additionally, the countersanctions, claimed Putin, forced Russians "to turn their brains on and to actively develop import substitution."[19]

The sanctions did hurt some Western producers, at least in the short term. The Italian government even tried to beg the Kremlin to make an exception for Parmesan cheese and remove it from the sanctioned products list, only to be unceremoniously rebuffed.[20] Others, like Polish apple growers, who suddenly lost 80 percent of their export market, coped by encouraging increased domestic consumption, asking Poles "to eat an apple to spite Putin." Yet, eventually, Polish apple growers simply reoriented their production to new markets without causing major long-term losses to the industry.[21] Most Western producers also found alternative markets for their products. The pain of losing access to the Russian market was thus minimal; according to Uzun and Loginova, in 2016, only Finland, Norway, Poland, and the Baltic states were still negatively affected by Russia's import ban.[22]

Still, financial harm to the West, though welcomed, was not the central goal of food countersanctions. Rather, it was to reduce Russia's dependence on imported, especially Western food items, and boost domestic production. Here, the results seemed to go Putin's way. Between 2014 and 2016, meat imports were down 40 percent compared to the period 2011–2013. The "dollar value of food imports fell from a post-Soviet high of $43 billion in 2013 to less than $25 billion in 2016."[23] In the meantime, domestic production increased. In 2015, production of poultry and cheese was 17–18 percent higher compared to 2013, pork production rose by 11 percent, and that of fruits and vegetables by 6–8 percent.[24] By 2018, the impact of the countersanctions on domestic production was even more pronounced. Production of pork grew by 70 percent and that of poultry by 23 percent compared to 2014. If 57 percent of beef consumed by Russians was imported then, in 2018, the number decreased to 38 percent. Moreover, only 3 percent of pork originated from outside of Russia (compared to 17 percent in 2014).[25] By 2020, Russia even became a significant meat exporter.[26] It is therefore not surprising that, when asked about the possibility of softening the food ban, Putin unequivocally replied "Hell no!" (*Fig im!*)[27]

Yet all Putin's bravado notwithstanding, measuring the real impact of the countersanctions is difficult; the ban coincided with the onset of a severe financial crisis that lasted until 2016. The crisis was primarily caused by a sharp decline in oil prices: between mid-2014 and early 2016, crude oil prices fell from their high of $108 per barrel to a low of $29, cutting deep into Russia's export revenue. The drop in oil prices removed a significant portion of Russia's foreign currency supply.[28] Between September 2014 and March 2016, the ruble declined a staggering 51 percent against the dollar. This benefited domestic food producers for it made food imports from nonsanctioned countries significantly more expensive. Yet, even though isolating the independent effect of the food import ban is challenging, we can clearly see who benefited from countersanctions and ruble depreciation, and who paid the price of such policies.

In conducting an in-depth analysis of the food import ban and its effect on producers, importers, and consumers, Volchkova and Kuznetsova found that the import substitution policies were only partially successful.[29] They focus on three categories of food production and measure success in terms of the domestic producers' market share, adjusted lower prices in comparison to 2013, and the growth in the domestic consumption of the product. According to their findings, import substitution was fully successful for basic staples, such as tomatoes, pork, and chicken. Both production and consumption significantly increased, while prices declined compared to 2013.

The second category contains the production and consumption of those food staples for which import substitution policies utterly failed to achieve their goals. It included apples, cheeses, fish, seafood products, and processed meat. Imports declined by 58 percent (cheese) and 33 percent (apples). At the same time, real prices substantially grew in comparison to 2013, consumption sharply declined, and domestic production remained flat. Thus, the consumption of apples, the main fruit for the majority of Russians, declined by 25 percent. Similarly, the consumption of cheese also fell by 15–20 percent relative to 2013, due to high prices, with no substantial improvement in domestic production.

Volchkova and Kuznetsova define the third, in-between category of products as "expensive import substitution." It includes milk and dairy products, such as yogurts, sour cream, butter, and cottage cheese. Local production and consumption substantially increased, but the adjusted prices were still much higher than in 2013. Because of the price hikes of the food staples in categories 2 and 3, in 2013–2018, the annual cost of the import ban to Russia's consumers amounted to 445 billion rubles. Local producers were the beneficiaries of the import substitution policies; they ramped up their input and enjoyed higher prices. According to Volchkova and Kuznetsova's estimates, the countersanctions brought Russian agribusiness an extra 374 billion rubles, while the Russian consumers ultimately paid the financial price for Putin's food independence policy and bore the brunt of supporting domestic agricultural production.[30]

Agricultural producers understood the meaning and implications of the countersanctions. Countersanctions increased state support for the industry, and according to Stefan Dürr, a German-born owner of a major Russian dairy producer, finally silenced those in the Russian government who still questioned the utility of providing money to less efficient domestic producers.[31] A Soyuzmoloko (Russia's dairy producers organization) representative pointed out that the import ban represented a "unique chance for the industry to take off" and that retail chains finally began paying attention to domestic producers.[32] In 2020, Soyuzmoloko CEO Artiom Belov explicitly stated that countersanctions stimulated the growth of the milk industry and should not be rescinded; representatives of the meat industry used almost identical language to describe the impact of the countersanctions.[33] And indeed, when in 2021 Italy tried to remove Parmesan from the list of sanctioned products, Russian cheesemakers vocally objected, claiming they needed at least five extra years of being shielded from competition before restrictions could be eased.[34] Even industry leaders who questioned the independent financial impact of the sanctions recognized their psychological effect on production growth.[35]

Politically, Putin's countersanctions gamble paid off, at least in the short term. True, import substitution failed to achieve the desired goals when it came to apples or seafood, but these mattered little for social stability, compared to staple food items, such as pork, chicken, and dairy products. Moreover, the disruption wrought by the sudden food export ban did not threaten the overall stability of the regime even when Western food was already unavailable, but domestic production was still insufficient. As Leifert et al. observed, "given that Russia imports mainly high-value products, such as meat, fruit, and vegetables, the import ban has not reduced the availability of staple foodstuffs, such as wheat and other grains, nor has it threatened the country's overall food security."[36]

After 2014, Russian citizens had to make do with fewer, more expensive options. However, this did not change attitudes, let alone trigger antigovernment protest mobilization. In fact, in November 2014, 80 percent of Russians claimed that the food import ban did not affect them in any meaningful way; only 15 percent stated it did. By late March 2016, the share of those unaffected declined but still remained high, amounting to 65 percent (while only 28 percent claimed to be affected).[37]

On social media, upper-middle-class individuals from major cities, where most imported food is consumed, grumbled about the disappearance of favorite meat or cheese products, or the lower quality of locally made substitutes. While visible, such complaints had a minimal political impact. When Viktor Linnik, a co-owner of Miratorg, a major meat producer and one of the main beneficiaries of the import substitution policies, dismissively called opponents of the countersanctions "hysterical blabbers" (*balaboly*), Russian liberal activists issued online calls to boycott Miratorg products,[38] but these were in vain and the company's bottom line did not suffer.

Beyond the dissatisfied members of the Moscow and St. Petersburg middle class, public opinion largely supported the food import ban. The limited economic impact of the countersanctions was not the only reason for the public approval. The government propaganda actively presented the policy as a patriotic measure of support for domestic producers, and the customers themselves were open to buying local.[39] The rally around the flag effect was most pronounced immediately after the policy was introduced and inevitably declined over time. Thus, in Moscow and St. Petersburg in 2021 only 45 percent of respondents supported countersanctions and 50 percent opposed them. But for Russia as a whole, the picture looked different. As many as 84 percent supported the countersanctions in 2014, 73 percent in 2015, and even in 2021 57 percent of Russians, a solid majority, backed the food import ban.[40] These numbers help explain why there were no food riots or protests in Russia.

Food Policy as the Domain of the *Siloviki*

Food and food supply policies were fully realized as a regime security domain, when, on May 18, 2018, the forty-year-old chairman of the Rosselkhozbank Dmitry Patrushev was appointed minister of agriculture, a position he still holds at the time of writing. All previous Putin-era ministers of agriculture either had substantial experience in the field or were seasoned politicians at the time of the appointment. Some, like Aleksandr Tkachev (April 2015–May 2018), a former governor of Krasnodar Krai and a major agricultural tycoon, combined both skill sets.[41] Patrushev had no previous political experience and his only expertise in the field of agriculture came from leading the Rosselkhozbank, a position to which he was appointed in 2010 at age thirty-three, with few objective qualifications to assume such a major role. Yet Patrushev made up for his lack of knowledge and professional experience with his background and connections. The minister is the son of Nikolai Patrushev, who replaced Putin in 1999 as the director of Russia's Federal Security Service (FSB), and left the FSB in 2008 to become the secretary of Russia's Security Council, a position he still occupies at the time of writing. As Security Council leader, Patrushev oversaw the drafting of the final text of the 2010 Food Security Doctrine. Ideologically, Patrushev senior is an extreme hawk who, as Galeotti aptly phrases, "makes Putin look like a moderate."[42]

The new minister of agriculture claimed to be a graduate of the State Management University (*Gosudarstvennyi Universitet Upravleniia*), though an investigation conducted by Russian journalists revealed that nobody at the school or among Patrushev's cohort remembered him. In 2003, Dmitry Patrushev defended a PhD (*kandidat nauk*) dissertation and, in 2008, a habilitation (*doktor nauk*) thesis. In Russia, the average time between the *kandidat* and habilitation theses is thirteen years, and the average age of becoming *doctor nauk* is forty-five. Patrushev managed to do this in just five years, obtaining the degree at thirty-one. Both theses contained multiple instances of plagiarism.[43]

In addition, Patrushev graduated from the FSB Academy (the service's own university) in 2006, though, at least publicly, he never held a position at the service. In 2007, he was appointed senior vice president of the state-controlled VTB Bank and from there transitioned to lead the Rosselkhozbank. During Patrushev's tenure, the bank substantially increased its lending activities, but the institution was also involved in numerous corruption scandals and lost substantial amounts of money, all covered by the state budget. Eleven of the bank's regional leaders faced criminal charges,[44] but neither financial losses nor corruption allegations affected Patrushev's career prospects. Indeed, in 2016, the Association of Russian Bankers recognized Patrushev as the Banker of the Year, and Putin awarded him the Order of Honor.[45]

Experts on Russia's agriculture found the appointment surprising, especially given that several more traditional candidates were serious contenders for the position. Patrushev himself, note Wegren, Nikulin, and Trotsuk, "stated that he was named minister, not because of his knowledge or experience in agriculture but because his father is a long-time colleague of Putin."[46] Patrushev's appointment also coincided with Gordeev's return to the government as vice prime minister in charge of agriculture, and therefore some expected him to indirectly run the industry,[47] with Patrushev being a nominal figurehead. Yet, in early 2020, Gordeev had become vice speaker of the State Duma, thus leaving Patrushev fully in charge of food production.

Patrushev's appointment, despite his obvious lack of qualifications, made perfect sense politically, strategically, and professionally. This was a logical result of the securitization of food that had begun with the 2010 Food Security Doctrine and integrated food production into Russia's security domain. It also fit Putin's third term pattern of making the *siloviki* a cornerstone of every important area of economic activity. Patrushev, who combined at least some exposure to agriculture with membership in the most prominent *siloviki* family, was thus a natural choice. His appointment also signaled that food policy, under the conditions of increasing confrontation with the West and the ongoing countersanctions, was too important to be left to more traditional agro-bureaucrats like Gordeev or Tkachev. Under Patrushev's watch, the new Food Security Doctrine was adopted in 2020, and the guidance for the Russian food industry for the years 2020–2030 was drafted.

Food Security Doctrine 2020 and Onward

On January 21, 2020, Putin signed Presidential Decree N20, the new version of the Food Security Doctrine. This document was meant to replace the 2010 Doctrine.[48] In reality, however, the 2020 Food Security Doctrine was a relatively minor revision of its 2010 predecessor. It added, in Paragraph 9, three new categories of food products to the list of those required for food independence: vegetables and melons (with a 90 percent domestic production target), fruits and berries (60 percent), and seeds (75 percent). Among the food items already listed in the 2010 Food Security Doctrine, five—grains, potatoes, meat, dairy products, and edible salt—retained at the same required level of domestic production. For sugar and vegetable oil, the domestic production target was raised to 90 percent, and for fish and fish-based products domestic production target rose to 85 percent. Like the 2010 Doctrine, the 2020 document neglected to explain how and when these figures would be achieved.

More important, the 2020 Doctrine conspicuously dropped any mention of WTO membership, a significant departure from the 2010 Doctrine, which presented WTO accession as a driver of Russian food security growth. This suggested that the countersanctions policies violated if not the letter, then certainly the spirit of the membership agreement and that, in the current situation, the return to open market policies was undesired. Instead, the 2020 Doctrine repeatedly mentions the Eurasian Economic Union (EEU), an organization of five former Soviet states (Russia, Belarus, Kazakhstan, Armenia, and Kyrgyzstan), created in 2014 to facilitate Russia-centered economic integration. In other words, the 2020 Doctrine signaled Putin's shift from greater integration into the world economy via the WTO to an extension of Russia's economic power in the post-Soviet space.[49] Finally, the 2020 document reconfirmed the food independence goals outlined in the 2010 Doctrine.

On November 20, 2019, even before Putin officially signed the 2020 Food Security Doctrine, the Ministry of Agriculture published its "Draft of the Strategy for the Development of the Food and Food Processing Industry of the Russian Federation to 2030" (hereafter 2030 Strategy Draft). This document assessed the progress toward the food independence thresholds established by the 2010 Doctrine. The 2016 Strategy Update already confirmed that grains, potatoes, vegetable oil, and sugar had reached the required thresholds. The 2030 Strategy Draft added meat and meat products to this list of import substitution success stories. At the same time, the Russian government also admitted that milk and dairy products and local edible salt production had failed to reach the targets. In other words, in five out of the seven key food categories listed by the 2010 Doctrine, the thresholds for food independence had been met.[50]

The 2030 Strategy Draft also boasted that food imports had declined by 20 percent from 2010 to 2019 without mentioning the countersanctions and the sharp devaluation of the ruble that had caused this. The 2030 Strategy Draft set more modest (but still ambitious) goals than earlier documents. Grain production was set to reach 124.5 million tons, slightly lower than the 2020 target (125 million tons). In other food categories, the government also lowered its ambitions, reflecting the limits of the domestic growth potential. Domestic meat production was projected to increase from 2019 to 2030 by 13.8 percent, milk by 15.7 percent, and sugar by 11.7 percent. Substantial production increases were maintained only for vegetable oil (by 33.8 percent) and edible salt (by 31.2 percent).

Finally, unlike prior documents, the 2030 Strategy Draft strongly emphasized the significance of food exports. The Strategy forecasted exports to grow from $25.6 billion to $37 billion by 2030. If achieved, Russian food exports would then outpace the weapons systems, for which the country is renowned, thereby enhancing Russia's prestige as one of the world's leading food producers. Overall, the 2030 Strategy Draft served as an ideological document that predicted the continuous success of Putin's food independence policies.

Yet by 2020, despite almost five years of countersanctions, Russia's food imports still remained significant. In fact, in 2019, Russia's total food imports exceeded its food exports by $5 billion.[51] These findings were further reinforced by the December 2020 report of the National Rating Agency (*Natsional'noe Reitingovoe Agenstvo*) company, which assessed the years of the countersanctions policies. It concluded that, in the food products banned under the countersanctions policies, the domestic industry increased its production by only 12.3 percent (25.2 million tons). Moreover, the authors compared the targets of the "Strategy for the Development of the Food and Food Processing Industry of the Russian Federation to 2020" to the actual performance of the Russian food industry in 2020, concluding that none of the key import substitution targets was fully achieved. Only meat and meat products came close to the government's target of reducing meat imports by 67.8 percent, with the actual import reduction amounting to 65 percent.

Additionally, the countersanctions, the authors concluded, changed the origins of the imported food. In 2013, the EU was the top food importer into Russia, but, by 2020, it was replaced by an allied Belarus, whose share of imports more than doubled from 12 percent (2013) to 24.2 percent (2020).[52] In the grand scheme of things, however, the import of Belarusian food was a geopolitically inferior outcome to fully domestic production but still a far superior option to reliance on the hostile West. In short, Russia was still quite far from complete food import substitution, but when it came to staple foods that the Kremlin cared the most about, the overall picture looked overall satisfying.

That the import substitution policies failed to fully achieve their ambitious goals should not come as a surprise; full food independence was no less utopian project than Stalin's goals for First Five Year Plan (1928–1932) to turn the USSR into a fully developed industrial society. Between 2014 and 2020, the Russian food-producing sector simply did not have the means to reach the desired target. Even if they had the resources, industries such as dairy require a longer time frame to yield results than grain. Belarusian and other non-Western food imports were therefore deemed good enough a solution to fill the shelves of the Russian supermarkets.

Concluding Remarks

This chapter focused on the radical escalation of the Kremlin's quest for nutritional independence. Western sanctions in the wake of the annexation of Crimea provided the Kremlin with an opening to bypass the expectations and the mechanisms of the free market, and Putin decided to center his retaliatory measure on food. The regime's aims in the realm of food supply shifted from isolationist to nearly autarkic. Import substitution became a key priority. This was highly unconventional; post–World War II history witnessed multiple attempts at import substitution but virtually all centered on industrial production, not food. In Russia, however, food was a key pillar of regime stability. Hence, when the geopolitical confrontation against the West became overt, Putin's willingness to use drastic measures to achieve nutritional independence made sense. The countersanctions failed to make Russia completely self-sufficient in food but spurred domestic production and switched the sources of imported foods from the hostile West to friendlier countries without triggering mass protests. The regime had good reasons to feel secure, nutritionally, and otherwise.

The 2030 Strategy Draft listed various potential dangers that threatened to undermine the achievement of the food production goals. This ranged from geopolitical to climatic risks and from ecological conditions to animal diseases. There was no mention, however, of a potential outbreak of a major pandemic. The coronavirus pandemic hit Russia in March 2020 and became a major test of Putin's strategy of food independence.

7

Top Feeders

The Government and Russia's Agro-Capitalism

In previous chapters, we discussed the political and security considerations that incentivized the Russian government to invest in domestic food production and the financial and physical infrastructure that allowed Russia to become a major, even if not entirely self-sufficient, food producer. Yet the state does not produce the vast majority of Russian food; Putin and his inner circle might be nostalgic for the Soviet Union in geopolitical terms but are also acutely aware of communism's disastrous food policies. Russian agriculture, especially its meat, dairy, and increasingly, grain sectors, is dominated by large private businesses, so-called agroholdings that benefit from economies of scale, political connections, and state support. With access to financing, advanced technologies, and close ties to the highest echelons of political and regulatory decision-making, these large businesses became the engine that propelled Russia's agricultural miracle. In exchange, these companies, which should provide Russia's cities with cheap, reliable, and abundant food, do not question the Kremlin's actions or oppose its policies. In some cases, they even line the pockets of politicians to which they are connected.

In this chapter, we provide a brief overview of agroholdings as a distinct business entity and zoom in on three industry titans: Agrocomplex, Rusagro, and Miratorg. Agrocomplex is the agroholding of Aleksandr Tkachev, a former governor of Krasnodar Krai in southern Russia (2001–2015) and minister of agriculture (2015–2018), as noted in the previous chapter. Agrocomplex produces a wide range of food products, including meat, dairy, vegetables, fruit, rice, sugar, and eggs. It is based primarily in the southern agrarian regions of Russia including Krasnodar, Stavropol, Rostov-on-Don, and Adygea.

Rusagro is owned by Vadim Moshkovich, a former member of the Federation Council (2006–2014), the upper house of the Russian parliament. It specializes in sugar, fats, and oil production, and operates primarily in Russia's Far East (Primor'ye), Belgorod, Tambov, Orel, Kursk, and Voronezh regions. Miratorg is owned by brothers Aleksandr and Viktor Linnik. The holding specializes in meat processing and production, and its main bases are Kaliningrad, Tula, Bryansk, Kaluga, Smolensk, Belgorod, and Kursk. These three agroholdings are among the largest agribusinesses in Russia in terms of landholding value. In 2021, Forbes Russia named Agrocomplex the largest agricultural landowner in Russia, with land valued at roughly $1.2 billion. Miratorg's is the third largest, with land valued at approximately $660 million, while Rusagro's lags behind slightly, with land valued at $590 million.[1]

These illustrative case descriptions, as we show, exemplify different modes of state-large agribusiness relations, yet each of them depends heavily on state funding and support. Over the years, they have benefited immensely from the Kremlin's desire to shore up domestic production and achieve nutritional self-sufficiency.

Russia's Agroholdings: An Overview

The emergence of agroholdings—large-scale, vertically integrated agricultural conglomerates—is central to Russia's food production during the Putin era. In a recent study, Uzun, Shagaida, and Lerman note that despite their key role in Russia's agriculture, there is no official definition of agroholdings "and the statistical agencies neither collect nor publish information about these organizations as a separate category." Uzun, Shagaida, and Lerman define an agroholding as "a group of legally independent entities that may include agricultural producers, agricultural processors, farm service providers, and other operators with links to agricultural activities. The group is controlled by a parent company or a physical person in virtue of their majority equity holdings."[2]

As the Russian government does not collect statistical data on agroholdings as a separate category, conducting a comprehensive analysis of agroholdings and their production profile, output, and revenue is challenging. According to Uzun, Shagaida, and Lerman, in 2016, there were about 1,000 agroholdings in Russia. These companies controlled about 25 percent of the country's agricultural land and generated 50 percent of the total sales and profit of the corporate farm sector. Roughly 10 percent stand out due to their size and importance, with 100 agroholdings earning revenue of at least two billion rubles.[3] While agroholdings cover almost the entire range of agriculture-related businesses, they are especially prominent in the production of meat and sugar and play an increasingly important role in the grain and dairy sectors.[4]

Contrary to the energy sector, where state ownership became the dominant model during Putin's years in power, it declined sharply in the agricultural sphere. State ownership fell from 59.4 percent in 2006 to just 8 percent in 2016, while private holdings grew from 40.6 percent to 92 percent in the same period. Moreover, agroholdings are predominantly Russian-owned, with foreign-owned companies constituting only 6.3 percent of the sector.[5]

Several reasons help explain the emergence and the dominance of agroholdings in Russia. The liberal market reforms of the 1990s destroyed the Soviet-era large state and collective farms, but the agricultural enterprises that succeeded them were "economically and financially weak, ripe targets for takeover," especially given that the existing legislation did not limit the excessive concentration of land.

> The rural population initially did not recognise the true long-term value of the land shares allocated in the process of land reform, often preferring to sell their land shares for quick cash rather than invest in farming.... All this created supply of agricultural land, whereas business entrepreneurs who had accumulated capital in other industries during privatisation sought new fields of activity.[6]

When, in the wake of the 1998 financial crisis, Russians increasingly bought local and the government signaled a strong commitment to food independence, investors began to favor the industry. These businesspeople and companies, which included industry titans such as Gazprom, Sibneft, and Norilsk Nickel, established agroholdings, bought up or leased land, and brought to the countryside capital, corporate management practices, market expertise, and a focus on profits that the former state and collective farms typically lacked.[7]

Unlike small and medium-sized farms, agroholdings benefit from economies of scale, reduced transaction costs, and the advantages of vertical integration. Additionally, agroholdings can use their extensive landholdings and advanced machinery as collateral to receive favorable loans from state and private banks. In contrast, as Sergei Iushin points out, in today's Russia few individual farmers could get a million-dollar loan from a bank to start a new farm. Most small-scale meat and poultry farmers also have great difficulty accessing appropriate animal feed.[8]

According to Wengle, agroholdings' success is also rooted in their adoption of "agricultural technologies that maximized yields and economic efficiency."[9] These mostly imported technologies and equipment allowed agroholdings to increase production and outcompete other Russian agricultural producers.[10]

But most important, the rise of agroholdings is directly linked to the Kremlin's and the regional elites' belief in and support for big business.[11] In 2004, Gordeev explicitly argued that "large, vertically integrated holdings" were the future of Russia's "powerful and modern agriculture."[12] Further, Putin's regime "saw agroholdings as the actors that could deliver on the political promise of more domestic production and less dependency on imports."[13] As with other sectors, the government's policy in food production centered on creating national champions and providing these with funding, subsidies, and preferential allocation of land that would cement their leadership of the industry. Thus, even though agroholdings account for just 10 percent of total agricultural land and employment in Russia, they receive almost a third of state subsidies allocated to agriculture; the eight largest agroholdings, combined, enjoy almost 10 percent of the state's support money.[14] Ultimately, the Kremlin made Russian agroholdings what they are, because the government believed (and not without reason!)[15] that they would provide the regime with the food independence it sought.

Putin's support for big business extends well beyond agriculture; Russia as a whole is "a country of big businesses."[16] The government believes a relatively small number of large agricultural businesses is easier to control than a much larger number of small farmers.[17] On their part, agroholdings "have consistently demonstrated a willingness to align themselves with dominant political priorities."[18] The Kremlin also perceives large enterprises as better positioned to produce what it needs than smaller companies. Agroholdings, therefore, recreated the basic model of large Soviet-era state farms but added to it ambition, an insatiable drive to expand, corporate bureaucracy, and industrial discipline, which the former lacked.[19]

The elites' ideological support is not the agroholdings' only political advantage. The large size of agroholdings and the sheer number of people they employ also make them important sociopolitical players, especially at the local and regional levels, thus leading to favorable legislation and regulatory measures as well as direct subsidies at the expense of other producers.

The symbiotic relationship between agroholdings and political elites is reinforced by the fact that some businesses are directly owned by top government officials and their families. Agrocomplex, owned by a former minister of agriculture, Tkachev, is the most notable instance of such a relationship but hardly the only one. Among the owners of agroholdings are members of Russia's parliament, federal government officials, and regional leaders who use their authority and power to benefit the companies they own and to enrich themselves.[20] Occasionally, their relatives or friends own the companies. For instance, Gordeev's son Nikita became a successful agricultural entrepreneur at the age of twenty-three. The agroholding he led was especially active in the Voronezh region, of which Gordeev senior became a governor in 2009.[21]

Close connection to and support of politicians benefit agroholdings in several ways. The agroholdings receive the lion's share of government subsidies and state- and regional-level financial support. This is especially pronounced in regions in which the governor or their relatives own locally dominant agroholdings. Proximity to (or direct ownership by) prominent politicians also helps agroholdings in securing credit and subsidized loans from state-owned financial institutions, such as Rosselkhozbank.

The government can also promote agroholdings and harm their competitors through various legislative, regulatory, and sanitary means. Russian agricultural experts are very explicit about the key role that government intervention and politics play in shaping agricultural policies and determining winners and losers on the ground.[22] Government interventions are especially consequential in the meat sector; the expansion of meat-producing agroholdings went hand in hand with "Russian veterinary watchdog *Rosselkhoznadzor* [culling] tens of thousands of pigs held on household farms,"[23] a policy that dealt a very painful blow to small farmers. In the Voronezh region, Governor Gordeev proceeded to destroy household and small farms' pigs with such a zeal that some observers even called the campaign a "swinecide" (*svinotsid*).[24]

Finally, politicians and politically connected agroholdings can rely on a wide range of non-agricultural state institutions such as compliant courts, corrupt law enforcement, tax collectors, and fire safety inspectors to harass, harm, and eventually put out of business their competitors, purchase their land and equipment, and consolidate their supremacy even further. This dominance can take almost monopolistic forms; according to the agricultural expert Dmitry Rylko, Russia even has a region in which practically all agricultural land is owned by the governor.[25]

A direct and inevitable outcome of such policies is the high concentration of land and resources in the hands of just a few mammoth companies. In 2020, the five largest agricultural landowners possessed more than 3.8 million hectares (14,700 square miles), slightly less than Massachusetts and New Jersey combined. Together, the sixty-one largest companies owned more land than the entire state of Wisconsin, or about half the size of Germany.[26] Russian agriculture has become the domain of "giants and midgets"—large agroholdings and tiny, subsistence-oriented household plots, whereas small and medium-sized farms are steadily declining in numbers and playing an increasingly negligible role in food production.[27]

The relations between agroholdings and the Russian state are hardly an equal partnership. In Putin's conception of Russian capitalism, the role of big business, agrobusiness included, is clearly defined as one that serves the state's goals. The state withdraws support when businesses' goals and practices do not align with those of the Kremlin. Thus, as long as agroholdings' growth was in line with the state's interest in creating a domestic food supply that assured Russia's food independence, the state-aided holdings' expansion and the agroholdings themselves became dependent on the government for financial, political, and regulatory support. Yet, as we show in Chapter 9, when the goals of the government and the food producers diverged, the Kremlin did not hesitate to crack down on large agribusiness and force agricultural tycoons to agree to food price freezes and export controls during the COVID-19 pandemic. Fully realizing their dependence on the government, food producers complied.

In the next sections, we demonstrate how various instruments of state support and connections with the government more generally were crucial in promoting the expansion of three key Russian food producers.

A Governor and a Minister as a Tycoon: Agrocomplex

In no Russian agricultural business is the link between the executive branch, at both the regional and the federal levels, and commercial success as pronounced as in the case of Agrocomplex, the agroholding of Aleksandr Tkachev. While Tkachev's business may have been able to achieve a measure of success even without government support, it was Tkachev's combination of executive office and business ownership that propelled Agrocomplex to a leading position in Russia's food production. Even though Tkachev's case might be extreme, it is hardly unique; agroholdings that are owned by or related to the governor, and thus reap the benefits of this connection, exist in many regions.

Aleksandr Tkachev was born in 1960 in Vyselki, a small town in Krasnodar Krai in southern Russia. Trained as a mechanical engineer, Tkachev began his professional career in 1983 at an animal feed factory located in his hometown and managed by his father, Nikolai Tkachev. After serving as the district head of the Komsomol, the Communist Party's youth branch, Tkachev junior replaced his aging father as the factory's director.[28] In 1993 the factory was privatized and reorganized as the joint stock company Agrocomplex with Aleksandr Tkachev as the CEO and Nikolai Tkachev as his deputy. Within several years the company expanded and took over additional land, a meat processing factory, and several grain storage elevators.

In 1994, Tkachev was elected to the Krasnodar regional parliament, and in the following year he won a seat at the State Duma, the lower house of Russia's parliament, on a left-wing, populist platform. In the Duma, Tkachev joined the Agrarian Deputies Group, allied with the KPRF. In 1999, he was re-elected, but this time as a KPRF representative, though he also managed to build close relations with Putin's advisors and allies such as Vladislav Surkov, the man behind the "sovereign democracy" doctrine. In December 2000, Tkachev was elected governor of the Krasnodar region with more than 82 percent of the votes.[29] He left the KPRF three years later and became the regional head of Putin's United Russia party. In 2014, in the wake of Russia's annexation of Crimea, Tkachev, who held nationalist views and was often accused of xenophobia, also became the target of Western sanctions. On April 22, 2015, Tkachev left Krasnodar to become the minister of agriculture, a position he held until 2018. He was officially not affiliated with Agrocomplex during that period but openly stated that it was owned by his family.[30] After Nikolai Tkachev died in 2014, Roman Batalov, the governor's son-in-law, became the Agrocomplex chairman of the board of directors. Finally, in 2021 all pretenses of Tkachev's non-involvement were dropped after Russian media revealed that the ex-governor and former minister controlled 77.5 percent of Agrocomplex shares, thus making him one of the world's largest landowners.[31]

According to multiple testimonies, "administrative resource," the Russian term for using government and official resources for private and political benefits, played a significant role in Agrocomplex's growth, first in its district, then in Krasnodar as a whole. In 2001, shortly after Tkachev became the governor, Aleksei Klimov, the head of a local agricultural enterprise, who actively resisted Agrocomplex's expansion attempts, became the subject of at least seven criminal investigations and several assassination attempts. Eventually, he gave up and retired.[32] To limit the competition in the meat market, the regional authorities forbade households to have more than two pigs—ostensible to fight the swine flu disease—and then started a massive culling campaign that predominantly targeted households and smaller enterprises.[33]

When Agrocomplex decided to expand its product portfolio and seize the neighboring Kristall sugar factory in 2005, a local court issued a ruling ordering the factory to suspend its operations, claiming these violated environmental regulations. The traffic police set up roadblocks near the factory and blocked trucks with sugar beets from entering the premises.[34] The company was also subject to constant inspections by various state bodies. "The FSB would visit the enterprise and order to install bars on the windows for security reasons. Once this was done, fire inspection would issue a fine and demand removing them because of fire safety. The cycle would start again thereafter."[35] Kristall's management resisted, appealed the court's decision, and even tried approaching Putin directly but eventually sold 90 percent of the company's shares.[36] Other agricultural producers in the region also complained of being deprived of state and regional subsidies, the lion's share of which went to Agrocomplex.[37]

By 2014, Agrocomplex had expanded to neighboring regions of southern Russia and the North Caucasus.[38] But the peak of its meteoric rise occurred when Tkachev served as the minister of agriculture: a large but still regional enterprise became a national one. During Tkachev's tenure, "barely a month passed without news about Agrocomplex's new acquisitions."[39] A substantial share of these acquisitions was funded by subsidized loans from state banks, and Tkachev's competitors explicitly linked this to the agroholding's growth. As a result, in 2015, the holding's debt was 192 times higher than in 2005 and four times higher than in 2012, the consequence of almost unrestricted access to subsidized long-term loans from state banks.[40] Some purchases came directly from the state. In 2015, Agrocomplex acquired one of the largest poultry enterprises in southern Russia for a third of the company's actual value. The state-owned Sberbank, which received the enterprise from its bankrupt previous owner, acted as the seller. Journalists uncovered that

Agrocomplex purchased additional entities from the state bank at a similar discount.[41]

Subsidized credit and preferential treatment were not the only sources of state support. In 2015, when Tkachev was appointed minister, Agrocomplex received subsidies from the state budget worth 1.13 billion rubles. Moreover, the holding secured roughly 20 percent of all government subsidies for the agriculture-centric Krasnodar. While some agroholdings received even higher levels of direct support from the state, the combination of massive subsidies, subsidized credit, and preferential treatment uniquely positioned Tkachev's agricultural empire to expand and thrive under his stewardship of the industry.[42] Unfortunately, Agrocomplex did not disclose its financial statements before Tkachev's ministerial appointment and therefore it is impossible to analyze the impact of ministerial position on the holding's performance. In 2017, Agrocomplex became the largest recipient of state subsidies in the dairy sector.[43]

Credit and subsidies fueled expansion. In 2015, Agrocomplex first entered the list of Russia's ten largest landowners, and in 2016, Tkachev's landholdings grew by more than 40 percent. During three short years (2014–2017), Agrocomplex's land bank tripled, and in 2017, it was the fourth largest landowner, just four thousand hectares behind the third.[44] By 2020, Agrocomplex became the largest with 660,000 hectares (slightly more than 2,500 sq. miles, larger than Delaware).[45]

In 2019, the Russian media published an undated, leaked video of Tkachev and Arkady Dvorkovich, Medvedev's aide and former deputy prime minister, flying on a private jet together with the wife of Gazprom head Aleksei Miller, singing, drinking, and toasting "the agricultural lobby."[46] As an agricultural tycoon, Tkachev had many reasons to thank the agricultural lobby and support the government's investment in and support of major agroholdings. When he was governor and minister of agriculture, he ensured that this state support, be it compliant government institutions, generous state funding, or corrupt ownership schemes, above all benefited him and his company.

A Legislator's Holding: Rusagro

Numerous sizable agroholdings owned by legislators at federal, regional, and local levels were similarly allied to the government. One was Agrocomplex before Tkachev's election as the governor of Krasnodar. Another was Rusagro, founded and controlled by Vadim Moshkovich.

Moshkovich was born in 1967 in Moscow. In 1992, just as Russia became a newly independent, food scarcity–obsessed state, Moshkovich graduated from university with a degree in radio engineering. His training and skills were in low demand in Russia's new economy, and thus Moshkovich, like many other Russians of his generation, went into business. After working at Moscow's stock exchange and importing US-made White Eagle vodka to Russia for a couple of years, Moshkovich cofounded Avgur Estate, a development company, and another enterprise named Sugar Trading Company.[47] Rusagro emerged out of these in 1995, later growing to become one of Russia's largest food producers. As of 2021, Moshkovich controlled 71 percent of the shares of the Cyprus-registered holding.[48]

In 2006, the Belgorod regional parliament selected Moshkovich (with no alternative candidates put forward) as the region's representative (colloquially referred to as "senator") in the Federation Council, the Russian parliament's upper house. This came as a surprise, for the move was not listed on the regional parliament's agenda, and the Belgorod legislators learned that the parliament's speaker had scheduled the vote just before the start of the session. Moshkovich was elected nonetheless, ostensibly in recognition of his contribution to the region's agriculture, but according to critics, simply to gain parliamentary immunity from criminal prosecution. At the time of the election, Rusagro owned seven sugar factories, six oils and fats enterprises, and oil-processing factories. It had an annual turnover of more than $800 million.[49] Moshkovich himself explained his transition from business to legislative office by claiming he desired to regulate the market and ensure that the government has "an understanding of agrarian policy."[50] He served in the Federation Council until December 2014.

The scandal from which Moshkovich might have sought protection occurred in 2003 and involved a nasty dispute between Rusagro and Russkaia Bakaleia, another agricultural company, over the ownership of Kropotkinskii, an oil extracting factory in Krasnodar. As Krasnodar was firmly Tkachev's domain, neither party had ready access to local institutions to prevail over the other. Thus, the struggle took the form of dueling accusations and lawsuits elsewhere. Moshkovich became the target of a Moscow-based criminal investigation. According to media reports, he was charged with fraud in February 2005,[51] though eventually the charges against him were dropped.

At the time of Moshkovich's election to the Federation Council, Rusagro's focus was sugar, oil, and fats, but by 2020, the holding expanded to grains, mayonnaise, and meat. In fact, by 2020, Rusagro had become Russia's largest producer of margarine, the second largest of mayonnaise, and the third largest in the pig sector. It was also a mammoth landowner, Russia's fourth largest, just slightly behind Agrocomplex.[52] That same year Rusagro was also included in the important list of the sixty-six "backbone" enterprises (*sistemoobrazuiuschie*) in the agricultural industry. Gruppa Rusagro, which belongs to the holding and is registered in Tambov in central Russia, had just a single employee but was nonetheless a recipient of the government's large COVID-19-related subsidy.[53]

While the expansion of Rusagro started even before Moshkovich became a senator, his position facilitated the agroholding's growth. Moshkovich's stated goal to regulate the market and shape agricultural policy and his membership in the Federation Council's economic policy committee inevitably affected the fate of the companies he owned. His "regulation of the market led to tens of companies [that processed raw cane sugar] exiting the market because [operations] became unprofitable."[54] This, in turn, created higher profits for those companies that, like Rusagro, relied on beets to produce sugar. Up until 2005, Moshkovich also owned 2.3 percent of the shares of the majority state-owned Sberbank. The bank eventually became the key provider of loans that fueled Rusagro's expansion when Moshkovich became a senator.[55]

Yet, despite the important legislative position, Moshkovich's powers were more limited than those of the executive branch leaders. Unlike Tkachev, Moshkovich was in no position to unleash the police or local courts on his competitors. Membership in the Federation Council, however, was a great springboard for cross-branch linkages and cooperation. For example, the wife of the Tambov region governor Sergei Ivanov has been employed by Tambovskii Bekon (Tambov Bacon), a part of the Rusagro holding.[56] In Belgorod, according to Moshkovich himself, Rusagro's initial projects received "unprecedented levels of support from the governor," generous credits from Sberbank, and state subsidies. In 2009, Rusagro received almost 900 million rubles from the state to repay loan interests, as well as direct subsidies for the purchase of machinery and fertilizers.[57] When, following Russia's WTO accession in 2012, meat prices fell and Rusagro experienced losses, the government "did not abandon the industry"[58] and used the African swine flu as the pretext to halt meat imports from the EU. The senator's profits swiftly returned.

Rusagro's annual reports also demonstrate the steady rise in state support. In 2013, the holding received 1.73 billion rubles in subsidies from the federal government and the regional governments of Belgorod (which Moshkovich represented in the Federation Council) and Tambov. This amount increased to 8.5 billion in 2020, though these direct subsidies were still somewhat lower than those received by Rusagro's peer companies. Moshkovich's holding also actively participates in the heavily subsidized development of food production in Russia's Far East. Other industry giants, such as Cherkizovo, tried to invest in the region before Rusagro but eventually withdrew. According to Iushin, Cherkizovo likely failed to receive the same level of [government] support that Moshkovich did.[59]

While Sberbank acts as the holding's main financial backer, Rosselkhozbank is yet another important partner. In November 2018, Rusagro bought from Rosselkhozbank the debt of Solnechnye Produkty, another oil-producing agroholding (and Rusagro's competitor) for 80 percent of its value, to be paid out in installments.[60] Acquiring the debt would allow Moshkovich to either seize Solnechnye Produkty's assets, thus enlarging his holding even further, to take a competitor out of business and, thus, increase Rusagro's market share. Some even alleged, though without any solid evidence, a conspiracy between Moshkovich and the then-head of Rosselkhozbank Dmitry Patrushev to bankrupt Solnechnye Produkty and split and siphon away its assets.[61]

Indeed, Rusagro itself was explicit about the impact of Moshkovich's position. In a document issued to potential investors, the holding openly admitted that "doing business in Russia often requires receiving formal permits as well as informal support of federal and local authorities" and that Rusagro "might be adversely impacted by a situation in which Mr. Moshkovich ceases to be a member of the Federation Council."[62] These fears, however, turned out to be unfounded, and the company continued its growth even after Moshkovich resigned from the parliament several months before the official end of his term.

The government's influence on the fate of agroholdings can also be gleaned from an altercation between Moshkovich and Putin during the COVID-19 pandemic in 2021. When, at a meeting with agribusiness leaders, Moshkovich dared to mildly criticize Putin's restrictions on exports, aimed at keeping domestic food prices low, the president berated Moshkovich while Patrushev, according to media reports, "was outraged." Immediately following the incident, Rusagro rushed to deny reports that its owner fled Russia, and the media reported that the agroholding's long-term future might now be in danger.[63]

Yet, Russia's 2022 invasion of Ukraine changed the fortunes of Moshkovich and Rusagro. In 2022, the company's profits rose by 8% and in April 2023, after such major international grain traders as Viterra, Cargill and Louis Dreyfus announced their withdrawal from Russia's grain exports, Rusagro announced its entrance into the Russian grain export business.[64]

Out of Office but Not out of Funding: Miratorg

When the owner of an agroholding is a member of the political elite, in either the executive or the legislative branch, they are well positioned to assist their enterprise through policies they promote and by virtue of their status and connections. Yet large producers that are, at least on paper, unaffiliated with high-ranking officials also depend on and benefit from large-scale government support. The best example of such a relationship is Miratorg.

The agroholding belongs to Viktor and Aleksandr Linnik, twin brothers born in Moscow in 1967. The Linnik brothers, like Moshkovich, were urbanites with engineering backgrounds and little experience in food production; both worked in the defense industry prior to the collapse of the USSR. The economic reforms and the contraction of Russia's defense spending forced the Linniks to explore new opportunities. According to the holding's origin story, the brothers moved from defense to tourism and organized Moscow tours for Westerners. One such tourist, whom they befriended, provided the Linniks with credit to purchase a Dutch milk powder machine. The twins moved from tourism to food production and have remained in the industry since. The Linnik brothers founded the Cyprus-registered Miratorg in 1995[65] when they decided to import meat from Latin America to Russia and built a meat-processing factory in Kaliningrad, Russia's exclave on the Baltic Sea.[66]

In the mid-2000s, after food production became a priority industry for the Kremlin, Miratorg purchased several pig farms in the Belgorod region. However, their further growth stalled and the Linniks experienced difficulty securing credit. The holding's fortunes changed dramatically in 2009 when Putin personally intervened on their behalf with VEB (formerly known as

Vneshekonombank), a state-owned development corporation. A 20 billion ruble loan that Miratorg received as the result of Putin's intervention became the engine of the holding's initial expansion.[67]

Miratorg's specialty is meat, a key item in the Kremlin's food independence agenda. According to Miratorg's own data, in 2019 it owned almost 630,000 heads of Aberdeen Angus, the world's largest angus stock, as well as the largest pig stock in Russia.[68] Miratorg also used to be Russia's largest landowner, but eventually lost this position to Tkachev's Agrocomplex.[69] The holding has almost forty thousand employees on its payroll and proudly presents itself as the largest investor in Russia's agriculture.[70] Numerous journalistic and expert accounts emphasize the Linniks' commercial acumen, efficiency, management skills, and enthusiastic willingness to adopt and learn from Western expertise.[71]

What explains this spectacular growth of a tiny milk powder producer to an agricultural titan? Unlike Tkachev or Moshkovich, neither of the Linnik twins ever held elected or executive office. Yet many in the agricultural sector and the media are convinced that the Linniks are cousins of Dmitry Medvedev's spouse Svetlana (nee Linnik). In response, the Russian government issued a statement denying any familial connection between the Miratorg owners and Medvedev, and no serious Russian media outlet has been able to prove such a relationship.[72] Moreover, an investigation conducted by Aleksei Navalny's Anti-Corruption Foundation (*Fond Bor'by s Korruptsiei*) also could not find any direct evidence of ties between the Linniks and Medvedev but suggested that they are quite likely to exist nonetheless.[73]

Other theories connect the Linniks to a different powerful patron, Sergei Dankvert, the head of Russia's veterinary watchdog *Rosselkhoznadzor* and Gordeev's former deputy minister.[74] A former governor of the Briansk region, where Miratorg is especially active, recalls that Dankvert directed him to the Linnik brothers. Viktor Linnik himself categorized Rosselkhoznadzor (in the context of veterinary control measures) as the holding's "forward operations base (*forpost*) in the Ministry of Agriculture."[75] Whatever the connection (or the lack thereof), the underlying assumption is that in Russia a privately owned company cannot reach such heights without close allies in very high places. This assumption, while conspiratorial and not backed by any solid evidence, is also not unreasonable, given the support Miratorg receives from the state. But at the same time, it is also not entirely impossible that Miratorg benefits from high levels of state support chiefly because of its massive size, presence in multiple regions, and the vital role it plays in promoting Putin's goal of food independence in meat, all outcomes of the Linniks outperforming their competitors' thanks to greater efficiency and skills.

Regardless of whether the Linnik brothers have powerful patrons in or near the Kremlin, it was the Russian government that enabled Miratorg's rise to the top. Part of this assistance is direct. Indeed, in Russia's food production, Miratorg is the largest recipient of state support, and in 2008 the holding was included in the list of Russia's 295 key enterprises (the so-called Putin's List) that receive preferential treatment from the state. The exact volume of direct subsidies and financial support that the holding receives from the state budget is unknown, but according to the agricultural scholar Natalia Shagaida, it amounted to tens of billions of rubles between 2016 and 2019, substantially more than almost all other food producers.[76]

Miratorg's subsidies also came from regional authorities. In 2011, a Miratorg-owned company received 625 million rubles out of the total 635 million that the Bryansk regional government allocated to agricultural subsidies. In 2014, Miratorg obtained 1.4 billion rubles out of a total of 1.419 billion of Bryansk agricultural subsidies, more than 98 percent.[77] In Kursk, the regional government provided Miratorg with an eye-popping 150 billion rubles for five years to develop the region's agriculture in 2018.[78] Additionally, the government assists Miratorg in increasing its land bank; the holding "often receives land under indefinite gratuitous bailments by order of the federal government.... After three years the land it leases free of charge is transferred from regional ownership to Miratorg's ownership."[79]

Furthermore, the holding benefits from access to large-scale, long-term subsidized loans from state banks and development bodies. Putin's facilitation of the loan from VEB was crucial for fueling Miratorg's expansion, but Linniks also benefited from additional long-term credits, namely, from Sberbank (several loans of more than eight billion rubles combined in 2012–2014), VEB (two loans in 2015 for about $742 million), and Gazprombank.[80] The loan that Miratorg received from Sberbank was the first given to an agricultural producer for a term of maturity of fifteen years, rather than the previously standard eight years.[81]

Miratorg also enjoys other types of government support, real and alleged. The Linniks were able to purchase large swaths of agricultural land in the Bryansk region at a fifth of its official value because local rumors speculated that the government was about to substantially increase land taxes and seize unused land. The source of these rumors is unclear, but Bryansk villagers found them credible enough, especially following Miratorg's move into the region. Moreover, the regional parliament quickly amended the law that capped the concentration of land when Miratorg reached the maximum limits of land ownership. Additionally, the holding relies on the local authorities' protection to physically harm neighboring, much smaller producers without facing any meaningful consequences for such actions.[82] To sum up, even the ostensibly politically unaffiliated agroholding that prides itself on modern production and management methods is, to a large degree, a product of the state's multifaceted and generous support.

Concluding Remarks

The growth of Russia's food production is largely due to government policies that started with grain and later expanded to other sectors. But these are private companies, not the state, that grow and produce the food required for achieving Putin's nutritional independence goals. This chapter shows how closely these private businesses are intertwined with the state and how government support—financial, regulatory, and administrative—drove and enabled the rise of industry titans.

Furthermore, Agrocomplex, Rusagro, and Miratorg demonstrate the different modes of state-agrobusiness relations and how corruption is part and parcel of Putin's effort to achieve regime stability through food. In that respect, food production shares multiple similarities with other types of Russia's crony capitalism of the 2010–2020s that replaced the state capitalism of Putin's early years.[83] We do not claim that the three agroholdings this chapter focuses on are representative of the industry as a whole. Rather, by centering on the industry's leaders and Russia's key food producers, we can better understand the full extent of the state's involvement in promoting food independence beyond ideological visions, framework documents, laws, and security strategies.

8
The COVID-19 Food Crisis, 2020–2021

On February 2, 2021, Aleksei Navalny, the leading Russian opposition activist, addressed the Moscow court that decided his sentence. Navalny, who survived a near-fatal poisoning by the Russian Federal Security Service (FSB) and recuperated in Germany, had been charged by authorities upon his return to Russia for not showing up for his parole hearing required as a part of his 2014 five-year suspended sentence for alleged money embezzlement. The Kremlin, determined to bar Navalny from exposing elite corruption and challenging President Vladimir Putin, had planned the trial's outcome well in advance. Addressing the court, Navalny forcefully rejected the charges levied against him and predicted that Putin would go down in history as "Vladimir the Poisoner of Underpants," a reference to Navalny's garment that the FSB presumably used to carry out the poisoning.

Navalny then pivoted to a topic that resonates with ordinary Russians stronger than democracy or the rule of law ever would: food prices. "I'm locked up in a prison cell and all I hear about on TV is that butter is getting more expensive. The price of eggs is rising. You've deprived these people of a future," he accused the government.[1]

What Navalny saw on TV in his prison cell was correct. Not only butter and eggs but also sugar, pasta, oil, meat, and other staple foods became more expensive in 2020–2021, many considerably so. The price of pasta increased by 10 percent, sunflower oil by 24 percent and sugar by more than 70 percent.[2] Navalny's main adversary, President Putin, also understood the political role of food and the danger of rising food prices. Despite two decades of heavy investment in agriculture, food shortages once again alarmed the Kremlin.

In previous chapters, we described the twenty-year evolution of Putin's food supply policies. His rhetoric was saturated with references to the principles of the open market economy. Still, the logic of his food policies was decidedly anti-market, driven primarily by the imperatives of regime survival. Putin, we showed, aimed to achieve two goals. The first goal was to create a loyal, regime-dependent agricultural industry capable of supplying the

Russian population with affordable and readily available staple foods. The second goal was to achieve food independence from the West through import substitution and countersanctions policies that closed Russian market to food imports from the United States and the EU. Together, these measures were intended to simultaneously shield Russia from foreign interference and protect the regime from a potentially disastrous supply crisis.

The goals adopted by the Kremlin inevitably pushed the country in opposite directions. Closing Russia to Western food imports fueled the rise of domestic food producers loyal to and dependent on the regime, but it also inevitably restricted competition and concentrated the market in the hands of several mammoth players. Thus, the danger of rising food prices, which the government hoped to avoid, increased. The most effective way to guarantee the supply of abundant food and keep prices low required opening the Russian market to Western imports, but this policy was incompatible with the Kremlin's goal of nutritional self-sufficiency.

The economic hardship triggered by the COVID-19 pandemic eventually exposed these inherent contradictions at the core of Russia's food policies. The outcome was a mixed bag for the regime. During a period marked by declining oil prices and plummeting real incomes, Russians were forced to reduce their food consumption. To compensate for the declining domestic demand, producers switched to exports. This led to a spiraling crisis of declining consumption and growing prices. The system designed to shield Russia from food shortages had faltered. But at the same time, the sheer volume of Russia's food production and the industry's dependence on the government gave Putin leverage. It allowed him to introduce painful intervention measures, such as export bans and price caps, without pushback from agricultural elites. There was food, and severe shortages and mass protests did not materialize. The regime, although gravely alarmed, held. This crisis also led to unprecedented levels of state intervention in the economy and potentially the emergence of command capitalism, which, history suggests, could extend beyond food to other sectors that the Kremlin considers politically important.

COVID-19 and the Return of Food Politics

The coronavirus pandemic catapulted food to the forefront of global political and social agendas. When COVID-19 disrupted international trade and states imposed travel restrictions, closing themselves off from the outside world, citizens throughout the globe emptied grocery store shelves. Governments from Algeria to Saudi Arabia to the Philippines also started stockpiling food.[3] In April 2020, David Beasley, the UN World Food Programme executive director, warned that COVID-19 might trigger a "'hunger pandemic,' which has the potential to engulf over a quarter of a billion people" in developing countries.[4] Luckily, this worst-case projection did not materialize. Yet, in July 2021, Oxfam, an organization dedicated to fighting hunger and poverty, reported that the number of people suffering from extreme food insecurity had increased by more than 20 million since the beginning of the pandemic. Moreover, the number of people living in famine-like conditions jumped sixfold. Oxfam calculated that the combined death toll of hunger, conflict, and climate change outpaced deaths directly caused by the coronavirus.[5]

Most of the suffering and food insecurity were concentrated in the poorest parts of the world, but rich states have not managed to escape the misery either. In the West, the pandemic pushed countless people into poverty and food insecurity. Governments and charitable organizations struggled to assist a growing number skipping meals and incapable of feeding their families.[6] Deprived of donations, food banks in the United States and the United Kingdom often failed to meet the skyrocketing demand, some even shutting down entirely.[7] In Italy, the mafia saw an opportunity to attract new loyalists and distributed groceries to struggling citizens.[8] Humanity was suffering, but each country, community, and family was forced to cope alone.

In May 2020, as the COVID-19 pandemic was spreading throughout the globe, *The Economist* published a cover titled "Goodbye Globalization: The Dangerous Lure of Self-sufficiency."[9] Russia, as we demonstrated, was years ahead of the emerging global tide. "Thanks to Sanctions, Russia Is Cushioned from Virus's Economic Shocks," a *New York Times* article boldly predicted.[10] The food supply system that Kremlin had been busy constructing for two decades seemed well equipped to protect the country, ostensibly validating Putin's actions. The system, however, also possessed inherent weaknesses that the cheerleaders of self-sufficiency failed to notice.

The Pandemic Comes to Russia: COVID-19 and Food Crises

The COVID-19 pandemic arrived in Russia relatively late in comparison to other countries and was initially confined to the Far East regions that border

China, creating an illusion of relative safety. Things took a more ominous turn in March 2020. On March 19, Russia recorded its first COVID-related death. Later that month and in early April, the number of confirmed cases skyrocketed in the country's major cities.[11]

As in the rest of the world, the pandemic caused a public health and economic crisis in Russia. The global economic downturn greatly affected the price of oil and gas, the country's key source of revenue. Russia's 2020 state budget predicted that the global price of oil would be about $42.45 for a barrel, but in March–April 2020, it plummeted to below $23. This caused a significant shortfall in state revenues and severely hurt the incomes of ordinary Russians. According to Rosstat, the country's official statistical agency, the real incomes of the Russian population declined by 4.5 percent in 2020. Given that incomes were already falling in previous years, the pandemic only exacerbated an already bad situation. According to official statistics, in 2020, Russians' real incomes were 10.1 percent lower than in 2013, before the annexation of Crimea.[12]

The decline of real incomes due to the COVID-19 pandemic, coupled with the devaluation of the ruble, which in 2020 alone lost 22.5 percent of its value vis-à-vis the US dollar, suppressed consumption throughout the country. Even staple foods were affected, as the average Russian began to buy less when incomes plummeted. To compensate for decreasing domestic demand, food producers switched to exports, mostly though not entirely to China, where the demand was high and they could recoup profits no longer available in Russia. In 2020, the country's agricultural exports hit a record-shattering $30.7 billion, $5 billion above the previous peak in 2018. For the first time in its post-communist history, Russian agricultural exports exceeded imports by $1 billion.[13] Domestic leaders proudly touted these numbers as evidence of agricultural success. In reality, they signaled growing troubles. Russia exported so much simply because its citizens could no longer afford domestic produce. More ominously, as domestic produce increasingly left the country, no food products entered from the West due to countersanctions.

Desperately scrambling to recoup lost profits, many retailers responded by raising prices. Cash-strapped Russians were thus forced to buy less, leading to even larger losses for the industry. But instead of changing tactics, retailers doubled down and continued to adjust prices upward stubbornly. A vicious cycle of rising prices, reduced consumption, and growing food insecurity evolved. In February–March 2021, the sales of fruits and vegetables declined by 30–60 percent compared to the previous year, bakery products by 40 percent, and meat sales by a quarter.[14] More than 9 million Russians, roughly

6 percent of the population, lacked sufficient amounts of food. By July 2021, about 400,000 were experiencing severe food insecurity.[15]

Russians ate less due to rising food prices, but they could not cease purchasing food entirely and were forced to pay more. According to the Russian Food Index, which measures the share of food in Russian households' total expenses, Russians spent more than 40 percent of their incomes on food at the height of the COVID-19 pandemic, a substantial increase from the 2017–2019 average of 31.6 percent.[16] From March 2020 to March 2021, the price of staple foods on average increased by 15.6 percent. The cost of several most popular products rose even more substantially. For example, the price of sugar went up by 47 percent, eggs by 32 percent, sunflower oil by 27 percent, groats, and chicken meat by almost 20 percent.[17]

Food availability soon became a major political concern for the government. In March 2021, Levada Center, the only independent public opinion research organization in Russia, reported that 58 percent of the population considered rising prices the most acute social problem. In contrast, a mere 6 percent classified Putin's crackdown on democratic rights and freedoms as a significant issue.[18] Furthermore, Levada Center pollsters observed a sizable decline in the proportion of Russians who believed that the country was headed in the right direction. In another blow to the government, Putin's approval rating took a painful hit and dropped from stunning yet nevertheless real 80 percent in March 2018 to just 59 percent.[19] Such a decrease in popular support must have been very concerning to Putin.

Parallel to the emerging food prices crisis, protests reignited in Russia. While food did not directly incite social mobilization in 2020–2021, rising prices provided a fertile ground for discontent. In the summer and fall of 2020, tens of thousands of Russians took to the streets in Khabarovsk, a major city in the Russian Far East. They protested against the arrest of Sergei Furgal, a popular local governor. Smaller yet vocal protests against the arrest and imprisonment of Aleksei Navalny swept across the country in the winter and spring of 2021. Navalny himself used the rising food prices to accuse Putin of robbing Russia of its wealth and the Russians of their future. Food availability became a threat the government could no longer ignore.

The Government's Response

In late 2020 and early 2021, Putin responded to protests with a harsh crackdown and brutal repression. Thousands were arrested, and media outlets critical of the government were labeled "foreign agents." With Navalny behind bars, his Anti-Corruption Foundation (FBK) was officially declared an "extremist organization" and dismantled.[20] Yet while the government cracked downed on political opposition, the more threatening popular discontent over rising prices received a different treatment.

During a Zoom discussion with government officials on December 9, 2020, Putin devoted a considerable portion of his remarks to the quickly growing food prices in the country. The president bitterly complained that staple foods were now inaccessible to most Russians.[21] The reason, Putin argued, was not the COVID-19 pandemic but the retailers' and producers' greed and attempts to align domestic prices to higher global ones. How, Putin thundered, could global price increases explain the rising food prices in Russia if the country is perfectly capable of producing these items on its own? Understandably, blaming the business community was politically more expedient for Putin than admitting that his food import bans contributed as much to the problem as the businesspeople's desire for profits.

Several days later, on December 13, 2020, Putin ordered the government to fix the problem within a week. "These are no jokes!," he publicly berated Minister of Economic Development Maxim Reshetnikov for allowing the situation to get out of control. The Soviet-era food shortages, Putin stressed, ought not to be repeated.[22]

During the president's annual press conference on December 17, Putin discussed skyrocketing food prices twice, more extensively than any other topic on the agenda. Russia's ruler was visibly concerned that the situation might escalate and threaten social stability. Once again, the food businesses that the regime nurtured and viewed as pliant servants bore the brunt of his ire.

> Manufacturers and exporters believe they should not be losing money with domestic prices. This is nonsense, of course, they must understand that they are not losing anything, since they are producing things here.... They forget how much the state has already invested and continues to invest in agriculture, and what they got from the budget in order to achieve these numbers.... A record-high harvest, 131 million [tonnes of grain] or maybe even 134 million—and bread and pasta prices are rising. This is nonsensical and is also related to exports and export incentives.... This is annoying. But it can be fixed.[23]

Putin reassured the public that the food price increases would be reversed "within days or weeks," and the government would pay close attention to future food price fluctuations. Despite openly reminding everyone how much agribusinesses depend on state support, the president also paid the necessary lip service to the market and its mechanisms. Putin promised not to interfere in market relations by administrative fiat, but it was clear to all that the "fixes" the government envisioned would inevitably do just that. The question was how extensive this new state intervention would be.[24]

The majority of Putin's responses to the food crisis were televised and broadly publicized by the state's PR machine. They were also clearly staged and screened just before Russians embarked on the holidays' food-shopping spree. Regulating food prices was the president's new year's present to the country. Putin's actions were meant to promote his image as the "good tsar" who is deeply concerned about the wellbeing of ordinary citizens. In light of slipping incomes and popular support, Putin needed to be seen and heard, and his image of a compassionate and decisive problem-solver omnipresent.

Following the widely advertised downplaying of the crisis, the government leaped into action. True to form, on December 11, the Russian Prosecutor-General office opened an investigation of staple food prices throughout the country and threatened criminal persecution of "all cartel arrangements," a clear sign that heads might roll.[25] More important, three days later, Prime Minister Mikhail Mishustin introduced a range of governmental regulations[26] designed to lower the cost of essential foods, primarily bread, sugar, and sunflower oil. The regulation was supposed to be a temporary, three-month measure and included a "voluntary" agreement between the Ministries of Agriculture and Trade and Industry, food producers, and retail chains. These new measures entailed restrictions on wholesale and retail prices and export tariffs on grains and corn.[27] Another official initiative envisioned a long-term mechanism to regulate the costs of staple, or "socially important," food products.[28] In late December 2020, the regulations were rushed through parliamentary approval and became laws. The new legislation allowed the government to set maximum food prices as it sees fit for up to ninety days.[29] Price caps were not totally unknown in Russia previously. For instance, during the 1998 crisis Moscow introduce price caps for bread produced by city-owned bakeries "along with stern warnings to private producers and retailers to refrain from increasing prices."[30] In 2007–2008 the government also coerced producers and retailers to agree to a price cap on several basic staple foods. Yet the scope and the ambition of restrictions went well beyond past measures.

A famous Russian saying states that the severity of the country's laws is compensated for by the lack of expectation to comply. This was different. The government ordered the Federal Tax Service (FNS) to monitor how diligently producers and retailers implemented the new decrees, just in case the Prosecutor General investigations were not frightening enough. On January 26, 2021, the FNS began ordering food producers to provide quarterly projections of price fluctuation until the end of the year.[31] The organization's role in enforcing the ostensibly voluntary agreements between private businesses and the government, coupled with the earlier actions by the Prosecutor General, clearly illustrated the highly coercive nature of these measures. But some politicians felt the government still did not go far enough and demanded an even more aggressive approach. Thus Vladimir Zhirinovsky, the leader of the populist LDPR (till his death in April 2022), suggested fixing the prices problem by simply compiling a list of people who would be arrested if prices did not go down.[32]

Cognizant of how much it owes to and depends on the regime, the business community knew better than openly pushing back even when their bottom lines were at stake. When Vadim Moshkovich, a major agricultural tycoon and former member of the Federation Council, dared to complain to Putin about the restrictions politely, the president grew irritated. The government, Putin shot back, has no interest in pressuring the business community by using "non-market methods," but Russian firms ought "to develop to benefit the citizens . . . and not to the detriment of our people." Shortly following this exchange, Moshkovich's company became subject to a tax audit, and according to some publications, the oligarch promptly left the country.[33] Thereafter, no other business leader spoke up again.

The economy recovered somewhat in 2021. In April, the oil price climbed to $62.5 per barrel and Putin's approval increased to a tolerable, if not stellar, 65 percent. The government, however, was still gravely concerned about food prices and in no mood to abandon its intervention in the food industry. In late March 2021, it extended the price freezes on sugar and sunflower until June 1 (sugar) and October 1 (sunflower oil). To partially compensate producers for lower retail prices, it also announced a nine billion ruble subsidy in April.[34]

The government adopted these decisions despite the growing price tag on such policies and emerging opposition to blatant state intervention in the economy. Elvira Nabiullina, the head of Russia's Central Bank, was the most vocal opponent within the Russian leadership. In December 2020, she asserted that adjusting food prices should only be a short-term measure since it greatly distorts supply and demand market mechanisms. Speaking at a forum sponsored by the Moscow Stock Exchange in April 2020, Nabiullina reiterated her objections to food price-fixing.[35] Aleksei Kudrin, Putin's longtime associate, former minister of finance, and the head of the government's Accounts Chamber, voiced similar concerns.[36]

Yet despite the (admittedly mild) opposition and the growing cost of intervention policies, Putin's government was determined to maintain the measures adopted in December 2020. Putin again referenced the food price increases in his annual address to the Russian parliament on April 21, 2021. He reluctantly admitted that high prices affect Russians' real incomes, but that the government knew, cared, and was committed to solving this problem. The president repeated his pledge to keep food prices affordable and paid the customary lip service to the importance of market-driven price formation, likely to appease the business community and internal dissenters, such as Nabiullina. Putin promised that commitment to the market economy would prevent acute shortages similar to the late 1980s. However, he remained silent on how price caps and massive state intervention were to be reconciled with market principles.[37]

But food prices kept climbing. The Kremlin's intervention managed to slow the pace at which food prices increased and, at least officially, froze the price tags of several staple foods. However, no government decree could magically eliminate the fundamental conditions affecting the industry. As long as Russia's domestic market remained shut to Western imports and real incomes declined, rising food prices were not going away unless the government took over the entire food sector. Many Russians understood this, and thus popular support for food countersanctions declined substantially, especially among the younger people.[38]

On May 12, 2021, Prime Minister Mishustin presented his annual report on the state of the economy to the Federal Assembly. He echoed the official rhetoric of coping with the rising food prices, reassuring the parliament that the government was doing its best to keep domestic food prices low. But he also acknowledged that thus far, the efforts had failed to have the desired impact. This, he maintained, was not the government's fault. According to the prime minister, rising prices were the consequence of the "greed" of "some" producers and supermarket chains. Like Putin, Mishustin warned the producers that exports could not come at the expense of domestic consumers and that the government has enough coercive tools to elicit compliance.[39] In other words, the solution to the failure of coercion was even more force.

Indeed, harsher measures followed. Alarmed by the government's inability to stem the rising prices, First Deputy Prime Minister Andrei Belousov called for an emergency meeting to discuss the costs of sugar, sunflower oil, pork, chicken, and eggs on May 18. Belousov, a rather conservative politician and Putin's former economic advisor, ordered the government to formulate recommendations for setting maximum prices on those food items within three days. The official statement published after the meeting did not even mention the need to consult food producers or retailers. In December 2020, there was at least the pretense of a "voluntary" agreement between producers, retailers, and the government. In contrast, in May 2021, the government openly acted as the lone price-setter.[40] No one else, be it producers, retailers, or industry associations, mattered. If businesses saw lower profits or even operated at a loss, then so be it. According to early estimates, sugar manufacturers alone lost about $130 million due to the restrictions. Dairy producers, the government admitted, kept prices constant throughout 2021 at their own expense.[41] But not even such severe measures could reverse the trend.

On May 21, 2021, instead of receiving the maximum food price recommendations, as Belousov requested, Russian leaders were forced to admit to their resounding failure to stop the crisis. On the same day, Rosstat, the government's official statistical agency, announced that food prices in the country had risen 4.7 percent from January through April 2021 and on an annual basis (April 2020–April 2021) by 16 percent.[42] Putin acknowledged the reality and, no longer blaming the greedy producers and retailers, admitted that the price increases in Russia related to higher global prices.[43] Simultaneously, the president showed no willingness to switch course. Whatever the cause of rising food prices, the Kremlin refused to relinquish nominal control of such a politically and socially crucial issue, the actual efficacy of its policies be damned. Price freezes, caps, and bans continued.

Food and Politics on the Screen

Putin and the Russian government doubled down on their crude intervention in the food market because they perceive food as primarily a political, not economic issue. They believe that the food supply is crucial for social stability. The regime's very survival justified even the harshest measures. To fully appreciate the political significance of food supplies, one must look beyond official policies, announcements, and resolutions. Culture, especially the officially sanctioned one, offers an equally illuminating perspective.

In September 2020, precisely when food prices were rising rapidly, *Dear Comrades!* (*Dorogie tovarishchi!*), a film devoted to the 1962 Novocherkassk Massacre, debuted in Russia. The movie, which recounts the communist government's bloody repression of food protests in the city, was widely discussed in Russian and foreign media. It became Russia's key cultural event of the year.[44] Critically acclaimed, *Dear Comrades!* won the Special Jury Prize at the Venice Film Festival and was selected as Russia's entry for the Academy Award. However, what made the film notable were not just its artistic qualities but also the people involved in the production and relevance of the topic.

The movie was directed by Andrei Konchalovsky, a celebrated filmmaker and a leading member of the country's official cultural elite. Konchalovsky's father, the writer Sergei Mikhalkov, authored the lyrics of both Soviet and Russian anthems. Konchalovsky is also the brother of Nikita Mikhalkov, an internationally renowned and vehemently nationalist actor and director. The production was funded by Alisher Usmanov, one of the wealthiest people in Russia and the world,[45] a "metals tycoon whose business had always gone hand in hand with the Russian state."[46]

When they produced the film, Konchalovsky and Usmanov naturally could not have predicted the COVID-19 pandemic and the food prices crisis that ensued. There is also no evidence that the film was produced in response to an explicit demand from above. Nevertheless, the topic and the timing of the film were hardly a coincidence. With food and protests so high up on the government's agenda post-2014, interest in the most famous episode of food-centered popular mobilization in living memory was only natural, especially when carried out by people with deep, long-standing ties to Russia's leadership.

Dear Comrades! focuses on the fictional story of Liudmila, a devoted communist official in Novocherkassk, who becomes increasingly disillusioned with the regime as she witnesses the bloody repression of ordinary Russians, massacred for simply demanding food. Viewed against the background of Putin's heavy response to the rising prices, the film confirms our key argument: Russian political elites are confident that food can mobilize Russians more effectively than any other topic.

Furthermore, the movie serves a clear propaganda purpose by focusing on the state's actions. *Dear Comrades!* demonstrates how the Soviet leadership ignored the problem of citizens' lack of access to affordable food, leading to the Novocherkassk tragedy. But not Putin. The state's PR machine reminded everyone that the president cares deeply about food supply and acts forcefully to address any problems in this realm.

Finally, *Dear Comrades!* was a warning to both the Russian people and the regime. The country's leaders should never forget that when food is lacking, people have no other choice but to take to the streets. Without food, the government might lose the support of even its most committed agents. But at the same time, in case ordinary Russians might have forgotten, mass protests are a risky, potentially bloody business. In times of food insecurity, the Kremlin and its allies preferred Russians to remember Novocherkassk 1962 rather than Petrograd 1917.

Roads Not Taken: The Food Certificates Debate

Price caps and direct state intervention in the economy were not the only available options to address the rising food prices. Lifting the food countersanctions and opening the Russian market to Western food imports and meaningful competition might have been the most sensible policy economically yet unthinkable politically. Another alternative was offering food assistance to disadvantaged Russians. Such aid, provided in food certificates or coupons, had been debated even before the onset of the COVID-19 pandemic, but the growing food crisis made it increasingly urgent.

Proposals to introduce food certificates for the poor can be traced back to the 2000s. However, the idea did not gain much traction within Russia during years of economic boom and declining poverty. In 2014–2015, following the decline in oil prices in the wake of the annexation of Crimea, the Russian Ministry of Industry and Trade began promoting a program modeled after American food stamps. A fixed amount of money would be deposited to designated cards, which could be used to purchase domestically grown produce. At the time, the government assumed that 15–16 million poor Russians would be eligible for such state support. It estimated that the programs would cost the state 240 to 300 billion rubles a year.[47] Some regions decided not to wait for Moscow and introduced their local-level food cards.[48]

The plan, presented as support to the vulnerable Russians and a booster of domestic food production, was widely discussed in the Russian media. However, its cost was perceived as prohibitively high for the traditionally fiscally conservative Putin,[49] and by 2019, the idea had effectively been shelved. The economic hardship caused by the COVID-19 pandemic revived the proposal. In December 2020, Yulia Ogloblina, the head of the Agro-Industrial Department of Russia's Civic Chamber, a state institution designed to serve as a bridge between the government and citizens, called for food cards for the poor to compensate for the rapidly rising food prices.[50]

The majority of Russians backed the introduction of food certificates. In April 2021, a Levada Center survey revealed that 54 percent of citizens approved the idea, whereas 39 percent opposed the plan.[51] The business community also voiced their support.[52] Massive government spending on social support programs promised a windfall for the industry, whereas price caps and restrictions spelled heavy financial losses. Food coupons were also the preferred action for many experts who believed that the poor and the industry would benefit from the proposal.[53]

Among political parties, Vladimir Zhirinovsky's nationalist, populist LDPR was the first to realize that it could gain political capital by promoting food certificates. Zhirinovsky himself had a long track record of advocating for domestically produced cheap food. The "Food Security" entry on the LDPR website rallies against the abundance of Chinese food on Russia's Far East markets and even calls for the nationalization of Russia's supermarket chains to boost food import substitution.[54] In February 2021, the politician voiced strong support for food certificates and lobbied Putin for their adoption.[55]

On the other hand, the communist KPRF strongly and consistently objected to food certificates since they were first discussed in 2008. This opposition might seem surprising for a socially oriented party heavily dependent on the votes of the most economically weak, especially older people. But the KPRF also desperately sought to shed any association with the social and economic failures of the USSR, first and foremost food shortages and the infamous Soviet food rationing coupons. Ivan Mel'nikov, the party second-in-command, condemned food certificates as evidence of the government's failure to combat poverty.[56] In 2017, KPRF continued its criticism of the idea, dubbing it "a bankruptcy of the current [economic] system."[57]

During the COVID-19 crisis, the communists reiterated their opposition to food certificates, correctly claiming that they would not fix the escalating price increases. KPRF instead advocated for permanent government regulation of prices in a wide range of spheres, such as medicine, transportation, and housing. As for food, the KPRF maintained that the state, not private companies, ought to be the main purchaser and distributor of agricultural products. The communists' solution to the food prices crisis thus presupposed a complete overhaul of Russia's post-Soviet economy and was therefore unrealistic.[58]

Yet Putin remained on the fence. In February 2021, during a meeting with the heads of Duma parliamentary factions, the president suggested that food certificates have advantages and disadvantages. He suggested that the idea might be discussed now but would be irrelevant in the post-pandemic era.[59] In April 2021, Putin eventually came out against the plan. In his address to the Federal Assembly, the president instead announced an increase in direct payments to low-income families to deal with rising living costs.[60]

We do not have direct knowledge of Putin's reasons for rejecting food certificates. Nevertheless, the current ruler of Russia likely wishes to avoid a policy, even a sensible one, that vividly evokes the worst aspects of Soviet life. Food coupons are just too closely associated with the economic crisis and state collapse to become a viable policy option.[61] "Our main impediment is that we are from the USSR," lamented Aleksei Kudrin, Putin's former liberal minister of finance and close associate, who disapproves of the ongoing state intervention in the economy.[62] For Putin, being from the USSR means not only seeking to revive Russia's status as a great power but also instinctively fearing anything similar to food rationing.

Concluding Remarks: An Advent of a New Model?

Despite Putin and Mishustin's reassurances that government measures to reduce food prices would not violate the basic principles of market-driven price formation, the reality was precisely the opposite. If anything, the Kremlin's reaction to the rising domestic food prices during the pandemic is nothing short of a move toward reviving the Soviet-style command economy. Repeated accusations of greed and price gouging, followed by the Prosecutor General and the Federal Tax Service investigations, represented a clear threat to unleash the security apparatus on those market actors who refuse to cooperate with the government. Severe long-term export restrictions followed by outright bans and especially the fixing of prices by fiat, hardly market mechanisms, are also reminiscent of Soviet-era policies. Putin's May 2021 admission that food price increases were, after all, due to the world market forces did not change the government's autarkic import substitution and heavy price regulations.

In 2020–2021, we potentially witnessed an advent of *command capitalism*, in which the government directly determines market activities by whim, in an ad hoc and occasionally repressive fashion. The food sector economy remains in private hands, but the government determines the prices even if this means long-term financial losses for businesses involved. "There is nothing terrible" about limiting businesses profits, Putin noted in March 2021.[63] This represents a mode of state-business relations incompatible with the principles of free market.[64] It is also fundamentally different from state capitalism, in which the government shapes the economy "either by owning majority or minority equity positions in companies or by providing subsidized credit and/or other privileges to private companies."[65] Nor does it fit the typical perceptions of crony capitalism, the essence of which is corrupt rent-seeking and private financial gains at the highest levels.[66]

Most states, even liberal ones, intervene in the economy to regulate the increasingly complex markets, protect consumers, or benefit some key actors. What makes the current situation in Russia to stand out is the simultaneous deployment of several heavy intervention measures, such as export bans and price caps, in peacetime, the manner in which these interventions are carried out—ad hoc, by fiat, and with explicit threats of repression to elicit compliance—and their longevity.

In the past, Putin practiced such interventions in a limited fashion,[67] but now he extended them to an entire industry and country. Even if the results of this approach are not exactly what the government had hoped for, Putin persists because the political importance of controlling food trumps other considerations. Assuming that the past is a helpful guide for understanding Russia, what begins in the food sector tends to spread to other parts of the economy quickly. Thus, Russia might be headed toward command capitalism well beyond agriculture and food retail.

In the short term the strategy seems to have achieved its basic goals. In summer 2021, a Reuters journalist visited Novocherkassk to understand why a city known for a mass protest in 1962 did not experience anti-government mobilization in 2020–2021. "Is there enough food? There's enough," a local leader summarized.[68]

But if we are correct, the more distant future spells trouble for the regime because the current model of nutritionally independent autocracy is unsustainable without ever-increasing political and financial state intervention. If the trend of introducing command capitalism continues, food shortages, which the Kremlin fears, would quickly become a reality. The regime will then face a substantially bigger threat than Navalny and the pro-democracy opposition. The Russian elites and society understand fully well that if severe food shortages return, no amount of propaganda, censorship, or coercion can save the government. And if a deadly pandemic was not enough of a challenge for the Kremlin, an even more existential crisis arrived in February 2022, when Russian troops invaded Ukraine.

9
The War in Ukraine and Russia's Food Politics

The goal of Russia's food independence drive was to protect the country and the regime from political instability, caused by food shortage in a case of a major political or social crisis. The system managed to survive the growing conflict with the West and an unexpected global pandemic. Yet the countersanctions in the wake of Russia's annexation of Crimea in 2014 were just a prelude to the system's key test—a major, potentially armed confrontation against the United States and NATO, for which the Kremlin actively has long prepared. Nutritional self-sufficiency was just a single component of such preparation, but clearly a major one. The clash came in the early morning of February 24, 2022, when Russian troops invaded Ukraine. While at the time of writing in May 2023, large-scale fighting was still ongoing and the eventual outcome of the war was still unknown, the first fifteen months of war do allow for the evaluation of how the food system that Putin built fares under extreme stress and how the Kremlin views and uses food during this confrontation.

Sanctions and Isolation

On February 24, 2022, while still in the midst of the COVID-19 pandemic, Putin launched a war on Ukraine in order topple its pro-Western, democratically elected government and bring the country back into Russia's sphere of influence. Unprecedented Western sanctions aimed at damaging Russia's economy and crippling its ability to wage war swiftly followed and have expanded ever since. Among the most significant ones affecting the financial sector were the freezing of some $300 billion of Russian Central Bank reserves, banning major Russian banks from accessing Western credits, and expelling many of them from the SWIFT global financial system.[1] In fact, the crippling sanctions impacted every major sector of Russia's economy,

Bread and Autocracy. Janetta Azarieva, Yitzhak M. Brudny, and Eugene Finkel, Oxford University Press.
© Oxford University Press 2023. DOI: 10.1093/oso/9780197684368.003.0010

from aviation and cars to luxury and consumer goods as well as Hollywood blockbusters. Western sanctions and Russia's growing isolation also led to the exodus of over a thousand Western companies operating in in the country.[2]

Western sanctions, expansive as they were, didn't target agriculture or the food sector. Still, many Western food chains or producers, including KFC, Pizza Hut, Burger King, McDonald's (the biggest fast-food company in Russia with 850 branches, 62,000 employees, and 160,000 suppliers), Starbucks, Coca-Cola, PepsiCo, Nestle, Carlsberg, and Mars left Russia, while the international food giant Danone suspended all further investments in the country. Four agriculture and food giants—Cargill, Archer Daniels Midland, Louis Dreyfus, and Bunge—all declared a scaling-down of their local activities yet decided to keep operating in Russia to continue "the production and transport of essential food commodities and ingredients."[3]

The war in Ukraine, Western sanctions, and sharp decline of the ruble vis-à-vis the dollar and the euro contributed to an atmosphere of panic buying in major Russian cities, resulting in the disappearance of such basic food staples as buckwheat, sugar, pasta, flour, rice, salt, and cooking oil from Russian supermarkets in March 2022.[4] Some supermarket chains declared limits on buying items in highest demand, and senior government officials rushed to reassure the public that there was plenty of food in the country and no reason for food hoarding.[5]

While food panic ended within weeks, the rise of food prices continued till the summer. As we described in the previous chapter, the government failed to stem the rise of food prices during the COVID-19 epidemic's peak (2020–2021). This trend continued and even accelerated during the early months of the war. According to Rosstat, the Russian Statistical Agency, between March 2021 and March 2022 the price of food rose by a staggering 19.6 percent, with such basic staples as sugar rising by 70.2 percent, fruits and vegetables by 35 percent, cereals and beans by 29 percent, pasta by 24.9 percent, butter by 22 percent, dairy products by 22 percent, meat (pork, beef, chicken) by 16 percent, and bread and bakery products by 15 percent.[6] The sharp rise in the price of sugar, which in the week of March 12–18, 2022, alone rose by 14 percent in Russia as a whole, and in some regions by 37 percent, brought the Russian Anti-Monopoly Agency (FAS) to open a price-fixing investigation against Prodimex, Russia's biggest sugar producer, and two major supermarket chains, Piatyorochka and Magnit.[7]

The Anti-Monopoly Agency investigation was not the only way the government tried to slow down the rise of food prices. On March 15, 2022, the

Russian government issued a temporary ban on the export of grain (including wheat, rye, barley, and corn) and sugar. The export ban expired on June 30, 2022, for the countries of the Eurasian Economic Union and on August 31, 2022, for the rest of the world as Russia restarted its grain exports worldwide. The measure was explained as a "defense of domestic food market."[8]

The absolute priority of the domestic food market over exports during the time of war was clearly expressed by Putin during an April 5, 2022, food industry conference. Russia's president boasted that the country had achieved food self-sufficiency and that Russian domestic food prices remain lower than those in the West. Yet Putin also added that "it goes without saying that this year, in view of the global food shortage, we will have to be more careful about food exports. . . . Food self-sufficiency is Russia's competitive advantage, and our citizens should feel its benefits. We must protect them from market fluctuations and price hikes on the global market."[9] To attain that goal, Putin promised that the government will ensure a reliable supply of fertilizers to Russian agriculture, thus limiting hard currency revenue from this important export item, allocate an additional 153 billion rubles (about $2 billion) from the federal budget to support the food industry, and add an additional 5 billion rubles (about $68 million) to support seed-growing and animal breeding centers.[10]

These promises were meant to reassure domestic producers and the public at large, but they also highlighted the inherent weakness of decades of nutritional independence policies. Whereas Russia centered its food policies on achieving self-sufficiency in production, the country still remained dependent on imports of seeds, about 80 percent of which came from the United States and EU. Russia is largely self-sufficient in seeds for such crops as winter and spring wheat, oats, and barley, but it is completely dependent on seed imports for sugar beets—the main source of sugar in Russia (98 percent imported)—sunflower seeds (73 percent imported), and potato seeds (65 percent imported). As far as animal breeding imports are concerned, such imports constitute about 40 percent of the Russian breeding material market.[11]

Following Russia's invasion of Ukraine, Russia's vulnerability in these spheres became even more acute. In early May 2022, the US-based Corteva Agriscience, a global leader in agricultural technology and a major exporter of corn, sunflower seeds, and herbicides into Russia, announced that it was leaving the country and would no longer sell its products there.[12] Limagrain, another industry giant, while deciding not to pull out of Russia, suspended its plans to build a seed factory in the country.[13]

Under condition of escalating economic warfare against the West, the government realized that this vulnerability needs to be addressed as fast as possible. Yet all the financial investment notwithstanding, rapid substitution of these crucial imports is physically impossible. This might also seriously endanger Russia's food independence project precisely when such independence is needed the most. According to an anonymous source cited by the *Kommersant* newspaper, it would take at least three years to develop local seed production for sugar beets, sunflowers, and potatoes. However, the government clearly does not wish to wait that long. Following the script of 2014 food countersanctions in July–August 2022, the *Rosselkhoznadzor* banned the import of seeds from French, Canadian, German, and Dutch companies. Predictably, the watchdog agency justified the ban by claiming that these companies had failed to comply with Russia phytosanitary requirements, the usual excuse to ban food products from countries the Kremlin views as hostile.[14]

Yet Russia also did not ban seed imports altogether. The targeting of French, Canadian, German, and Dutch companies was just the first step in the Ministry of Agriculture's plan to lessen dependence on Western companies by imposing quotas on imported seeds from the EU, United States, and other "non-friendly" Western countries. As the first deputy minister of agriculture, Oksana Lut, stated, "[Russia] will move to a quota system for imported seeds, gradually lowering the quotas." This plan, however, will hurt Russian producers who as on now heavily rely on imported seeds, especially corn and sunflower growers.[15]

The war also created additional problems that Russian food and agriculture industries had not faced in decades. One major example was food packaging. In late March 2022, the Swedish company Tetra Pak, the biggest producer of food packages in Russia, announced a radical scaling-down of its activities in Russia, leaving only milk and baby food packages in production. In July 2022, Tetra Pak announced that was ceasing its remaining operations in Russia after sixty-two years of activity in the country.[16]

Tetra Pak technologies, which allow packaged food to be kept up to one year, are currently unavailable in Russia. Russia's deputy prime minister, Viktoria Abramchenko, promised to develop a Russia-made alternative to Tetra Pak packages by the end of 2022. It is not clear, however, whether the target date is real or whether Russian import-substituted packing technology, if ever developed, would be as good as the original Swedish one or as affordable to the food producers. Meanwhile, the shortage of high-quality packing material has already forced many Russian food producers to switch to lower-quality plastic and glass packages.[17]

Another major problem caused by the war was service and maintenance of Western agricultural machinery widely used in Russia. Among Western companies that left the country in the aftermath of the invasion of Ukraine, Deere & Company clearly stands out. Deere & Company is the world's largest manufacturer of agricultural machinery and its products range from iconic John Deere tractors to planters and combines. At the time of company's decision, in March 2022 to pull out Russia, business in the country provided 3 percent of the company's annual sales. While this might look small on the global scale, Deere & Company had significant investments in Russia with a major distribution center in Domodedovo near Moscow, its own production facility in the city of Orenburg, and a leasing company, John Deere Financial, which allowed Russian agro-businesses to lease the Deere & Company machinery directly, bypassing the state-owned Rossagroleasing. Between 2012 and 2022, John Deere Financial financed the leasing of about 5,000 agricultural machines of all types.[18] In May 2022, Deere & Co. went a step further in its willingness to help Ukraine when it remotely disabled $5 million worth of tractors stolen by Russian troops in the occupied city of Melitopol and moved to Chechnya.[19]

The departure of Deere & Company is bound to cause significant damage to Russian agriculture since its agricultural machinery is difficult to replace by locally manufactured ones or imports from China. According to a *Kommersant* report, obtaining spare parts for John Deere and other Western agricultural machinery became an acute problem by the summer 2022. Andrei Neduzhko, head of Step agroholding, complained that Deere & Company spare parts now cost three times as much as before the war. Aleksandr Altynov, the head of the Russian agricultural machinery dealers' association, also pointed out that the problem of spare parts for John Deere machines is most acute and predicted the inevitability in "year and a half to two years" of disassembling existing Deere & Company machinery for necessary spare parts.[20]

Western agricultural machinery constitutes 30–40 percent of entire fleet involved in Russian agriculture, but in some of the major agroholdings this percentage is much higher. For instance, in Rusagro, the agroholding discussed in Chapter 8, Western agricultural machinery constitutes about

85 percent of its fleet. An unnamed Rusagro executive pleaded with the Ministry of Agriculture to allow parallel import of spare parts for these machines through third countries. Yet despite the clear need, Deere & Company dealers in Kazakhstan were reluctant to sell the Russians the necessary spare parts, for fear of being subjected to secondary sanctions.[21]

These two examples show the consequences of war on the Russian agro-industrial complex. The longer the war draws out, the Western sanctions remain in place or even escalate, and Western companies leave the Russian market, the more difficult it would be for the Putin regime to maintain its cherished "food independence."

The War in Ukraine and the Russian Domestic Food Market

After the initial months of the war, a combination of high energy prices and Russian Central Bank's policies helped prevent collapse of the economy and limited the decline of Russia's GDP to an estimated 4–6 percent in 2022, a much better outcome than 10–16 percent in the wake of the invasion. While some sectors of the economy that were crucially dependent on Western components, such as the car industry, experienced sharp decline,[22] the agrarian sector was doing exceptionally well, reporting a production increase in all main food categories.[23] This production increase combined with government policies to stabilize the domestic food market and successfully prevent food supply disruptions, thus allowing Putin to continue his war effort without fear of food riots in the major Russian urban centers.

No less significant was the beginning of deflation, which brought food prices down. Until summer 2022 and the onset of deflation, Russian food prices were rising above the annual inflation rate.[24] Yet once deflation began in summer 2022, food prices began to decline. In July–August 2022, food prices declined by 1.5 percent, with fruits and vegetables leading the way with 11.5 percent. According to Rosstat, the decline of food prices was more significant than in other areas of the economy: the overall price decline was 0.4 percent during this period.[25] While deflation is bad for the economy in general, the decline of food prices is politically important at the time of war. Readily available food and prices below those preceding the invasion thus further lowered the likelihood of public pressure on the government to stop its aggression in Ukraine.

The Invasion of Ukraine and Grain Exports

Decades-long Russian government investment in food production turned the country into a leader in the global grain trade. Putin, as we shall see below, certainly wanted to leverage Russia's major share of the global grain market as tool in support of Russia's war efforts. Yet, as we saw in other areas of economic activities, the Kremlin also certainly underestimated the Western counties' ability to land a serious blow to the Russian economy.

Domestically, the war and subsequent Western sanctions affected the ability of Russian grain producers to export their grain. The 2022 Russian grain harvest was exceptionally good and estimated to be about 152 million tons, including about 101 million tons of wheat, Russia's most important export commodity.[26] In light of such a bountiful harvest, Russia was projected to export a record 50 million tons of grain, including 43.1 million tons of wheat.[27]

In 2021, grain exports brought Russia $11 billion in revenues.[28] With rising wheat prices, the grain export revenues should have been much higher in 2022. Moreover, until August 2022, Russia blockaded Ukrainian ports and effectively prevented Ukrainian grain export. Given that export markets for Ukrainian and Russian grain are similar, one should have expected Russia to benefit from Ukraine's inability to export its grain. Yet in reality, from July through early September 2022, Russia was able to export just about 7 million tons of wheat, which was the lowest figure since the 2017–2018 season and 16 percent lower than the same period in 2021. Figures for exports of all types of grains were even worse: Russia's United Grain Company projected a decline of 47 percent in July–August 2022 in comparison to the previous year.[29] According to the analyst Aleksandra Prokopenko, the inability to export grain directly affected the revenues of the Russia's agroholdings heavily involved in grain production, including Tkachev's Agrocomplex and the Linnik brothers–owned Miratorg, both discussed in Chapter 8.[30]

It is important to remember that are no Western sanctions targeting the export of Russian grain. Instead, Russian officials involved in the grain trade blame high transportation costs, the refusal of international shipping companies such as Maersk, CGM, and Hapag-Lloyd, to enter Russian ports, and the unwillingness of international insurance companies to insure ships and of Western banks to execute the grain-related transactions as the main reasons for the grain export decline. Dmitry Patrushev, the Russian agriculture minister, called these actions by Western insurance and shipping companies "the hidden sanctions."[31] Russia's difficulties in exporting its grain paled, however, in comparison with the deliberate damage it caused to Ukraine's agricultural sector.

Since the beginning of Russia's invasion, the Kremlin used food as a potent weapon of war. Until August 2022, over 20 million tons of Ukrainian grain were held up in the country's Black Sea ports because of a Russian naval blockade, thus denying Ukraine valuable foreign currency income. Moreover, according to the Conflict Observatory, an American NGO that analyzes Russian war crimes in Ukraine, approximately 14.57 percent of Ukraine's estimated 58 million tons of crop storage capacity has been impacted by the conflict.[32] Russia is also actively engaged in stealing Ukrainian grain from the areas it occupied and tries to sell it in the Middle East as its own. According to investigative reporting of the Associated Press and the Public Broadcasting Service (PBS), in 2022 Russia was running a sophisticated smuggling operation "that has used falsified manifests and seaborne subterfuge to steal Ukrainian grain worth at least $530 million—cash that has helped feed President Vladimir Putin's war machine."[33] This is clearly a case of a war crime, one of many Russia committed in Ukraine. On May 19, 2023, the UK announced a new wave of sanctions against Russian companies and individuals connected to the theft of Ukrainian grain in the temporarily occupied territories in Ukraine and its further resale.[34]

Contrary to hydrocarbon-rich Russia, Ukraine's economy is heavily dependent on its agriculture: in 2021, it received $27.8 billion from agricultural exports. This figure accounted for 41 percent of Ukraine's $68 billion in overall exports.[35] The damage to Ukrainian agriculture caused by Russia's invasion is therefore highly impactful on the country's economy as a whole.[36]

Yet the desire to ease Russian grain export which was also hurting, as well as international pressure to prevent global food shortages, forced Russia to sign on July 22, 2022, the Black Sea Grain Initiative agreement, which finally allowed the export of Ukrainian grain.

Russian and Ukrainian Grain as a Global Problem: The Black Sea Grain Initiative Agreement

According to FAO, Egypt, Turkey, Bangladesh, Iran, Lebanon, Tunisia, Yemen, Libya, and Pakistan purchase at least 50 percent of their wheat from Russia and Ukraine.[37] These countries therefore might be expected to provide Russia with important political support during its growing confrontation with the West, or face reduction or even cancellation of their grain import contracts. After all, if Russia can stop gas supplies to the EU countries, it is equally capable of suspending grain deliveries to Turkey, a NATO member state, or to key regional powers such as Egypt or Pakistan.

Indeed, on April 1, 2022, Russia's former president and current deputy chairman of the Security Council, Dmitry Medvedev, explicitly issued such a threat via his Telegram channel, saying that food sales are Russia's powerful weapon and that Russia should use this weapon by supplying food only to "friendly countries" while denying it to the unfriendly ones. On April 24, this warning was reiterated by the Russian state-owned news agency, RIA Novosti. Russia's food weapon, the article argued, is more potent than its missiles, for Russia controls 24 percent of the global market in wheat and nearly 50 percent in sunflower oil. After all, it posited, "one can survive without [mobile] phones and the internet, but not without bread, even if it is baked from totalitarian Russian wheat."[38]

These threats to global food security were taken seriously enough. In addition to weaponizing its own food exports as a tool of geopolitics, Russian actions were also triggering, likely deliberately so, a wider global food crisis by stealing massive amounts of Ukrainian grain and agricultural machinery and preventing the export of Ukrainian grain by blockading its maritime ports. The main destinations of Ukrainian grain exports are Middle Eastern and African countries, and the UN World Food Programme warned on May 6, 2022, that the blockage of Ukrainian grain exports might cause widespread hunger in those already vulnerable regions.

On May 14, 2022, speaking at a meeting of G-7 Foreign Ministers, German foreign minister Annalena Baerbock directly accused Russia of deliberately turning the war against Ukraine into a global "grain war" and cynically using food as "a deliberately chosen instrument in a hybrid war that is being waged right now." Russia's goal, according to Baerbock, is to manufacture a global humanitarian crisis that will pressure the international community to give in to Kremlin's demands. Putin, in the meantime, blamed the potential famine on Western elites who "are ready to sacrifice the rest of the world to maintain their global dominance," thus utilizing food as a propaganda tool.[39]

In this global "grain war," Putin has powerful weapons both as a food provider to the Russian population and as a food denier to the nutritionally vulnerable Global South. For the ultimate outcome of Russia's confrontation with the West, Russia's ability to cause a major hunger crisis in the Global South is as crucial as its military performance on the battlefield in Ukraine.

According to the US Department of Agriculture, Russia's five-year average (2017–2021) share of global wheat trade was 19 percent.[40] By blockading Ukrainian ports and thus preventing Ukrainian export of its wheat (a 10 percent share of global trade based on five-year average), Russia heavily contributed to the meteoric rise of wheat prices in the world market for the short term. Thus, on April 6, 2022, the price of a metric ton of US wheat was $481, an annual increase of 52 percent, while Russian wheat cost $395 per metric ton, which a constituted a 60 percent annual rise.[41] As the economist Paul Krugman observed, from March 2021 to March 2022 the price increases in wheat were much bigger than the surge in oil prices.[42] Moreover, Russia's early restrictions on wheat exports and the inability of Ukraine to export its own wheat were adversely affecting Turkey, Iran, and other Middle East counties that are the main importers of Russian and Ukrainian grain. Many of these countries are Russia's allies but they abstained during the vote on March 2, 2022, UN General Assembly resolution to condemn Russia for its invasion of Ukraine. Rising wheat prices might have played a major role in their decision.

It is also not surprising that Turkey was the main player in initiating the UN-sponsored agreement, the so-called Black Sea Grain Initiative, which allowed Ukraine to resume exporting its grain through the Black Sea ports blockaded by the Russian navy since February 24, 2022, in exchange for removing obstacles to Russian grain exports.[43] The mere announcement of the deal led to the decline of wheat prices on the Chicago Commodities Exchange by 5 percent, thus bringing it back to the early February 2022 levels and assuaging the concerns of countries dependent on grain export.[44] Russia, on its part, hoped that the agreement would lead to the full resumption of its own grain exports.

Starting in early August 2022, ships with Ukrainian grain were regularly leaving Ukrainian ports. By mid-October 2022, Ukraine was able to export 7.7 million tons of grain via its ports on the Black Sea. However, this represents only about 39 percent of grain intended for export. According to the BBC, 20 million tons of grain along with other foodstuffs, such as maize and sunflower oil, were still waiting to be exported.[45] The data published by the Ministry of Agrarian Policy and Food of Ukraine show that from March to November 2022, Ukraine exported an average of 3.5 million metric tons of grains and oilseeds per month, a steep decline from the 5 million to

7 million metric tons per month it exported prior to the February 2022 invasion. Moreover, on October 22, 2022, Russia began systematic attacks on the Ukrainian energy infrastructure that caused significant damage to the country's grain terminals which process loading of wheat and corn into ships.[46]

To remind Ukraine and the world that the Black Sea Grain Initiative cannot guarantee the uninterrupted flow of Ukrainian grain to world markets, Russia heavily bombarded the port of Odesa the day after it signed the agreement. By September 2022, Russia resumed its grain blackmail of Ukraine and the world by threatening to not resume the agreement since its initial 120-day term was due to expire in mid-November 2022. Senior Russian diplomats and ultimately Putin himself threatened to end the agreement unless Western shipping and insurance companies return to the Russian grain markets and allow uninterrupted export of Russian grain and fertilizers.[47] Yet, on November 17, 2022, under heavy pressure from Turkey, one of the main beneficiaries of the Initiative, Russia agreed to extend the agreement for another 120 days without receiving firm guarantees on its own exports of grain and fertilizers. The agreement was renewed on March 19, 2023 and again on May 17, 2023 (only for 60 days) despite Russia's threats not to do so.[48]

Russian Agroholdings at War

Since the 2014 occupation of Crimea, no major Russian business dared to conduct business on the peninsula or in other parts of Ukraine not under control of the legitimate government in Kyiv from fear of Western sanctions. This included major Russian agroholdings. The Russian invasion of Ukraine and Western sanctions changed the situation for many businesses. In the agro-industrial complex, Tkachev's Agrocomplex was the first and so far the only major agroholding that openly decided to expand its business to occupied Ukrainian territory. The fact that the head of the agroholding, Aleksandr Tkachev, was already under Western sanctions since 2014 probably made this expansion easier.

In early June 2022, Russian media announced that Tkachev had acquired one of Crimea's biggest agroholdings, "Friendship of the People." This agroholding controls 49,421 acres of land which are used for meat processing and fruit growing. It also has a retail network of stores through which it sells its food products.[49] In December 2022, it was reported that Agrocomplex seized 400,000 acres of agricultural land in Donbas from three Ukrainian agrobusinesses without any compensation and likely under the threat of violence.[50]

Tkachev's Agrocomplex expansion into Crimea and Donbas might be the first step of Russian agroholdings setting up businesses in the occupied agrarian regions of Ukraine. If Russian agroholdings do indeed expand their businesses into occupied and annexed regions of Ukraine, this would be a clear sign that large agrobusiness dependence on the state is so deep that state orders have a higher priority than sound business practices and fear of sanctions. Expanding into occupied Ukraine will likely lead to Western sanctions not just on specific owners and CEOs but on Russian agroholdings as a whole.

Concluding Remarks

In early October 2022, Russia's minister of agriculture, Dmitry Patrushev, gave an extended interview to the Russian business publication *RBK*. In the interview, Patrushev summed up the state of the Russian agro-industrial complex seven and a half months after start of the war. The picture he painted was rosy. Russia's agro-industrial complex, he claimed, showed itself to be immune to Western sanctions. The food production in January–September 2022 did not decline and even showed a moderate growth. Most of the numerical targets of the 2020 Food Security Doctrine have been achieved; for some indicators, Russian producers even surpassed the targets. The price rises of food staples were contained and food availability was no longer an acute concern. There are no food shortages either. As far as the Russian food exports are concerned, despite the problems of exporting Russian grain, Patrushev projected an increase in revenues from $37.1 billion in 2021 to $40 billion in 2022.

This rosy picture came with an admission that the Russian agro-industrial complex is one of the most subsidized sectors of the economy. Patrushev also asserted that the import substitution policies would continue and even intensify since the West cannot be trusted: "If we endlessly keep our market open, then our dependence [on Western imports] would be permanent. Our Western partners are very inconsistent. Today, they say that they are not imposing sanctions on the food product exports, tomorrow, [the sanctions] will appear and without any warning and we will simply remain with nothing."[51] In short, the war in Patrushev's eyes proved the correctness of the policies of import substitution. The mere possibility of Western sanctions justified further expansion of such policies into the areas (such as seeds) where Russia agro-industrial complex so far was dependent on imports.

Patrushev's rhetoric and bravado were not false. Indeed, nutritional self-sufficiency shielded Russia from severe food disruptions during the early stages of the war and even when the fighting was dragging on for months, it came under increasing strain but did not collapse. The drawbacks of these policies, as well as the full impact of Western sanctions would take much longer to fully manifest themselves. The future of Putin's nutritional self-sufficiency project will ultimately depend on the ability of Russian food producers to fully insulate themselves from global supply chains and overcome the disappearance of traditional trading partners. It will also depend on the Russian state's ability to back up its rhetoric with massive financial support for the agro-industrial complex, or on consumer food subsidies to keep staple foods even minimally affordable.

The willingness of international food giants to remain in Russia and continue their operations in the country would also play an important role, because Russia needs their expertise, global trade networks, and capabilities. Grain is still the key to Russia's domestic food production and the country has it aplenty. Grain is also an easily stored product and thus even if the system eventually unravels, it might take years before serious food shortages appear in the country. The system that Putin built struggled, but at least as of fall 2022, did survive its ultimate test and fulfill its original purpose.

10
Conclusion

Food availability and affordability is an important factor in the politics of democratic and authoritarian states alike. Empty shelves or high prices of basic food items could trigger various forms of political protest, from peaceful demonstrations to riots to revolutionary uprisings.[1] Therefore, all regime types want to prevent contentious collective action driven by food shortages or high prices. While the problem of food availability and affordability is common regardless of regime type, the ways democratic and authoritarian regimes cope with this problem do differ. The repertoire of authoritarian state responses to crises caused by high food prices or food unavailability have historically included widespread use of repression, curtailment of food exports, expansion of food imports, and encouragement of local producers to increase production for the domestic market.

Whereas many developing countries adopted policies of industrial import substitution in the 1950s and 1960s,[2] coordinated state programs of agrarian import substitution were virtually unheard of until Putin launched one in the early 2000s. This drive proceeded in phases starting with attainment of self-sufficiency in grains, especially wheat, and ending with radical import substitution policies, dubbed "countersanctions," enacted in response to Western sanctions imposed in the wake of Russia's 2014 annexation of Crimea. These countersanctions, still in force at the time of writing (May 2023), banned the import of Western food products whose estimated value was $9.1 billion in 2014. The banned products constituted 21 percent of Russia's imported food at the time. The domestic food industry was encouraged through subsidies to replace the imported items with domestically produced ones. This was not only a radical policy choice but also a bold social experiment that tested the willingness of urban Russians who, since the collapse of communism, got used to a great variety of affordable imported food and to accepting higher prices, lower food quality, and more limited choices of the domestic food they had to increasingly consume.

Putin's drive for agrarian import substitution also coincided with the transformation of his regime. In the early 2000s, Putin's Russia was a competitive

Bread and Autocracy. Janetta Azarieva, Yitzhak M. Brudny, and Eugene Finkel, Oxford University Press.
© Oxford University Press 2023. DOI: 10.1093/oso/9780197684368.003.0011

autocracy, a hybrid regime in which meaningful democratic institutions and serious incumbent abuse of power coexist, and in which electoral competition is real even if unfair.[3] By 2022, competitive autocracy had been replaced with domestically repressive and externally aggressive full-blown personal dictatorship. This is not merely a coincidence. Barrington Moore in his classic *Social Origins of Dictatorship and Democracy* demonstrated a connection between regime type and the kind of agriculture developed in democratic and non-democratic states. Alexander Gerschenkron in his now largely forgotten *Society and Democracy in Germany* argued that a particular kind of agriculture and the social forces it represented—big grain-producing estates in East Prussia and the agrarian elites who controlled them, the Junkers—generated political outcomes that were highly adversarial to democracy.[4]

These classic studies on the connection between autocracy and food policy led us to explore the linkage between a nutritional independence drive, the nature of Russia's authoritarian regime, and the consequences of such policies for regime survival. In this book we focus on policies the Putin's regime designed and implemented in the years 2000–2022, policies that sought to achieve Russia's independence from Western food imports. As we argue, food availability and affordability can be crucial for authoritarian regimes' legitimacy and survival. The 2011 riots in Egypt and Tunisia that followed the sharp increases in bread prices led to regime collapse in both countries. Putin's regime in Russia was able to withstand the challenge of war in Ukraine in no small part by ensuring a so far uninterrupted food supply and combating sharp price increases.

The prevailing literature on authoritarian regimes emphasizes institutions, leaders, and political survival strategies. Policies of food provision as legitimation or regime survival strategies are largely outside the scope of most key analyses of autocracy.[5] Even the studies of authoritarianism in the Middle East, where food riots occurred frequently and were a trigger of the Arab Spring, also rarely incorporate the food factor into their explanations. As Eva Bellin points out, scholars of authoritarian regimes in the Middle East tend to explain the persistence of the region's authoritarianism by "weakness of civil society; the deliberate manipulation and division of opposition forces; the cooptation of social forces through the distribution of rent, cronyism, and stunted economic liberalization . . . and the effective manipulation of political institutions such as parties and electoral laws." To this list she adds "an exceptionally muscular coercive apparatus endowed with both the capacity and will to repress democratic initiatives originating from society." Even studies of the Arab Spring in Egypt typically refer to food as a source of corruption, a venue of state subsidies, and a mere trigger of protests, rather than a significant policy area and a key driver of political developments.[6]

Understanding Russia through Food

Focusing on food is also important for better understanding Putin's Russia. Food, as we showed, is vital for comprehending the regime's policymaking and survival strategy. The existing treatments of Putin and his regime offer conflicting, often diametrically opposed perspectives. According to a view popular among many Western Kremlinologists, politicians, and security experts, Putin is a grand strategist who plays a long game, has a well-defined master plan, predicts several moves, and skillfully and meticulously manipulates domestic and global affairs.[7] An opposing view is that of Putin "the *adhocrat*," an opportunistic, swift, but reactive and not always coherent tactician who does not have a grand vision but exploits his opponents' mistakes.[8] In fact, we argue, Putin is neither, or, rather, a combination of both perspectives. Not a grandmaster of multidimensional chess, Putin is nevertheless too strategic and consistent for an incoherent and improvising adhocrat.

Food-centered import substitution as a key pillar of regime stability and national security was almost certainly not part of his original master plan or long-term vision; it was an initiative that first emerged from the bowels of agricultural bureaucracy. Nevertheless, making a country of Russia's size (and history) self-sufficient in grain, and, increasingly, other food products was impossible without a clear strategic vision, long time horizons, and commitment that do not fit the view of Putin as an adhocrat.

Several accounts present Putin as an omnipotent master of Russia, the "new Tsar" who controls everything and faces no obstacles internally.[9] On the opposite side are those who view Putin as a "weak strongman," more a product of Russians' desires and beliefs than their shaper.[10] Our analysis of Putin's food policies suggests a middle road. The idea of nutritional autarky originated outside of Putin's inner circle; the president was neither the mastermind nor the original chief promoter of the strategy. But at the same time, the transformation of the country's agriculture could not have been achieved without Putin's approval, active support, and ability to shape policies in even the most far-flung parts of Russia.

Furthermore, the president's actions during the 2020–2021 food crisis demonstrated both his weakness and strength. Putin the "weak strongman" clearly fears the popular discontent that food shortages might spark. At the same time, the ease with which he browbeat entire industries into submission signals his unequaled power. As Brian Taylor argues, Putin and his closest allies share several central beliefs: statism, conservatism, and anti-Westernism.[11] We move beyond these and focus on the elite's primal fear of food shortages and the conviction that food is crucial for national security and regime survival.

Other key studies try to understand Russia through the lens of formal and informal institutions, primarily the presidency,[12] markets, governance, and corruption.[13] All these explanations are important and yet are not sufficient to fully explain the nature of Putin's hold on power and political survival. We believe that a lot can be learned about Russian politics by focusing on specific policies and industries other than natural resources.[14]

Our research suggests that authoritarianism in general, and Putin's autocracy in particular, cannot be explained by just focusing on policies and practices of repression and cooptation, propaganda, political institutions, or natural resources management. Two decades of deliberate policies aimed at securing domestic food supply at reasonable prices transformed Russia politics and economics. Food production became an issue of national security, and national security considerations became paramount, overriding the economic ones. Recent scholarship that centers on popular support for Russia's autocracy by highlighting topics such as nostalgia, values, and psychological needs[15] or the middle class's dependency on the state[16] would also benefit from paying attention to fears, expectations, and uncertainties related to "bread and butter" issues, the availability and affordability of food. In Putin's Russia, having food on the table and in stores strengthens the trust in the government and allows the public to move beyond the worst aspects of Soviet life and focus instead on continuities such as great power status and security.

Food policies are also an increasingly important topic for those interested in security issues and agencies. As Putin's regime began to be increasingly dominated by the security apparatus, food supply and provision also became a part of security services portfolio. In 2010, the regime's drive to achieve independence from food imports was elevated to the status of official doctrine. Subsequent documents, including the 2020 Food Security Doctrine, further entrenched securitization of the food production industry and making the goal of food independence as an important ideological tenet of the regime.[17]

The May 2018 appointment of Dmitry Patrushev, son of the powerful head of the National Security Council Nikolai Patrushev, as the minister of agriculture sealed the *siloviki* control of agro-industrial policymaking and also transferred the ministry's resources to the hands of the security apparatus.

It is reasonable to ask whether the securitization of the nutritional independence drive and especially the 2014 countersanctions were enacted with the forthcoming war with Ukraine in mind. While we still do not know when the decision to invade Ukraine was taken, it is clear that Russia's security services saw a confrontation with the West as inevitable and sought to achieve Russia's independence from food imports originating in hostile countries. Viewed from this vantage point, Putin's import substitution drive and its radical escalation in the wake of Crimea's annexation and the war in the Donbas makes perfect sense.

Putin's policies also reshaped the Russian agro-industrial complex, now dominated by giant agroholdings that control most of the country's food production. These agroholdings fulfill the role assigned to them by the regime, namely by guaranteeing an uninterrupted supply of food to the major urban centers. At the same time, they are dependent on the state for generous loans and subsidies while being protected from external competition by the countersanctions and other protectionist measures.

While the Kremlin and the agroholdings are dependent on each other, it is clear that the government is the dominant actor in these relations. During the COVID-19 pandemic and the war in Ukraine, the state showed great willingness to intervene in food production and forced producers to scale down price increases by threatening judicial persecution, publicly shaming producers and reminding the business how much of its success is owed to the state. We view this form of economic relations as "command capitalism." This form of economic relations between the state and the business is one of Putin regime's most important features. With the war in Ukraine dragging on and forcing transformation of the Russian economy into a war economy, this command capitalism has become the dominant feature of the Russian economy as a whole. In this war economy, food production is playing a key role and is therefore even more tightly controlled by the state.

Putin's two-decade-long policies aimed at ending dependency on food imports also had important international dimensions. From 2000 to 2008, Russia gradually ended its dependence on grain imports. Yet the food independence agenda inadvertently catapulted the country to a leading position in the global market. By 2018, Russia had become the dominant player in the world grain market, controlling about a quarter of the world's wheat market. During the war in Ukraine, Russia began weaponizing its own food exports as a tool of geopolitics, threatening hunger and a humanitarian crisis in Asia and Africa. In Putin's arsenal of weapons employed against what he calls "the global West" to force it to abandon its support for Ukraine, the use of food will in the long run be more important than his use of oil and gas.

Outlook for the Future

The COVID-19 pandemic and Russia's war on Ukraine tested the success of Putin's food independence project. The results, we show, are thus far mixed. As of now, the Kremlin has good reasons to view its focus on nutritional independence as a tool of regime survival as a success. Even a combination of monumental crises—a global pandemic, large-scale war, and an open confrontation with the West—have not led to Soviet-era empty shelves, breadlines, and chronic food shortages, thus vindicating the investment in nutritional self-sufficiency. In the major Russian cities, supermarket shelves are full of food staples whose prices are still quite affordable despite a decline in incomes caused by the war. There were no food riots in the first fifteen months of the war. Moreover, the ability to feed Russia as the war rages on strengthened the regime's will to expand its import substitution into those areas of food production—such as seeds—which until then relied on Western imports. The readiness of the population in the major cities to accept shrinkage food choices only encourages the regime to continue its relentless drive for food independence. In short, Putin's Russia managed to neutralize the threats that had destroyed both the Romanov Empire and the USSR.

However, due to the system's inherent weaknesses such as limited competition, inefficiency, and heavy state intervention, the regime, all its desires notwithstanding, simply cannot completely isolate Russians from trends of the global food market and subsequently from food price increases caused by the pandemic and energy price rises. As long as the Kremlin is able to ensure plentiful domestic food supply and keep the most basic food staples, first and foremost bread, minimally affordable, either thanks to price controls or subsidies, Putin should not fear a repeat of the 1917 food riots or the 1962 Novocherkassk-type demonstrations that required violent use of force to suppress, or a collapse of popular support as occurred in the early 1990s. However, if the drive toward complete autarky continues long enough to either impede domestic production or make staple foods unaffordable, the regime would be in severe danger. Excessive mobilization, a war necessity, can definitely impede food production and thus threaten regime survival.

Another challenge that Russian food production will have to contend with is climate change. The more optimistic outlook suggests that Russia might benefit from climate change as previously unsuitable areas, especially at higher latitudes, will increasingly open up to farming production because of rising temperatures.[18] Yet the effects of climate change, such as droughts, excessive rains, or floods, are also bound to negatively affects the country's current key agricultural regions, located mostly in southern Russia.[19] Even more important, writes Gustafson, "most players in the [Russian] food sector do not yet believe climate change is real."[20] This lack of proper attention, coupled with the shift of government's attention and resources to the war in Ukraine will severely limit Russia's ability to adapt to the changing climate. Thus, on balance, the negative effects of climate change on Russia's food production will substantially outweigh any potential benefits and the "world of climate change will be highly unfavorable inside Russia."[21]

Taken together, the system's inherent inefficiencies and the effects of climate change thus pose a grave danger to Putin's food independence system. Writing about earlier empires, Scott Nelson asserted that "empires survive only as long as they control the sources of food needed to feed soldiers and citizens."[22] The war in Ukraine is certainly Putin's attempt at empire restoration. Nelson's statement is therefore quite relevant to the future of Putin's Russia and his imperial ambitions. In 2014, Vyacheslav Volodin, one of Putin's key officials, famously stated "No Putin, no Russia." As we argue, "no food, no Putin."

Finally, it is reasonable to ask whether other authoritarian regimes see the Russian model of food independence as something worth imitating. The answer to this question is definitely yes. China's Xi Jinping is clearly following in Putin's footsteps. If in prior decades China heavily relied on food imports, especially from the United States, and on purchasing food-producing companies abroad as a way to feed its population, in recent years the Xi-led regime began to follow Putin's path of equating food security with national security.

As in Russia, China's current conception of food security prioritizes domestic food production with the goal of maintaining self-sufficiency in grain production (95 percent) and reaching self-sufficiency in seed production, a clear lesson drawn from Russia's dependency on imported seeds. If the People's Republic of China considers the invasion of Taiwan a realistic possibility, Beijing must also understand that this would undoubtedly trigger a major confrontation with the West, especially the United States. Thus, imitating Putin's food independence policies is a reasonable policy choice. In short, Putin's model of nutritional independence is now also being adopted by the world's most important authoritarian regime. Other authoritarian leaders will no doubt take notice.[23] Policymakers and scholars in the West thus should also view food for what it is: political power.

Notes

Introduction: Russia's Nutritional Autocracy

1. "Valdai Discussion Club Meeting" (President of Russia, October 21, 2021), http://en.kremlin.ru/events/president/news/66975.
2. Andrei Kolesnikov, "Zernopoddanicheskie nastroeniia," Kommersant, May 21, 2020, https://www.kommersant.ru/doc/4349683.
3. Michael Bieseker, Sarah El Deeb, and Beatrice Dupuy, "Russia Smuggling Ukrainian Grain to Help Pay for Putin's War," AP News, October 3, 2022, https://apnews.com/article/russia-ukraine-putin-business-lebanon-syria-87c3b6fea3f4c326003123b21aa78099.
4. Sergei Savchuk, "Protiv Zapada u Rossii est' oruzhie namnogo strashnee raket," RIA Novosti, April 22, 2022, https://ria.ru/20220422/eda-1784835298.html.
5. Andrea Palasciano, "Putin Urges Food Price Cap as Russian Economy Falters," Moscow Times, December 16, 2020, https://www.themoscowtimes.com/2020/12/16/putin-urges-food-price-cap-as-russian-economy-falters-a72378.
6. "Food Security," Policy Brief (Food and Agriculture Organization, June 1996), http://www.fao.org/fileadmin/templates/faoitaly/documents/pdf/pdf_Food_Security_Cocept_Note.pdf; Robert Paarlberg, Food Politics: What Everyone Needs to Know (New York: Oxford University Press, 2013).
7. Mark Bittman, Animal, Vegetable, Junk: A History of Food, from Sustainable to Suicidal (New York: Houghton Mifflin Harcourt, 2021).
8. Ceylan Yeginsu, "'It's Very Scary': U.K. Food Banks Close as Coronavirus Stalls Donations," New York Times, March 19, 2020, https://www.nytimes.com/2020/03/19/world/europe/coronavirus-uk-food-banks.html; Kenneth Rosen, "Stoking Unrest and Distributing Groceries: Italy's Mafias Gain Ground in Fight for Loyalty during Pandemic Lockdown," Newsweek, April 18, 2020, https://www.newsweek.com/italy-mafias-coronavirus-pandemic-support-1498726; Manny Fernandez, "Coronavirus and Poverty: A Mother Skips Meals so Her Children Can Eat," New York Times, March 20, 2020, https://www.nytimes.com/2020/03/20/us/coronavirus-poverty-school-lunch.html.
9. Andrew E. Kramer, "Thanks to Sanctions, Russia Is Cushioned From Virus's Economic Shocks," New York Times, March 20, 2020, https://www.nytimes.com/2020/03/20/world/europe/russia-coronavirus-covid-19.html.
10. Tom Standage, An Edible History of Humanity (New York: Bloomsbury, 2009), 32.
11. James Suzman, Work: A Deep History, from the Stone Age to the Age of Robots (New York: Penguin, 2021), 276.

12. Jean-Jacques Rousseau, Of the Social Contract and Other Political Writings, ed. Christopher Bertram (London: Penguin, 2012), 195.
13. Standage, *An Edible History of Humanity*, 145.
14. Alexander Gerschenkron, Bread and Democracy in Germany (Berkeley: University of California Press, 1943).
15. Barrington Moore, Social Origins of Dictatorship and Democracy: Lord and Peasant in the Making of the Modern World (Boston: Beacon Press, 1966).
16. Amartya Sen, Poverty and Famines: An Essay on Entitlement and Deprivation (Oxford: Oxford University Press, 1982).
17. Robert H. Bates, Markets and States in Tropical Africa (Berkeley: University of California Press, 1981); Henry Thomson, "Food and Power: Agricultural Policy under Democracy and Dictatorship," Comparative Politics 49, no. 2 (2017): 273–96; Jan H. Pierskalla, "The Politics of Urban Bias: Rural Threats and the Dual Dilemma of Political Survival," Studies in Comparative International Development 51, no. 3 (2016): 286–307.
18. Standage, *An Edible History of Humanity*, 193.
19. "How Is Poverty Measured?" (The Institute for Research on Poverty [IRP], University of Wisconsin), accessed July 21, 2021, https://www.irp.wisc.edu/resources/how-is-poverty-measured.
20. Rami Zurayk, "Global Views of Local Food Systems: Civil War and the Devastation of Syria's Food System," Journal of Agriculture, Food Systems, and Community Development 3, no. 2 (2013): 7–9.
21. Christopher B. Barrett, "Food or Consequences: Food Security and Its Implications for Global Sociopolitical Stability," in Food Security and Sociopolitical Stability, ed. Christopher B Barrett (Oxford: Oxford University Press, 2013), 4.
22. Marco Lagi, Karla Z. Bertrand, and Yaneer Bar-Yam, "The Food Crises and Political Instability in North Africa and the Middle East," 2011, doi: 10.2139/ssrn.1910031.
23. Marc F. Bellemare, "Rising Food Prices, Food Price Volatility, and Social Unrest," American Journal of Agricultural Economics 97, no. 1 (2015): 1–21; Cullen S. Hendrix and Stephan Haggard, "Global Food Prices, Regime Type, and Urban Unrest in the Developing World," Journal of Peace Research 52, no. 2 (2015): 143–57; Edward Newman, "Hungry, or Hungry for Change? Food Riots and Political Conflict, 2005–2015," Studies in Conflict & Terrorism 43, no. 4 (2020): 300–24.
24. Anzhelina Rogozhina, "'Chtoby tsena khleba vsegda v moikh rukakh byla': Ekaterina II i formirovanie khlebozapasnoi sistemy v Rossii," Vestnik arkhivista, no. 1 (2020): 131–35.
25. Lars T. Lih, Bread and Authority in Russia, 1914–1921 (Berkeley: University of California Press, 1990).
26. Sheila Fitzpatrick, Stalin's Peasants: Resistance and Survival in the Russian Village after Collectivization (New York: Oxford University Press, 1996); Nancy Qian, Andrei Markevich, and Natalya Naumenko, "The Political-Economic Causes of the Soviet Great Famine, 1932–33," National Bureau of Economic Research Working Paper 29089 (Cambridge, MA: NBER, 2021).

27. Chris Miller, Putinomics: Power and Money in Resurgent Russia (Chapel Hill: University of North Carolina Press, 2018), 3.
28. Jennifer Gandhi and Ellen Lust-Okar, "Elections under Authoritarianism," Annual Review of Political Science 12 (2009): 403–22; Natasha M. Ezrow and Erica Frantz, Dictators and Dictatorships: Understanding Authoritarian Regimes and Their Leaders (New York: Bloomsbury Publishing, 2011); Barbara Geddes et al., How Dictatorships Work: Power, Personalization, and Collapse (Cambridge: Cambridge University Press, 2018); Milan W. Svolik, The Politics of Authoritarian Rule (Cambridge: Cambridge University Press, 2012).
29. Daron Acemoglu and James A. Robinson, Economic Origins of Dictatorship and Democracy (Cambridge: Cambridge University Press, 2006); Carles Boix, Democracy and Redistribution (Cambridge: Cambridge University Press, 2003); Steven Levitsky and Lucan A. Way, Competitive Authoritarianism: Hybrid Regimes after the Cold War (Cambridge: Cambridge University Press, 2010); Jason Brownlee, Authoritarianism in an Age of Democratization (Cambridge: Cambridge University Press, 2007).
30. Jeremy Wallace, Cities and Stability: Urbanization, Redistribution, and Regime Survival in China (New York: Oxford University Press, 2014).
31. Henry Thomson, Food and Power: Regime Type, Agricultural Policy, and Political Stability (New York: Cambridge University Press, 2019).
32. Natalia Mamonova, "Understanding the Silent Majority in Authoritarian Populism: What Can We Learn from Popular Support for Putin in Rural Russia?," Journal of Peasant Studies 46, no. 3 (2019): 570.
33. Henry J. Bruton, "A Reconsideration of Import Substitution," Journal of Economic Literature 36, no. 2 (1998): 903–36.
34. Miller, Putinomics; Brian D. Taylor, The Code of Putinism (New York: Oxford University Press, 2018).
35. Jessica Allina-Pisano, The Post-Soviet Potemkin Village: Politics and Property Rights in the Black Earth (New York: Cambridge University Press, 2008); Stephen K. Wegren, Agriculture and the State in Soviet and Post-Soviet Russia (Pittsburgh: University of Pittsburgh Press, 1998); Stephen K. Wegren, Russia's Food Revolution: The Transformation of the Food System (London: Routledge, 2020); Susanne A. Wengle, "The New Plenty; Why Are Some Post-Soviet Farms Thriving?," Governance 33, no. 4 (2020): 915–33.
36. Aldo Musacchio and Sergio G. Lazzarini, Reinventing State Capitalism: Leviathan in Business, Brazil and Beyond (Cambridge, MA: Harvard University Press, 2014), 2.
37. Anders Åslund, Russia's Crony Capitalism: The Path from Market Economy to Kleptocracy (New Haven, CT: Yale University Press, 2019); Timothy Frye, Weak Strongman: The Limits of Power in Putin's Russia (Princeton, NJ: Princeton University Press, 2021), 18.
38. Jennifer Clapp, "Food Self-Sufficiency: Making Sense of It, and When It Makes Sense," Food Policy 66 (2017): 88–96.
39. "Ob obespechenii prodovol'stvennoi bezopasnosti Rossiĭskoi Federatsii" (Sovet Bezopasnosti RF, December 4, 2009), http://www.scrf.gov.ru/council/session/2045.

40. Frye, *Weak Strongman*, 109.
41. Mark Galeotti, We Need to Talk about Putin: How the West Gets Him Wrong (London: Random House, 2019).
42. Bryn Rosenfeld, "Reevaluating the Middle-Class Protest Paradigm: A Case-Control Study of Democratic Protest Coalitions in Russia," American Political Science Review 111, no. 4 (2017): 637–52; Samuel A. Greene and Graeme B. Robertson, Putin v. the People (London: Yale University Press, 2019); Miller, *Putinomics*.
43. Wegren, *Agriculture and the State in Soviet and Post-Soviet Russia*; Stephen K. Wegren, Land Reform in Russia: Institutional Design and Behavioral Responses (New Haven, CT: Yale University Press, 2009); Wegren, *Russia's Food Revolution*; Grigory Ioffe, Tatyana Nefedova, and Ilya Zaslavsky, The End of Peasantry? The Disintegration of Rural Russia (Pittsburgh: University of Pittsburgh Press, 2006); Susanne A. Wengle, Black Earth, White Bread: A Technopolitical History of Russian Agriculture and Food (Madison: University of Wisconsin Press, 2022); Natalya Shagaida and Vasilii Uzun, "Tendentsii razvitiia i osnovnye vyzovy agrarnogo sektora Rossii" (RANKhiGS, 2017), https://papers.ssrn.com/sol3/papers.cfm?abstract_id=3090839; Natalya Shagaida and Vasilii Uzun, "Draivery rosta i strukturnykh sdvigov v sel'skom khoziaistve Rossii" (Moscow, 2019), https://papers.ssrn.com/sol3/papers.cfm?abstract_id=3337794.

Chapter 1

1. Norman Stone, *The Eastern Front 1914–1917* (London: Penguin, 2008).
2. Lars T. Lih, *Bread and Authority in Russia, 1914–1921* (Berkeley: University of California Press, 1990), 8–9.
3. Zhores A. Medvedev, *Soviet Agriculture* (New York: W. W. Norton, 1987), 18.
4. Lih, *Bread and Authority in Russia*, 1, 8–9.
5. St. Petersburg was renamed Petrograd in August 1914. In 1924 the city's name was changed to Leningrad. In September 1991 the original name was returned.
6. Scott Reynolds Nelson, *Oceans of Grain: How American Wheat Remade the World* (New York: Basic Books, 2022), 255; Barbara Alpern Engel, "Not by Bread Alone: Subsistence Riots in Russia during World War I," *Journal of Modern History* 69, no. 4 (1997): 697–98.
7. Engel, "Not by Bread Alone," 717.
8. Lih, *Bread and Authority in Russia*.
9. Medvedev, *Soviet Agriculture*, 23.
10. Lih, *Bread and Authority in Russia*, chaps. 3, 5.
11. Melissa L. Caldwell, *Not by Bread Alone: Social Support in the New Russia* (Berkeley: University of California Press, 2004), 9–10.
12. Caldwell, *Not by Bread Alone*, 9–10.
13. Medvedev, *Soviet Agriculture*, 32; Lih, *Bread and Authority in Russia*, 126, 130, 133; Douglas Smith, *The Russian Job: The Forgotten Story of How America Saved the Soviet Union from Famine* (New York: Farrar, Straus & Giroux, 2019), 12.

14. Anne Applebaum, *Red Famine: Stalin's War on Ukraine* (New York: Doubleday, 2017).
15. Medvedev, *Soviet Agriculture*, 37–39.
16. Smith, *The Russian Job*, 16.
17. Applebaum, *Red Famine*.
18. Smith, *The Russian Job*, 36.
19. Sheila Fitzpatrick, *Stalin's Peasants*: Resistance and Survival in the Russian Village after Collectivization (New York: Oxford University Press, 1996), 4.
20. Fitzpatrick, *Stalin's Peasants*, 38–39.
21. Lynne Viola, *Peasant Rebels under Stalin: Collectivization and the Culture of Peasant Resistance* (New York: Oxford University Press, 1999).
22. Grigory Ioffe, Tatyana Nefedova, and Ilya Zaslavsky, *The End of Peasantry? The Disintegration of Rural Russia* (Pittsburgh: University of Pittsburgh Press, 2006), 23.
23. Fitzpatrick, *Stalin's Peasants*, 5.
24. Applebaum, *Red Famine*; Sarah Cameron, *The Hungry Steppe: Famine, Violence, and the Making of Soviet Kazakhstan* (Ithaca, NY: Cornell University Press, 2018); Natalya Naumenko, "The Political Economy of Famine: The Ukrainian Famine of 1933," *Journal of Economic History* 81, no. 1 (2021): 156–97.
25. Lesley A. Rimmel, "Another Kind of Fear: The Kirov Murder and the End of Bread Rationing in Leningrad," *Slavic Review* 56, no. 3 (1997): 481–99.
26. Donald Filtzer, "Starvation Mortality in Soviet Home-Front Industrial Regions during World War II," in *Hunger and War: Food Supply in the Soviet Union during the Second World War*, ed. Wendy Goldman and Donald Filtzer (Bloomington: Indiana University Press, 2015), 270.
27. Wendy Goldman, "Not by Bread Alone: Food, Workers, and the State," in *Hunger and War: Food Supply in the Soviet Union during the Second World War*, ed. Wendy Goldman and Donald Filtzer (Bloomington: Indiana University Press, 2015), 45.
28. Medvedev, *Soviet Agriculture*, 139.
29. Stephen K. Wegren, *Agriculture and the State in Soviet and Post-Soviet Russia* (Pittsburgh: University of Pittsburgh Press, 1998), 36–37.
30. Wegren, *Agriculture and the State in Soviet and Post-Soviet Russia*, 37.
31. William Taubman, *Khrushchev: The Man and His Era* (New York: W. W. Norton, 2003), 364–65.
32. Taubman, *Khrushchev*, 372–74.
33. Taubman, *Khrushchev*, 305.
34. Daniel Kahneman and Amos Tversky, "Prospect Theory: An Analysis of Decision under Risk," in *Handbook of the Fundamentals of Financial Decision Making: Part I*, ed. Leonard C. MacLean and William T. Ziemba (Hackensack, NJ: World Scientific, 2013), 99–127.
35. Robert Hornsby, *Protest, Reform and Repression in Khrushchev's Soviet Union* (Cambridge: Cambridge University Press, 2013), chap. 6.
36. According to a different version, the suggestion was to eat pasties with cabbage.
37. Outside of the USSR, especially in Poland, food price increases were also catalysts of workers strikes and occasional riots. See Archie Brown, *The Rise and Fall of Communism* (London: Random House, 2009), chap. 21.

38. Samuel H. Baron, *Bloody Saturday in the Soviet Union: Novocherkassk, 1962* (Stanford, CA: Stanford University Press, 2001); Tat'iana Bocharova, *Novocherkassk. Krovavyi Polden'* (Rostov-on-Don: Izdatel'stvo Rostovskogo Universiteta, 2002).
39. Aleksandr Solzhenitsyn, *The Gulag Archipelago, 1918–56: An Experiment in Literary Investigation*, vol. 3 (New York: Harper & Row, 1974), 507.
40. Evgenia Serova, Authors' Interview, January 29, 2021.
41. Taubman, *Khrushchev*, 606–7; Medvedev, *Soviet Agriculture*, 191–97.
42. Taubman, *Khrushchev*, 4–5.
43. Linda J. Cook, *The Soviet Social Contract and Why It Failed: Welfare Policy and Workers' Politics from Brezhnev to Yeltsin* (Cambridge, MA: Harvard University Press, 1993); Stephen White, "Economic Performance and Communist Legitimacy," *World Politics: A Quarterly Journal of International Relations* 38, no. 3 (1986): 462–82.
44. Linda J. Cook and Martin K. Dimitrov, "The Social Contract Revisited: Evidence from Communist and State Capitalist Economies," *Europe-Asia Studies* 69, no. 1 (2017): 10.
45. Iurii Zhukov, "Zapiska Iu. Zhukova na imia A. Aleksandrova s prilozheniem podborki pisem," November 20, 1972, 80-1-331, RGANI.
46. Cook, *The Soviet Social Contract and Why It Failed*, 40–41.
47. Cook, *The Soviet Social Contract and Why It Failed*, 43.
48. Medvedev, *Soviet Agriculture*, 210.
49. Medvedev, *Soviet Agriculture*, 210, 386, 391.
50. Anatolii Chernyaev, "Diary," January 6, 1976, National Security Archive, https://nsarchive.gwu.edu/rus/text_files/Chernyaev/1976.pdf.
51. Philip Hanson, *The Rise and Fall of the Soviet Economy: An Economic History of the USSR 1945–1991* (London: Routledge, 2014), 150.
52. Carol S. Leonard, *Agrarian Reform in Russia: The Road from Serfdom* (Cambridge: Cambridge University Press, 2010), 79.
53. CIA, "Overview of an Intelligence Assessment Prepared in the Central Intelligence Agency," in *Foreign Relations of the United States. 1977–1980. Soviet Union*, ed. Melissa Jane Taylor, vol. VI (Washington, DC: Department of State, 2013), 723–25.
54. Walter Mondale, "Memorandum from Vice President Mondale to President Carter, 01/03/1980," in *Foreign Relations of the United States. 1977–1980. Soviet Union*, ed. Melissa Jane Taylor, vol. VI (Washington, DC: Department of State, 2013), 730–31.
55. Anatolii Chernyaev, "Diary," January 28, 1980, National Security Archive, https://nsarchive.gwu.edu/rus/text_files/Chernyaev/1980.pdf.
56. Leon Aron, *Yeltsin: A Revolutionary Life* (New York: HarperCollins, 2000), 101.
57. Georgy Arbatov, "K voprosu ob otmene amerikanskim pravitel'stvom embargo na postavki zerna v SSSR," June 3, 1981, 80/1/225, RGANI.
58. Hanson, *The Rise and Fall of the Soviet Economy*, 149–51.
59. Anton F. Malish, "Soviet Agricultural Policy in the 1980s," *Review of Policy Research* 4, no. 2 (1984): 301–10.
60. David Gale Johnson and Karen McConnell Brooks, *Prospects for Soviet Agriculture in the 1980s* (Bloomington: Indiana University Press, 1983), 92.
61. Leonard, *Agrarian Reform in Russia*, 79.

62. William Taubman, *Gorbachev: His Life and Times* (New York: Simon & Schuster, 2017), 238.
63. Peter Hauslohner, "Gorbachev's Social Contract," *Soviet Economy* 3, no. 1 (1987): 66; Taubman, *Gorbachev*, 236.
64. Wegren, *Agriculture and the State in Soviet and Post-Soviet Russia*, 44.
65. Anatolii Chernyaev, "Diary," November 12, 1987, National Security Archive, https://nsarchive.gwu.edu/rus/text_files/Chernyaev/1987.pdf.
66. Iurii Pominov, *Khronika smutnogo vremeni: Zapiski redaktora* (Pavlodar: Eko, 2007), http://ypominov.ru/books/7/.
67. Anatolii Chernyaev, "Diary," May 28, 1989, National Security Archive, http://www2.gwu.edu/~nsarchiv/rus/text_files/Chernyaev/1989.pdf.
68. Taubman, *Gorbachev*, 242; Aron, *Yeltsin*, 151.
69. Aron, *Yeltsin*, 325–29.
70. Taubman, *Gorbachev*, 373, 435.
71. Aron, *Yeltsin*, 397.
72. Taubman, *Gorbachev*, 503.
73. Wegren, *Land Reform in Russia*, 34.
74. Cook, *The Soviet Social Contract and Why It Failed*, 140.
75. Anatolii Chernyaev, "Diary," 1991, National Security Archive, https://nsarchive.gwu.edu/rus/text_files/Chernyaev/1991.pdf.
76. "Talony i otavarka: kak tyumentsy dobyvali propitanie v nachale 1990kh," Tyumen Online, October 3, 2020, https://72.ru/text/gorod/2020/10/03/69479411/.
77. William Liefert, "Distribution Problems in the Food Economy of the Former Soviet Union," in *The Former Soviet Union in Transition*, ed. Richard F. Kaufman and John P. Hardt (Armonk: M. E. Sharpe, 1993), 495.
78. Ioffe, Nefedova, and Zaslavsky, *The End of Peasantry?*, 20–21.

Chapter 2

1. Yegor Gaidar and Anatoly Chubais, *Razvilki noveishei istorii Rossii* (Moscow: OGI, 2011), 53–54.
2. Vladimir Putin et al., *First Person: An Astonishingly Frank Self-Portrait by Russia's President Vladimir Putin* (New York: Public Affairs, 2000), 87.
3. Yegor Gaidar, *Dni porazhenii i pobed* (Moscow: Vagrius, 1996), 88, 133–34, 139.
4. Stephen Handelman, *Comrade Criminal: Russia's New Mafiya* (New Haven, CT: Yale University Press, 1995), 60.
5. Gaidar, *Dni porazhenii i pobed*, 88.
6. William M. Liefert, "The Food Problem in the Republics of the Former USSR," in *The "Farmer Threat": The Political Economy of Agrarian Reform in Post-Soviet Russia*, ed. Don Van Atta (Boulder, CO: Westview Press, 1993), 27; Stephen K. Wegren, *Agriculture and the State in Soviet and Post-Soviet Russia* (Pittsburgh: University of Pittsburgh Press, 1998), 60.

7. Werner Hahn, "The Farms' Revolt and Grain Shortages in 1991," in *The "Farmer Threat": The Political Economy of Agrarian Reform in Post-Soviet Russia*, ed. Don Van Atta (Boulder, CO: Westview Press, 1993), 43.
8. Andrey Nechaev, Authors' Interview, October 27, 2020.
9. Nechaev, Authors' Interview.
10. Hahn, "The Farms' Revolt and Grain Shortages in 1991," 43.
11. Gaidar, *Dni porazhenii i pobed*, 136; Andrey Vavilov, *The Russian Public Debt and Financial Meltdowns* (London: Palgrave Macmillan, 2010), 20–25.
12. Hahn, "The Farms' Revolt and Grain Shortages in 1991," 50.
13. Nechaev, Authors' Interview.
14. Liefert, "The Food Problem in the Republics of the Former USSR," 34–35.
15. Anders Åslund, *How Russia Became a Market Economy* (Washington, DC: Brookings Institution, 1995), 139–40; Anders Åslund, *Russia's Crony Capitalism: The Path from Market Economy to Kleptocracy* (New Haven, CT: Yale University Press, 2019), 21.
16. Susanne A. Wengle, *Black Earth, White Bread: A Technopolitical History of Russian Agriculture and Food* (Madison: University of Wisconsin Press, 2022), 3.
17. Åslund, *How Russia Became a Market Economy*, 148–49; Nechaev, Authors' Interview.
18. Gaidar and Chubais, *Razvilki noveishei istorii Rossii*, 39.
19. Russian liberals of early 1990s shared a belief that in the long run free market would lead to low prices. In a telling anecdote, in April 1990s one of the authors, then a postdoctoral researcher at Harvard was assigned as a chaperone to Vasilii Seliunin, a prominent Russian liberal public intellectual who was visiting the United States. What shocked Seliunin the most was not the abundance of food in American stores, but the high prices, which were inconsistent with the liberals' perceptions.
20. Åslund, *How Russia Became a Market Economy*, 140.
21. Skokov was Yeltsin's advisor on security issues and would become in May 1992 the chairman of the Russian Security Council.
22. Nechaev, Authors' Interview; see also Gaidar and Chubais, *Razvilki noveishei istorii Rossii*, 53–55.
23. Listed in Gaidar's memoir as Munford.
24. For the West, Russia's status as a major exporter of oil, gas, and other natural resources made the terms justified. The authors thank Peter Rutland for pointing this out.
25. Gaidar, *Dni porazhenii i pobed*, 143–44, 215.
26. Nikolai Koniaev, "Pokhmel'e," *Diary*, January 4, 1992, https://prozhito.org/note/528310.
27. Genrikh Ioffe, "Diary Entry," *Diary*, January 7, 1992, https://prozhito.org/note/197711.
28. Lev Osterman, *Intelligentsiia i vlast' v Rossii (1985–1996)* (Moscow: Monolit, 2000), diary entry January 10, 1992.
29. Debra Javeline, *Protest and the Politics of Blame: The Russian Response to Unpaid Wages* (Ann Arbor: University of Michigan Press, 2009); Sarah Ashwin, *Russian Workers: The Anatomy of Patience* (Manchester: Manchester University Press, 1999).
30. Ashwin, *Russian Workers*.
31. Liefert, "The Food Problem in the Republics of the Former USSR," 36.

32. Nechaev, Authors' Interview.
33. Gaidar, *Dni porazhenii i pobed*, 85.
34. Gaidar, *Dni porazhenii i pobed*, 132.
35. Karen Dawisha, *Putin's Kleptocracy: Who Owns Russia?* (New York: Simon & Schuster, 2015), 108; according to Catherine Belton, *Putin's People: How the KGB Took Back Russia and Then Took On the West* (New York: Farrar, Straus & Giroux, 2020), 89, the permission was given by Piotr Aven, the minister of foreign trade.
36. Belton, *Putin's People*, 89.
37. Belton, *Putin's People*, 90.
38. Belton, *Putin's People*, 19–20.
39. Dawisha, *Putin's Kleptocracy*, 109, 117–18.
40. Belton, *Putin's People*, 91–93.
41. Putin et al., *First Person*; Dawisha, *Putin's Kleptocracy*, 123–25.
42. Don Van Atta, "Russian Food Supplies in 1992," in *The "Farmer Threat": The Political Economy of Agrarian Reform in Post-Soviet Russia*, ed. Don Van Atta (Boulder, Co: Westview Press, 1993), 55.
43. "Talony i otavarka: kak Tyumentsy dobyvali propitanie v nachale 1990kh," *Tyumen Online*, October 3, 2020, https://72.ru/text/gorod/2020/10/03/69479411/.
44. Evgenia Serova, Authors' Interview, January 29, 2021.
45. Yoshiko M. Herrera, *Imagined Economies: The Sources of Russian Regionalism* (New York: Cambridge University Press, 2005), 2006.
46. "Talony i otavarka."
47. Van Atta, "Russian Food Supplies in 1992," 62.
48. Carol S. Leonard, *Agrarian Reform in Russia: The Road from Serfdom* (Cambridge: Cambridge University Press, 2010), 91.
49. Karin M. Ekström et al., "Changes in Food Provision in Russian Households Experiencing Perestroika," *International Journal of Consumer Studies* 27, no. 4 (2003): 294–301.
50. Neala Schleuning, "Family Economics in Russia: Women's Perspectives on the Transition to a Market Economy," *Journal of Consumer Studies & Home Economics* 22, no. 1 (1998): 51–64.
51. Stephen K. Wegren, *Russia's Food Revolution: The Transformation of the Food System* (London: Routledge, 2020), 144.
52. Stephen Lovell, *Summerfolk: A History of the Dacha, 1710–2000* (Ithaca, NY: Cornell University Press, 2003), 163, 216.
53. Jerker Nilsson et al., "Governance of Production Co-operatives in Russian Agriculture," *Annals of Public and Cooperative Economics* 87, no. 4 (2016): 545.
54. Judith Pallot and Tat'yana Nefedova, *Russia's Unknown Agriculture: Household Production in Post-Communist Russia* (Oxford: Oxford University Press, 2007), 17–18.
55. Wegren, *Russia's Food Revolution*, 106.
56. Wegren, *Agriculture and the State in Soviet and Post-Soviet Russia*, 116.
57. Axel Wolz et al., "Reviewing Changing Institutional Conditions for Private Farming in Russia," *Outlook on Agriculture* 45, no. 2 (2016): 113.
58. Nilsson et al., "Governance of Production Co-operatives in Russian Agriculture," 544.

59. Leonard, *Agrarian Reform in Russia*, 251.
60. Leonard, *Agrarian Reform in Russia*, 181, Table 5.3.
61. Wegren, *Agriculture and the State in Soviet and Post-Soviet Russia*, 1.
62. Ira Lindsay, "A Troubled Path to Private Property: Agricultural Land Law in Russia," *Columbia Journal of European Law* 16 (2010): 268–69; Nikolai Dronin and Andrei Kirilenko, "Climate Change, Food Stress, and Security in Russia," *Regional Environmental Change* 11, no. 1 (2011): 167–78.
63. Grigory Ioffe, Tatyana Nefedova, and Ilya Zaslavsky, *The End of Peasantry?: The Disintegration of Rural Russia* (Pittsburgh: University of Pittsburgh Press, 2006), 28.
64. Alexander V. Prishchepov et al., "Effects of Institutional Changes on Land Use: Agricultural Land Abandonment during the Transition from State-Command to Market-Driven Economies in Post-Soviet Eastern Europe," *Environmental Research Letters* 7, no. 2 (2012): 024021.
65. Grigory Ioffe, Tatyana Nefedova, and Ilya Zaslavsky, "From Spatial Continuity to Fragmentation: The Case of Russian Farming," *Annals of the Association of American Geographers* 94, no. 4 (2004): 938.
66. Lindsay, "A Troubled Path to Private Property," 268.
67. Amartya Sen, *Poverty and Famines: An Essay on Entitlement and Deprivation* (Oxford: Oxford University Press, 1982).

Chapter 3

1. Michael R. Gordon, "Food Crisis Forces Russia to Swallow Its Pride," *New York Times*, November 7, 1998, sec. A; Michael R. Gordon, "Facing Severe Shortage of Food, Russia Seeks Foreign Relief Aid," *New York Times*, October 10, 1998, sec. A.
2. Stephen K. Wegren, *Land Reform in Russia*: Institutional Design and Behavioral Responses (New Haven, CT: Yale University Press, 2009); Jessica Allina-Pisano, *The Post-Soviet Potemkin Village*: Politics and Property Rights in the Black Earth (New York: Cambridge University Press, 2008); Carol S. Leonard, *Agrarian Reform in Russia*: The Road from Serfdom (Cambridge: Cambridge University Press, 2010).
3. Nechaev, Authors' Interview.
4. Allina-Pisano, *The Post-Soviet Potemkin Village*, 54.
5. Wegren, *Land Reform in Russia*.
6. Donna Bahry, "The New Federalism and the Paradoxes of Regional Sovereignty in Russia," *Comparative Politics* 37, no. 2 (2005): 135.
7. Aleksandr Rutskoi, *Agrarnaia reforma v Rossii* (Moscow: RAU-Korporatsiia, 1993), 5.
8. Yegor Gaidar, *Dni porazhenii i pobed* (Moscow: Vagrius, 1996), 160–61.
9. Rutskoi, *Agrarnaia reforma v Rossii*, 6.
10. Gaidar, *Dni porazhenii i pobed*, 296.
11. Rutskoi, *Agrarnaia reforma v Rossii*, 19.
12. Rutskoi, *Agrarnaia reforma v Rossii*, 137.
13. Ivan Starikov, Authors' Interview, October 27, 2020.
14. Nechaev, Authors' Interview.

15. Leonard, *Agrarian Reform in Russia*, 91–92; Lindsay, "A Troubled Path to Private Property," Columbia Journal of European Law 16 (2010): 264.
16. Wegren, *Land Reform in Russia*, 53. Readers interested in a comprehensive discussion of the land reform in Russia are encouraged to consult this book.
17. Yegor Gaidar and Anatoly Chubais, *Razvilki noveishei istorii Rossii* (Moscow: OGI, 2011), 39.
18. Aron, *Yeltsin: A Revolutionary Life*, 589; Åslund, *How Russia Became a Market Economy* (Washington, DC: Brookings Institution, 1995), 261.
19. Aron, *Yeltsin*, 496.
20. Åslund, *How Russia Became a Market Economy*, 261.
21. Zvi Lerman, Csaba Csaki, and Gershon Feder, *Agriculture in Transition: Land Policies and Evolving Farm Structures in Post-Soviet Countries* (Lanham, MD: Lexington Books, 2004), 69; Stephen K. Wegren, "Institutional Impact and Agricultural Change in Russia," *Journal of Eurasian Studies* 3, no. 2 (2012): 195.
22. Timothy J. Colton, *Yeltsin: A Life* (New York: Basic Books, 2008), 402.
23. Gaidar, *Dni porazhenii i pobed*, 296; Vasilii Uzun, "Otsenka rezul'tatov Yel'tsinskoi agrarnoi reformy," *EKO*, 3, 2013, 6–30.
24. Gaidar, *Dni porazhenii i pobed*, 170.
25. Gaidar, *Dni porazhenii i pobed*, 119.
26. Aron, *Yeltsin*, 587.
27. Caldwell, *Not by Bread Alone: Social Support in the New Russia* (Berkeley: University of California Press, 2004), 11.
28. Aron, *Yeltsin*, 524.
29. Vilia Gel'bras, *Kto est' chto: Politicheskie partii i bloki, obshchestvennye organizatsii* (Moscow: RAN, 1994), 13.
30. Wegren, *Agriculture and the State in Soviet and Post-Soviet Russia* (Pittsburgh: University of Pittsburgh Press, 1998), 144–45.
31. Serova, Authors' Interview.
32. Compare Article 3 of the draft law (http://council.gov.ru/activity/documents/6126/) to the final text approved by Yeltsin (http://www.szrf.ru/szrf/doc.phtml?nb=100&issid=1001996026000&docid=5186).
33. http://www.kremlin.ru/acts/bank/11189.
34. Allina-Pisano, *The Post-Soviet Potemkin Village*, 9.
35. Ulrich Koester, "A Revival of Large Farms in Eastern Europe—How Important Are Institutions?," *Agricultural Economics* 32 (2005): 104.
36. Oane Visser, "Insecure Land Rights, Obstacles to Family Farming, and the Weakness of Protest in Rural Russia," *Laboratorium* 2, no. 3 (2010): 281.
37. Rutskoi, *Agrarnaia reforma v Rossii*, 48.
38. Don Van Atta, "Russian Food Supplies in 1992," in *The "Farmer Threat": The Political Economy of Agrarian Reform in Post-Soviet Russia*, ed. Don Van Atta (Boulder, CO: Westview Press, 1993), 61.
39. Visser, "Insecure Land Rights, Obstacles to Family Farming, and the Weakness of Protest in Rural Russia," 283.
40. Åslund, *How Russia Became a Market Economy*, 260.

41. Stephen K. Wegren and Frank A. Durgin, "The Political Economy of Private Farming in Russia," *Comparative Economic Studies* 39, no. 3 (1997): 8.
42. Maria Amelina, "Why Russian Peasants Remain in Collective Farms: A Household Perspective on Agricultural Restructuring," *Post-Soviet Geography and Economics* 41, no. 7 (2000): 483–511.
43. Allina-Pisano, *The Post-Soviet Potemkin Village*, 3.
44. Allina-Pisano, *The Post-Soviet Potemkin Village*, 190.
45. Evgeny Finkel and Scott Gehlbach, *Reform and Rebellion in Weak States* (New York: Cambridge University Press, 2020).
46. Andriy Matyukha, Peter Voigt, and Axel Wolz, "Agro-Holdings in Russia, Ukraine and Kazakhstan: Temporary Phenomenon or Permanent Business Form? Farm-Level Evidence from Moscow and Belgorod Regions," *Post-Communist Economies* 27, no. 3 (2015): 370–94.
47. Wegren, *Agriculture and the State in Soviet and Post-Soviet Russia*, 93.
48. Oane Visser, Natalia Mamonova, and Max Spoor, "Oligarchs, Megafarms and Land Reserves: Understanding Land Grabbing in Russia," *Journal of Peasant Studies* 39, no. 3–4 (2012): 899–931.
49. Wegren, *Agriculture and the State in Soviet and Post-Soviet Russia*, 88.
50. Wegren, *Agriculture and the State in Soviet and Post-Soviet Russia*, 116.
51. Stephen K. Wegren, "Private Farming in Russia: An Emerging Success?," *Post-Soviet Affairs* 27, no. 3 (2011): 211–40; Wolz et al., "Reviewing Changing Institutional Conditions for Private Farming in Russia."
52. Jerker Nilsson et al., "Governance of Production Co-operatives in Russian Agriculture," Annals of Public and Cooperative Economics 87, no. 4 (2016): 541–62.
53. Nilsson et al., "Governance of Production Co-operatives in Russian Agriculture."
54. Leonard, *Agrarian Reform in Russia*, 218.
55. Quoted in Grigory Ioffe, Tatyana Nefedova, and Ilya Zaslavsky, *The End of Peasantry? The Disintegration of Rural Russia* (Pittsburgh: University of Pittsburgh Press, 2006), 93.
56. Ioffe, Nefedova, and Zaslavsky, *The End of Peasantry?*, 93.
57. Wegren, *Agriculture and the State in Soviet and Post-Soviet Russia*, 60.
58. Grigory Ioffe, Tatyana Nefedova, and Ilya Zaslavsky, "From Spatial Continuity to Fragmentation: The Case of Russian Farming," Annals of the Association of American Geographers 94, no. 4 (2004): 938.
59. Arkadii Zlochevskii, Authors' Interview, October 16, 2020; Sergei Iushin, Authors' Interview, September 24, 2020.
60. For annual harvest data by year see https://www.agroinvestor.ru/upload/iblock/ec9/ec924135514c801d88fde47c5ee07fa4.jpg.
61. Chris Miller, *Putinomics: Power and Money in Resurgent Russia* (Chapel Hill: University of North Carolina Press, 2018), 1.
62. Miller, *Putinomics*, 19.
63. Caldwell, *Not by Bread Alone*, 163.
64. Miller, *Putinomics*, 19.
65. Caldwell, *Not by Bread Alone*, 165.

66. Zlochevskii, Authors' Interview.
67. Victor Semenov, "Nuzhny li nam mezhregional'nye torgovye voiny?," *Rossiiskaia gazeta*, October 14, 1999.
68. Caldwell, *Not by Bread Alone*, 164.
69. Putin was appointment to lead the FSB on July 25, 1998, just before the crisis broke out.
70. Gordon, "Facing Severe Shortage of Food, Russia Seeks Foreign Relief Aid."
71. Aleksandr Gavriliuk, "Prazdnik so slezami v zakromakh," *Rossiiskaia gazeta*, November 14, 1998.

Chapter 4

1. Aleksandr Gavriliuk, "Prazdnik so slezami v zakromakh," *Rossiiskaia gazeta*, November 14, 1998.
2. On August 16, 1998, 1 US dollar was worth 6.8 rubles. On January 1, 1999, its value rose to 22 rubles.
3. A 400 percent profit margin was almost certainly a perception rather than a precise estimate. Marat Isangazin, "Zerno daet 400% godovykh a neft' v luchshem sluchae 80%," *Kommercheskie vesti*, November 21, 2002, https://kvnews.ru/gazeta/2002/11/45/evgeniya_serova_zerno_daet_400__godovih__a_neft_v_luchshem_sluchae_80.
4. Stephen K. Wegren, "Observations on Russia's New Agricultural Land Legislation," *Eurasian Geography and Economics* 43, no. 8 (2002): 651–60.
5. Janetta Azarieva, "Grain and Power in Russia 2001–2011" (PhD diss., Hebrew University of Jerusalem, 2015), 16.
6. World Bank, *Russian Federation: Agriculture Support Policies and Performance* (Washington, DC: World Bank, 2020), 80.
7. Svetlana Ulybkina, "Gosudarstvo ob"avilo zernovuiu interventsiiu v podderzhku sobstvennykh tovaroproizvoditelei," *Rossiiskaia gazeta*, September 11, 2001.
8. Evgenii Arsiukhin, "Bitva s rublem do poslednego zerna," *Rossiiskaia gazeta*, August 21, 2002.
9. Anders Åslund, *Russia's Crony Capitalism: The Path from Market Economy to Kleptocracy* (New Haven, CT: Yale University Press, 2019).
10. Aleksei Gordeev, *Russia's Food Supply: Problems of Theory and Practice* (Moscow: Kolos, 1999) (in Russian).
11. The fifty-page summary of the thesis is available online at https://rusneb.ru/catalog/000199_000009_000796050. The dissertation research was conducted at the Agriculture Ministry's own research arm, the Research Institute of Economics, Labor and Management in Agriculture. However, this body is not allowed to grant doctoral degrees, so the dissertation was submitted to and defended at the Institute of the Agrarian Studies of the Russian Academy of Sciences.
12. Valerie Strauss, "Russia's Plagiarism Problem: Even Putin Has Done It!," *Washington Post*, March 18, 2014, https://www.washingtonpost.com/news/answer-sheet/wp/2014/03/18/russias-plagiarism-problem-even-putin-has-done-it/.

13. Additionally, Gordeev is listed as a coauthor of two books that focus on the importance of grains to the Russian economy: *Russian Grain: Strategic Commodity of the 21st Century* (2007) and *Russia: Grain Power* (2009).
14. Evgenii Arsiukhin, "Aleksei Gordeev: V Rossii ne dolzhno byt' golodnykh," *Rossiiskaia gazeta*, August 19, 2004, https://rg.ru/2004/08/19/gordeev.html.
15. "Sel'skoe khoziaistvo," Personal site of Aleksei Gordeev, June 28, 2009, https://web.archive.org/web/20090628214512/http://gordeev.su:80/.
16. "Cherez 10 let na zemli RF budut pretendovat' drugie strany," *RBC.ru*, July 26, 2005, https://www.rbc.ru/economics/26/07/2005/5703c2479a7947dde8e09b37.
17. Evgenii Arsiukhin, "Aleksei Gordeev: Gosudarstvo ne uidet s rynka prodovol'stviia," *Rossiiskaia gazeta*, December 5, 2003.
18. "Internet-konferentsiia Ministra sel'skogo khoziaiistva Rossiiskoi Federatsii Alekseiia Gordeeva," November 22, 2006, https://www.agroyug.ru/news/id-4280.
19. "A. Gordeev: VTO—vrednaia dlia mirovoi ekonomiki organizatsiia," *RBC.ru*, September 25, 2008, https://www.rbc.ru/economics/25/09/2008/5703cf2a9a79473dc8149323.
20. Åslund, *Russia's Crony Capitalism*; Natalya Shagaida, "Agricultural Land Market in Russia: Living with Constraints," *Comparative Economic Studies* 47, no. 1 (2005): 127–40.
21. "Vystuplenie Zamestitelia Predsedatelia Pravitel'stva Rossiiskoi Federatsii—Ministra sel'skogo khoziaiiistva Rossiiskoi Federatsii Gordeeva A.V. na zasedanii Pravitel'stva Rossiiskoi Federatsii 27 iulia 2000g.," July 27, 2000, http://www.vasilievaa.narod.ru/gu/Konst_zak/PPr/Agrpol_01-10.htm.
22. "Osnovnye napravleniia agroprodovol'stvennoi politiki Pravitel'stva Rossiiskoi Federatsii na 2001–2010 gody" (Government of the Russian Federation, July 27, 2000), https://rulaws.ru/goverment/Osnovnye-napravleniya-agroprodovolstvennoy-politiki-Pravitelstva-Rossiyskoy-Federatsii-na-2001—-201/.
23. Victor Semenov, "Nuzhny li nam mezhregional'nye torgovye voiny?," *Rossiiskaia gazeta*, October 14, 1999.
24. Susanne A. Wengle, *Black Earth, White Bread: A Technopolitical History of Russian Agriculture and Food* (Madison: University of Wisconsin Press, 2022), 68.
25. "Pravila osuchshestvleniia gosudarstvenykh zakupochnykh i tovarnykh interventsii dlia regulirovaniia rynka sel'skohoziaistvenoi produktsii, syria i prodovolstviia" (Government of the Russian Federation, August 3, 2001), http://pravo.gov.ru/proxy/ips/?docbody=&prevDoc=102167464&backlink=1&&nd=102072342.
26. Nataliia Evdokimova, "Zakupochnye interventsii na zernovom rynke," *APK: Ekonomika, upravlenie* 3 (2011): 64–67.
27. Arkadii Zlochevskii, Authors' Interview, October 16, 2020.
28. Anfisa Voronina, "Vskryli neeffektivnost' i neorganizovannost'"—Sergei Levin, general'nyi direktor Ob"edinennoi zernovoi kompanii," *Vedomosti*, April 2, 2010, https://www.top-personal.ru/pressissue.html?22335.
29. "Gendirektor OZK S. Levin: Kachestvo zerna interventsionnogo fonda v tselom normal'noe," *Agrarnoe obozrenie*, December 16, 2010, https://agroobzor.ru/stati/a-588.html.

30. Evdokimova, "Zakupochnye interventsii na zernovom rynke."
31. Henry Thomson, "Food and Power: Agricultural Policy under Democracy and Dictatorship," *Comparative Politics* 49, no. 2 (2017): 273–96; Natalia Mamonova, "Naive Monarchism and Rural Resistance in Contemporary Russia," *Rural Sociology* 81, no. 3 (2016): 316–42; Natalia Mamonova and Oane Visser, "State Marionettes, Phantom Organisations or Genuine Movements? The Paradoxical Emergence of Rural Social Movements in Post-Socialist Russia," *Journal of Peasant Studies* 41, no. 4 (2014): 491–516.
32. Samuel A. Greene, *Moscow in Movement: Power and Opposition in Putin's Russia* (Stanford, CA: Stanford University Press, 2014); Stephen K. Wegren, *Russia's Food Revolution: The Transformation of the Food System* (London: Routledge, 2020), 15.
33. William M. Liefert and Olga Liefert, "Russian Agriculture during Transition: Performance, Global Impact, and Outlook," *Applied Economic Perspectives and Policy* 34, no. 1 (2012): 44.
34. Svetlana Barsukova, "Vekhi agrarnoi politiki Rossii v 2000-e gody," *Mir Rossii* 1 (2013): 3–28.
35. Aleksei Makarkin and Peter M. Oppenheimer, "The Russian Social Contract and Regime Legitimacy," *International Affairs* 87, no. 6 (2011): 1459–74; Samuel A. Greene, "From Boom to Bust: Hardship, Mobilization & Russia's Social Contract," *Daedalus* 146, no. 2 (2017): 113–27.
36. Barsukova, "Vekhi agrarnoi politiki Rossii v 2000-e gody," 5.
37. World Bank, *Russian Federation*, 12–13.
38. Vladimir Gel'man, *The Politics of Bad Governance in Contemporary Russia* (Ann Arbor: University of Michigan Press, 2022), 59.
39. SBS Agro Bank was Russia's second biggest private bank and collapsed during Russia's 1998 financial crash.
40. Sergei Iushin, Authors' Interview, September 24, 2020.
41. "Interview with Iurii Trushin" (Rosselkhozbank), accessed April 10, 2022, https://www.rshb.ru/press/releases/16177.
42. Zlochevskii, Authors' Interview; Wegren, *Russia's Food Revolution*, 66–67.
43. Barsukova, "Vekhi agrarnoi politiki Rossii v 2000-e gody."
44. Rinat Sagdiev, "Rassledovanie 'Vedomoste': Biznes interesy Elena Skynnik," *Vedomosti*, November 28, 2012, https://www.vedomosti.ru/library/articles/2012/11/28/biznesinteresy_elena_skynnik; Iuliia Kotova, "Skrynnik rasskazala o 'khischenniakh' v Rosagrolizinge," *Vedomosti*, December 2, 2012, https://www.vedomosti.ru/politics/articles/2012/12/02/skrynnik_rasskazala; "Schweiz stellt Geldwäscherei-Verfahren gegen Putin-Vertraute ein," *Blick*, August 5, 2017, https://www.blick.ch/schweiz/geldwaescherei-schweiz-stellt-geldwaescherei-verfahren-gegen-putin-vertraute-ein-id7100388.html.
45. Zlochevskii, Authors' Interview.
46. Anatolii Altukhov, Authors' Interview, Zoom, February 16, 2021.
47. Dmitrii Buturin, "Pravitel'stvo natsional'nogo proekta," *Kommersant*, December 30, 2005, https://www.kommersant.ru/doc/639704.

184 NOTES

48. Marlene Laruelle, *Is Russia Fascist?: Unraveling Propaganda East and West* (Ithaca, NY: Cornell University Press, 2021); Dima Kortukov, "'Sovereign Democracy' and the Politics of Ideology in Putin's Russia," *Russian Politics* 5, no. 1 (2020): 81–104.
49. Susanne A. Wengle, "Local Effects of the New Land Rush: How Capital Inflows Transformed Rural Russia," *Governance* 31, no. 2 (2018): 259–77; Barsukova, "Vekhi agrarnoi politiki Rossii v 2000-e gody."
50. Mark Galeotti, *We Need to Talk about Putin* (London: Penguin, 2019).
51. Timothy Frye, *Weak Strongman: The Limits of Power in Putin's Russia* (Princeton, NJ: Princeton University Press, 2021).
52. Brian D. Taylor, *The Code of Putinism* (New York: Oxford University Press, 2018).
53. Åslund, *Russia's Crony Capitalism*; Chris Miller, *Putinomics: Power and Money in Resurgent Russia* (Chapel Hill: University of North Carolina Press, 2018).
54. Ian Bremmer, "State Capitalism Comes of Age—The End of the Free Market," *Foreign Affairs* 88, no. 3 (2009): 40–55; Aldo Musacchio and Sergio G. Lazzarini, *Reinventing State Capitalism: Leviathan in Business, Brazil and Beyond* (Cambridge, MA: Harvard University Press, 2014).

Chapter 5

1. According to Russia's Constitution, Putin was limited to two terms in office. He stepped down in 2008 and was appointed by Medvedev as prime minister. Putin returned to presidency in 2012 and has occupied it since.
2. "Ukaz Prezidenta Rossiiskoi Federatsii 'Ob utverzhdenii doktriny prodovol'stvennoi bezopasnosti Rossiiskoi Federatsii,'" January 30, 2010, https://rg.ru/2010/02/03/prod-dok.html.
3. Russia's Security Council is the institution responsible for creating documents with "Doctrine" status. The Doctrines are: Military Doctrine (adopted in 2000, updated in 2014), Information Security Doctrine (adopted in 2000, revised in 2016), Naval Doctrine (adopted in 2001, updated in 2015), Ecological Doctrine (adopted in 2002), Climate Doctrine (adopted in 2009), Food Security Doctrine (adopted in 2010, updated in 2020), and the Energy Security Doctrine (adopted in 2012, updated in 2019).
4. Svetlana Barsukova, "Vekhi agrarnoi politiki Rossii v 2000-e gody," *Mir Rossii* 1 (2013): 3–28; Svetlana Barsukova, "Doktrina Prodovol'svennoi Bezopasnosti: Otsenka ekspertov," *Terra Economicus* 10, no. 4 (2012): 37–38.
5. Andrey Nechaev, Authors' Interview, October 27, 2020; Ivan Starikov, Authors' Interview, October 27, 2020.
6. Evgenia Serova, Authors' Interview, January 29, 2021.
7. "Food Security," Policy Brief (Food and Agriculture Organization, June 1996), http://www.fao.org/fileadmin/templates/faoitaly/documents/pdf/pdf_Food_Security_Cocept_Note.pdf.
8. According to Evgenia Serova, all her colleagues at the FAO objected linking food security to domestic production. Serova, Authors' Interview.

9. Raj Patel, "Food Sovereignty," *Journal of Peasant Studies* 36, no. 3 (2009): 663–706.
10. Stephen K. Wegren and Christel Elvestad, "Russia's Food Self-Sufficiency and Food Security: An Assessment," *Post-Communist Economies* 30, no. 5 (2018): 565–87; Jennifer Clapp, "Food Self-Sufficiency: Making Sense of It, and When It Makes Sense," *Food Policy* 66 (2017): 88–96.
11. Stephen K. Wegren, Alexander M. Nikulin, and Irina Trotsuk, "The Russian Variant of Food Security," *Problems of Post-Communism* 64, no. 1 (2017): 48.
12. Anatolii Altukhov, Authors' Interview, Zoom, February 16, 2021; Arkadii Zlochevskii, Authors' Interview, October 16, 2020.
13. Aleksei Greshonkov, "Permanentnost' strategicheskikh prioritetov ekonomicheskoi bezopasnosti Rossii v prodovol'stvennoi sfere" (PhD diss., Tambovskii Gosudarstvennyi Universitet imeni G.R. Derzhavina, 2015), 25, https://www.dissercat.com/content/permanentnost-strategicheskikh-prioritetov-ekonomicheskoi-bezopasnosti-rossii-v-prodovolstve.
14. Concurrent with the 2008 draft law initiative, KPRF organized a large public panel whose speakers attempted to delegitimize the government agricultural policies by emphasizing Russia's continuing dependence on low-quality food imports, the sharp decline of agricultural support budgets from the Soviet era, the continuous depopulation of the countryside, the steep rise of food prices, and the dire economic situation of many agro-industrial enterprises; see Vladimir Vishniakov and Elena Krasnolutskaia, "Prodovol'stvennaia bezopasnost'—Glavnaia zabota kommunistov," *Pravda*, June 6, 2008, https://kprf.ru/dep/57612.html.
15. The Great Recession led to a plunge in Russia's oil and gas revenues. The Russian government's strategy to cope with the situation was gradual devaluation of the ruble, and as a result the ruble weakened 35 percent against the dollar from August 2008 to January 2009.
16. Aleksei Mikhailov, "Kasha iz topora," *Gazeta.ru*, April 4, 2011, https://www.gazeta.ru/column/mikhailov/3573933.shtml; "V Sankt-Peterburge sroki 'zamorazhivaiushchikh' tseny soglashenii prodleny do marta," *Regnum.ru*, January 28, 2008, https://regnum.ru/news/economy/948853.html.
17. "Kudrin: Zamorazhivat' tseny na prodovol'stvennom rynke byli by oshibkoi," *RIA Novosti*, October 24, 2007, https://ria.ru/20071024/85292984.html; "Kholodil'nik dlia tsen. Pravitel'stvo dogovorilos' o zamorazhivanii tsen na produkty pitaniia," *Lenta.ru*, October 27, 2007, https://m.lenta.ru/articles/2007/10/22/cold; "Minsel'khoz prodlil zamorozku tsen na produkty do maia 2008 goda," *Lenta.ru*, January 31, 2008, https://lenta.ru/news/2008/01/31/freeze.
18. "Putin poruchil provesti inventarizatsiiu vneshnetorgovykh soglashenii v sfere APK," *Interfax*, May 19, 2022, https://www.interfax.ru/russia/13737; "Rossiia dolzhna stat' krupnym igrokom na mirovom rynke prodovol'stviia," *DagPravda*, May 20, 2008, https://dagpravda.ru/politika/rossiya-dolzhna-stat-krupnym-igrokom-na-mirovom-rynke-prodovolstviya/; "V.V. Putin provel soveshchanie po voprosu povysheniia effektivnosti gosudarstvennoi agrarnoi politiki" (Arkhiv saita Predsedatelia Pravitel'stva RF V.V. Putina, May 2008), http://archive.premier.gov.ru/visits/ru/6038/events/1382/.

19. "Vystuplenie A.V. Gordeeva na soveshchanii po voprosu povysheniia effektivnosti gosudarstvennoi agrarnoi politiki" (Agroyug, May 19, 2008), https://www.agroyug.ru/page/item/_id-2358.
20. Mikhail Chkanikov, "My za edoi ne postoim. V Rossii gotoviat zakon o prodovol'stvennoi bezopasnosti," *Rossiiskaia gazeta*, May 21, 2008, https://rg.ru/2008/05/21/minselhoz.html.
21. Zlochevskii, Authors' Interview.
22. Boris Chernyakov, *Aiova—Prodovol'stvennaia stolitsa mira* (Moscow: Tipografiia Rosselkhozakademii, 2011); Boris Chernyakov, "Politika prodovol'stvennoi bezopasnosti zarubezhnykh stran i interesy Rossii," *Ekonomika sel'skokhoziastvennykh i pererabatyvaiushchikh predpriiatii* 5 (2002): 11–13; Boris Chernyakov, "Zakonodatel'nye i administrativnye osnovy prodovol'stvennoi bezopasnosti SShA: Opyt dlia Rossii," *SShA-Kanada* 8 (2001): 89–104.
23. "Predlozheniia uchenykh o reformakh v zemel'noi i agrarnoi sferakh—uchet zemel' i chetkoe gosudartvennoe planirovanie" (Soyuz Zemleustroitelei, 2013), http://roszemproekt.ru/newsx/predlozheniya/.
24. Serova, Authors' Interview; Zlochevskii, Authors' Interview.
25. "Proekt Doktriny Prodovol'stvennoi Bezopasnosti Rossiiskoi Federatsii" (Dairy News, October 31, 2008), https://dairynews.today/news/projekt_doktriny_prodovolstvennoj_bezopasnosti_ros.html; "Ukaz Prezidenta Rossiiskoi Federatsii N120 ob utverzhdenii Doktriny prodovol'stvennoi bezopasnosti Rossiiskoi Federatsii" (President of Russia, January 2010), http://kremlin.ru/acts/bank/30563.
26. On May 12, 2009, President Medvedev also signed a Presidential Decree N 537 "On the Strategy of National Security of the Russian Federation through or to 2020." While this document's prime concern was foreign and security policy, Article 49 explicitly included the concept of "food security" in a wider concept of Russia's national security. Article 50 included such policies as import substitution in major food staples, and protection of the Russian grain market from domination by foreign companies. The 2010 Food Security Doctrine explicitly states that it develops the ideas mentioned in the 2009 National Security Strategy. See the text: https://www.garant.ru/products/ipo/prime/doc/95521/?ysclid=lhj15i34jo616762618.
27. Gordeev remained in this position until December 2017.
28. Chkanikov, "My za edoi ne postoim." Kudrin consistently opposed price freezes on food products as anti-market device but supported strategies of price stabilization, which he viewed as appropriate market mechanism; see "Kudrin schitaet oshibochnymi zamorazhivat' tseny na produkty," www.ria.ru/20071024/85304625.html.
29. Altukhov, Authors' Interview.
30. Aleksandr Kukolevskii, "Tak poedim!," *Kommersant*, February 8, 2010, https://www.kommersant.ru/doc/1315512; Starikov, Authors' Interview; Nechaev, Authors' Interview.
31. Barsukova, "Vekhi agrarnoi politiki Rossii v 2000-e gody"; Dmitrii Buturin, "Minsel'khoz pochustvoval golod," *Kommersant*, March 29, 2008, https://www.kommersant.ru/doc/872786.

32. Quoted in Stephen K. Wegren, "Food Security and Russia's 2010 Drought," *Eurasian Geography and Economics* 52, no. 1 (2011): 142.
33. Zlochevskii, Authors' Interview.
34. Wegren, "Food Security and Russia's 2010 Drought," 142.
35. Sergei Iushin, Authors' Interview, September 24, 2020.
36. Artiom Belov, Authors' Interview, Zoom, October 7, 2020.
37. Altukhov, Authors' Interview.
38. Iushin, Authors' Interview.
39. "Ob utverzhdenii Strategii razvitiia pishchevoi i pererabatyvaiushchei promyshlennosti do 2020 goda" (Government of the Russian Federation, April 17, 2012), http://government.ru/docs/23574/. The 2012 figures turned out to be too ambitious and were revised downward in the 2016 update of the Strategy.
40. "O vnesenii izmenenii v Strategiiu razvitiia pishchevoi i pererabatyvaiuschei promyshlennosti" (Government of the Russian Federation, July 5, 2016), http://government.ru/docs/23608/.
41. Wegren, "Food Security and Russia's 2010 Drought," 148.
42. Janetta Azarieva, "Grain and Power in Russia 2001–2011" (PhD diss., Hebrew University of Jerusalem, 2015), 96.
43. "Elena Skynnik: O masshtabakh bedy zaranee ne znali ni Rosgidromet, ni nashi uchenye," *Rossiiskaia gazeta*, August 29, 2010, https://rg.ru/2010/08/30/skrynnik.html; Iuliia Shestoperova, "Defitsita prodovol'stviia ne budet: Pravitel'stvo sozdast gruppu dlia monitoringa tsen na produkty," *MK.ru*, July 23, 2010, https://www.mk.ru/economics/article/2010/07/23/518641-defitsita-prodovolstviya-ne-budet.html; George Welton, "The Impact of Russia's 2010 Grain Export Ban," *Oxfam Policy and Practice: Agriculture, Food and Land* 11, no. 5 (2011): 15.
44. "Predsedatel' Pravitel'stva Rossiiskoi Federatsii V.V. Putin provel zasedanie Prezidiuma Pravitel'stva" (Government of the Russian Federation, 2010), http://archive.government.ru/docs/11633/print/.
45. Welton, "The Impact of Russia's 2010 Grain Export Ban."
46. Giulia Soffiantini, "Food Insecurity and Political Instability during the Arab Spring," *Global Food Security* 26 (2020): 100400; Willeke Veninga and Rico Ihle, "Import Vulnerability in the Middle East: Effects of the Arab Spring on Egyptian Wheat Trade," *Food Security* 10, no. 1 (2018): 183–94.
47. Oleg Gladunov, "Embargo Putina: Dva goda bez urozhaia," *Svobodnaia pressa*, March 18, 2011, https://svpressa.ru/economy/article/40640/; "Itogi goda: Utomlennyi solntsev APK," *Interfax*, December 27, 2010, https://www.interfax.ru/business/171113; Welton, "The Impact of Russia's 2010 Grain Export Ban."
48. Welton, "The Impact of Russia's 2010 Grain Export Ban," 3.
49. Wegren, "Food Security and Russia's 2010 Drought"; Zlochevskii, Authors' Interview.
50. The United States formally repealed the Jackson-Vanik amendment in December 2012.
51. William M. Liefert et al., "The Effect of Russia's Economic Crisis and Import Ban on Its Agricultural and Food Sector," *Journal of Eurasian Studies* 10, no. 2 (2019): 119–35;

William M. Liefert and Olga Liefert, "Russia's Economic Crisis and Its Agricultural and Food Economy," *Choices* 30, no. 1 (2015): 1–6.
52. Sergey F. Sutyrin, "Russia's Accession to the WTO: Major Commitments, Possible Implications" (International Trade Centre, 2012), 6, https://intracen.org/sites/default/files/uploadedFiles/Russia_WTO_Accession_English.pdf.
53. Stephen K. Wegren, "The Impact of WTO Accession on Russia's Agriculture," *Post-Soviet Affairs* 28, no. 3 (2012): 299; see also David Sedik, Zvi Lerman, and Vasilii Uzun, "Agricultural Policy in Russia and WTO Accession," *Post-Soviet Affairs* 29, no. 6 (2013): 500–27.
54. Susanne Wengle, "The Domestic Effects of the Russian Food Embargo," *Demokratizatsiya: The Journal of Post-Soviet Democratization* 24, no. 3 (2016): 281–89; Susanne A. Wengle, "Local Effects of the New Land Rush: How Capital Inflows Transformed Rural Russia," *Governance* 31, no. 2 (2018): 259–77.
55. "Ob obespechenii prodovol'stvennoi bezopasnosti Rossi'skoi Federatsii" (Sovet Bezopasnosti RF, December 4, 2009), http://www.scrf.gov.ru/council/session/2045/.
56. Evgeny Finkel and Yitzhak M. Brudny, "Russia and the Colour Revolutions," *Democratization* 19, no. 1 (2012): 15–36; Evgeny Finkel and Yitzhak M. Brudny, "No More Colour! Authoritarian Regimes and Colour Revolutions in Eurasia," *Democratization* 19, no. 1 (February 1, 2012): 1–14, https://doi.org/10.1080/13510347.2012.641298.

Chapter 6

1. "Address by President of the Russian Federation" (President of Russia, March 18, 2014), http://en.kremlin.ru/events/president/news/20603; Ishaan Tharoor, "Why Putin Says Crimea Is Russia's 'Temple Mount,'" *Washington Post*, December 14, 2014, https://www.washingtonpost.com/news/worldviews/wp/2014/12/04/why-putin-says-crimea-is-russias-temple-mount/.
2. For the details on individuals, companies and nature of sanctions against them, as well as the timeline of US and EU sanctions, see Ivan Gutterman and Wojtec Grojec, "A Timeline of All Russia-Related Sanctions," *Radio Free Europe/Radio Liberty*, September 19, 2018, https://www.rferl.org/a/russia-sanctions-timeline/29477179.html.
3. The only country taken out of the sanctioned list was Turkey. Turkey was added to the list in 2016 and removed in 2017. However, Russia imposed an import quota of 50,000 tons of tomatoes, Turkey's main food export item to Russia. This quota was lifted to 250,000 tons and then to 300,000 tons in June 2021; see "Russia Raises Turkey's Tomato Import Quota to 300,000 Tons," *Hortidaily*, June 2, 2021, https://www.hortidaily.com/article/9326467/russia-raises-turkey-s-tomato-import-quota-to-300-000-tons/.
4. "Ukaz N560 O priminenii otdel'nykh spetsial'nykh ekonomicheskikh mer v tseliakh obespecheniia bezopasnosti Rossiiskoi Federatsii" (President of Russia, August 6, 2014), http://www.kremlin.ru/acts/bank/38809; "Ukaz N391 Ob otdel'nykh

spetsial'nykh ekonomicheskikh merakh v tseliakh obespecheniia bezopasnosti Rossiiskoi Federatsii" (President of Russia, July 29, 2015), http://www.kremlin.ru/acts/bank/39975; "Bolee 36 tys. tonn produktov unichtozhil Rosselkhoznadzor za 5 let," *Agronews*, August 6, 2020, https://agronews.com/ru/ru/news/breaking-news/2020-08-06/46206; for a video recording of food destruction see "Uzhe tri goda v Rossii daviat i szhigaiut produkty" (TV Rain, August 13, 2018), https://youtu.be/6ECA8RyMiQU.

5. Elena Mukhametshina, "Rossiiane ne podderzhivaiut unichtozhenie sanktsionnykh produktov—'Levada-Tsentr,'" *Vedomosti*, August 12, 2015, https://www.vedomosti.ru/politics/articles/2015/08/13/604601-rossiyane-ne-podderzhivayut-unichtozhenie-sanktsionnih-produktov; Rustem Faliakhov, "Parmezanskie voiny: pochem embargo dlia naroda," *Gazeta.ru*, August 6, 2020, https://www.gazeta.ru/business/2020/08/06/13184413.shtml.

6. Susanne Wengle, "The Domestic Effects of the Russian Food Embargo," *Demokratizatsiya: The Journal of Post-Soviet Democratization* 24, no. 3 (2016): 281–89; Smutka Lubos et al., "Agrarian Import Ban and Its Impact on the Russian and European Union Agrarian Trade Performance," *Agricultural Economics* 62, no. 11 (2016): 493–506; Paulina Pospieszna, Joanna Skrzypczyńska, and Beata Stępień, "Hitting Two Birds with One Stone: How Russian Countersanctions Intertwined Political and Economic Goals," *PS: Political Science & Politics* 53, no. 2 (2020): 243–47.

7. Nicholas Mulder, *The Economic Weapon: The Rise of Sanctions as a Tool of Modern War* (New Haven, CT: Yale University Press, 2022), 4.

8. Mulder, *The Economic Weapon*, 11.

9. Risa A. Brooks, "Sanctions and Regime Type: What Works, and When?," *Security Studies* 11, no. 4 (2002): 1–50; Kerim Can Kavaklı, J. Tyson Chatagnier, and Emre Hatipoğlu, "The Power to Hurt and the Effectiveness of International Sanctions," *Journal of Politics* 82, no. 3 (2020): 879–94.

10. "Internet-konferentssiia Ministra sel'skogo khoziiaistva Rossiiskoi Federatsii Alekseiia Gordeeva," November 22, 2006, https://www.agroyug.ru/news/id-4280; Mikhail Chkanikov, "Kolbasnyi krug," *Rossiiskaia gazeta*, April 24, 2008, https://dlib.eastview.com/browse/doc/14300039.

11. Mikhail Chkanikov, "Molchanie teliat," *Rossiiskaia gazeta*, July 13, 2009, https://dlib.eastview.com/browse/doc/20346477.

12. Richard Connolly and Philip Hanson, "Import Substitution and Economic Sovereignty in Russia," *Research Paper*, 2016, 3–5.

13. Not only beer but other alcoholic products, such as wine, brandy, sparkling wine, and hard liquor, were not included in banned products despite the fact that in prior years Russia had banned wine imports from Moldova (2006–2007, 2011, 2013–2017) and Georgia (2006–2013) as a form of political punishment.

14. Masha Hedberg, "The Target Strikes Back: Explaining Countersanctions and Russia's Strategy of Differentiated Retaliation," *Post-Soviet Affairs* 34, no. 1 (2018): 36.

15. Shortly after announcing the food import ban, Russia lifted import restrictions on beef, poultry, pork, and milk from Brazil. Hedberg, "The Target Strikes Back," 41.

16. There is no evidence that any food-related Western sanctions against Russia were planned or even considered.
17. "Plan meropriiatii ('dorozhnaia karta') po importzameshcheniiu v sel'skom khoziaistve na 2014–2015 gody" (Government of the Russian Federation, October 2, 2014), http://static.government.ru/media/files/hZ8xLKjTbJk.pdf; Vladimir Putin, "Poslanie Prezidenta Federal'nomu Sobraniiu" (President of Russia, December 3, 2015), http://kremlin.ru/events/president/news/50864.
18. Taras Fomchenkov, "Poteri stran Zapada ot prodembargo sostavili 8,8 milliarda dollarov," *Rossiiskaia gazeta*, August 8, 2016, https://rg.ru/2016/08/02/poteri-stran-zapada-ot-prodembargo-sostavili-86-milliarda-dollarov.html; Elena Gosteva, "Putin podshchital poteri: kto bol'she postradal ot sanktsii," *Gazeta.ru*, June 20, 2019, https://www.gazeta.ru/business/2019/06/20/12429169.shtml?updated; "Finlandiia otsenila poteri ot sanktsionnoi voiny ES i Rossii," *Regnum.ru*, May 5, 2016, https://regnum.ru/news/economy/2128693.html.
19. Elena Mukhametshina, "Bol'shinstvo rossiian ne chustvuet problem ot zapadnykh sanktsii," *Vedomosti*, March 17, 2020, https://www.vedomosti.ru/society/articles/2020/03/17/825343-bolshinstvo-chuvstvuet.
20. Viktoriia Poliakova, "Posol Italii poprosil po druzhbe otmenit' ogranicheniia na parmezan v Rossii," *RBC.ru*, March 26, 2021, https://www.rbc.ru/business/26/03/2021/605d75809a79478894e60792; "Posol Italii prizval Rossiiu razreshit' vvoz parmezana," *Meduza*, March 26, 2021, https://meduza.io/news/2021/03/26/posol-italii-prizval-rossiyu-razreshit-vvoz-parmezana-odin-iz-rossiyskih-syrovarov-poprosil-ne-delat-etogo-esche-pyat-shest-let.
21. Mariia Sikorskaia, "Kto teper' est pol'skie iabloki," *Novaya polsha*, July 11, 2019, https://novayapolsha.pl/article/kto-teper-est-polskie-yabloki/.
22. Evgeny Andreev, "Popali mimo iablochka," *Novaya gazeta*, May 13, 2016, https://novayagazeta.ru/articles/2016/05/13/68573-popali-mimo-yablochka; Vasilii Uzun and Dariia Loginova, "Rossiiskoe prodovol'stvennoe embargo: poteri zapadnykh stran nesushchestvenny," *Russian Economic Development* 23, no. 9 (2016): 17–23.
23. Stephen K. Wegren and Christel Elvestad, "Russia's Food Self-Sufficiency and Food Security: An Assessment," *Post-Communist Economies* 30, no. 5 (2018): 574.
24. Andreev, "Popali mimo iablochka"; William M. Liefert et al., "The Effect of Russia's Economic Crisis and Import Ban on Its Agricultural and Food Sector," *Journal of Eurasian Studies* 10, no. 2 (2019): 119–35.
25. Evgeny Gaiva, "Est' svoe," *Rossiiskaia gazeta*, August 6, 2019, https://dlib.eastview.com/browse/doc/54175574.
26. Tatiana Karabut, "Za miluiu tushu," *Rossiiskaia gazeta*, July 20, 2020, https://dlib.eastview.com/browse/doc/60657650.
27. Faliakhov, "Parmezanskie voiny."
28. Sergey Aleksashenko, "The Ruble Currency Storm Is Over, but Is the Russian Economy Ready for the Next One?," *Brookings* (blog), May 18, 2015, https://www.brookings.edu/blog/up-front/2015/05/18/the-ruble-currency-storm-is-over-but-is-the-russian-economy-ready-for-the-next-one/.

29. Natal'ia Volchkova and Polina Kuznetsova, "Skol'ko stoiat Kontrsanktsii: Analiz Blagosostoianiia," *Zhurnal Novoi Ekonomicheskoi Assotsiatsii* 43, no. 3 (2019): 173–83, https://doi.org/10.31737/2221-2264-2019-43-3-9.
30. Natalia Shagaida and Vasilii Uzun, "Tendentsii razvitiia i osnovnye vyzovy agrarnogo sektora Rossii" (2017).
31. Irina Skrynnik, "V Rossii khotiat ukazanii: delaem raz, dva, tri," *Vedomosti*, July 20, 2015, https://www.vedomosti.ru/business/characters/2015/07/21/601427-v-rossii-hotyat-ukazanii-delaem-raz-dva-tri; William M. Liefert and Olga Liefert, "Russia's Economic Crisis and Its Agricultural and Food Economy," *Choices* 30, no. 1 (2015): 1–6.
32. Aleksandr Andriukhin, "Mlechnyi put'," *Kul'tura*, September 30, 2014, https://portal-kultura.ru/articles/country/59169-mlechnyy-put/.
33. Belov, Authors' Interview; Evgeny Gaiva, "So svoim karavaem," *Rossiiskaia gazeta*, July 13, 2018, https://dlib.eastview.com/browse/doc/51449849.
34. "Posol Italii prizval Rossiiu razreshit' vvoz parmezana."
35. Iushin, Authors' Interview.
36. Liefert et al., "The Effect of Russia's Economic Crisis and Import Ban on Its Agricultural and Food Sector," 131.
37. "Dinamika otnoshenii k sanktsiiam i kontrsanktsiiam" (Fond Obshestvennoe Mnenie, April 12, 2016), https://fom.ru/Ekonomika/12599.
38. Ekaterina Kravchenko, "'Iz nichego isteriku zakatily, balaboly'. Viktor Linnik i Vadim Dymov o zaprete na vvoz khamona i parmezana v Rossiiu," *Forbes*, April 30, 2019, https://www.forbes.ru/biznes/375489-iz-nichego-isteriku-zakatili-balaboly-viktor-linnik-i-vadim-dymov-o-zaprete-na-vvoz; "Izvestnye rossiiskie polittekhnologi ob"iavili 'Miratorgu' i 'Dymovu' boikot za 'balabolov,'" *EAN News*, April 30, 2019, https://eanews.ru/news/izvestnyye-rossiyskiy-polittekhnologi-ob-yavili-miratorgu-i-dymovu-boykot-za-balabolov_30-04-2019.
39. Susanne A. Wengle, *Black Earth, White Bread*: A Technopolitical History of Russian Agriculture and Food (Madison: University of Wisconsin Press, 2022), 173.
40. Kirill Rodin, "Spetsifika vospriiatiia zhiteliami Rossii otechestvennykh i importnykh produktov pitaniia na fone ekonomicheskikh sanktsii" (VTSIOM, 2021), https://wciom.ru/presentation/prezentacii/specifika-vosprijatija-zhiteljami-rossii-otechestvennykh-i-importnykh-produktov-pitanija-na-fone-ehkonomicheskikh-sankcii. On the impact of the economic sanctions imposed by the West on Russians' attitudes see Timothy Frye, "Economic Sanctions and Public Opinion: Survey Experiments from Russia," *Comparative Political Studies* 52, no. 7 (2019): 967–94.
41. We discuss Tkachev and his business more in depth in Chapter 8.
42. Mark Galeotti, *We Need to Talk about Putin*: How the West Gets Him Wrong (London: Random House, 2019), chap. "Cast of Characters."
43. "Ekspertiza kandidatskoi dissertatsii Dmitriia Nikolaevicha Patrusheva" (Dissernet), accessed August 22, 2022, https://www.dissernet.org/expertise/patrushevdn2003.htm; "Ekspertiza doktorskoi dissertatsii Dmitriia Nikolaevicha Patrusheva" (Dissernet), accessed August 22, 2022, https://www.dissernet.org/expertise/patrushevdn2008.htm.

192 NOTES

44. Stephen K. Wegren, Alexander M. Nikulin, and Irina Trotsuk, "Russian Agriculture during Putin's Fourth Term: A SWOT Analysis," *Post-Communist Economies* 31, no. 4 (2019): 422.
45. Amy Knight, "Anti-Putin Campaigners: It's Time to Sanction the Large Adult Sons of Oligarchs and Cronies," *Daily Beast*, March 2, 2021, sec. world, https://www.thedailybeast.com/anti-putin-campaigners-say-its-time-to-sanction-sons-of-oligarchs-and-cronies; "Putin nagradil syna Patrusheva ordenom Pocheta," *RBC.ru*, October 27, 2016, https://www.rbc.ru/rbcfreenews/5811e8729a7947610dfa2b6d.
46. Wegren, Nikulin, and Trotsuk, "Russian Agriculture during Putin's Fourth Term: A SWOT Analysis," 422.
47. Wegren, Nikulin, and Trotsuk, "Russian Agriculture during Putin's Fourth Term," 422.
48. "Ukaz Prezidenta Rossiiskoi Federatsii N120 Ob utverzhdenii Doktriny prodovol'stvennoi bezopasnosti Rossiiskoi Federatsii."
49. While the WTO is not mentioned in the text even once, the Eurasian Economic Union appears nine times.
50. "Proekt: Strategiia razvitiia pishchevoi i pererabatyvaiushchei promyshlennosti Rossiiskoi Federatsii na period do 2030 goda" (Ministry of Agriculture, 2019), barley-malt.ru/wp-content/uploads/2019/11/proekt-strategyy-razvytyja-pyschevoj-y-pererabatyvajuschej-promyshlennosty-rf.pdf.
51. Alesia Anishchenko and Anatolii Shut'kov, "Problemy realizatsii Doktriny Prodovol'stvennoi Bezopasnosti Rossii," *Prodovol'stvennaia politika i bezopasnost'* 8, no. 1 (2021): 15, https://doi.org/10.18334/ppib.8.1.111777.
52. Mariia Sulima and Sergei Grishunin, "Importzameshchenie ili peremeshchenie?" (Natsional'noe Reitingovoe Agenstvo, December 2020), https://www.ra-national.ru/sites/default/files/Review_Import%20substitution_NRA_Dec.%202020_0.pdf.

Chapter 7

1. "Top 10 Russian Most Expensive Landholders 2021" (The Leibniz Institute of Agricultural Development in Transition Economies, March 8, 2021), https://www.largescaleagriculture.com/home/news-details/top-10-russian-most-expensive-landholders-2021/.
2. Vasily Uzun, Natalya Shagaida, and Zvi Lerman, "Russian Agroholdings and Their Role in Agriculture," *Post-Communist Economies* 33, no. 8 (2021): 3–4.
3. Uzun, Shagaida, and Lerman, "Russian Agroholdings and Their Role in Agriculture."
4. Natalia Shagaida and Vasilii Uzun, "Draivery rosta i strukturnykh sdvigov v sel'skom khoziaistve Rossii" (Moscow, 2019), 36.
5. Uzun, Shagaida, and Lerman, "Russian Agroholdings and Their Role in Agriculture."
6. Uzun, Shagaida, and Lerman, "Russian Agroholdings and Their Role in Agriculture," 3; see also Oane Visser, Natalia Mamonova, and Max Spoor, "Oligarchs, Megafarms and Land Reserves," *Journal of Peasant Studies* 39, no. 3–4 (2012): 899–931.
7. "Noveishaia gigantomaniia," *Krestianskie vedomosti*, October 20, 2009, https://kvedomosti.ru/pressa/novejshaya-gigantomaniya.html.

8. Iushin, Authors' Interview.
9. Wengle, *Black Earth, White Bread: A Technopolitical History of Russian Agriculture and Food* (Madison: University of Wisconsin Press, 2022), 59.
10. Wengle, *Black Earth, White Bread*, 123.
11. Wengle, *Black Earth, White Bread*, 42.
12. Evegnii Arsiukhin, "Aleksei Gordeev: V Rossii ne dolzhno byt' golodnykh," *Rossiiskaia gazeta*, December 5, 2003.
13. Wengle, *Black Earth, White Bread*, 29.
14. Uzun, Shagaida, and Lerman, "Russian Agroholdings and Their Role in Agriculture," 9–10; Shagaida and Uzun, "Draivery rosta i strukturnykh sdvigov v sel'skom khoziaistve Rossii," 42.
15. Tatyana Nefedova, "Dvadtsat' piat' let postsovetskomu sel'skomu khoziaistvu Rossii: Geograficheskie tendentsii i protivorechiia," *Izvestiia RAN. Seriia geograficheskaia* 5 (2017): 7–18, https://doi.org/10.7868/S0373244417050012.
16. Il'ia Matveev, "Krupnyi biznes v Putinskoi Rossii: Starye i novye istochniki vliianiia na vlast'," *Mir Rossii* 28, no. 1 (2019): 55, https://doi.org/0.17323/1811-038X-2019-28-1-54-74.
17. Starikov, Authors' Interview.
18. Wengle, *Black Earth, White Bread*, 188.
19. Svetlana Barsukova, "Dilemma 'fermery-Agroholdingi' v kontekste importzamescheniia," *Obschestvennye nauki i sovremennost'* 5 (2016): 63–74; Susanne A. Wengle, "Agroholdings, Technology, and the Political Economy of Russian Agriculture," *Laboratorium* 13, no. 1 (2021): 57–80.
20. David Szakonyi, *Politics for Profit: Business, Elections, and Policymaking in Russia* (New York: Cambridge University Press, 2020).
21. "Syn voronezhskogo gubernatora Nikita Gordeev prodaet agrokholding Okaagro Stefanu Diurru," *Chetyre pera: Nezavisimyi obschestvenno-politicheskii portal Voronezha*, December 2017, http://4pera.com/news/picture_of_the_day/syn_voronezhskogo_gubernatora_nikita_gordeev_prodaet_agrokholding_okaagro_shtefanu_dyurru/.
22. Aleksandr Trushin, "Agrokholdingi—detishche nashei ekonomiki," *Kommersant*, October 31, 2016, https://www.kommersant.ru/doc/3127445.
23. Wengle, *Black Earth, White Bread*, 131.
24. Andrei Markov, "Svinotsid Gubernatora Gordeeva," *Moscow Post*, September 30, 2013, http://www.compromat.ru/page_33817.htm.
25. Trushin, "Agrokholdingi—detishche nashei ekonomiki."
26. "Krupneishie vladel'tsy sel'skokhoziaistvennoi zemli v Rossii v Rossii na 2020 god" (BEFL, May 2020), https://www.befl.ru/upload/iblock/d6a/d6a4b0dde4f8168cdb5dda65b3910d33.pdf.
27. Shagaida and Uzun, "Draivery rosta i strukturnykh sdvigov v sel'skom khoziaistve Rossii," 7; Anastasiia Bashkatova, "Rossiia prevraschaetsia v stranu gigantskikh agroholdingov," *Nezavisimaia gazeta*, November 14, 2016, https://www.ng.ru/economics/2016-11-14/1_6859_agro.html.
28. Evgeny Titov, "Tkachev. Krestnyi otets zemli Russkoi," *Novaya gazeta*, January 13, 2011, https://novayagazeta.ru/politics/7575.html.

29. "Tkachev, Aleksandr" (Lenta.ru, December 9, 2004), https://lenta.ru/lib/14173927/full.
30. Aleksei Titkov, "Kruche 'tsapkov' na Kubani tol'ko 'tkachi,'" *Osobaia bukva*, January 14, 2011, https://www.specletter.com/corruption/2011-01-14/kruche-tsapkov-na-kubani-tolko-tkachi.html; Rinat Sagdiev, "Kak agrokholding ministra Tkacheva vybilsia v lidery rynka," *Vedomosti*, August 7, 2016, https://www.vedomosti.ru/business/articles/2016/08/08/652058-kak-agroholding-ministra-selskogo-hozyaistva-aleksandra-tkacheva-vibilsya-lideri-rinka.
31. Aleksandr Piatin, "Eks-glava Minsel'khoza okazalsia kontroliruiushchim aktsionerom krupneishego zemlevladel'tsa v Rossii," *Forbes Russia*, April 15, 2021, https://www.forbes.ru/newsroom/biznes/426511-eks-glava-minselhoza-okazalsya-kontroliruyushchim-akcionerom-krupneyshego.
32. Pavel Sheremet, "Kazak s partbiletami," *Kommersant*, November 29, 2000, https://www.kommersant.ru/doc/1544834.
33. Il'ia Azar, "Ugod'ia markiza Karabasa," *Meduza*, April 29, 2015, https://meduza.io/feature/2015/04/29/ugodya-markiza-karabasa.
34. Pavel Sedakov and Igor Popov, "Brat, svat i shtrafbat: kak ustroen biznes sem'i Aleksandra Tkacheva," *Forbes Russia*, August 10, 2015, https://www.forbes.ru/sobytiya/vlast/296467-brat-svat-i-shtrafbat-kak-ustroen-biznes-semi-aleksandra-tkacheva.
35. Sagdiev, "Kak agrokholding ministra Tkacheva vybilsia v lidery rynka."
36. Titov, "Tkachev. Krestnyi otets zemli Russkoi."
37. Sedakov and Popov, "Brat, svat i shtrafbat."
38. Aleksandr Vorob'ev, "Sel'khozaktivy Valinor Group pokupaet Krasnodarskii 'Agrokompleks,'" *Vedomosti*, November 14, 2014, https://www.vedomosti.ru/business/articles/2014/11/14/agrokompleks-sobiraet-zemli.
39. Sagdiev, "Kak agrokholding ministra Tkacheva vybilsia v lidery rynka."
40. Sagdiev, "Kak agrokholding ministra Tkacheva vybilsia v lidery rynka."
41. Sagdiev, "Kak agrokholding ministra Tkacheva vybilsia v lidery rynka."
42. Sagdiev, "Kak agrokholding ministra Tkacheva vybilsia v lidery rynka."
43. "'Agrocomplex' im. Tkacheva poluchit rekordnye subsidii na moloko," *RBC Kuban'*, April 5, 2017, https://kuban.rbc.ru/krasnodar/freenews/58e49b6e9a7947cc504e3d0d.
44. Ekaterina Burlakova, "Agrokompleks imeni Tkacheva stal chetvertym vladel'tsem sel'khozzemel' v Rossii," *Vedomosti*, April 24, 2017, https://www.vedomosti.ru/business/articles/2017/04/24/687150-agrokompleks.
45. "Agrokompleks imeni Tkacheva podtverdil status krupneishego zemlevladel'tsa Rossii" (Expert Yug, March 3, 2021), https://expertsouth.ru/news/agrokompleks-imeni-tkacheva-podtverdil-status-krupneyshego-zemlevladeltsa-rossii-/.
46. "Kto i zachem opublikoval video s poiushchimi v samolete Dvorkovichem, Tkachevym i Timakovoi," *BFM.ru*, February 14, 2019, https://www.bfm.ru/news/406879.
47. Aleksandr Sazonov, "Sladkaia zhizn'. Vadim Moshkovich," *Forbes Russia*, December 2, 2006, https://www.forbes.ru/forbes/issue/2006-12/16614-sladkaya-zhizn.

48. "'Rusagro' i l'goty dlia kiprskikh offshorov," *Polit.ru*, accessed August 29, 2022, https://polit.ru/article/2021/04/05/rusagro/.
49. Matvey Sergeev, "Gendirektor Rusagro obzavelsia immunitetom," *Kommersant*, February 26, 2006, https://www.kommersant.ru/doc/652646.
50. Sazonov, "Sladkaia zhizn."
51. Sergei Kisin, "Glavu 'Rusagro' obvinili v moshennichestve," *Kommersant*, February 1, 2005, https://www.kommersant.ru/doc/543213.
52. "'Rusagro' i l'goty dlia kiprskikh offshorov"; "Krupneishie vladel'tsy sel'skokhoziaistvennoi zemli v Rossii na 2020 god"; Wengle, *Black Earth, White Bread*, 114.
53. "'Rusagro' i l'goty dlia kiprskikh offshorov"; "Minsel'khoz RF vkliuchil v svoi perechen' 66 sistemoobrazuiushchikh predpriiatii," *Kommersant*, April 21, 2020, https://www.interfax.ru/business/705378.
54. Sazonov, "Sladkaia zhizn."
55. Sazonov, "Sladkaia zhizn."
56. "'Rusagro' i l'goty dlia kiprskikh offshorov."
57. Irina Gruzinova and Galina Zinchenko, "Bekon vmesto betona: Pochemu Vadim Moshkovich ushel iz stroitel'nogo biznesa," *Forbes Russia*, September 25, 2015, https://www.forbes.ru/milliardery/301229-bekon-vmesto-betona-pochemu-vladimir-moshkovich-ushel-iz-stroitelnogo-biznesa.
58. Gruzinova and Zinchenko, "Bekon vmesto betona."
59. Gruzinova and Zinchenko, "Bekon vmesto betona."
60. Inga Pavskaia, "Siloviki sdvinut Moshkovicha s mesta 'pod solntsem'?," *Utro News*, December 30, 2019, https://utro-news.ru/siloviki-sdvinut-moshkovicha-s-mesta-pod-solncem/; Irina Kondrat'eva, "Bankrotstvo kak sredstvo ot konkurentov: 'Solnechnye Produkty' doshli do VS," *Pravo.ru*, September 14, 2020, https://pravo.ru/story/225655/.
61. Ruslan Orlianskii, "'Spetsoperatsiia-kooperatsiia' Patrusheva," *Moscow Post*, July 10, 2019, http://www.moscow-post.su/economics/specoperaciya_kooperaciya_patrusheva30069/.
62. Gruzinova and Zinchenko, "Bekon vmesto betona."
63. Evgeny Safronov and Elene Vinogradova, "Gendirektor 'Rusagro' oproverg ot"ezd za granitsu sovladel'tsa kompanii Vadima Moshkovicha posle spora s Putinym," *Otkrytye media*, May 19, 2021, https://openmedia.io/news/n2/gendirektor-rusagro-oproverg-otezd-za-granicu-sovladelca-kompanii-vadima-moshkovicha-posle-spora-s-putinym/; "Begi, Vadik, begi: Vadim Moshkovich pokinul Rossiu?," *Biznes-Vektor*, May 19, 2021, https://www.business-vector.info/begi-vadik-begi-vadim-120532/.
64. Anatolii Kostyrev, "V pshenitse prorastayut prodavtsy," *Kommersant*, April 20, 2023, https://www.kommersant.ru/doc/5941249.
65. According to the Russian Registrar of Companies, APH Miratorg, the holding company of Miratorg Group, is owned by two Cyprus entities: Agromir Ltd. and Saudade Enterprises Ltd. These are limited liability companies, and information on their shareholders and ultimate beneficial owners is not publicly disclosed.

66. Aleksandr Levinskii, "Kak Miratorg s pomoshch'iu gosudarstva stal prodovol'stvennym gigantom," *Forbes Russia*, April 8, 2019, https://www.forbes.ru/biznes/374459-kak-miratorg-s-pomoshchyu-gosudarstva-stal-prodovolstvennym-gigantom.
67. Levinskii, "Kak Miratorg s pomoshch'iu gosudarstva stal prodovol'stvennym gigantom"; Wengle, *Black Earth, White Bread*, 76.
68. Levinskii, "Kak Miratorg s pomoshch'iu gosudarstva stal prodovol'stvennym gigantom."
69. "Krupneishie vladel'tsy sel'skokhoziaistvennoi zemli v Rossii v Rossii na 2020 god."
70. https://miratorg.ru/investors/.
71. Irina Skrynnik, "Nastuplenie svinei: kak Miratorg zavoeval rossiiskii produktovyi rynok," *Forbes Russia*, October 16, 2014, https://www.forbes.ru/kompanii/potrebi telskii-rynok/270697-nastuplenie-svinei-kak-miratorg-zavoeval-rossiiskii-produkto vyi; Levinskii, "Kak Miratorg s pomoshch'iu gosudarstva stal prodovol'stvennym gigantom."
72. Roman Streletskii, "Dmitry Medvedev ne spaset brat'ev Linnikov," *Kompromat*, February 19, 2021, https://compromat.group/main/economics/39768-dmitriy-medvedev-ne-spaset-bratev-linnikov.html; "Pravitel'stvo RF oproverglo rodstvo zheny Medvedeva i glav Miratorga," *Interfax*, May 3, 2019, https://www.interfax.ru/russia/660058.
73. "Stoit li Medvedev za Miratorgom," *Gde den'gi* (Navalny LIVE, April 19, 2019), https://www.youtube.com/watch?v=Zc1k0eMSUUI.
74. Aleksandr Pirogov, "Top-100—Miratorg: miasom naruzhu," *Abireg.Ru*, November 23, 2018, https://abireg.ru/n_71911.html.
75. Levinskii, "Kak Miratorg s pomoshch'iu gosudarstva stal prodovol'stvennym gigantom"; Aleksandra Koreneva, "Rosselkhoznadzor voz'met vsekh v svoi ruki: raionnykh veterinarov obvinili v neblagonadezhnosti," *AgroBook*, May 22, 2019, https://agrobook.ru/blog/user/aleksandra-koreneva/rosselhoznadzor-vozmyot-vseh-v-svoi-ruki-rayonnyh-veterinarov-obvinili.
76. Levinskii, "Kak Miratorg s pomoshch'iu gosudarstva stal prodovol'stvennym gigantom."
77. Skrynnik, "Nastuplenie svinei."
78. Pirogov, "Top-100—Miratorg: miasom naruzhu."
79. Dmitry Zhuravsky, "Nastiness Is a Warm Gun: The Kremlin's Cowboys," *Russian Reader*, May 7, 2019, https://therussianreader.com/2019/05/07/miratorg/.
80. Elena Loktiononva, "Koroli i miaso," *Kommersant*, February 8, 2010, https://www.kommersant.ru/doc/1310339; Skrynnik, "Nastuplenie svinei"; Irina Skrynnik, "'Miratorg' poluchit ot VEBa $425.8 mln na 15 let na proizvodstvo goviadiny," *Vedomosti*, January 27, 2015, https://www.vedomosti.ru/business/articles/2015/01/27/miratorg-poluchit-ot-veba-4258-mln-na-15-let-na-proizvodstvo.
81. "Miratorg i Sberbank CIB podpisali pervoe v istorii APK Rossii kreditnoe soglashenie srokom na 15 let" (Sberbank, June 6, 2013), https://cbonds.ru/news/655263.
82. Levinskii, "Kak Miratorg s pomoshch'iu gosudarstva stal prodovol'stvennym gigantom."

83. Anders Åslund, *Russia's Crony Capitalism: The Path from Market Economy to Kleptocracy* (New Haven, CT: Yale University Press, 2019).

Chapter 8

1. Kevin Rothrock, "'Vladimir the Poisoner': A Translation of Alexey Navalny's Speech in Court on February 2," *Meduza* (blog), February 2, 2021, https://meduza.io/en/feature/2021/02/02/vladimir-the-poisoner.
2. Andrea Palasciano, "Putin Urges Food Price Cap as Russian Economy Falters," *Moscow Times*, December 16, 2020.
3. Emiko Terazono, Heba Saleh, and John Reed, "Countries Follow Consumers in Stockpiling Food," *Financial Times*, April 5, 2020, https://www.ft.com/content/5c8cbc60-aec0-4f3d-b0e2-a5e44f0c6f74.
4. David M. Beasley, "Covid-19 Could Detonate a 'Hunger Pandemic.' with Millions at Risk, the World Must Act," *Washington Post*, April 22, 2020, https://www.washingtonpost.com/opinions/2020/04/22/covid-19-could-detonate-hunger-pandemic-with-millions-risk-world-must-act/.
5. "The Hunger Virus Multiplies: Deadly Recipe of Conflict, COVID-19 and Climate Accelerate World Hunger," Oxfam Media Briefing (Oxfam, July 9, 2021), https://oi-files-d8-prod.s3.eu-west-2.amazonaws.com/s3fs-public/2021-07/The%20Hunger%20Virus%202.0_media%20brief_EN.pdf.
6. Manny Fernandez, "Coronavirus and Poverty: A Mother Skips Meals So Her Children Can Eat," *New York Times*, March 20, 2020.
7. Ceylan Yeginsu, "'It's Very Scary': U.K. Food Banks Close as Coronavirus Stalls Donations," *New York Times*, March 19, 2020; Kyle Swenson, "Coronavirus Could Push 250,000 into Hunger in D.C. Region, Report Says," *Washington Post*, July 22, 2020, https://www.washingtonpost.com/local/social-issues/dc-coronavirus-hunger-report/2020/07/22/ad6f33b0-cad4-11ea-b0e3-d55bda07d66a_story.html.
8. Kenneth Rosen, "Stoking Unrest and Distributing Groceries: Italy's Mafias Gain Ground in Fight for Loyalty during Pandemic Lockdown," *Newsweek*, April 18, 2020.
9. Eric Helleiner, "The Return of National Self-Sufficiency? Excavating Autarkic Thought in a De-Globalizing Era," *International Studies Review* 23, no. 3 (2021): 933–57.
10. Andrew E. Kramer, "Thanks to Sanctions, Russia Is Cushioned From Virus's Economic Shocks," *New York Times*, March 20, 2020.
11. Jeffrey Mankoff, "Russia's Response to Covid-19" (Center for Strategic and International Studies, April 10, 2020), https://www.csis.org/analysis/russias-response-covid-19.
12. Iuliia Starostina and Ivan Tkachev, "Rosstat otsenil mashtab snizhennia real'nykh raspologaemykh dokhodov rossiian," *RBC.ru*, January 28, 2021, https://www.rbc.ru/economics/28/01/2021/60129a749a7947cf1ca85d53.

13. Elena Sukhorukova, "Rossiia v 2020 godu pokazala rekord po postavkam prodovol'stviia za rubezh," *RBC.ru*, March 9, 2021, https://www.rbc.ru/business/09/03/2021/604217269a79471196c1131b.
14. Dar'ia Andrianova, Aleksei Polukhin, and Khalil Aminov, "Plody stabil'nosti," *Kommersant*, April 23, 2021, https://www.kommersant.ru/doc/4783655.
15. "UNICEF: Bolee 9 mln rossiian ekonomiat na ede i nedoedaiut," *BBC*, July 14, 2021, https://www.bbc.com/russian/news-57807139.
16. "Food Index vernulsia k dokarantinnym znacheniiam" (Romir, July 9, 2020), https://romir.ru/studies/food-index-vernulsya-k-dokarantinnym-znacheniyam.
17. "Dorogoi minimum," April 22, 2021, https://finexpertiza.ru/press-service/researches/2021/dorogoy-minimum/.
18. "Problemy obshchestva" (Levada-Tsentr, March 9, 2021), https://www.levada.ru/2021/03/09/problemy-obshhestva/.
19. Timothy Frye et al., "Is Putin's Popularity Real?," *Post-Soviet Affairs* 33, no. 1 (2017): 1–15.
20. "Activities at Navalny Offices Suspended by Russian Court" (RFERL, April 26, 2021), https://www.rferl.org/a/russia-navalny-foundation-extremist-label-court/31222994.html.
21. Isabelle Khurshudyan, "Putin Is Boiling over Rising Pasta Prices in Russia. It Seems More about Populism than Penne," *Washington Post*, December 16, 2021, https://www.washingtonpost.com/world/europe/russia-pasta-food-prices-putin/2020/12/16/0c0cde72-3ed9-11eb-b58b-1623f6267960_story.html.
22. Maria Lisitsyna, "Putin raskritikoval Reshetnikova za 'eksperimenty' s tsenami na produkty," *RBC.ru*, December 13, 2020, https://www.rbc.ru/society/13/12/2020/5fd5ea339a79474886223f5f.
23. "Ezhegodnaia press-konferentsiia Vladimira Putina" (Office of the President of Russia, December 17, 2020), http://kremlin.ru/events/president/news/64671.
24. "Ezhegodnaia press-konferentsiia Vladimira Putina."
25. Georgii Tadtaev, "Genprokuratura nachala proverku rosta tsen na produkty," *RBC.ru*, December 11, 2020, https://www.rbc.ru/society/11/12/2020/5fd37d009a794742ef97893d.
26. Government Decrees N. 2094, 2095, 2096, 2097.
27. "Mikhail Mishustin podpisal riad postanovlenii dlia stabilizatsii situatsii na rynke prodovol'stviia" (Government of the Russian Federation, December 15, 2020), http://government.ru/news/41118/.
28. "Maksim Reshetnikov: nuzhno sozdat' predskazuemyi i poniatnyi mekhanizm reagirovaniia na kolebaniia tsen na produkty" (Ministerstvo ekonomicheskogo razvitiia Rossiiskoi Federatsii, December 16, 2020), https://www.economy.gov.ru/material/news/maksim_reshetnikov_nuzhno_sozdat_predskazuemyy_i_ponyatnyy_mehanizm_reagirovaniya_na_kolebaniya_cen_na_produkty.html; "Pravitel'stvo RF podderzhalo zakonoproekt o vozmozhnosti gosregulirovaniia tsen na produkty v sluchae rosta tsen" (Ministerstvo ekonomicheskogo razvitiia Rossiiskoi Federatsii, December 16, 2020), https://www.economy.gov.ru/material/news/

pravitelstvo_rf_podderzhalo_zakonoproekt_o_vozmozhnosti_gosregulirovaniya_cen_na_produkty_v_sluchae_rosta_cen.html.
29. Draft Law 1024255-7, signed by Putin and published December 30, 2020.
30. Susanne A. Wengle, *Black Earth, White Bread: A Technopolitical History of Russian Agriculture and Food* (Madison: University of Wisconsin Press, 2022), 4.
31. "FSN podkliuchilas' k kontroliu za tsenami na produkty," *Interfax*, January 26, 2021, https://www.interfax.ru/business/746852.
32. "Zhirinovsky predlozhil sposob 'navesti poriadok' s tsenami na produkty," *Lenta.ru*, December 17, 2020, https://lenta.ru/news/2020/12/17/poryadok/.
33. Evgeny Safronov and Elene Vinogradova, "Gendirektor 'Rusagro' oproverg ot"ezd za granitsu sovladel'tsa kompanii Vadima Moshkovicha posle spora s Putinym," *Otkrytye media*, May 19, 2021.
34. Vitalii Miagkii, "Mishustin vydelil na zamorozku tsen eshche 9 milliardov rublei," *URA.ru*, April 7, 2021, https://ura.news/news/1052479417; Andrei Zlobin, "Pravitel'stvo prodlilo zamorozku tsen na sakhar i podsolnechnoe maslo," *Forbes*, March 30, 2021, https://www.forbes.ru/newsroom/biznes/424883-pravitelstvo-prodlilo-zamorozku-cen-na-sahar-i-podsolnechnoe-maslo.
35. Anastasiia Batmanova, "Nabiullina prizvala bystree otkazat'sia ot ogranicheniia tsen vlastiami," *RBC.ru*, April 7, 2021, https://www.rbc.ru/economics/07/04/2021/606d7f199a7947a153bb00e2.
36. Ivan Tkachev, "Kudrin-RBK: 'Neskol'ko sot milliardov mogli by snizit' bednost' vdvoe,'" *RBC.ru*, August 3, 2021, https://www.rbc.ru/economics/03/08/2021/610522849a7947d3e7f40be8?from=column_1.
37. "Poslanie Prezidenta Federal'nomu Sobraniiu" (President of Russia, April 21, 2021), http://kremlin.ru/events/president/news/65418.
38. Evgeniia Kuznetsova and Elena Sukhorukova, "Rossiiane stali khuzhe otnosit'sia k prodovol'stvennomu embargo," *RBC.ru*, July 6, 2021, https://www.rbc.ru/society/06/07/2021/60e31b1e9a79474492a76c32.
39. "Ezhegodnyi otchet pravitel'stva v Gosudarstvennoi Dume" (The Government of the Russian Federation, May 12, 2021), http://government.ru/news/42158/.
40. "Andrei Belousov provel soveshchanie po situatsii s tsenami na sotsial'no znachimye tovary" (Government of the Russian Federation, May 18, 2021), http://government.ru/news/42238/.
41. "Ubytki sakharnoi promyshlennosti ot fiksatsii tsen sostaviat okolo 10 milliardov rublei," *Sugar.ru*, April 1, 2021, https://sugar.ru/node/35171; Sakina Nurieva, "Minsel'khoz zaiavil o sderzhivanii rosta tsen proizvoditeliami molochnoi produktsii," *Gazeta.ru*, November 3, 2021, https://m.gazeta.ru/business/news/2021/11/03/n_16795585.shtml.
42. "Rosstat soobschil o roste tsen na produkty s nachala goda," *News.ru*, May 21, 2021, https://news.ru/economics/proizvoditeli-produktov-s-nachala-goda-podnyali-ceny-na-6-4/.
43. "Zasedanie Vysshego Evraziiskogo ekonomicheskogo soveta" (President of Russia, May 21, 2021), http://www.kremlin.ru/events/president/news/65626.

44. Andrew Pulver, "Andrei Konchalovsky: 'I'm Very Glad I Failed in Hollywood,'" *The Guardian*, April 8, 2021, https://www.theguardian.com/film/2021/apr/08/andrei-konchalovsky-im-very-glad-i-failed-in-hollywood. See also Peter Rutland, "Workers against the Worker's State," Part 1: https://jordanrussiacenter.org/news/workers-againstthe-workers-state-part-i/#.Y7GU—xBx26; Part 2: https://jordanrussiacenter.org/news/workers-against-theworkers-state-part-ii/#.Y7GUv-xBx24
45. According to the 2021 Bloomberg Billionaires Index, Usmanov's net worth is $21.1 billion and he occupies the ninety-first spot on the list.
46. Catherine Belton, *Putin's People: How the KGB Took Back Russia and Then Took on the West* (New York: Farrar, Straus & Giroux, 2020), 364.
47. Marat Seleznev, "Talonnaia bednost'," *Lenta.ru*, May 12, 2017, https://lenta.ru/articles/2017/05/12/foodcard; Maksim Builov, "Produktovye kartochki dlia rosta VVP," *Kommersant*, November 2, 2017, https://www.kommersant.ru/doc/3213996; "Minpromtorg podgotovil kontseptsiiu sistemy prodovol'stvennykh kartochek," *Forbes*, September 15, 2015, https://www.forbes.ru/news/299705-minpromtorg-pod gotovil-kontseptsiyu-sistemy-prodovolstvennykh-kartochek.
48. Viktoriia Chernysheva, "Izuchaiut karty," *Rossiiskaia gazeta*, February 24, 2015, https://rg.ru/2015/02/25/karti.html.
49. Chris Miller, *Putinomics: Power and Money in Resurgent Russia* (Chapel Hill: University of North Carolina Press, 2018).
50. Vitalii An'kov, "V Rossii predlozhili vvesti produktovye kartochki dlia maloimushchikh," *RIA Novosti*, December 21, 2020, https://ria.ru/20201221/pitanie-1590151393.html.
51. "Produktovye Sertifikaty," April 23, 2021, https://www.levada.ru/2021/04/23/prod uktovye-sertifikaty/.
52. Andrei Zlobin, "Putin predlozhil podumat' nad produktovymi kartochksmi dlia bednykh," *Forbes*, February 17, 2021, https://www.forbes.ru/newsroom/obshchestvo/421393-putin-predlozhil-podumat-nad-produktovymi-kartochkami-dlya-bednyh.
53. Serova, Authors' Interview.
54. "Prodovol'stvennaia Bezopasnost'" (LDPR, October 13, 2020), https://ldpr.ru/event/98759.
55. "Initsiativy LDPR o sertifikatakh na produkty i semeinom biznese podderzhali v Kremle" (LDPR, February 17, 2021), https://ldpr.ru/event/110284.
56. "I.I. Mel'nikov: V KPRF udivilis' uslyshav predlozhenie 'edinorossov' vvesti prodovol'stvennye talony dlia maloimushchikh" (KPRF, May 23, 2008), https://kprf.ru/rus_soc/57303.html.
57. "Talony na bednost' ili opravdanie 'Mira'?" (KPRF, May 14, 2017), https://msk.kprf.ru/2017/05/14/27052/.
58. "Khroniki velikoi derzhavy: Produktovye kartochki na podkhode?" (KPRF, December 22, 2020), https://msk.kprf.ru/2020/12/22/151713/.
59. "Putin predlozhil podumat' o vvedenii sertifikatov na produkty dlia maloimushchikh," *Kommersant*, February 17, 2021, https://www.kommersant.ru/doc/4693892.
60. "Poslanie Prezidenta Federal'nomu Sobraniiu."

61. Maksim Konnov, "Sovetskii podkhod," *Lenta.ru*, April 2, 2021, https://lenta.ru/articles/2021/04/02/coupons/.
62. Tkachev, "Kudrin-RBK."
63. Lada Shamardina, "Putin nazval 'ne strashnym' ogranichenie pribyli biznesa iz-za kontrolia tsen," *The Bell*, March 11, 2021, https://thebell.io/putin-nazval-ne-strashnym-ogranichenie-pribyli-biznesa-iz-za-kontrolya-tsen.
64. Cook and Dimitrov write about market social contract, "a set of state policies and practices that shield some population strata from the effects of market competition, at the cost of economic efficiency and productivity, in order to maintain social stability." Command capitalism more clearly deviates from the principles of market economy and is much more extensive in its scope and ambition. Linda J. Cook and Martin K. Dimitrov, "The Social Contract Revisited: Evidence from Communist and State Capitalist Economies," *Europe-Asia Studies* 69, no. 1 (2017): 9.
65. Aldo Musacchio and Sergio G. Lazzarini, *Reinventing State Capitalism: Leviathan in Business, Brazil and Beyond* (Cambridge, MA: Harvard University Press, 2014), 2.
66. Paul Dragos Aligica and Vlad Tarko, *Capitalist Alternatives: Models, Taxonomies, Scenarios* (Abingdon: Routledge, 2014), chap. 2.
67. Stephen Fortescue, "Putin in Pikalevo: PR or Watershed?," *Australian Slavonic and East European Studies* 23, no. 1–2 (2010): 19–38.
68. Polina Ivanova, "Protesting No More," *Reuters*, July 30, 2021, https://www.reuters.com/investigates/special-report/russia-navalny-protest-city/?2.

Chapter 9

1. Artur Arutyonov, "ES otkliuchil ot SWIFT 'Sber,' MKB i RSKhB: chto eto znachit," *Forbes Russia*, June 14, 2022, https://www.forbes.ru/finansy/464803-es-gotovitsa-otklucit-ot-swift-sber-i-dva-drugih-krupnyh-banka-cto-eto-znacit.
2. "Russia Sanctions Tracker" (Ashurst), accessed May 10, 2022, https://www.ashurst.com/en/news-and-insights/hubs/sanctions-tracker/; "Almost 1,000 Companies Have Curtailed Operations in Russia—But Some Remain" (Yale School of Management, May 10, 2022), https://som.yale.edu/story/2022/almost-1000-companies-have-curtailed-operations-russia-some-remain.
3. Asim Anand, "The Big 4 of Agriculture Unlikely to Exit Russia despite Mounting Pressure," *S&P Global: Commodity Insights*, April 19, 2022, https://www.spglobal.com/commodityinsights/en/market-insights/blogs/agriculture/041922-russia-ukraine-war-food-adm-bunge-cargill-louis-dreyfus; John Reidy, "Cargill, ADM Scale Back Operations in Russia | World Grain," *World Grain*, March 11, 2022, https://www.world-grain.com/articles/16613-cargill-scales-back-operations-in-russia; "Starbucks, McDonald's Exit Russia as Ukraine War Rages On," *Time*, accessed October 24, 2022, https://time.com/6180652/starbucks-mcdonalds-russia-ukraine/. In March–April 2023, Western agricultural giants, Cargill, Viterra, and Louis Drefus,

announced the end of their involvement in Russia's grain exports, https://news.bloomberglaw.com/international-trade/three-top-western-wheat-traders-exit-russia-as-moscow-takes-hold.

4. Inna Degot'kova and Ekaterina Vinogradova, "Real'nye dokhody vozobnovili snizhenie," *RBC.ru*, April 27, 2022, https://www.rbc.ru/newspaper/2022/04/28/62693bde9a7947022f9ed92a.

5. "Outflow Possibly Overstated," *Moscow Times*, June 19, 2011, https://www.themoscowtimes.com/2011/06/19/outflow-possibly-overstated-a7699; "Largest Hypermarket Chain in Russia's Far East Imposes Limits amid Buying Frenzy," *Radio Free Europe/Radio Liberty*, March 12, 2022, https://www.rferl.org/a/russia-hypermarket-chain-restricting-sales-panic/31749947.html.

6. "Rost tsen v Rossii za mesiats voiny stal maksimal'nym s 1999 goda. Chto podorozhalo v marte?," *BBC News Russian Service*, April 8, 2022, https://www.bbc.com/russian/news-61045710.

7. Anna Gromova, "Sakharnyi sgovor: FAS vyiasniaet, kto stoial za podorozhaniem 'belogo zolota,'" *Gazeta.ru*, March 29, 2022, https://www.gazeta.ru/business/2022/03/29/14677837.shtml.

8. "Mishustin podpisal postanovlenie o zaprete na vyvoz zerna v EAES i sakhara za predely soiuza," *Interfax*, March 14, 2022, https://www.interfax.ru/business/828166.

9. Aleksei Polukhin, "Kazakhstanu ne khvatilo pschenitsy," *Kommersant*, April 22, 2022, https://www.kommersant.ru/doc/5326323.

10. "Meeting on Developing Agriculture and Fisheries" (President of Russia, April 5, 2022), http://en.kremlin.ru/events/president/news/68141.

11. Federation Council of the Russian Federation, "Senatory obsudili realizatsiiu Federal'noi nauchno-technicheskoi programmy razvitiia sel'skogo khoziaistva," February 1, 2022, http://council.gov.ru/events/news/133020/; Natuur en Voedselkwaliteit Ministerie van Landbouw, "Situation with Potato Seeds in Russia Is Catastrophic—Nieuwsbericht—Agroberichten Buitenland," nieuwsbericht (Ministerie van Landbouw, Natuur en Voedselkwaliteit, February 7, 2022), https://www.agroberichtenbuitenland.nl/actueel/nieuws/2022/02/07/situation-with-potato-seeds-in-russia-is-catastrophic; Natuur en Voedselkwaliteit Ministerie van Landbouw, "Russian Animal Breeders Concerned about Reduction in Genetic Material Imports—Nieuwsbericht—Agroberichten Buitenland," nieuwsbericht (Ministerie van Landbouw, Natuur en Voedselkwaliteit, January 20, 2022), https://www.agroberichtenbuitenland.nl/actueel/nieuws/2022/01/20/russian-animal-breeders-concerned-about-reduction-in-genetic-material-imports.

12. "Corteva to Withdraw from Russia," April 28, 2022, https://www.corteva.com/resources/media-center/corteva-decides-to-withdraw-from-russia.html.

13. "Situation in Ukraine and in Russia," *Limagrain.com*, accessed October 24, 2022, https://www.limagrain.com/en/situation-in-ukraine-and-in-russia.

14. Natalya Demchenko, "'Kommersant' uznal o predlozhenii Minsel'khoza zapretit' import semian," *RBC.ru*, August 5, 2022, https://www.rbc.ru/society/05/08/2022/62ecba889a79471276a9cb15; "Russia to Ban Some Imports of Seeds from Europe and Canada," *Euronews*, August 12, 2022, https://www.euronews.com/next/2022/08/12/ukraine-crisis-russia-seeds.

15. Aleksei Polukhin, "Chto poseesh', to pozhnesh'," *Kommersant*, August 5, 2022, https://www.kommersant.ru/doc/5493536; "Russia May Limit Seed Imports—Interfax," *Reuters*, August 5, 2022, sec. Commodities News, https://www.reuters.com/article/ukraine-crisis-russia-seeds-idUSKBN2PB1AC.
16. "Tetra Pak to Leave Russia after 62 Years in Blow to Packaging Industry," *Reuters*, July 26, 2022, sec. Retail & Consumer, https://www.reuters.com/business/retail-consumer/tetra-pak-leave-russia-after-62-years-blow-packaging-industry-2022-07-26/.
17. Kseniia Kapustinskaia, "'Serogo tsveta, zato otechestvennaia': v Rossii pytaiutsia sozdat' upakovku, kotoraia zamenit Tetra Pak," *Obozrevatel'*, June 15, 2022, https://news.obozrevatel.com/economics/economy/serogo-tsveta-zato-otechestvennaya-v-rossii-pyitayutsya-sozdat-upakovku-kotoraya-zamenit-tetra-pak.htm.
18. Joe Deaux, "Caterpillar, Deere Join Firms Suspending Business in Russia," *Bloomberg.com*, March 9, 2022, https://www.bloomberg.com/news/articles/2022-03-09/deere-suspends-shipments-of-farm-equipment-to-russia-and-belarus.
19. Oleksandr Fylyppov and Tim Lister, "Russians Plunder $5M Farm Vehicles from Ukraine—to Find They've Been Remotely Disabled," *CNN*, May 1, 2022, https://www.cnn.com/2022/05/01/europe/russia-farm-vehicles-ukraine-disabled-melitopol-intl/index.html.
20. "John Deere Suspends Shipments to Russia," *Deere.com*, accessed October 24, 2022, https://www.deere.com/en/stories/featured/john-deere-suspends-shipments-to-russia/; Deaux, "Caterpillar, Deere Join Firms Suspending Business in Russia."
21. Olga Nikitina and Anatolii Kostyrev, "Defitsit vyshel na polia," *Kommersant*, June 23, 2022, https://www.kommersant.ru/doc/5423867.
22. "Russia's Car Manufacturing Collapses by 97% in May," *Moscow Times*, June 30, 2022, sec. news, https://www.themoscowtimes.com/2022/06/30/russias-car-manufacturing-collapses-by-97-in-may-a78151.
23. Aleksei Plugov, "Rynok prodovol'stviia Rossii: Nekotorye tendentsii za pervoe polugodie 2022 goda," *AB Centre*, July 6, 2022, https://ab-centre.ru/news/rynok-prodovolstviya-rossii-nekotorye-tendencii-pervogo-polugodiya-2022-goda.
24. "Tseny na produkty pitaniia v Rossii i ikh izmenenie za god, dannye na mai 2022 goda," *AB Centre*, June 15, 2022, https://ab-centre.ru/news/ceny-na-produkty-pitaniya-v-rossii-i-ih-izmenenie-za-god-dannye-na-may-2022-goda.
25. Maria Kokoreva, "Tseny v Rossii snizhaiutsia dva mesiatsa podriad vpervye za tri goda: Chto proiskhodit," *Forbes.ru*, August 10, 2022, https://www.forbes.ru/finansy/474061-ceny-v-rossii-snizautsa-dva-mesaca-podrad-vpervye-za-tri-goda-cto-proishodit.
26. For comparison, Russia harvested 85 million tons of wheat in 2020. Arvin Donley, "The Fall and Rise of Russian Wheat," *World-Grain.com*, December 27, 2021, https://www.world-grain.com/articles/16273-the-fall-and-rise-of-russian-wheat.
27. Aleks Budris, "Rossiya ozhidaet rekordnyi urozhai zerna: chto budet s eksportom?," *Forbes Russia*, November 21, 2022, https://www.forbes.ru/biznes/481264-rossia-ozidaet-rekordnyj-urozaj-zerna-cto-budet-seksportom.
28. Polina Martynova, "Vlasti pereveli rasschety poshliny za eksport zerna v rubli," *RBC.ru*, July 1, 2022, https://www.rbc.ru/economics/01/07/2022/62bf32e89a7947a0d3fac3c3.

29. Anatolii Kostyrev, "Postavshchiki peregruzili zerno," *Kommersant*, September 1, 2022, https://www.kommersant.ru/doc/5537182; Olesia Pavlenko, "Eksport pshenitsy iz Rossii rukhnul na 27%," *Kommersant*, August 23, 2022, https://www.kommersant.ru/doc/5525340; Anatolii Kostyrev, "Pshenitsu rezhut pod koren," *Kommersant*, August 29, 2022, https://www.kommersant.ru/doc/5535904; "Sovecon Raises Forecast for 2022 Russian Wheat Crop," *Reuters*, August 16, 2022, sec. Commodities, https://www.reuters.com/article/russia-grains-idUSKBN2PM0VS.
30. Aleksandra Prokopenko, "Pochemu Rossiia soglasilas' razblokirovat' ukrainskii eksport zerna" (The Carnegie Endowment, July 25, 2022), https://carnegieendowment.org/politika/87559; Kostyrev, "Pshenitsu rezhut pod koren."
31. Elena Sukhorukova, "Glava Minsel'khoza zaiavil o skrytykh sanktsiakh na eksport prodovol'stviia," *RBC.ru*, October 3, 2022, https://www.rbc.ru/business/03/10/2022/6339675a9a794779a06116cd; Sof'ia Ermakova, "Eksport pshenitsy iz Rossii rukhnul," *Lenta.ru*, August 23, 2022, https://lenta.ru/news/2022/08/23/psheno/?ysclid=l81x4ecqoq779417061.
32. "Ukraine's Crop Storage Infrastructure: Post-Invasion Impact Assessment" (Conflict Observatory, September 15, 2022), https://hub.conflictobservatory.org/portal/sharing/rest/content/items/67cc4b8ff2124d3bbd5b8ec2bdaece4f/data.
33. Michael Biesecker, Sarah El Deeb, and Beatrice Dupuy, "Russia Smuggling Ukrainian Grain to Help Pay for Putin's War," *AP News*, October 3, 2022, https://apnews.com/article/russia-ukraine-putin-business-lebanon-syria-87c3b6fea3f4c326003123b21aa78099.
34. "UK sanctions target Russia's theft of Ukrainian grain, advanced military technology, and remaining revenue sources." GOV.UK, May 19, 2023. https://www.gov.uk/government/news/uk-sanctions-target-russias-theft-of-ukrainian-grain-advanced-military-technology-and-remaining-revenue-source.
35. "Ukraine Agricultural Production and Trade" (US Department of Agriculture, April 2022), https://www.fas.usda.gov/sites/default/files/2022-04/Ukraine-Factsheet-April2022.pdf.
36. According to the Ukrainian Grain Association, in 2022, due to the war, Ukraine harvested 40 percent less grain than in the previous year, see: "Na Ukraine zayavili o snizhenii urozhaya na 40%," https://www.rbc.ru/rbcfreenews/63a6e8e59a7947b3fa1642c6.
37. "The Importance of Ukraine and the Russian Federation for Global Agricultural Markets and the Risks Associated with the Current Conflict" (UN Food and Agriculture Organization, March 25, 2022), https://www.fao.org/3/cb9236en/cb9236en.pdf.
38. Dmitry Medvedev, "Nasha eda protiv ikh sanktsii," *Telegram Kanal: Dmitry Medvedev*, April 1, 2022, https://t.me/medvedev_telegram/29; Sergei Savchuk, "Protiv Zapada u Rossii est' oruzhie namnogo strashnee raket," *RIA Novosti*, April 22, 2022, https://ria.ru/20220422/eda-1784835298.html.
39. "War in Ukraine: WFP Calls for Ports to Reopen as World Faces Deepening Hunger Crisis," *World Food Programme*, May 6, 2022, https://www.wfp.org/stories/war-ukraine-wfp-calls-ports-reopen-world-faces-deepening-hunger-crisis; "G7: Russia

Extending Ukraine Military War to 'Grain War,' Says German FM Baerbock," *Euronews*, May 14, 2022, 7, https://www.euronews.com/2022/05/14/ukraine-war-grain-exports-blocked-by-russia-threaten-to-bring-hunger-and-famine-g7-warns; "Putin: West's Russia Sanctions Triggering Global Economic Crisis," *Al Jazeera*, May 12, 2022, https://www.aljazeera.com/economy/2022/5/12/putin-wests-russia-sanctions-triggering-global-economic-crisis.

40. Anand, "The Big 4 of Agriculture Unlikely to Exit Russia despite Mounting Pressure."
41. Calculations are based on "Grain: World Markets and Trade" (Washington, DC: US Department of Agriculture, December 10, 2022), https://www.fas.usda.gov/data/grain-world-markets-and-trade.
42. Paul Krugman, "Food, Fertilizer and the Future," *New York Times*, April 26, 2022, sec. Opinion, https://www.nytimes.com/2022/04/26/opinion/ukraine-russia-food-crisis.html.
43. The Black Sea Grain Initiative agreement was signed in Istanbul on July 22, 2022, by Turkey, Russia, and Ukraine. For the full text of the agreement, see: https://www.un.org/sites/un2.un.org/files/black_sea_grain_initiative_full_text.pdf.
44. Prokopenko, "Pochemu Rossiia soglasilas' razblokirovat' ukrainskii eksport zerna."
45. Andrei Sapozhnikov, "Ukraina eksportirovala 7.7 millionov tonn agroproduktsii v ramkakh 'zernovoi sdelki,'" *Kommersant*, October 16, 2022, https://www.kommersant.ru/doc/5619075; "How Much Grain Is Being Shipped from Ukraine?," *BBC News*, August 22, 2022, sec. World, https://www.bbc.com/news/world-61759692; "Ukraine Grain Deal: Where Are the Ships Going?," *BBC News*, August 30, 2022, sec. Europe, https://www.bbc.com/news/world-europe-62717010.
46. Edward Wong and Ana Swanson, "How Russia's War on Ukraine Is Worsening Global Starvation," *New York Times*, January 2, 2023, sec. U.S., https://www.nytimes.com/2023/01/02/us/politics/russia-ukraine-food-crisis.html.
47. Lusine Balasian, "Rossiia mozhet otkazat'sia ot zernovoi sdelki iz-za sokhraniaiushchikhsia ogranichenii na eksport," *Kommersant*, October 13, 2022, https://www.kommersant.ru/doc/5609022; "Russian Diplomat Says Moscow Prepared to Reject Renewal of Grain Export Deal," *Radio Free Europe/Radio Liberty*, October 13, 2022, https://www.rferl.org/a/russia-reject-grain-deal-ukraine/32081082.html.
48. According to the Office of the UN Coordinator for the Black Sea Grain Initiative, between August 2022 and May 8, 2023, Ukraine was able to export almost 30 million tons of grain and foodstaffs, see: "Update from the Office of the UN Coordinator for the Black Sea Grain Initiative (May 8, 2023)," https://www.un.org/sg/en/content/sg/note-correspondents/2023-05-08/update-the-office-of-the-un-coordinator-for-the-black-sea-grain-initiative%C2%A0.
49. Natalia Anisimova, "Agrokompleks sem'i eks-glavy Minsel'khoza Tkacheva priobrel biznes v Krymu," *RBC.ru*, June 6, 2022, https://www.rbc.ru/business/06/06/2022/629d8ea69a794775d5c8d76d; Anatolii Kostyrev, "Eks-Ministr ukrepit 'Druzhbu Narodov,'" *Kommersant*, June 6, 2022, https://www.kommersant.ru/doc/5391928.
50. Alistair MacDonald and Oksana Pyrozhok, "Russian Oligarch Seizes 400,000 Acres of Ukrainian Farmland, Owners Say," *Wall Street Journal*, December 6, 2022, https://

www.wsj.com/articles/russian-oligarch-seizes-400-000-acres-of-ukrainian-farml and-owners-say-11670338956.

51. Petr Kanaev and Elena Sukhorukova, "Dmitry Patrushev—RBK: 'Ot nashei produktsii voobshche ne otkazyvaiutsia,'" *RBC.ru*, October 3, 2022, https://www.rbc.ru/interview/business/03/10/2022/633291d79a794719ca093b90.

Chapter 10

1. Christopher B. Barrett, ed., *Food Security and Sociopolitical Stability* (New York: Oxford University Press, 2013).
2. Werner Baer, "Import Substitution and Industrialization in Latin America: Experiences and Interpretations," *Latin American Research Review* 7, no. 1 (1972): 95–122; Meredith Woo-Cumings, *The Developmental State* (Ithaca, NY: Cornell University Press, 2019); Albert O. Hirschman, "The Political Economy of Import-Substituting Industrialization in Latin America," *Quarterly Journal of Economics* 82, no. 1 (1968): 1–32.
3. Steven Levitsky and Lucan A. Way, *Competitive Authoritarianism: Hybrid Regimes after the Cold War* (Cambridge: Cambridge University Press, 2010).
4. Barrington Moore, *Social Origins of Dictatorship and Democracy* (New York: Beacon Press, 1966); Alexander Gerschenkron, *Bread and Democracy in Germany* (Berkeley: University of California Press, 1943).
5. Barbara Geddes et al., *How Dictatorships Work: Power, Personalization, and Collapse* (Cambridge: Cambridge University Press, 2018); Jason Brownlee, *Authoritarianism in an Age of Democratization* (Cambridge: Cambridge University Press, 2007); Jennifer Gandhi, *Political Institutions under Dictatorship* (New York: Cambridge University Press, 2008); Milan W. Svolik, *The Politics of Authoritarian Rule* (Cambridge: Cambridge University Press, 2012).
6. Eva Bellin, "Reconsidering the Robustness of Authoritarianism in the Middle East: Lessons from the Arab Spring," *Comparative Politics* 44, no. 2 (2012): 127–49; Kira D. Jumet, *Contesting the Repressive State: Why Ordinary Egyptians Protested during the Arab Spring* (New York: Oxford University Press, 2018); Marsha Pripstein Posusney and Michele Penner Angrist, eds., *Authoritarianism in the Middle East: Regimes and Resistance* (Boulder, CO: Lynne Rienner Publishers, 2005); Mona El-Ghobashy, *Bread and Freedom: Egypt's Revolutionary Situation* (Stanford, CA: Stanford University Press, 2021).
7. Anne-Marie Slaughter and Heather Ashby, "Countering Putin's Grand Strategy," *Project Sindicate* (blog), July 27, 2021, https://www.project-syndicate.org/commentary/biden-needs-strategy-to-counter-russia-by-anne-marie-slaughter-and-heather-ashby-2021-07; Douglas E. Schoen, *Putin's Master Plan: To Destroy Europe, Divide NATO, and Restore Russian Power and Global Influence* (New York: Encounter Books, 2016); Rebekah Koffler, *Putin's Playbook: Russia's Secret Plan to Defeat America* (New York: Simon & Schuster, 2021).

8. Mark Galeotti, *We Need to Talk about Putin: How the West Gets Him Wrong* (London: Random House, 2019); Angela Stent, *Putin's World: Russia against the West and with the Rest* (New York: Twelve, 2019).
9. Steven Lee Myers, *The New Tsar: The Rise and Reign of Vladimir Putin* (New York: Simon & Schuster, 2015); Masha Gessen, *The Man without a Face: The Unlikely Rise of Vladimir Putin* (New York: Riverhead Books, 2013).
10. Timothy Frye, *Weak Strongman: The Limits of Power in Putin's Russia* (Princeton, NJ: Princeton University Press, 2021); Samuel A. Greene and Graeme B. Robertson, *Putin v. the People* (London: Yale University Press, 2019).
11. Brian D. Taylor, *Politics and the Russian Army: Civil-Military Relations, 1689–2000* (Cambridge: Cambridge University Press, 2003).
12. Henry E. Hale, *Patronal Politics: Eurasian Regime Dynamics in Comparative Perspective* (New York: Cambridge University Press, 2014); M. Steven Fish, *Democracy Derailed in Russia: The Failure of Open Politics* (New York: Cambridge University Press, 2005); Vladimir Gel'man, "The Dynamics of Subnational Authoritarianism," *Russian Politics and Law* 48, no. 2 (2010): 7–26.
13. Anders Åslund, *Russia's Crony Capitalism: The Path from Market Economy to Kleptocracy* (New Haven, CT: Yale University Press, 2019); Karen Dawisha, *Putin's Kleptocracy: Who Owns Russia?* (New York: Simon & Schuster, 2015); Vladimir Gel'man, *Authoritarian Russia: Analyzing Post-Soviet Regime Changes* (Pittsburgh: University of Pittsburgh Press, 2015); Chris Miller, *Putinomics: Power and Money in Resurgent Russia* (Chapel Hill: University of North Carolina Press, 2018).
14. Thane Gustafson, *Wheel of Fortune* (Cambridge, MA: Harvard University Press, 2012); Marshall I. Goldman, *Petrostate: Putin, Power, and the New Russia* (New York: Oxford University Press, 2008).
15. Greene and Robertson, *Putin v. the People*; Gulnaz Sharafutdinova, *The Red Mirror: Putin's Leadership and Russia's Insecure Identity* (New York: Oxford University Press, 2020).
16. Bryn Rosenfeld, "Reevaluating the Middle-Class Protest Paradigm: A Case-Control Study of Democratic Protest Coalitions in Russia," *American Political Science Review* 111, no. 4 (2017): 637–52; Bryn Rosenfeld, *The Autocratic Middle Class: How State Dependency Reduces the Demand for Democracy* (Princeton, NJ: Princeton University Press, 2020).
17. Elevation of the import substitution drive into an ideological tenet of Putin's regime is strikingly similar to the elevation of industrial import substitution drive into an ideology of "developmentalism" in the 1950s–1960s in Latin America; see Kathryn Sikkink, *Developmentalism and Democracy: Ideas, Institutions, and Economic Policy-Making in Brazil and Argentina* (Ithaca, NY: Cornell University Press, 1991).
18. Nikolai Dronin and Andrei Kirilenko, "Climate Change, Food Stress, and Security in Russia," *Regional Environmental Change* 11, no. 1 (2011): 167–78.
19. Georgiy Safonov and Yulia Safonova, *Economic Analysis of the Impact of Climate Change on Agriculture in Russia* (Oxfam International, 2013); Dronin and Kirilenko, "Climate Change, Food Stress, and Security in Russia."

20. Thane Gustafson, *Klimat: Russia in the Age of Climate Change* (Cambridge, MA: Harvard University Press, 2021), 157.
21. Gustafson, *Klimat*, 6, 14.
22. Scott Reynolds Nelson, *Oceans of Grain: How American Wheat Remade the World* (New York: Basic Books, 2022), 39.
23. James Kynge, Sun Yu, and Leo Lewis, "Fortress China: Xi Jinping's Plan for Economic Independence," *Financial Times*, September 15, 2022, https://www.ft.com/content/0496b125-7760-41ba-8895-8358a7f24685; Leo Lewis, "China Is on a Mission to Ensure Its Food Security," *Financial Times*, September 1, 2022, https://www.ft.com/content/363c94c1-afed-49b3-aa09-f31227819791. On China's food security policy see Bishwajit Ghose, "Food Security and Food Self-sufficiency in China: From Past to 2050," *Food and Energy Security* 3, no. 2 (2014): 86–95.

Bibliography

"A. Gordeev: VTO—vrednaia dlia mirovoi ekonomiki organizatsiia." *RBC.ru*, September 25, 2008. https://www.rbc.ru/economics/25/09/2008/5703cf2a9a79473dc8149323.

Acemoglu, Daron, and James A. Robinson. *Economic Origins of Dictatorship and Democracy*. Cambridge: Cambridge University Press, 2006.

"Activities at Navalny Offices Suspended by Russian Court." RFERL, April 26, 2021. https://www.rferl.org/a/russia-navalny-foundation-extremist-label-court/31222994.html.

"Address by President of the Russian Federation." President of Russia, March 18, 2014. http://en.kremlin.ru/events/president/news/20603.

"'Agrocomplex' im. Tkacheva poluchit rekordnye subsidii na moloko." *RBC Kuban'*, April 5, 2017. https://kuban.rbc.ru/krasnodar/freenews/58e49b6e9a7947cc504e3d0d.

"Agrokompleks imeni Tkacheva podtverdil status krupneishego zemlevladel'tsa Rossii." Expert Yug, March 3, 2021. https://expertsouth.ru/news/agrokompleks-imeni-tkacheva-podtverdil-status-krupneyshego-zemlevladeltsa-rossii-/.

Aleksashenko, Sergey. "The Ruble Currency Storm Is Over, but Is the Russian Economy Ready for the Next One?" *Brookings* (blog), May 18, 2015. https://www.brookings.edu/blog/up-front/2015/05/18/the-ruble-currency-storm-is-over-but-is-the-russian-economy-ready-for-the-next-one/.

Aligica, Paul Dragos, and Vlad Tarko. *Capitalist Alternatives: Models, Taxonomies, Scenarios*. Abingdon: Routledge, 2014.

Allina-Pisano, Jessica. *The Post-Soviet Potemkin Village: Politics and Property Rights in the Black Earth*. New York: Cambridge University Press, 2008.

"Almost 1,000 Companies Have Curtailed Operations in Russia—But Some Remain." Yale School of Management, May 10, 2022. https://som.yale.edu/story/2022/almost-1000-companies-have-curtailed-operations-russia-some-remain.

Altukhov, Anatolii. Authors' Interview. Zoom, February 16, 2021.

Amelina, Maria. "Why Russian Peasants Remain in Collective Farms: A Household Perspective on Agricultural Restructuring." *Post-Soviet Geography and Economics* 41, no. 7 (2000): 483–511.

Anand, Asim. "The Big 4 of Agriculture Unlikely to Exit Russia despite Mounting Pressure." S&P Global: Commodity Insights, April 19, 2022. https://www.spglobal.com/commodityinsights/en/market-insights/blogs/agriculture/041922-russia-ukraine-war-food-adm-bunge-cargill-louis-dreyfus.

Andreev, Evgeny. "Popali mimo iablochka." *Novaya gazeta*, May 13, 2016. https://novayagazeta.ru/articles/2016/05/13/68573-popali-mimo-yablochka.

"Andrei Belousov provel soveshchanie po situatsii s tsenami na sotsial'no znachimye tovary." Government of the Russian Federation, May 18, 2021. http://government.ru/news/42238/.

Andrianova, Dar'ia, Aleksei Polukhin, and Khalil Aminov. "Plody stabil'nosti." *Kommersant*, April 23, 2021. https://www.kommersant.ru/doc/4783655.

Andriukhin, Aleksandr. "Mlechnyi put'." *Kul'tura*, September 30, 2014. https://portal-kult ura.ru/articles/country/59169-mlechnyy-put/.
Anishchenko, Alesia, and Anatolii Shut'kov. "Problemy realizatsii Doktriny prodovol'stvennoi bezopasnosti Rossii." *Prodovol'stvennaia politika i bezopasnost'* 8, no. 1 (2021): 9–22. https://doi.org/10.18334/ppib.8.1.111777.
Anisimova, Natalia. "Agrokompleks sem'i eks-glavy Minsel'khoza Tkacheva priobrel biznes v Krymu." *RBC.ru*, June 6, 2022. https://www.rbc.ru/business/06/06/2022/629d8ea69a794775d5c8d76d.
An'kov, Vitalii. "V Rossii predlozhili vvesti produktovye kartochki dlia maloimushchikh." *RIA Novosti*, December 21, 2020. https://ria.ru/20201221/pitanie-1590151393.html.
Applebaum, Anne. *Red Famine: Stalin's War on Ukraine*. New York: Doubleday, 2017.
Arbatov, Georgy. "K voprosu ob otmene amerikanskim pravitel'stvom embargo na postavki zerna v SSSR." June 3, 1981. 80/1/225. RGANI.
Aron, Leon. *Yeltsin: A Revolutionary Life*. New York: HarperCollins, 2000.
Arsiukhin, Evgenii. "Aleksei Gordeev: Gosudarstvo ne uidet s rynka prodovol'stviia." *Rossiiskaia gazeta*, December 5, 2003.
Arsiukhin, Evgenii. "Aleksei Gordeev: V Rossii ne dolzhno byt' golodnykh." *Rossiiskaia gazeta*, August 19, 2004. https://rg.ru/2004/08/19/gordeev.html.
Arsiukhin, Evgenii. "Bitva s rublem do poslednego zerna." *Rossiiskaia gazeta*, August 21, 2002.
Arutyonov, Artur. "ES otkliuchil ot SWIFT 'Sber', MKB i RSKhB: chto eto znachit." *Forbes Russia*, June 14, 2022. https://www.forbes.ru/finansy/464803-es-gotovitsa-otklucit-ot-swift-sber-i-dva-drugih-krupnyh-banka-cto-eto-znacit.
Ashwin, Sarah. *Russian Workers: The Anatomy of Patience*. Manchester: Manchester University Press, 1999.
Åslund, Anders. *How Russia Became a Market Economy*. Washington, DC: Brookings Institution, 1995.
Åslund, Anders. *Russia's Crony Capitalism: The Path from Market Economy to Kleptocracy*. New Haven, CT: Yale University Press, 2019.
Azar, Il'ia. "Ugod'ia markiza Karabasa." *Meduza*, April 29, 2015. https://meduza.io/feature/2015/04/29/ugodya-markiza-karabasa.
Azarieva, Janetta. "Grain and Power in Russia 2001–2011." PhD diss., Hebrew University of Jerusalem, 2015.
Baer, Werner. "Import Substitution and Industrialization in Latin America: Experiences and Interpretations." *Latin American Research Review* 7, no. 1 (1972): 95–122.
Bahry, Donna. "The New Federalism and the Paradoxes of Regional Sovereignty in Russia." *Comparative Politics* 37, no. 2 (2005): 127–46.
Balasian, Lusine. "Rossiia mozhet otkazat'sia ot zernovoi sdelki iz-za sokhraniaiushchikhsia ogranichenii na eksport." *Kommersant*, October 13, 2022. https://www.kommersant.ru/doc/5609022.
Baron, Samuel H. *Bloody Saturday in the Soviet Union: Novocherkassk, 1962*. Stanford, CA: Stanford University Press, 2001.
Barrett, Christopher B. "Food or Consequences: Food Security and Its Implications for Global Sociopolitical Stability." In *Food Security and Sociopolitical Stability*, edited by Christopher B. Barrett, 1–34. Oxford: Oxford University Press, 2013.
Barrett, Christopher B., ed. *Food Security and Sociopolitical Stability*. New York: Oxford University Press, 2013.

Barsukova, Svetlana. "Dilemma 'fermery-Agroholdingi' v kontekste importzameshcheniia." *Obshchestvennye nauki i sovremennost'* 5 (2016): 63–74.
Barsukova, Svetlana. "Doktrina prodovol'svennoi bezopasnosti: Otsenka ekspertov." *Terra Economicus* 10, no. 4 (2012): 34–46.
Barsukova, Svetlana. "Vekhi agrarnoi politiki Rossii v 2000-e gody." *Mir Rossii* 1 (2013): 3–28.
Bashkatova, Anastasiia. "Rossiia prevrashchaetsia v stranu gigantskih agroholdingov." *Nezavisimaia gazeta*, November 14, 2016. https://www.ng.ru/economics/2016-11-14/1_6859_agro.html.
Bates, Robert H. *Markets and States in Tropical Africa*. Berkeley: University of California Press, 1981.
Batmanova, Anastasiia. "Nabiullina prizvala bystree otkazat'sia ot ogranicheniia tsen vlastiami." *RBC.ru*, April 7, 2021. https://www.rbc.ru/economics/07/04/2021/606d7f199a7947a153bb00e2.
Beasley, David M. "Covid-19 Could Detonate a 'Hunger Pandemic.' With Millions at Risk, the World Must Act." *Washington Post*, April 22, 2020. https://www.washingtonpost.com/opinions/2020/04/22/covid-19-could-detonate-hunger-pandemic-with-millions-risk-world-must-act/.
"Begi, Vadik, begi: Vadim Moshkovich pokinul Rossiu?" *Biznes-Vektor*, May 19, 2021. https://www.business-vector.info/begi-vadik-begi-vadim-120532/.
Bellemare, Marc F. "Rising Food Prices, Food Price Volatility, and Social Unrest." *American Journal of Agricultural Economics* 97, no. 1 (2015): 1–21.
Bellin, Eva. "Reconsidering the Robustness of Authoritarianism in the Middle East: Lessons from the Arab Spring." *Comparative Politics* 44, no. 2 (2012): 127–49.
Belov, Artiom. Authors' Interview. Zoom, October 7, 2020.
Belton, Catherine. *Putin's People: How the KGB Took Back Russia and Then Took On the West*. New York: Farrar, Straus & Giroux, 2020.
Bieseker, Michael, Sarah El Deeb, and Beatrice Dupuy. "Russia Smuggling Ukrainian Grain to Help Pay for Putin's War." *AP News*, October 3, 2022. https://apnews.com/article/russia-ukraine-putin-business-lebanon-syria-87c3b6fea3f4c326003123b21aa78099.
Bittman, Mark. *Animal, Vegetable, Junk: A History of Food, from Sustainable to Suicidal*. New York: Houghton Mifflin Harcourt, 2021.
Bocharova, Tat'iana. *Novocherkassk. Krovavyi polden'*. Rostov-on-Don: Izdatel'stvo Rostovskogo Universiteta, 2002.
Boix, Carles. *Democracy and Redistribution*. Cambridge: Cambridge University Press, 2003.
"Bolee 36 tys. tonn produktov unichtozhil Rosselkhoznadzor za 5 let." *Agronews*, August 6, 2020. https://agronews.com/ru/ru/news/breaking-news/2020-08-06/46206.
Bremmer, Ian. "State Capitalism Comes of Age—The End of the Free Market." *Foreign Affairs* 88, no. 3 (2009): 40–55.
Brooks, Risa A. "Sanctions and Regime Type: What Works, and When?" *Security Studies* 11, no. 4 (2002): 1–50.
Brown, Archie. *The Rise and Fall of Communism*. London: Random House, 2009.
Brownlee, Jason. *Authoritarianism in an Age of Democratization*. Cambridge: Cambridge University Press, 2007.
Bruton, Henry J. "A Reconsideration of Import Substitution." *Journal of Economic Literature* 36, no. 2 (1998): 903–36.

Budris, Aleks. "Rossiya ozhidaet rekordnyi urozhai zerna: chto budet s eksportom?" *Forbes Russia*, November 21, 2022. https://www.forbes.ru/biznes/481264-rossiya-ozid aet-rekordnyj-urozaj-zerna-cto-budet-seksportom.

Builov, Maksim. "Produktovye kartochki dlia rosta VVP." *Kommersant*, November 2, 2017. https://www.kommersant.ru/doc/3213996.

Burlakova, Ekaterina. "Agrokompleks imeni Tkacheva stal chetvertym vladel'tsem sel'khozzemel' v Rossii." *Vedomosti*, April 24, 2017. https://www.vedomosti.ru/busin ess/articles/2017/04/24/687150-agrokompleks.

Buturin, Dmitrii. "Minsel'khoz pochustvoval golod." *Kommersant*, March 29, 2008. https://www.kommersant.ru/doc/872786.

Buturin, Dmitrii. "Pravitel'stvo natsional'nogo proekta." *Kommersant*, December 30, 2005. https://www.kommersant.ru/doc/639704.

Caldwell, Melissa L. *Not by Bread Alone: Social Support in the New Russia*. Berkeley: University of California Press, 2004.

Cameron, Sarah. *The Hungry Steppe: Famine, Violence, and the Making of Soviet Kazakhstan*. Ithaca, NY: Cornell University Press, 2018.

"Cherez 10 let na zemli RF budut pretendovat' drugie strany." *RBC.ru*, July 26, 2005. https://www.rbc.ru/economics/26/07/2005/5703c2479a7947dde8e09b37.

Chernyaev, Anatolii. "Diary." January 6, 1976. https://nsarchive.gwu.edu/rus/text_files/Chernyaev/1976.pdf.

Chernyaev, Anatolii. "Diary." January 28, 1980. https://nsarchive.gwu.edu/rus/text_files/Chernyaev/1980.pdf.

Chernyaev, Anatolii. "Diary." November 12, 1987. National Security Archive. https://nsarchive.gwu.edu/rus/text_files/Chernyaev/1987.pdf.

Chernyaev, Anatolii. "Diary." May 28, 1989. National Security Archive. http://www2.gwu.edu/~nsarchiv/rus/text_files/Chernyaev/1989.pdf.

Chernyaev, Anatolii. "Diary." 1991. National Security Archive. https://nsarchive.gwu.edu/rus/text_files/Chernyaev/1991.pdf.

Chernyakov, Boris. *Aiova—Prodovol'stvennaia stolitsa mira*. Moscow: Tipografiia Rosselkhozakademii, 2011.

Chernyakov, Boris. "Politika prodovol'stvennoi bezopasnosti zarubezhnykh stran i interesy Rossii." *Ekonomika sel'skokhoziastvennykh i pererabatyvaiushchikh predpriiatii* 5 (2002): 11–13.

Chernyakov, Boris. "Zakonodatel'nye i administrativnye osnovy prodovol'stvennoi bezopasnosti SShA: Opyt dlia Rossii." *SShA-Kanada* 8 (2001): 89–104.

Chernysheva, Viktoriia. "Izuchaiut karty." *Rossiiskaia gazeta*, February 24, 2015. https://rg.ru/2015/02/25/karti.html.

Chkanikov, Mikhail. "Kolbasnyi krug." *Rossiiskaia gazeta*, April 24, 2008. https://dlib.eastview.com/browse/doc/14300039.

Chkanikov, Mikhail. "Molchanie teliat." *Rossiiskaia gazeta*, July 13, 2009. https://dlib.eastview.com/browse/doc/20346477.

Chkanikov, Mikhail. "My za edoi ne postoim. V Rossii gotoviat zakon o prodovol'stvennoi bezopasnosti." *Rossiiskaia gazeta*, May 21, 2008. https://rg.ru/2008/05/21/minsel hoz.html.

CIA. "Overview of an Intelligence Assessment Prepared in the Central Intelligence Agency." In *Foreign Relations of the United States. 1977–1980. Soviet Union*, edited by Melissa Jane Taylor, VI:723–25. Washington, DC: Department of State, 2013.

Clapp, Jennifer. "Food Self-Sufficiency: Making Sense of It, and When It Makes Sense." *Food Policy* 66 (2017): 88–96.
Colton, Timothy J. *Yeltsin: A Life*. New York: Basic Books, 2008.
Connolly, Richard, and Philip Hanson. "Import Substitution and Economic Sovereignty in Russia." *Research Paper*, 2016, 3–5.
Cook, Linda J. *The Soviet Social Contract and Why It Failed: Welfare Policy and Workers' Politics from Brezhnev to Yeltsin*. Cambridge, MA: Harvard University Press, 1993.
Cook, Linda J., and Martin K. Dimitrov. "The Social Contract Revisited: Evidence from Communist and State Capitalist Economies." *Europe-Asia Studies* 69, no. 1 (2017): 8–26.
"Corteva to Withdraw from Russia." April 28, 2022. https://www.corteva.com/resources/media-center/corteva-decides-to-withdraw-from-russia.html.
Dawisha, Karen. *Putin's Kleptocracy: Who Owns Russia?* New York: Simon & Schuster, 2015.
Deaux, Joe. "Caterpillar, Deere Join Firms Suspending Business in Russia." *Bloomberg.com*, March 9, 2022. https://www.bloomberg.com/news/articles/2022-03-09/deere-suspends-shipments-of-farm-equipment-to-russia-and-belarus.
Degot'kova, Inna, and Ekaterina Vinogradova. "Real'nye dokhody vozobnovili snizhenie." *RBC.ru*, April 27, 2022. https://www.rbc.ru/newspaper/2022/04/28/62693bde9a7947022f9ed92a.
Demchenko, Natalya. "'Kommersant' uznal o predlozhenii Minsel'khoza zapretit' import semian." *RBC.ru*, August 5, 2022. https://www.rbc.ru/society/05/08/2022/62ecba889a79471276a9cb15.
"Dinamika otnoshenii k sanktsiiam i kontrsanktsiiam." Fond Obshestvennoe Mnenie, April 12, 2016. https://fom.ru/Ekonomika/12599.
Donley, Arvin. "The Fall and Rise of Russian Wheat." *World-Grain.com*, December 27, 2021. https://www.world-grain.com/articles/16273-the-fall-and-rise-of-russian-wheat.
"Dorogoi minimum." April 22, 2021. https://finexpertiza.ru/press-service/researches/2021/dorogoy-minimum/.
Dronin, Nikolai, and Andrei Kirilenko. "Climate Change, Food Stress, and Security in Russia." *Regional Environmental Change* 11, no. 1 (2011): 167–78.
"Ekspertiza doktorskoi dissertatsii Dmitriia Nikolaevicha Patrusheva." Dissernet. Accessed August 22, 2022. https://www.dissernet.org/expertise/patrushevdn2008.htm.
"Ekspertiza kandidatskoi dissertatsii Dmitriiia Nikolaevicha Patrusheva." Dissernet. Accessed August 22, 2022. https://www.dissernet.org/expertise/patrushevdn2003.htm.
Ekström, Karin M., Marianne P. Ekström, Marina Potapova, and Helena Shanahan. "Changes in Food Provision in Russian Households Experiencing Perestroika." *International Journal of Consumer Studies* 27, no. 4 (2003): 294–301.
"Elena Skrynnik: O masshtabakh bedy zaranee ne znali ni Rosgidromet, ni nashi uchenye." *Rossiiskaia gazeta*, August 29, 2010. https://rg.ru/2010/08/30/skrynnik.html.
El-Ghobashy, Mona. *Bread and Freedom: Egypt's Revolutionary Situation*. Stanford, CA: Stanford University Press, 2021.
Engel, Barbara Alpern. "Not by Bread Alone: Subsistence Riots in Russia during World War I." *Journal of Modern History* 69, no. 4 (1997): 696–721.
Ermakova, Sof'ia. "Eksport pshenitsy iz Rossii rukhnul." *Lenta.ru*, August 23, 2022. https://lenta.ru/news/2022/08/23/psheno/?ysclid=l81x4ecqoq779417061.

Evdokimova, Nataliia. "Zakupochnye interventsii na zernovom rynke." *APK: Ekonomika, upravlenie* 3 (2011): 64–67.

"Ezhegodnaia press-konferentssia Vladimira Putina." Office of the President of Russia, December 17, 2020. http://kremlin.ru/events/president/news/64671.

"Ezhegodnyi otchet pravitel'stva v Gosudarstvennoi Dume." Government of the Russian Federation, May 12, 2021. http://government.ru/news/42158/.

Ezrow, Natasha M., and Erica Frantz. *Dictators and Dictatorships: Understanding Authoritarian Regimes and Their Leaders.* New York: Bloomsbury, 2011.

Faliakhov, Rustem. "Parmezanskie voiny: pochem embargo dlia naroda." *Gazeta.ru*, August 6, 2020. https://www.gazeta.ru/business/2020/08/06/13184413.shtml.

Fernandez, Manny. "Coronavirus and Poverty: A Mother Skips Meals so Her Children Can Eat." *New York Times*, March 20, 2020. https://www.nytimes.com/2020/03/20/us/coronavirus-poverty-school-lunch.html.

Filtzer, Donald. "Starvation Mortality in Soviet Home-Front Industrial Regions during World War II." In *Hunger and War: Food Supply in the Soviet Union during the Second World War*, edited by Wendy Goldman and Donald Filtzer, 265–335. Bloomington: Indiana University Press, 2015.

Finkel, Evgeny, and Yitzhak M. Brudny. "No More Colour! Authoritarian Regimes and Colour Revolutions in Eurasia." *Democratization* 19, no. 1 (February 1, 2012): 1–14. https://doi.org/10.1080/13510347.2012.641298.

Finkel, Evgeny, and Yitzhak M. Brudny. "Russia and the Colour Revolutions." *Democratization* 19, no. 1 (2012): 15–36.

Finkel, Evgeny, and Scott Gehlbach. *Reform and Rebellion in Weak States.* New York: Cambridge University Press, 2020.

"Finlandiia otsenila poteri ot sanktsionnoi voiny ES i Rossii." *Regnum.ru*, May 5, 2016. https://regnum.ru/news/economy/2128693.html.

Fish, M. Steven. *Democracy Derailed in Russia: The Failure of Open Politics.* New York: Cambridge University Press, 2005.

Fitzpatrick, Sheila. *Stalin's Peasants: Resistance and Survival in the Russian Village after Collectivization.* New York: Oxford University Press, 1996.

Fomchenkov, Taras. "Poteri stran Zapada ot prodembargo sostavili 8,8 milliarda dollarov." *Rossiiskaia gazeta*, August 8, 2016. https://rg.ru/2016/08/02/poteri-stran-zapada-ot-prodembargo-sostavili-86-milliarda-dollarov.html.

"Food Index vernulsia k dokarantinnym znacheniiam." *Romir*, July 9, 2020. https://romir.ru/studies/food-index-vernulsya-k-dokarantinnym-znacheniyam.

"Food Security." Policy Brief. Food and Agriculture Organization, June 1996. http://www.fao.org/fileadmin/templates/faoitaly/documents/pdf/pdf_Food_Security_Cocept_Note.pdf.

Fortescue, Stephen. "Putin in Pikalevo: PR or Watershed?" *Australian Slavonic and East European Studies* 23, no. 1–2 (2010): 19–38.

Frye, Timothy. "Economic Sanctions and Public Opinion: Survey Experiments from Russia." *Comparative Political Studies* 52, no. 7 (2019): 967–94.

Frye, Timothy. *Weak Strongman: The Limits of Power in Putin's Russia.* Princeton, NJ: Princeton University Press, 2021.

Frye, Timothy, Scott Gehlbach, Kyle L. Marquardt, and Ora John Reuter. "Is Putin's Popularity Real?" *Post-Soviet Affairs* 33, no. 1 (2017): 1–15.

"FSN podkliuchilas' k kontroliu za tsenami na produkty." *Interfax*, January 26, 2021. https://www.interfax.ru/business/746852.

Fylyppov, Oleksandr, and Tim Lister. "Russians Plunder $5M Farm Vehicles from Ukraine—to Find They've Been Remotely Disabled." *CNN*, May 1, 2022. https://www.cnn.com/2022/05/01/europe/russia-farm-vehicles-ukraine-disabled-melitopol-intl/index.html.

"G7: Russia Extending Ukraine Military War to 'Grain War,' Says German FM Baerbock." *Euronews*, May 14, 2022. https://www.euronews.com/2022/05/14/ukraine-war-grain-exports-blocked-by-russia-threaten-to-bring-hunger-and-famine-g7-warns.

Gaidar, Yegor. *Dni porazhenii i pobed*. Moscow: Vagrius, 1996.

Gaidar, Yegor, and Anatoly Chubais. *Razvilki noveishei istorii Rossii*. Moscow: OGI, 2011.

Gaiva, Evgeny. "Est' svoe." *Rossiiskaia gazeta*, August 6, 2019. https://dlib.eastview.com/browse/doc/54175574.

Gaiva, Evgeny. "So svoim karavaem." *Rossiiskaia gazeta*, July 13, 2018. https://dlib.eastview.com/browse/doc/51449849.

Galeotti, Mark. *We Need to Talk about Putin: How the West Gets Him Wrong*. London: Random House, 2019.

Gandhi, Jennifer. *Political Institutions under Dictatorship*. New York: Cambridge University Press, 2008.

Gandhi, Jennifer, and Ellen Lust-Okar. "Elections under Authoritarianism." *Annual Review of Political Science* 12 (2009): 403–22.

Gavriliuk, Aleksandr. "Prazdnik so slezami v zakromakh." *Rossiiskaia gazeta*, November 14, 1998.

Geddes, Barbara, Joseph George Wright, Joseph Wright, and Erica Frantz. *How Dictatorships Work: Power, Personalization, and Collapse*. Cambridge: Cambridge University Press, 2018.

Gel'bras, Vilia. *Kto est' chto: Politicheskie partii i bloki, obshchestvennye organizatsii*. Moscow: RAN, 1994.

Gel'man, Vladimir. *Authoritarian Russia: Analyzing Post-Soviet Regime Changes*. Pittsburgh: University of Pittsburgh Press, 2015.

Gel'man, Vladimir. "The Dynamics of Subnational Authoritarianism." *Russian Politics and Law* 48, no. 2 (2010): 7–26.

Gel'man, Vladimir. *The Politics of Bad Governance in Contemporary Russia*. Ann Arbor: University of Michigan Press, 2022.

"Gendirektor OZK S. Levin: Kachestvo zerna interventsionnogo fonda v tselom normal'noe." *Agrarnoe obozrenie*, December 16, 2010. https://agroobzor.ru/stati/a-588.html.

Gerschenkron, Alexander. *Bread and Democracy in Germany*. Berkeley: University of California Press, 1943.

Gessen, Masha. *The Man without a Face: The Unlikely Rise of Vladimir Putin*. New York: Riverhead Books, 2013.

Ghose, Bishwajit. "Food Security and Food Self-sufficiency in China: From Past to 2050." *Food and Energy Security* 3, no. 2 (2014): 86–95.

Gladunov, Oleg. "Embargo Putina: Dva goda bez urozhaia." *Svobodnaia pressa*, March 18, 2011. https://svpressa.ru/economy/article/40640/.

Goldman, Marshall I. *Petrostate: Putin, Power, and the New Russia*. New York: Oxford University Press, 2008.

Goldman, Wendy. "Not by Bread Alone: Food, Workers, and the State." In *Hunger and War: Food Supply in the Soviet Union during the Second World War*, edited by Wendy Goldman and Donald Filtzer, 44–97. Bloomington: Indiana University Press, 2015.

Gordeev, Aleksei. *Russia's Food Supply: Problems of Theory and Practice*. Moscow: Kolos, 1999. In Russian.

Gordon, Michael R. "Facing Severe Shortage of Food, Russia Seeks Foreign Relief Aid." *New York Times*, October 10, 1998, sec. A.

Gordon, Michael R. "Food Crisis Forces Russia to Swallow Its Pride." *New York Times*, November 7, 1998, sec. A.

Gosteva, Elena. "Putin podshchital poteri: kto bol'she postradal ot sanktsii." *Gazeta.ru*, June 20, 2019. https://www.gazeta.ru/business/2019/06/20/12429169.shtml?updated.

"Grain: World Markets and Trade." December 10, 2022. Washington, DC: US Department of Agriculture. https://www.fas.usda.gov/data/grain-world-markets-and-trade.

Greene, Samuel A. "From Boom to Bust: Hardship, Mobilization & Russia's Social Contract." *Daedalus* 146, no. 2 (2017): 113–27.

Greene, Samuel A. *Moscow in Movement: Power and Opposition in Putin's Russia*. Stanford, CA: Stanford University Press, 2014.

Greene, Samuel A., and Graeme B. Robertson. *Putin v. the People*. London: Yale University Press, 2019.

Greshonkov, Aleksei. "Permanentnost' strategicheskikh prioritetov ekonomicheskoi bezopasnosti Rossii v prodovol'stvennoi sfere." Doctoral diss., Tambovskii Gosudartvennyi Universitet imeni G.R. Derzhavina, 2015. https://www.dissercat.com/content/permanentnost-strategicheskikh-prioritetov-ekonomicheskoi-bezopasnosti-rossii-v-prodovolstve.

Gromova, Anna. "Sakharnyi sgovor: FAS vyiasniaet, kto stoial za podorozhaniem 'belogo zolota.'" *Gazeta.ru*, March 29, 2022. https://www.gazeta.ru/business/2022/03/29/14677837.shtml.

Gruzinova, Irina, and Galina Zinchenko. "Bekon vmesto betona: Pochemu Vadim Moshkovich ushel iz stroitel'nogo biznesa." *Forbes Russia*, September 25, 2015. https://www.forbes.ru/milliardery/301229-bekon-vmesto-betona-pochemu-vladimir-moshkovich-ushel-iz-stroitelnogo-biznesa.

Gustafson, Thane. *Klimat: Russia in the Age of Climate Change*. Cambridge, MA: Harvard University Press, 2021.

Gustafson, Thane. *Wheel of Fortune*. Cambridge, MA: Harvard University Press, 2012.

Gutterman, Ivan, and Wojtec Grojec. "A Timeline of All Russia-Related Sanctions." *Radio Free Europe/Radio Liberty*, September 19, 2018. https://www.rferl.org/a/russia-sanctions-timeline/29477179.html.

Hahn, Werner. "The Farms' Revolt and Grain Shortages in 1991." In *The "Farmer Threat": The Political Economy of Agrarian Reform in Post-Soviet Russia*, edited by Don Van Atta, 43–54. Boulder, CO: Westview Press, 1993.

Hale, Henry E. *Patronal Politics: Eurasian Regime Dynamics in Comparative Perspective*. New York: Cambridge University Press, 2014.

Handelman, Stephen. *Comrade Criminal: Russia's New Mafiya*. New Haven, CT: Yale University Press, 1995.

Hanson, Philip. *The Rise and Fall of the The Soviet Economy: An Economic History of the USSR 1945-1991*. London: Routledge, 2014.

Hauslohner, Peter. "Gorbachev's Social Contract." *Soviet Economy* 3, no. 1 (1987): 54–89.

Hedberg, Masha. "The Target Strikes Back: Explaining Countersanctions and Russia's Strategy of Differentiated Retaliation." *Post-Soviet Affairs* 34, no. 1 (2018): 35–54.

Helleiner, Eric. "The Return of National Self-Sufficiency? Excavating Autarkic Thought in a De-Globalizing Era." *International Studies Review* 23, no. 3 (2021): 933–57.

Hendrix, Cullen S., and Stephan Haggard. "Global Food Prices, Regime Type, and Urban Unrest in the Developing World." *Journal of Peace Research* 52, no. 2 (2015): 143–57.

Herrera, Yoshiko M. *Imagined Economies: The Sources of Russian Regionalism.* New York: Cambridge University Press, 2005.

Hirschman, Albert O. "The Political Economy of Import-Substituting Industrialization in Latin America." *Quarterly Journal of Economics* 82, no. 1 (1968): 1–32.

Hornsby, Robert. *Protest, Reform and Repression in Khrushchev's Soviet Union.* Cambridge: Cambridge University Press, 2013.

"How Is Poverty Measured?" Institute for Research on Poverty (IRP), University of Wisconsin. Accessed July 21, 2021. https://www.irp.wisc.edu/resources/how-is-poverty-measured/.

"How Much Grain Is Being Shipped from Ukraine?" *BBC News*, August 22, 2022, sec. World. https://www.bbc.com/news/world-61759692.

"The Hunger Virus Multiplies: Deadly Recipe of Conflict, COVID-19 and Climate Accelerate World Hunger." Oxfam Media Briefing. Oxfam, July 9, 2021. https://oi-files-d8-prod.s3.eu-west-2.amazonaws.com/s3fs-public/2021-07/The%20Hunger%20Virus%202.0_media%20brief_EN.pdf.

"I.I. Mel'nikov: V KPRF udivilis' uslyshav predlozhenie 'edinorossov' vvesti prodovol'stvennye talony dlia maloimushchikh." *KPRF*, May 23, 2008. https://kprf.ru/rus_soc/57303.html.

"The Importance of Ukraine and the Russian Federation for Global Agricultural Markets and the Risks Associated with the Current Conflict." UN Food and Agriculture Organization, March 25, 2022. https://www.fao.org/3/cb9236en/cb9236en.pdf.

"Initsiativy LDPR o sertifikatakh na produkty i semeinom biznese podderzhali v Kremle." *LDPR*, February 17, 2021. https://ldpr.ru/event/110284.

"Internet-konferentsiia ministra sel'skogo khoziaistva Rosiiskoi Federatsii Alekseiia Gordeeva." November 22, 2006, https://www.agroyug.ru/news/id-4280.

"Interview with Iurii Trushin." Rosselkhozbank. Accessed April 10, 2022. https://www.rshb.ru/press/releases/16177.

Ioffe, Genrikh. "Diary Entry." *Diary* (blog), January 7, 1992. https://prozhito.org/note/197711.

Ioffe, Grigory, Tatyana Nefedova, and Ilya Zaslavsky. "From Spatial Continuity to Fragmentation: The Case of Russian Farming." *Annals of the Association of American Geographers* 94, no. 4 (2004): 913–43.

Ioffe, Grigory, Tatyana Nefedova, and Ilya Zaslavsky. *The End of Peasantry? The Disintegration of Rural Russia.* Pittsburgh: University of Pittsburgh Press, 2006.

Isangazin, Marat. "Zerno daet 400% godovykh a neft' v luchshem sluchae 80%." *Kommercheskie vesti*, November 21, 2002. https://kvnews.ru/gazeta/2002/11/45/evgenia_serova_zerno_daet_400__godovih__a_neft_v_luchshem_sluchae_80.

"Itogi goda: Utomlennyi solntsev APK." *Interfax*, December 27, 2010. https://www.interfax.ru/business/171113.

Iushin, Sergei. Authors' Interview, September 24, 2020.

Ivanova, Polina. "Protesting No More." *Reuters*, July 30, 2021. https://www.reuters.com/investigates/special-report/russia-navalny-protest-city/?2.

"Izvestnye rossiiskie polittekhnologi ob"iavili 'Miratorgu' i 'Dymovu' boikot za 'balabolov.'" *EAN News*, April 30, 2019. https://eanews.ru/news/izvestnyye-rossiyskiy-polittekhnologi-ob-yavili-miratorgu-i-dymovu-boykot-za-balabolov_30-04-2019.

Javeline, Debra. *Protest and the Politics of Blame: The Russian Response to Unpaid Wages*. Ann Arbor: University of Michigan Press, 2009.

"John Deere Suspends Shipments to Russia." *Deere.com*. Accessed October 24, 2022. https://www.deere.com/en/stories/featured/john-deere-suspends-shipments-to-russia/.

Johnson, David Gale, and Karen McConnell Brooks. *Prospects for Soviet Agriculture in the 1980s*. Bloomington: Indiana University Press, 1983.

Jumet, Kira D. *Contesting the Repressive State: Why Ordinary Egyptians Protested during the Arab Spring*. New York: Oxford University Press, 2018.

Kahneman, Daniel, and Amos Tversky. "Prospect Theory: An Analysis of Decision under Risk." In *Handbook of the Fundamentals of Financial Decision Making: Part I*, edited by Leonard C. MacLean and William T. Ziemba, 99–127. Hackensack, NJ: World Scientific, 2013.

Kanaev, Petr, and Elena Sukhorukova. "Dmitry Patrushev— RBK: 'Ot nashei produktsii voobshche ne otkazyvaiutsia.'" *RBC.ru*, October 3, 2022. https://www.rbc.ru/interview/business/03/10/2022/633291d79a794719ca093b90.

Kapustinskaia, Kseniia. "'Serogo tsveta, zato otechestvennaia': v Rossii pytaiutsia sozdat' upakovku, kotoraia zamenit Tetra Pak." *Obozrevatel'*, June 15, 2022. https://news.obozrevatel.com/economics/economy/serogo-tsveta-zato-otechestvennaya-v-rossii-pyitayutsya-sozdat-upakovku-kotoraya-zamenit-tetra-pak.htm.

Karabut, Tatiana. "Za miluiu tushu." *Rossiiskaia gazeta*, July 20, 2020. https://dlib.eastview.com/browse/doc/60657650.

Kavaklı, Kerim Can, J. Tyson Chatagnier, and Emre Hatipoğlu. "The Power to Hurt and the Effectiveness of International Sanctions." *Journal of Politics* 82, no. 3 (2020): 879–94.

"Kholodil'nik dlia tsen. Pravitel'stvo dogovorilos' o zamorazhivanii tsen na produkty pitaniia." *Lenta.ru*, October 27, 2007. https://m.lenta.ru/articles/2007/10/22/cold.

"Khroniki velikoi derzhavy: Produktovye kartochki na podkhode?" *KPRF*, December 22, 2020. https://msk.kprf.ru/2020/12/22/151713/.

Khurshudyan, Isabelle. "Putin Is Boiling over Rising Pasta Prices in Russia. It Seems More about Populism than Penne." *Washington Post*, December 16, 2021. https://www.washingtonpost.com/world/europe/russia-pasta-food-prices-putin/2020/12/16/0c0cde72-3ed9-11eb-b58b-1623f6267960_story.html.

Kisin, Sergei. "Glavu 'Rusagro' obvinili v moshennichestve." *Kommersant*, February 1, 2005. https://www.kommersant.ru/doc/543213.

Knight, Amy. "Anti-Putin Campaigners: It's Time to Sanction the Large Adult Sons of Oligarchs and Cronies." *Daily Beast*, March 2, 2021, sec. world. https://www.thedailybeast.com/anti-putin-campaigners-say-its-time-to-sanction-sons-of-oligarchs-and-cronies.

Koester, Ulrich. "A Revival of Large Farms in Eastern Europe—How Important Are Institutions?" *Agricultural Economics* 32 (2005): 103–13.

Koffler, Rebekah. *Putin's Playbook: Russia's Secret Plan to Defeat America*. New York: Simon & Schuster, 2021.

Kokoreva, Maria. "Tseny v Rossii snizhaiutsia dva mesiatsa podriad vpervye za tri goda: Chto proiskhodit." *Forbes.ru*, August 10, 2022. https://www.forbes.ru/finansy/474061-ceny-v-rossii-snizautsa-dva-mesaca-podrad-vpervye-za-tri-goda-cto-proishodit.

Kolesnikov, Andrei. "Zernopoddanicheskie nastroeniia." *Kommersant*. May 21, 2020. https://www.kommersant.ru/doc/4349683.

Kondrat'eva, Irina. "Bankrotstvo kak sredstvo ot konkurentov: 'Solnechnye Produkty' doshli do VS." *Pravo.ru*, September 14, 2020. https://pravo.ru/story/225655/.

Koniaev, Nikolai. "Pokhmel'e." *Diary* (blog), January 4, 1992. https://prozhito.org/note/528310.

Konnov, Maksim. "Sovetskii podkhod." *Lenta.ru*, April 2, 2021. https://lenta.ru/articles/2021/04/02/coupons/.

Koreneva, Aleksandra. "Rosselkhoznadzor voz'met vsekh v svoi ruki: raionnykh veterinarov obvinili v neblagonadezhnosti." *AgroBook*, May 22, 2019. https://agrobook.ru/blog/user/aleksandra-koreneva/rosselhoznadzor-vozmyot-vseh-v-svoi-ruki-rayonnyh-veterinarov-obvinili.

Kortukov, Dima. "'Sovereign Democracy' and the Politics of Ideology in Putin's Russia." *Russian Politics* 5, no. 1 (2020): 81–104.

Kostyrev, Anatolii. "Eks-Ministr ukrepit 'Druzhbu Narodov.'" *Kommersant*, June 6, 2022. https://www.kommersant.ru/doc/5391928.

Kostyrev, Anatolii. "Postavshchiki peregruzili zerno." *Kommersant*, September 1, 2022. https://www.kommersant.ru/doc/5537182.

Kostyrev, Anatolii. "Pshenitsu rezhut pod koren'." *Kommersant*, August 29, 2022. https://www.kommersant.ru/doc/5535904.

Kostyrev, Anatolii. "V pshenitse prorastayut prodavtsy," *Kommersant*, April 20, 2023. https://www.kommersant.ru/doc/5941249.

Kotova, Iuliia. "Skrynnik rasskazala o 'khishchenniakh' v Rosagrolizinge." *Vedomosti*, December 2, 2012. https://www.vedomosti.ru/politics/articles/2012/12/02/skrynnik_rasskazala.

Kramer, Andrew E. "Thanks to Sanctions, Russia Is Cushioned from Virus's Economic Shocks." *New York Times*. March 20, 2020. https://www.nytimes.com/2020/03/20/world/europe/russia-coronavirus-covid-19.html.

Kravchenko, Ekaterina. "'Iz nichego isteriku zakatily, balaboly'. Viktor Linnik i Vadim Dymov o zaprete na vvoz khamona i parmezana v Rossiiu." *Forbes*, April 30, 2019. https://www.forbes.ru/biznes/375489-iz-nichego-isteriku-zakatili-balaboly-viktor-linnik-i-vadim-dymov-o-zaprete-na-vvoz.

Krugman, Paul. "Food, Fertilizer and the Future." *New York Times*, April 26, 2022, sec. Opinion. https://www.nytimes.com/2022/04/26/opinion/ukraine-russia-food-crisis.html.

"Krupneishie vladel'tsy sel'skokhoziaistvennoi zemli v Rossii v Rossii na 2020 god." *BEFL*, May 2020. https://www.befl.ru/upload/iblock/d6a/d6a4b0dde4f8168cdb5dda65b3910d33.pdf.

"Kto i zachem opublikoval video s poiushchimi v samolete Dvorkovichem, Tkachevym i Timakovoi." *BFM.ru*, February 14, 2019. https://www.bfm.ru/news/406879.

"Kudrin: Zamorazhivat' tseny na prodovol'stvennom rynke byli by oshibkoi." *RIA Novosti*, October 24, 2007. https://ria.ru/20071024/85292984.html.

Kukolevskii, Aleksandr. "Tak poedim!" *Kommersant*, February 8, 2010. https://www.kommersant.ru/doc/1315512.

Kuznetsova, Evgeniia, and Elena Sukhorukova. "Rossiiane stali khuzhe otnosit'sia k prodovol'stvennomu embargo." *RBC.ru*, July 6, 2021. https://www.rbc.ru/society/06/07/2021/60e31b1e9a79474492a76c32.

Kynge, James, Sun Yu, and Leo Lewis. "Fortress China: Xi Jinping's Plan for Economic Independence." *Financial Times*, September 15, 2022. https://www.ft.com/content/0496b125-7760-41ba-8895-8358a7f24685.

Lagi, Marco, Karla Z. Bertrand, and Yaneer Bar-Yam. "The Food Crises and Political Instability in North Africa and the Middle East." 2011. doi: 10.2139/ssrn.1910031
"Largest Hypermarket Chain in Russia's Far East Imposes Limits amid Buying Frenzy." *Radio Free Europe/Radio Liberty*, March 12, 2022. https://www.rferl.org/a/russia-hypermarket-chain-restricting-sales-panic/31749947.html.
Laruelle, Marlene. *Is Russia Fascist?: Unraveling Propaganda East and West*. Ithaca, NY: Cornell University Press, 2021.
Leonard, Carol S. *Agrarian Reform in Russia: The Road from Serfdom*. Cambridge: Cambridge University Press, 2010.
Lerman, Zvi, Csaba Csaki, and Gershon Feder. *Agriculture in Transition: Land Policies and Evolving Farm Structures in Post-Soviet Countries*. Lanham, MD: Lexington Books, 2004.
Levinskii, Aleksandr. "Kak Miratorg s pomoshch'iu gosudarstva stal prodovol'stvennym gigantom." *Forbes Russia*, April 8, 2019. https://www.forbes.ru/biznes/374459-kak-miratorg-s-pomoshchyu-gosudarstva-stal-prodovolstvennym-gigantom.
Levitsky, Steven, and Lucan A. Way. *Competitive Authoritarianism: Hybrid Regimes after the Cold War*. Cambridge: Cambridge University Press, 2010.
Lewis, Leo. "China Is on a Mission to Ensure Its Food Security." *Financial Times*, September 1, 2022. https://www.ft.com/content/363c94c1-afed-49b3-aa09-f31227819791.
Liefert, William. "Distribution Problems in the Food Economy of the Former Soviet Union." In *The Former Soviet Union in Transition*, edited by Richard F. Kaufman and John P. Hardt, 491–505. Armonk, NY: M. E. Sharpe, 1993.
Liefert, William M. "The Food Problem in the Republics of the Former USSR." In *The "Farmer Threat": The Political Economy of Agrarian Reform in Post-Soviet Russia*, edited by Don Van Atta, 25–42. Boulder, CO: Westview Press, 1993.
Liefert, William M., and Olga Liefert. "Russian Agriculture during Transition: Performance, Global Impact, and Outlook." *Applied Economic Perspectives and Policy* 34, no. 1 (2012): 37–75.
Liefert, William M., and Olga Liefert. "Russia's Economic Crisis and Its Agricultural and Food Economy." *Choices* 30, no. 1 (2015): 1–6.
Liefert, William M., Olga Liefert, Ralph Seeley, and Tani Lee. "The Effect of Russia's Economic Crisis and Import Ban on Its Agricultural and Food Sector." *Journal of Eurasian Studies* 10, no. 2 (2019): 119–35.
Lih, Lars T. *Bread and Authority in Russia, 1914–1921*. Berkeley: University of California Press, 1990.
Lindsay, Ira. "A Troubled Path to Private Property: Agricultural Land Law in Russia." *Columbia Journal of European Law* 16 (2010): 261–302.
Lisitsyna, Maria. "Putin raskritikoval Reshetnikova za 'eksperimenty' s tsenami na produkty." *RBC.ru*, December 13, 2020. https://www.rbc.ru/society/13/12/2020/5fd5ea339a79474886223f5f.
Loktiononva, Elena. "Koroli i miaso." *Kommersant*, February 8, 2010. https://www.kommersant.ru/doc/1310339.
Lovell, Stephen. *Summerfolk: A History of the Dacha, 1710–2000*. Ithaca, NY: Cornell University Press, 2003.
Lubos, Smutka, Spicka Jindrich, Ishchukova Natalia, and Selby Richard. "Agrarian Import Ban and Its Impact on the Russian and European Union Agrarian Trade Performance." *Agricultural Economics* 62, no. 11 (2016): 493–506.

MacDonald, Alistair, and Oksana Pyrozhok. "Russian Oligarch Seizes 400,000 Acres of Ukrainian Farmland, Owners Say." *Wall Street Journal*, December 6, 2022, https://www.wsj.com/articles/russian-oligarch-seizes-400-000-acres-of-ukrainian-farmland-owners-say-11670338956.

Makarkin, Aleksei, and Peter M. Oppenheimer. "The Russian Social Contract and Regime Legitimacy." *International Affairs* 87, no. 6 (2011): 1459–74.

"Maksim Reshetnikov: nuzhno sozdat' preskazuemyi i poniatnyi mekhanizm reagirovaniia na kolebaniia tsen na produkty." Ministerstvo ekonomicheskogo razvitiia Rossiiskoi Federatsii, December 16, 2020. https://www.economy.gov.ru/material/news/maksim_reshetnikov_nuzhno_sozdat_predskazuemyy_i_ponyatnyy_mehanizm_reagirovaniya_na_kolebaniya_cen_na_produkty.html.

Malish, Anton F. "Soviet Agricultural Policy in the 1980s." *Review of Policy Research* 4, no. 2 (1984): 301–10.

Mamonova, Natalia. "Naive Monarchism and Rural Resistance in Contemporary Russia." *Rural Sociology* 81, no. 3 (2016): 316–42.

Mamonova, Natalia. "Understanding the Silent Majority in Authoritarian Populism: What Can We Learn from Popular Support for Putin in Rural Russia?" *Journal of Peasant Studies* 46, no. 3 (2019): 561–85.

Mamonova, Natalia, and Oane Visser. "State Marionettes, Phantom Organisations or Genuine Movements? The Paradoxical Emergence of Rural Social Movements in Post-Socialist Russia." *Journal of Peasant Studies* 41, no. 4 (2014): 491–516.

Mankoff, Jeffrey. "Russia's Response to Covid-19." Center for Strategic and International Studies, April 10, 2020. https://www.csis.org/analysis/russias-response-covid-19.

Markov, Andrei. "Svinotsid gubernatora Gordeeva." *Moscow Post*, September 30, 2013. http://www.compromat.ru/page_33817.htm.

Martynova, Polina. "Vlasti pereveli rasshchety poshliny za eksport zerna v rubli." *RBC.ru*, July 1, 2022. https://www.rbc.ru/economics/01/07/2022/62bf32e89a7947a0d3fac3c3.

Matveev, Il'ia. "Krupnyi biznes v putinskoi Rossii: Starye i novye istochniki vliianiia na vlast'." *Mir Rossii* 28, no. 1 (2019): 54–74. https://doi.org/0.17323/1811-038X-2019-28-1-54-74.

Matyukha, Andriy, Peter Voigt, and Axel Wolz. "Agro-Holdings in Russia, Ukraine and Kazakhstan: Temporary Phenomenon or Permanent Business Form? Farm-Level Evidence from Moscow and Belgorod Regions." *Post-Communist Economies* 27, no. 3 (2015): 370–94.

Medvedev, Dmitry. "Nasha eda protiv ikh sanktsii." *Telegram Kanal: Dmitry Medvedev*, April 1, 2022. https://t.me/medvedev_telegram/29.

Medvedev, Zhores A. *Soviet Agriculture*. New York: W. W. Norton, 1987.

"Meeting on Developing Agriculture and Fisheries." President of Russia, April 5, 2022. http://en.kremlin.ru/events/president/news/68141.

Miagkii, Vitalii. "Mishustin vydelil na zamorozku tsen eshche 9 milliardov rublei." *URA.ru*, April 7, 2021. https://ura.news/news/1052479417.

"Mikhail Mishustin podpisal riad postanovlenii dlia stabilizatsii situatsii na rynke prodovol'stviia." Government of the Russian Federation, December 15, 2020. http://government.ru/news/41118/.

Mikhailov, Aleksei. "Kasha iz topora." *Gazeta.ru*, April 4, 2011. https://www.gazeta.ru/column/mikhailov/3573933.shtml.

Miller, Chris. *Putinomics: Power and Money in Resurgent Russia*. Chapel Hill: University of North Carolina Press, 2018.

Ministerie van Landbouw, Natuur en Voedselkwaliteit. "Russian Animal Breeders Concerned about Reduction in Genetic Material Imports—Nieuwsbericht—Agroberichten Buitenland." Nieuwsbericht. Ministerie van Landbouw, Natuur en Voedselkwaliteit, January 20, 2022. https://www.agroberichtenbuitenland.nl/actueel/nieuws/2022/01/20/russian-animal-breeders-concerned-about-reduction-in-genetic-material-imports.

Ministerie van Landbouw, Natuur en Voedselkwaliteit. "Situation with Potato Seeds in Russia Is Catastrophic—Nieuwsbericht—Agroberichten Buitenland." Nieuwsbericht. Ministerie van Landbouw, Natuur en Voedselkwaliteit, February 7, 2022. https://www.agroberichtenbuitenland.nl/actueel/nieuws/2022/02/07/situation-with-potato-seeds-in-russia-is-catastrophic.

"Minpromtorg podgotovil kontseptsiiu sistemy prodovol'stvennykh kartochek." *Forbes*, September 15, 2015. https://www.forbes.ru/news/299705-minpromtorg-podgotovil-kontseptsiyu-sistemy-prodovolstvennykh-kartochek.

"Minsel'khoz prodlil zamorozku tsen na produkty do maia 2008 goda." *Lenta.ru*, January 31, 2008. https://lenta.ru/news/2008/01/31/freeze.

"Minsel'khoz RF vkliuchil v svoi perechen' 66 sistemoobrazuiushchikh predpriiatii." *Kommersant*, April 21, 2020. https://www.interfax.ru/business/705378.

"Miratorg i Sberbank CIB podpisali pervoe v istorii APK Rossii kreditnoe soglashenie srokom na 15 let." Sberbank, June 6, 2013. https://cbonds.ru/news/655263.

"Mishustin podpisal postanovlenie o zaprete na vyvoz zerna v EAES i sakhara za predely soiuza." *Interfax*, March 14, 2022. https://www.interfax.ru/business/828166.

Mondale, Walter. "Memorandum from Vice President Mondale to President Carter, 01/03/1980." In *Foreign Relations of the United States. 1977-1980. Soviet Union*, edited by Melissa Jane Taylor, VI:730–31. Washington, DC: Department of State, 2013.

Moore, Barrington. *Social Origins of Dictatorship and Democracy: Lord and Peasant in the Making of the Modern World*. Boston: Beacon Press, 1966.

Mukhametshina, Elena. "Bol'shinstvo rossiian ne chustvuet problem ot zapadnykh sanktsii." *Vedomosti*, March 17, 2020. https://www.vedomosti.ru/society/articles/2020/03/17/825343-bolshinstvo-chuvstvuet.

Mukhametshina, Elena. "Rossiiane ne podderzhivaiut unichtozhenie sanktsionnykh produktov—'Levada-Tsentr.'" *Vedomosti*, August 12, 2015. https://www.vedomosti.ru/politics/articles/2015/08/13/604601-rossiyane-ne-podderzhivayut-unichtozhenie-sanktsionnih-produktov.

Mulder, Nicholas. *The Economic Weapon: The Rise of Sanctions as a Tool of Modern War*. New Haven, CT: Yale University Press, 2022.

Musacchio, Aldo, and Sergio G. Lazzarini. *Reinventing State Capitalism: Leviathan in Business, Brazil and Beyond*. Cambridge, MA: Harvard University Press, 2014.

Myers, Steven Lee. *The New Tsar: The Rise and Reign of Vladimir Putin*. New York: Simon & Schuster, 2015.

Naumenko, Natalya. "The Political Economy of Famine: The Ukrainian Famine of 1933." *Journal of Economic History* 81, no. 1 (2021): 156–97.

Nechaev, Andrey. Authors' Interview, October 27, 2020.

Nefedova, Tatyana. "Dvadtsat' piat' let postsovetskomu sel'skomu khoziaistvu Rossii: Geograficheskie tendentsii i protivorechiia." *Izvestiia RAN. Seriia geograficheskaia* 5 (2017): 7–18. https://doi.org/10.7868/S0373244417050012.

Nelson, Scott Reynolds. *Oceans of Grain: How American Wheat Remade the World*. New York: Basic Books, 2022.

Newman, Edward. "Hungry, or Hungry for Change? Food Riots and Political Conflict, 2005–2015." *Studies in Conflict & Terrorism* 43, no. 4 (2020): 300–24.

Nikitina, Olga, and Anatolii Kostyrev. "Defitsit vyshel na polia." *Kommersant*, June 23, 2022. https://www.kommersant.ru/doc/5423867.

Nilsson, Jerker, Svetlana Golovina, Sebastian Hess, and Axel Wolz. "Governance of Production Co-operatives in Russian Agriculture." *Annals of Public and Cooperative Economics* 87, no. 4 (2016): 541–62.

"Noveishaia gigantomaniia." *Krestianskie vedomosti*, October 20, 2009. https://kvedomosti.ru/pressa/novejshaya-gigantomaniya.html.

Nurieva, Sakina. "Minsel'khoz zaiavil o sderzhivanii rosta tsen proizvoditeliami molochnoi produktsii." *Gazeta.ru*, November 3, 2021. https://m.gazeta.ru/business/news/2021/11/03/n_16795585.shtml.

"O vnesenii izmenenii v Strategiiu razvitiia pishchevoi i pererabatyvaiuschchei promyshlennosti." Government of the Russian Federation, July 5, 2016. http://government.ru/docs/23608/.

"Ob obespechenii prodovol'stvennoi bezopasnosti Rossi'skoi Federatsii." Sovet Bezopasnosti RF, December 4, 2009. http://www.scrf.gov.ru/council/session/2045/.

"Ob utverzhdenii Strategii razvitiia pishchevoi i pererabatyvaiushchei promyshlennosti do 2020 goda." Government of the Russian Federation, April 17, 2012. http://government.ru/docs/23574/.

Office of the UN Coordinator for the Black Sea Grain Initiative, May 8, 2023 update: https://www.un.org/sg/en/content/sg/note-correspondents/2023-05-08/update-the-office-of-the-un-coordinator-for-the-black-sea-grain-initiative%C2%A0.

Orlianskii, Ruslan. "'Spetsoperatsiia-kooperatsiia' Patrusheva." *Moscow Post*, July 10, 2019. http://www.moscow-post.su/economics/specoperaciya_kooperaciya_patrusheva30069/.

"Osnovnye napravleniia agroprodovol'stvennoi politiki pravitel'stva Rossiiskoi Federatsii na 2001–2010 gody." Government of the Russian Federation, July 27, 2000. https://rulaws.ru/goverment/Osnovnye-napravleniya-agroprodovolstvennoy-politiki-Pravitelstva-Rossiyskoy-Federatsii-na-2001---201/.

Osterman, Lev. *Intelligentsiia i vlast' v Rossii (1985–1996)*. Moscow: Monolit, 2000.

"Outflow Possibly Overstated." *Moscow Times*, June 19, 2011. https://www.themoscowtimes.com/2011/06/19/outflow-possibly-overstated-a7699.

Paarlberg, Robert. *Food Politics: What Everyone Needs to Know*. New York: Oxford University Press, 2013.

Palasciano, Andrea. "Putin Urges Food Price Cap as Russian Economy Falters." *Moscow Times*, December 16, 2020. https://www.themoscowtimes.com/2020/12/16/putin-urges-food-price-cap-as-russian-economy-falters-a72378.

Pallot, Judith, and Tat'yana Nefedova. *Russia's Unknown Agriculture: Household Production in Post-Communist Russia*. Oxford: Oxford University Press, 2007.

Patel, Raj. "Food Sovereignty." *Journal of Peasant Studies* 36, no. 3 (2009): 663–706.

Pavlenko, Olesia. "Eksport pshenitsy iz Rossii rukhnul na 27%." *Kommersant*, August 23, 2022. https://www.kommersant.ru/doc/5525340.

Pavskaia, Inga. "Siloviki sdvinut Moshkovicha s mesta 'pod solntsem'?" *Utro News*, December 30, 2019. https://utro-news.ru/siloviki-sdvinut-moshkovicha-s-mesta-pod-solncem/.

Piatin, Aleksandr. "Eks-glava Minsel'khoza okazalsia kontroliruiushchim aktsionerom krupneishego zemlevladel'tsa v Rossii." *Forbes Russia*, April 15, 2021. https://www.for

bes.ru/newsroom/biznes/426511-eks-glava-minselhoza-okazalsya-kontroliruyushc him-akcionerom-krupneyshego.

Pierskalla, Jan H. "The Politics of Urban Bias: Rural Threats and the Dual Dilemma of Political Survival." *Studies in Comparative International Development* 51, no. 3 (2016): 286–307.

Pirogov, Aleksandr. "Top-100—Miratorg: miasom naruzhu." *Abireg.ru*, November 23, 2018. https://abireg.ru/n_71911.html.

"Plan meropriiatii ('dorozhnaia karta') po importzameshcheniiu v sel'skom khoziaistve na 2014–2015 gody." Government of the Russian Federation, October 2, 2014. http://static.government.ru/media/files/hZ8xLKjTbJk.pdf.

Plugov, Aleksei. "Rynok prodovol'stviia Rossii: Nekotorye tendentsii za pervoe polugodie 2022 goda." AB Centre, July 6, 2022. https://ab-centre.ru/news/rynok-prodovolstviya-rossii-nekotorye-tendencii-pervogo-polugodiya-2022-goda.

Poliakova, Viktoriia. "Posol Italii poprosil po druzhbe otmenit' ogranicheniia na parmezan v Rossii." *RBC.ru*, March 26, 2021. https://www.rbc.ru/business/26/03/2021/605d75809a79478894e60792.

Polukhin, Aleksei. "Chto poseesh', to pozhnesh'." *Kommersant*, August 5, 2022. https://www.kommersant.ru/doc/5493536.

Polukhin, Aleksei. "Kazakhstanu ne khvatilo pshenitsy." *Kommersant*, April 22, 2022. https://www.kommersant.ru/doc/5326323.

Pominov, Iurii. *Khronika smutnogo vremeni: Zapiski redaktora*. Pavlodar: Eko, 2007. http://ypominov.ru/books/7/.

"Poslanie prezidenta federal'nomu sobraniiu." President of Russia, April 21, 2021. http://kremlin.ru/events/president/news/65418.

"Posol Italii prizval Rossiiu razreshit' vvoz parmezana." *Meduza*, March 26, 2021. https://meduza.io/news/2021/03/26/posol-italii-prizval-rossiyu-razreshit-vvoz-parmezana-odin-iz-rossiyskih-syrovarov-poprosil-ne-delat-etogo-esche-pyat-shest-let.

Pospieszna, Paulina, Joanna Skrzypczyńska, and Beata Stępień. "Hitting Two Birds with One Stone: How Russian Countersanctions Intertwined Political and Economic Goals." *PS: Political Science & Politics* 53, no. 2 (2020): 243–47.

"Pravila osushchestvleniia gosudarstvenykh zakupochnykh i tovarnykh interventsii dlya regulirovaniia rynka selskohozyaistvenoi produktsii, syr'a i prodovolstviia." Government of the Russian Federation, August 3, 2001. http://pravo.gov.ru/proxy/ips/?docbody=&prevDoc=102167464&backlink=1&&nd=102072342.

"Pravitel'stvo RF oproverglo rodstvo zheny Medvedeva i glav Miratorga." *Interfax*, May 3, 2019. https://www.interfax.ru/russia/660058.

"Pravitel'stvo RF podderzhalo zakonoproekt o vozmozhnosti gosregulirovaniii tsen na produkty v sluchae rosta tsen." Ministerstvo ekonomicheskogo razvitiia Rossiiskoi Federatsii, December 16, 2020. https://www.economy.gov.ru/material/news/pravitelstvo_rf_podderzhalo_zakonoproekt_o_vozmozhnosti_gosregulirovaniya_cen_na_produkty_v_sluchae_rosta_cen.html.

"Predlozheniia uchenykh o reformakh v zemel'noi i agrarnoi sferakh—uchet zemel' i chetkoe gosudartvennoe planirovanie." Soyuz Zemleustroitelei, 2013. http://roszemproekt.ru/newsx/predlozheniya/.

"Predsedatel' Pravitel'stva Rossiiskoi Federatsii V.V. Putin provel zasedanie Prezidiuma Pravitel'stva." Government of the Russian Federation, 2010. http://archive.government.ru/docs/11633/print/.

Pripstein Posusney, Marsha, and Michele Penner Angrist, eds. *Authoritarianism in the Middle East: Regimes and Resistance*. Boulder, CO: Lynne Rienner Publishers, 2005.

Prishchepov, Alexander V., Volker C Radeloff, Matthias Baumann, Tobias Kuemmerle, and Daniel Müller. "Effects of Institutional Changes on Land Use: Agricultural Land Abandonment during the Transition from State-Command to Market-Driven Economies in Post-Soviet Eastern Europe." *Environmental Research Letters* 7, no. 2 (2012): 024021.

"Problemy obshchestva." Levada-Tsentr, March 9, 2021. https://www.levada.ru/2021/03/09/problemy-obshhestva/.

"Prodovol'stvennaia bezopasnost'." *LDPR*, October 13, 2020. https://ldpr.ru/event/98759.

"Produktovye sertifikaty." April 23, 2021. https://www.levada.ru/2021/04/23/produktovye-sertifikaty/.

"Proekt Doktriny prodovol'stvennoi bezopasnosti Rossiiskoi Federatsii." *Dairy News*, October 31, 2008. https://dairynews.today/news/projekt_doktriny_prodovolstvennoj_bezopasnosti_ros.html.

"Proekt: Strategiia razvitiia pishchevoi i pererabatyvaiushchei promyshlennosti Rossiiskoi Federatsii na period do 2030 goda." Ministry of Agriculture, 2019. barley-malt.ru/wp-content/uploads/2019/11/proekt-strategyy-razvytyja-pyschevoj-y-pererabatyvajuschej-promyshlennosty-rf.pdf.

Prokopenko, Aleksandra. "Pochemu Rossiia soglasilas' razblokirovat' ukrainskii eksport zerna." The Carnegie Endowment, July 25, 2022. https://carnegieendowment.org/politika/87559.

Pulver, Andrew. "Andrei Konchalovsky: 'I'm Very Glad I Failed in Hollywood.'" *The Guardian*, April 8, 2021. https://www.theguardian.com/film/2021/apr/08/andrei-konchalovsky-im-very-glad-i-failed-in-hollywood.

"Putin nagradil syna Patrusheva ordenom Pocheta." *RBC.ru*, October 27, 2016. https://www.rbc.ru/rbcfreenews/5811e8729a7947610dfa2b6d.

"Putin poruchil provesti inventarizatsiiu vneshnetorgovykh soglashenii v sfere APK." *Interfax*, May 19, 2022. https://www.interfax.ru/russia/13737.

"Putin predlozhil podumat' o vvedenii sertifikatov na produkty dlia maloimushchikh." *Kommersant*, February 17, 2021. https://www.kommersant.ru/doc/4693892.

Putin, Vladimir. "Poslanie Prezidenta Federal'nomu Sobraniiu." President of Russia, December 3, 2015. http://kremlin.ru/events/president/news/50864.

Putin, Vladimir, Nataliya Gevorkyan, Natalya Timakova, and Andrei Kolesnikov. *First Person: An Astonishingly Frank Self-Portrait by Russia's President Vladimir Putin*. New York: Public Affairs, 2000.

"Putin: West's Russia Sanctions Triggering Global Economic Crisis." *Al Jazeera*, May 12, 2022. https://www.aljazeera.com/economy/2022/5/12/putin-wests-russia-sanctions-triggering-global-economic-crisis.

Qian, Nancy, Andrei Markevich, and Natalya Naumenko. "The Political-Economic Causes of the Soviet Great Famine, 1932–33." National Bureau of Economic Research Working Paper 290189. Cambridge, MA: NBER, 2021.

Reidy, John. "Cargill, ADM Scale Back Operations in Russia | World Grain." World Grain, March 11, 2022. https://www.world-grain.com/articles/16613-cargill-scales-back-operations-in-russia.

Rimmel, Lesley A. "Another Kind of Fear: The Kirov Murder and the End of Bread Rationing in Leningrad." *Slavic Review* 56, no. 3 (1997): 481–99.

Rodin, Kirill. "Spetsifika vospriiatiia zhiteliami Rossii otechestvennykh i importnykh produktov pitaniia na fone ekonomicheskikh sanktsii." VTSIOM, 2021. https://wciom.ru/presentation/prezentacii/specifika-vosprijatija-zhiteljami-rossii-otechestvennykh-i-importnykh-produktov-pitanija-na-fone-ehkonomicheskikh-sankcii.

Rogozina, Anzhelina. " 'Chtoby tsena khleba vsegda v moikh rukakh byla'. Ekaterina II i formirovanie khlebozapasnoi sistemy v Rossii." *Vestnik arkhivista*, no. 1 (2020): 131–44.

Rosen, Kenneth. "Stoking Unrest and Distributing Groceries: Italy's Mafias Gain Ground in Fight for Loyalty during Pandemic Lockdown." *Newsweek*, April 18, 2020. https://www.newsweek.com/italy-mafias-coronavirus-pandemic-support-1498726.

Rosenfeld, Bryn. *The Autocratic Middle Class: How State Dependency Reduces the Demand for Democracy*. Princeton, NJ: Princeton University Press, 2020.

Rosenfeld, Bryn. "Reevaluating the Middle-Class Protest Paradigm: A Case-Control Study of Democratic Protest Coalitions in Russia." *American Political Science Review* 111, no. 4 (2017): 637–52.

"Rossiia dolzhna stat' krupnym igrokom na mirovom rynke prodovol'stviia." *DagPravda*, May 20, 2008. https://dagpravda.ru/politika/rossiya-dolzhna-stat-krupnym-igrokom-na-mirovom-rynke-prodovolstviya/.

"Rosstat soobshchil o roste tsen na produkty s nachala goda." *News.ru*, May 21, 2021. https://news.ru/economics/proizvoditeli-produktov-s-nachala-goda-podnyali-ceny-na-6-4/.

"Rost tsen v Rossii za mesiats voiny stal maksimal'nym s 1999 goda. Chto podorozhalo v marte?" *BBC News Russian Service*, April 8, 2022. https://www.bbc.com/russian/news-61045710.

Rothrock, Kevin. "'Vladimir the Poisoner': A Translation of Alexey Navalny's Speech in Court on February 2." *Meduza* (blog), February 2, 2021. https://meduza.io/en/feature/2021/02/02/vladimir-the-poisoner.

Rousseau, Jean-Jacques. *Of the Social Contract and Other Political Writings*. Edited by Christopher Bertram. London: Penguin, 2012.

"'Rusagro' i l'goty dlia kiprskikh offshorov." *Polit.Ru*, Accessed August 29, 2022. https://polit.ru/article/2021/04/05/rusagro/.

"Russia May Limit Seed Imports—Interfax." *Reuters*, August 5, 2022, sec. Commodities News. https://www.reuters.com/article/ukraine-crisis-russia-seeds-idUSKBN2PB1AC.

"Russia Raises Turkey's Tomato Import Quota to 300,000 Tons." *Hortidaily*, June 2, 2021. https://www.hortidaily.com/article/9326467/russia-raises-turkey-s-tomato-import-quota-to-300-000-tons/.

"Russia Sanctions Tracker." Ashurst. Accessed May 10, 2022. https://www.ashurst.com/en/news-and-insights/hubs/sanctions-tracker/.

"Russia to Ban Some Imports of Seeds from Europe and Canada." *Euronews*, August 12, 2022. https://www.euronews.com/next/2022/08/12/ukraine-crisis-russia-seeds.

"Russian Diplomat Says Moscow Prepared to Reject Renewal of Grain Export Deal." *Radio Free Europe/Radio Liberty*, October 13, 2022. https://www.rferl.org/a/russia-reject-grain-deal-ukraine/32081082.html.

"Russia's Car Manufacturing Collapses by 97% in May." *Moscow Times*, June 30, 2022, sec. news. https://www.themoscowtimes.com/2022/06/30/russias-car-manufacturing-collapses-by-97-in-may-a78151.

Rutskoi, Aleksandr. *Agrarnaia Reforma v Rossii*. Moscow: RAU-Korporatsiia, 1993.

Safonov, Georgiy, and Yulia Safonova. *Economic Analysis of the Impact of Climate Change on Agriculture in Russia*. Oxfam International, 2013.

Safronov, Evgeny, and Elene Vinogradova. "Gendirektor 'Rusagro' oproverg ot"ezd za granitsu sovladel'tsa kompanii Vadima Moshkovicha posle spora s Putinym." *Otkrytye media*, May 19, 2021. https://openmedia.io/news/n2/gendirektor-rusagro-oproverg-otezd-za-granicu-sovladelca-kompanii-vadima-moshkovicha-posle-spora-s-putinym/.

Sagdiev, Rinat. "Kak agrokholding ministra Tkacheva vybilsia v lidery rynka." *Vedomosti*, August 7, 2016. https://www.vedomosti.ru/business/articles/2016/08/08/652058-kak-agroholding-ministra-selskogo-hozyaistva-aleksandra-tkacheva-vibilsya-lideri-rinka.

Sagdiev, Rinat. "Rassledovanie 'Vedomostei': Biznes interesy Elena Skynnik." *Vedomosti*, November 28, 2012. https://www.vedomosti.ru/library/articles/2012/11/28/biznesinteresy_eleny_skrynnik.

Sapozhnikov, Andrei. "Ukraina eksportirovala 7.7 millionov tonn agroproduktsii v ramkakh 'zernovoi sdelki.'" *Kommersant*, October 16, 2022. https://www.kommersant.ru/doc/5619075.

Savchuk, Sergei. "Protiv Zapada u Rossii est' oruzhie namnogo strashnee raket." *RIA Novosti*. April 22, 2022. https://ria.ru/20220422/eda-1784835298.html.

Sazonov, Aleksandr. "Sladkaia zhizn'. Vadim Moshkovich." *Forbes Russia*, December 2, 2006. https://www.forbes.ru/forbes/issue/2006-12/16614-sladkaya-zhizn.

Schleuning, Neala. "Family Economics in Russia: Women's Perspectives on the Transition to a Market Economy." *Journal of Consumer Studies & Home Economics* 22, no. 1 (1998): 51–64.

Schoen, Douglas E. *Putin's Master Plan: To Destroy Europe, Divide NATO, and Restore Russian Power and Global Influence*. New York: Encounter Books, 2016.

"Schweiz stellt Geldwäscherei-Verfahren gegen Putin-Vertraute ein." *Blick*, August 5, 2017. https://www.blick.ch/schweiz/geldwaescherei-schweiz-stellt-geldwaescherei-verfahren-gegen-putin-vertraute-ein-id7100388.html.

Sedakov, Pavel, and Igor Popov. "Brat, svat i shtrafbat: kak ustroen biznes sem'i Aleksandra Tkacheva." *Forbes Russia*, August 10, 2015. https://www.forbes.ru/sobytiya/vlast/296467-brat-svat-i-shtrafbat-kak-ustroen-biznes-semi-aleksandra-tkacheva.

Sedik, David, Zvi Lerman, and Vasilii Uzun, "Agricultural Policy in Russia and WTO Accession." *Post-Soviet Affairs* 29, no. 6 (2013): 500–27.

Seleznev, Marat. "Talonnaia bednost'." *Lenta.ru*, May 12, 2017. https://lenta.ru/articles/2017/05/12/foodcard.

"Sel'skoe khoziaistvo." Personal site of Aleksei Gordeev, June 28, 2009. https://web.archive.org/web/20090628214512/http://gordeev.su:80/.

Semenov, Viktor. "Nuzhny li nam mezhregional'nye torgovye voiny?" *Rossiiskaia gazeta*, October 14, 1999.

Sen, Amartya. *Poverty and Famines: An Essay on Entitlement and Deprivation*. Oxford: Oxford University Press, 1982.

"Senatory obsudili realizatsiiu Federal'noi nauchno-technicheskoi programmy razvitiia sel'skogo khoziaistva." Federation Council of the Russian Federation, February 1, 2022. http://council.gov.ru/events/news/133020/.

Sergeev, Matvey. "Gendirektor Rusagro obzavelsia immunitetom." *Kommersant*, February 26, 2006. https://www.kommersant.ru/doc/652646.

Serova, Evgenia. Authors' Interview, January 29, 2021.

Shagaida, Natalya. "Agricultural Land Market in Russia: Living with Constraints." *Comparative Economic Studies* 47, no. 1 (2005): 127–40.

Shagaida, Natalya, and Vasilii Uzun. "Draivery rosta i strukturnykh sdvigov v sel'skom khoziaistve Rossii." Moscow, 2019. https://papers.ssrn.com/sol3/papers.cfm?abstract_id=3337794.

Shagaida, Natalya, and Vasilii Uzun. "Tendentsii razvitiia i osnovnye vyzovy agrarnogo sektora Rossii." RANKhiGS, 2017. https://papers.ssrn.com/sol3/papers.cfm?abstract_id=3090839.

Shamardina, Lada. "Putin nazval 'ne strashnym' ogranichenie pribyli biznesa iz-za kontrolia tsen." *The Bell*, March 11, 2021. https://thebell.io/putin-nazval-ne-strashnym-ogranichenie-pribyli-biznesa-iz-za-kontrolya-tsen.

Sharafutdinova, Gulnaz. *The Red Mirror: Putin's Leadership and Russia's Insecure Identity*. New York: Oxford University Press, 2020.

Sheremet, Pavel. "Kazak s partbiletami." *Kommersant*, November 29, 2000. https://www.kommersant.ru/doc/1544834.

Shestoperova, Iuliia. "Defitsita prodovol'stviia ne budet: Pravitel'stvo sozdast gruppu dlia monitoringa tsen na produkty." *MK.ru*, July 23, 2010. https://www.mk.ru/economics/article/2010/07/23/518641-defitsita-prodovolstviya-ne-budet.html.

Sikkink, Kathryn. *Developmentalism and Democracy: Ideas, Institutions, and Economic Policy-Making in Brazil and Argentina*. Ithaca, NY: Cornell University Press, 1991.

Sikorskaia, Mariia. "Kto teper' est pol'skie iabloki." *Novaya polsha*, July 11, 2019. https://novayapolsha.pl/article/kto-teper-est-polskie-yabloki/.

"Situation in Ukraine and in Russia." *Limagrain.com*. Accessed October 24, 2022. https://www.limagrain.com/en/situation-in-ukraine-and-in-russia.

Skrynnik, Irina. "'Miratorg' poluchit ot VEBa $425.8 mln na 15 let na proizvodstvo goviadiny." *Vedomosti*, January 27, 2015. https://www.vedomosti.ru/business/articles/2015/01/27/miratorg-poluchit-ot-veba-4258-mln-na-15-let-na-proizvodstvo.

Skrynnik, Irina. "Nastuplenie svinei: kak Miratorg zavoeval rossiiskii produktovyi rynok." *Forbes Russia*, October 16, 2014. https://www.forbes.ru/kompanii/potrebitelskii-rynok/270697-nastuplenie-svinei-kak-miratorg-zavoeval-rossiiskii-produktovyi.

Skrynnik, Irina. "V Rossii khotiat ukazanii: delaem raz, dva, tri." *Vedomosti*, July 20, 2015. https://www.vedomosti.ru/business/characters/2015/07/21/601427-v-rossii-hotyat-ukazanii-delaem-raz-dva-tri.

Slaughter, Anne-Marie, and Heather Ashby. "Countering Putin's Grand Strategy." *Project Sindicate* (blog), July 27, 2021. https://www.project-syndicate.org/commentary/biden-needs-strategy-to-counter-russia-by-anne-marie-slaughter-and-heather-ashby-2021-07.

Smith, Douglas. *The Russian Job: The Forgotten Story of How America Saved the Soviet Union from Famine*. New York: Farrar, Straus & Giroux, 2019.

Soffiantini, Giulia. "Food Insecurity and Political Instability during the Arab Spring." *Global Food Security* 26 (2020): 100400.

Solzhenitsyn, Aleksandr. *The Gulag Archipelago, 1918–56: An Experiment in Literary Investigation*. Vol. 3. New York: Harper & Row, 1974.

"Sovecon Raises Forecast for 2022 Russian Wheat Crop." *Reuters*, August 16, 2022, sec. Commodities. https://www.reuters.com/article/russia-grains-idUSKBN2PM0VS.

Standage, Tom. *An Edible History of Humanity*. New York: Bloomsbury, 2009.

"Starbucks, McDonald's Exit Russia as Ukraine War Rages On." *Time*. Accessed October 24, 2022. https://time.com/6180652/starbucks-mcdonalds-russia-ukraine/.

Starikov, Ivan. Authors' Interview, October 27, 2020.
Starostina, Iuliia, and Ivan Tkachev. "Rosstat otsenil mashtab snizhennia real'nykh raspologaemykh dokhodov rossiian." *RBC.ru*, January 28, 2021. https://www.rbc.ru/economics/28/01/2021/60129a749a7947cf1ca85d53.
Stent, Angela. *Putin's World: Russia against the West and with the Rest*. New York: Twelve, 2019.
"Stoit li Medvedev za Miratorgom." *Gde den'gi. Navalny LIVE*, April 19, 2019. https://www.youtube.com/watch?v=Zc1k0eMSUUI.
Stone, Norman. *The Eastern Front 1914–1917*. London: Penguin, 2008.
Strauss, Valerie. "Russia's Plagiarism Problem: Even Putin Has Done It!" *Washington Post*, March 18, 2014. https://www.washingtonpost.com/news/answer-sheet/wp/2014/03/18/russias-plagiarism-problem-even-putin-has-done-it/.
Streletskii, Roman. "Dmitry Medvedev ne spaset brat'ev Linnikov." *Kompromat*, February 19, 2021. https://compromat.group/main/economics/39768-dmitriy-medvedev-ne-spaset-bratev-linnikov.html.
Sukhorukova, Elena. "Glava Minsel'khoza zaiavil o skrytykh sanktsiakh na eksport prodovol'stviia." *RBC.ru*, October 3, 2022. https://www.rbc.ru/business/03/10/2022/6339675a9a794779a06116cd.
Sukhorukova, Elena. "Rossiia v 2020 godu pokazala rekord po postavkam prodovol'stviia za rubezh." *RBC.ru*, March 9, 2021. https://www.rbc.ru/business/09/03/2021/604217269a79471196c1131b.
Sulima, Mariia, and Sergei Grishunin. "Importzameshchenie ili peremeshchenie?" Natsional'noe Reitingovoe Agenstvo, December 2020. https://www.ra-national.ru/sites/default/files/Review_Import%20substitution_NRA_Dec.%202020_0.pdf.
Sutyrin, Sergey F. "Russia's Accession to the WTO: Major Commitments, Possible Implications." International Trade Centre, 2012. https://intracen.org/sites/default/files/uploadedFiles/Russia_WTO_Accession_English.pdf.
Suzman, James. *Work: A Deep History, from the Stone Age to the Age of Robots*. New York: Penguin, 2021.
Svolik, Milan W. *The Politics of Authoritarian Rule*. Cambridge: Cambridge University Press, 2012.
Swenson, Kyle. "Coronavirus Could Push 250,000 into Hunger in D.C. Region, Report Says." *Washington Post*. July 22, 2020. https://www.washingtonpost.com/local/social-issues/dc-coronavirus-hunger-report/2020/07/22/ad6f33b0-cad4-11ea-b0e3-d55bda07d66a_story.html.
"Syn voronezhskogo gubernatora Nikita Gordeev prodaet agroholding Okaagro Shtefanu Diurru." *Chetyre pera: Nezavisimyi obschestvenno-politicheskii portal Voronezha*, December 2017. http://4pera.com/news/picture_of_the_day/syn_voronezhskogo_gubernatora_nikita_gordeev_prodaet_agrokholding_okaagro_shtefanu_dyurru/.
Szakonyi, David. *Politics for Profit: Business, Elections, and Policymaking in Russia*. New York: Cambridge University Press, 2020.
Tadtaev, Georgii. "Genprokuratura nachala proverku rosta tsen na produkty." *RBC.ru*, December 11, 2020. https://www.rbc.ru/society/11/12/2020/5fd37d009a794742ef97893d.
"Talony i otavarka: kak Tyumentsy dobyvali propitanie v nachale 1990kh." *Tyumen Online*, October 3, 2020. https://72.ru/text/gorod/2020/10/03/69479411/.
"Talony na bednost' ili opravdanie 'Mira'?" *KPRF*, May 14, 2017. https://msk.kprf.ru/2017/05/14/27052/.

Taubman, William. *Gorbachev: His Life and Times*. New York: Simon & Schuster, 2017.
Taubman, William. *Khrushchev: The Man and His Era*. New York: W. W. Norton, 2003.
Taylor, Brian D. *The Code of Putinism*. New York: Oxford University Press, 2018.
Taylor, Brian D. *Politics and the Russian Army: Civil-Military Relations, 1689–2000*. Cambridge: Cambridge University Press, 2003.
Terazono, Emiko, Heba Saleh, and John Reed. "Countries Follow Consumers in Stockpiling Food." *Financial Times*, April 5, 2020. https://www.ft.com/content/5c8cbc60-aec0-4f3d-b0e2-a5e44f0c6f74.
"Tetra Pak to Leave Russia after 62 Years in Blow to Packaging Industry." *Reuters*, July 26, 2022, sec. Retail & Consumer. https://www.reuters.com/business/retail-consumer/tetra-pak-leave-russia-after-62-years-blow-packaging-industry-2022-07-26/.
Tharoor, Ishaan. "Why Putin Says Crimea Is Russia's 'Temple Mount.'" *Washington Post*, December 14, 2014. https://www.washingtonpost.com/news/worldviews/wp/2014/12/04/why-putin-says-crimea-is-russias-temple-mount/.
Thomson, Henry. "Food and Power: Agricultural Policy under Democracy and Dictatorship." *Comparative Politics* 49, no. 2 (2017): 273–96.
Thomson, Henry. *Food and Power: Regime Type, Agricultural Policy, and Political Stability*. New York: Cambridge University Press, 2019.
Titkov, Aleksei. "Kruche 'tsapkov' na Kubani tol'ko 'tkachi.'" *Osobaia bukva*, January 14, 2011. https://www.specletter.com/corruption/2011-01-14/kruche-tsapkov-na-kubani-tolko-tkachi.html.
Titov, Evgeny. "Tkachev. Krestnyi otets zemli Russkoi." *Novaya gazeta*, January 13, 2011. https://novayagazeta.ru/politics/7575.html.
"Tkachev, Aleksandr." *Lenta.ru*, December 9, 2004. https://lenta.ru/lib/14173927/full.
Tkachev, Ivan. "Kudrin-RBK: 'Neskol'ko sot milliardov mogli by snizit' bednost' vdvoe.'" *RBC.ru*, August 3, 2021. https://www.rbc.ru/economics/03/08/2021/610522849a7947d3e7f40be8.
"Top 10 Russian Most Expensive Landholders 2021." The Leibniz Institute of Agricultural Development in Transition Economies, March 8, 2021. https://www.largescaleagriculture.com/home/news-details/top-10-russian-most-expensive-landholders-2021/.
Trushin, Aleksandr. "Agrokholdingi—detishche nashei ekonomiki." *Kommersant*, October 31, 2016. https://www.kommersant.ru/doc/3127445.
"Tseny na produkty pitaniia v Rossii i ikh izmenenie za god, dannye na mai 2022 goda." AB Centre, June 15, 2022. https://ab-centre.ru/news/ceny-na-produkty-pitaniya-v-rossii-i-ih-izmenenie-za-god-dannye-na-may-2022-goda.
"Ubytki sakharnoi promyshlennosti ot fiksatsii tsen sostaviat okolo 10 milliardov rublei." *Sugar.ru*, April 1, 2021. https://sugar.ru/node/35171.
"UK sanctions target Russia's theft of Ukrainian grain, advanced military technology, and remaining revenue sources." GOV.UK, May 19, 2023. https://www.gov.uk/government/news/uk-sanctions-target-russias-theft-of-ukrainian-grain-advanced-military-technology-and-remaining-revenue-sources.
"Ukaz N391 Ob otdel'nykh spetsial'nykh ekonomicheskikh merakh v tseliakh obespecheniia bezopasnosti Rossiiskoi Federatsii." President of Russia, July 29, 2015. http://www.kremlin.ru/acts/bank/39975.
"Ukaz N560 O priminenii otdel'nykh spetsial'nykh ekonomicheskikh mer v tseliakh obespecheniia bezopasnosti Rossiiskoi Federatsii." President of Russia, August 6, 2014. http://www.kremlin.ru/acts/bank/38809.

"Ukaz Prezidenta Rossiiskoi Federatsii N120 Ob utverzhdenii Doktriny prodovol'stvennoi bezopasnosti Rossiiskoi Federatsii." President of Russia, Jaanuary 2010. http://kremlin.ru/acts/bank/30563.

"Ukaz Prezidenta Rossiiskoi Federatsii 'Ob utverzhdenii doktriny prodovol'stvennoi bezopasnosti Rossiiskoi Federatsii,'" January 30, 2010. https://rg.ru/2010/02/03/prod-dok.html.

"Ukraine Agricultural Production and Trade." US Department of Agriculture, April 2022. https://www.fas.usda.gov/sites/default/files/2022-04/Ukraine-Factsheet-April2022.pdf.

"Ukraine Grain Deal: Where Are the Ships Going?" *BBC News*, August 30, 2022, sec. Europe. https://www.bbc.com/news/world-europe-62717010.

"Ukraine's Crop Storage Infrastructure: Post-Invasion Impact Assessment." Conflict Observatory, September 15, 2022. https://hub.conflictobservatory.org/portal/sharing/rest/content/items/67cc4b8ff2124d3bbd5b8ec2bdaece4f/data.

Ulybkina, Svetlana. "Gosudarstvo ob"avilo zernovuiu interventsiiu v podderzhku sobstvennykh tovaroproizvoditelei." *Rossiiskaia gazeta*, September 11, 2001.

"UNICEF: Bolee 9 mln rossiian ekonomiat na ede i nedoedaiut." *BBC*, July 14, 2021. https://www.bbc.com/russian/news-57807139.

"Uzhe tri goda v rossii daviat i szhigaiut produkty." *TV Rain*, August 13, 2018. https://youtu.be/6ECA8RyMiQU.

Uzun, Vasilii. "Otsenka rezul'tatov yeltsinskoi agrarnoi reformy." *EKO*, 2013.

Uzun, Vasilii, and Dariia Loginova. "Rossiiskoe prodovol'stvennoe embargo: poteri zapadnykh stran nesushchestvenny." *Russian Economic Development* 23, no. 9 (2016): 17–23.

Uzun, Vasily, Natalya Shagaida, and Zvi Lerman. "Russian Agroholdings and Their Role in Agriculture." *Post-Communist Economies* 33, no. 8 (2021): 1035–55.

"V Sankt-Peterburge sroki 'zamorazhivaiushchikh' tseny soglashenii prodleny do marta." *Regnum.ru*, January 28, 2008. https://regnum.ru/news/economy/948853.html.

"Valdai Discussion Club Meeting." President of Russia, October 21, 2021. http://en.kremlin.ru/events/president/news/66975.

Van Atta, Don. "Russian Food Supplies in 1992." In *The "Farmer Threat": The Political Economy of Agrarian Reform in Post-Soviet Russia*, edited by Don Van Atta, 55–70. Boulder, CO: Westview Press, 1993.

Vavilov, Andrey. *The Russian Public Debt and Financial Meltdowns*. London: Palgrave Mcmillan, 2010.

Veninga, Willeke, and Rico Ihle. "Import Vulnerability in the Middle East: Effects of the Arab Spring on Egyptian Wheat Trade." *Food Security* 10, no. 1 (2018): 183–94.

Viola, Lynne. *Peasant Rebels under Stalin: Collectivization and the Culture of Peasant Resistance*. New York: Oxford University Press, 1999.

Vishniakov, Vladimir, and Elena Krasnolutskaia. "Prodovol'stvennaia bezopasnost'— Glavnaia zabota kommunistov." *Pravda*. June 6, 2008. https://kprf.ru/dep/57612.html.

Visser, Oane. "Insecure Land Rights, Obstacles to Family Farming, and the Weakness of Protest in Rural Russia." *Laboratorium* 2, no. 3 (2010): 275–95.

Visser, Oane, Natalia Mamonova, and Max Spoor. "Oligarchs, Megafarms and Land Reserves: Understanding Land Grabbing in Russia." *Journal of Peasant Studies* 39, no. 3–4 (2012): 899–931.

Volchkova, Natal'ia, and Polina Kuznetsova. "Skol'ko stoiat kontrsanktsii: Analiz blagosostoianiia." *Zhurnal Novoi Ekonomicheskoi Assotsiatsii* 43, no. 3 (2019): 173–83. https://doi.org/10.31737/2221-2264-2019-43-3-9.

Vorob'ev, Aleksandr. "Sel'khozaktivy Valinor Group pokupaet krasnodarskii 'Agrokompleks.'" *Vedomosti*, November 14, 2014. https://www.vedomosti.ru/business/articles/2014/11/14/agrokompleks-sobiraet-zemli.

Voronina, Anfisa. "'Vskryli neeffektivnost' i neorganizovannost'—Sergei Levin, general'nyi direktor Ob''edinennoi zernovoi kompanii." *Vedomosti*, April 2, 2010. https://www.top-personal.ru/pressissue.html?22335.

"V.V. Putin provel soveshchanie po voprosu povysheniia effektivnosti gosudarstvennoi agrarnoi politiki." Arkhiv saita Predsedatelia Pravitel'stva RF V.V. Putina, May 2008. http://archive.premier.gov.ru/visits/ru/6038/events/1382/.

"Vystuplenie A.V. Gordeeva na soveshchanii po voprosu povysheniia effektivnosti gosudarstvennoi agrarnoi politiki." *Agroyug*, May 19, 2008. https://www.agroyug.ru/page/item/_id-2358.

"Vystuplenie Zamestitelia Predsedatelia Pravitel'stva Rossiiskoi Federatsii—Ministra Sel'skogo Khoziaiistva Rossiiskoi Federatsii Gordeeva A.V. na zasedanii Pravitel'stva Rossiiskoi Federatsii 27 iulia 2000g." July 27, 2000. http://www.vasilievaa.narod.ru/gu/Konst_zak/PPr/Agrpol_01-10.htm.

Wallace, Jeremy. *Cities and Stability: Urbanization, Redistribution, and Regime Survival in China*. New York: Oxford University Press, 2014.

Wegren, Stephen K. *Agriculture and the State in Soviet and Post-Soviet Russia*. Pittsburgh: University of Pittsburgh Press, 1998.

Wegren, Stephen K. "Food Security and Russia's 2010 Drought." *Eurasian Geography and Economics* 52, no. 1 (2011): 140–56.

Wegren, Stephen K. "The Impact of WTO Accession on Russia's Agriculture." *Post-Soviet Affairs* 28, no. 3 (2012): 296–318.

Wegren, Stephen K. "Institutional Impact and Agricultural Change in Russia." *Journal of Eurasian Studies* 3, no. 2 (2012): 193–202.

Wegren, Stephen K. *Land Reform in Russia: Institutional Design and Behavioral Responses*. New Haven, CT: Yale University Press, 2009.

Wegren, Stephen K. "Observations on Russia's New Agricultural Land Legislation." *Eurasian Geography and Economics* 43, no. 8 (2002): 651–60.

Wegren, Stephen K. "Private Farming in Russia: An Emerging Success?" *Post-Soviet Affairs* 27, no. 3 (2011): 211–40.

Wegren, Stephen K. *Russia's Food Revolution: The Transformation of the Food System*. London: Routledge, 2020.

Wegren, Stephen K., and Frank A. Durgin. "The Political Economy of Private Farming in Russia." *Comparative Economic Studies* 39, no. 3 (1997): 1–24.

Wegren, Stephen K., and Christel Elvestad. "Russia's Food Self-Sufficiency and Food Security: An Assessment." *Post-Communist Economies* 30, no. 5 (2018): 565–87.

Wegren, Stephen K., Alexander M. Nikulin, and Irina Trotsuk. "Russian Agriculture during Putin's Fourth Term: A SWOT Analysis." *Post-Communist Economies* 31, no. 4 (2019): 419–50.

Wegren, Stephen K., Alexander M. Nikulin, and Irina Trotsuk. "The Russian Variant of Food Security." *Problems of Post-Communism* 64, no. 1 (2017): 47–62.

Welton, George. "The Impact of Russia's 2010 Grain Export Ban." *Oxfam Policy and Practice: Agriculture, Food and Land* 11, no. 5 (2011): 76–107.

Wengle, Susanne A. "The Domestic Effects of the Russian Food Embargo." *Demokratizatsiya: The Journal of Post-Soviet Democratization* 24, no. 3 (2016): 281–89.

Wengle, Susanne A. "Agroholdings, Technology, and the Political Economy of Russian Agriculture." *Laboratorium* 13, no. 1 (2021): 57–80.

Wengle, Susanne A. *Black Earth, White Bread: A Technopolitical History of Russian Agriculture and Food.* Madison: University of Wisconsin Press, 2022.

Wengle, Susanne A. "Local Effects of the New Land Rush: How Capital Inflows Transformed Rural Russia." *Governance* 31, no. 2 (2018): 259–77.

Wengle, Susanne A. "The New Plenty; Why Are Some Post-Soviet Farms Thriving?" *Governance* 33, no. 4 (2020): 915–33.

"Wheat Prices—40 Year Historical Chart." Accessed August 3, 2022. https://www.macrotrends.net/2534/wheat-prices-historical-chart-data.

White, Stephen. "Economic Performance and Communist Legitimacy." *World Politics: A Quarterly Journal of International Relations* 38, no. 3 (1986): 462–82.

Wolz, Axel, Svetlana Golovina, Jerker Nilsson, and Sebastian Hess. "Reviewing Changing Institutional Conditions for Private Farming in Russia." *Outlook on Agriculture* 45, no. 2 (2016): 111–16.

Wong, Edward, and Ana Swanson, "How Russia's War on Ukraine Is Worsening Global Starvation." *New York Times*, January 2, 2023. https://www.nytimes.com/2023/01/02/us/politics/russia-ukraine-food-crisis.html.

Woo-Cumings, Meredith. *The Developmental State.* Ithaca, NY: Cornell University Press, 2019.

World Bank. *Russian Federation: Agriculture Support Policies and Performance.* Washington, DC: World Bank, 2020.

World Food Programme. "War in Ukraine: WFP Calls for Ports to Reopen as World Faces Deepening Hunger Crisis." May 6, 2022. https://www.wfp.org/stories/war-ukraine-wfp-calls-ports-reopen-world-faces-deepening-hunger-crisis.

Yeginsu, Ceylan. "'It's Very Scary': U.K. Food Banks Close as Coronavirus Stalls Donations." *New York Times*, March 19, 2020. https://www.nytimes.com/2020/03/19/world/europe/coronavirus-uk-food-banks.html.

"Zasedanie Vysshego Evraziiskogo ekonomicheskogo soveta." President of Russia, May 21, 2021. http://www.kremlin.ru/events/president/news/65626.

"Zhirinovsky predlozhil sposob 'navesti poriadok' s tsenami na produkty." *Lenta.Ru*, December 17, 2020. https://lenta.ru/news/2020/12/17/poryadok/.

Zhukov, Iurii. "Zapiska Iu. Zhukova na imia A. Aleksandrova s prilozheniem podborki pisem." November 20, 1972. 80-1-331. RGANI.

Zhuravsky, Dmitry. "Nastiness Is a Warm Gun: The Kremlin's Cowboys." *The Russian Reader*, May 7, 2019. https://therussianreader.com/2019/05/07/miratorg/.

Zlobin, Andrei. "Pravitel'stvo prodlilo zamorozku tsen na sakhar i podsolenechnoe maslo." *Forbes*, March 30, 2021. https://www.forbes.ru/newsroom/biznes/424883-pravitelstvo-prodlilo-zamorozku-cen-na-sahar-i-podsolnechnoe-maslo.

Zlobin, Andrei. "Putin predlozhil podumat' nad produktovymi kartochksmi dlia bednykh." *Forbes*, February 17, 2021. https://www.forbes.ru/newsroom/obshchestvo/421393-putin-predlozhil-podumat-nad-produktovymi-kartochkami-dlya-bednyh.

Zlochevskii, Arkadii. Authors' Interview, October 16, 2020.

Zurayk, Rami. "Global Views of Local Food Systems: Civil War and the Devastation of Syria's Food System." *Journal of Agriculture, Food Systems, and Community Development* 3, no. 2 (2013): 7–9.

Index

For the benefit of digital users, indexed terms that span two pages (e.g., 52–53) may, on occasion, appear on only one of those pages.

adhocrat, view of Putin as, 162
Afghanistan, war in, 30–31
agrarian elites, 10–11, 118–19
Agrarian Party (AP), 54–55
agrarian reforms
    attempts at, 50–53
    crisis of 1998 and origins of rebound, 60–62
    failure of, 56–58
    overview, 49
    persistence of Soviet farms, 58–60
    political backlash against, 53–56
agriculture. *See also* agroholdings; USSR, political role of food in
    collapse during transition to market economy, 46–47
    collectivization policy, 23–24
    de-collectivization of farms, 51–52, 56
    economic drivers of recovery in, 64–67
    food production policies, 10–11
    Gordeev's role in boom, 67–70
    growth in self-sufficiency and exportation, 1, 3, 8
    impact of new approach to, 75–76
    instruments of state support, 79–81
    perestroika and, 33–34
    Putin's role in boom, 81–83
    return of state intervention, 70–73
    state capitalism and, 13–14
    Western machinery in, 151–52
Agrocomplex
    decline in grain exports after War in Ukraine, 153
    expansion into occupied Ukraine, 157–58
    general discussion, 120–23
    overview, 115

agroholdings. *See also* Agrocomplex
    agrarian elites, 10–11
    decline in grain exports after War in Ukraine, 153
    defined, 116
    emergence and dominance of, 116–20
    expansion into occupied Ukraine, 157–58
    Miratorg, 108, 116, 127–30, 153
    overview, 115–16
    Rusagro, 115–16, 123–27, 151–52
Allina-Pisano, Jessica, 57–58
Altynov, Aleksandr, 151
American Relief Administration (ARA), 22
animal feed, 76–79
Anti-Monopoly Agency (FAS), 148–49
AP (Agrarian Party), 54–55
Arab Spring, 161–62
Åslund, Anders, 52
Associated Press, 154
authoritarianism
    conflict theory of, 9–10
    nutritional independence and, 160–62
    outlook for the future, 165–67
    understanding Russia through food, 162–65
autocracy in Russia, 9–11, 160–62

Baerbock, Annalena, 155
bans
    on food imports, 98–99, 103–9
    on grain exports, 95–97, 148–49
bartering, 42–44
Bates, Robert H., 5
Beasley, David, 132–33
Bellin, Eva, 161–62

Belousov, Andrey, 140
Belov, Artiom, 93–94, 107–8
big business, support for, 118, 120
Black Sea Grain Initiative agreement, 154–57, 205n.44
Bloody Saturday in Novocherkassk. *See* Novocherkassk Massacre
Bolshevik Revolution, 6, 19–21
Bread and Democracy in Germany (Gerschenkron), 4
Brezhnev, food shortages during years of, 28–32
Budennyi Electric Locomotive Works (NEVZ), 26–28

Caldwell, Melissa, 61
Chernyaev, Anatolii, 30, 31, 33, 34–35
Chernyakov, Boris, 89–90
Chernyshev, Aleksei, 55–56
China, 9, 166–67
climate change, 166
code of Putinism, 83
coercion in food supply policies, 21–22, 23–24, 137–38, 139–40
collectivization policy, 23–24
command capitalism, 2, 11, 132, 144–46, 201n.64
Communist Party of the Russian Federation (KPRF), 86, 87–88, 143–44, 185n.14
Communist Revolution, 6, 19–21
competitive autocracy, 160–61
Conflict Observatory, 154
conflict theory of authoritarianism, 9–10
Cook, Linda J., 201n.64
cooperatives, persistence of Soviet farms as, 59
corn cultivation, 24–26
corruption scandals
 Moshkovich in, 47
 Patrushev in, 42–44
 Putin in, 42–44
 Skrynnik in, 81
Corteva Agriscience, 149–50
countersanctions
 after annexation of Crimea, 98–99
 choice of food import ban as, 103–5
 failure to meet goals, 112–13
 impact of, 105–8
 overview, 101–3
 public opinion of, 108–9
 2030 Strategy Draft, 111–12
countryside, reinvigoration of, 68–69
COVID-19 food crisis
 advent of command capitalism, 144–46
 economic impacts in Russia, 133–35
 food affordability crisis and, 15–16
 food and politics on screen, 140–42
 food certificates debate, 142–44
 government response, 135–40
 impact on food security, 3
 overview, 131–32
 return of food politics, 132–33
Crimea, annexation of, 98–99, 101–3, 111–13
crony capitalism, 130, 145

dachas, 45–46, 61
dairy industry
 goals in Food Security Doctrine, 94–95
 growth of, 66
 import bans and, 107–8
 2030 Strategy Draft, 111–12
Dankvert, Sergey, 128–29
Dear Comrades! (*Dorogie tovarishchi!*) (film), 140–42
debt negotiations, 40
de-collectivization of farms, 51–52, 56
Deere & Company, 151–52
deflation, 152
deregulation of prices, 39–40
devaluation of ruble, 60–62, 64–65, 88, 134, 185n.15
developmentalism, 207n.17
dictatorship, 160–61
Dimitrov, Martin K., 201n.64
Doctrines of Russian Federation, 85, 184n.3. *See also* Food Security Doctrine
domestic food market, prioritization of, 148–49, 152
Dorogie tovarishchi! (*Dear Comrades!*) (film), 140–42
drought, 60–61, 75–76, 95–97
Dürr, Stefan, 107–8
Dvorkovich, Arkady, 123

INDEX 237

Dzhikop, 42–44

early states, food in politics of, 3–6
economic crisis of 1998, 60–62, 64–65
economic drivers of agricultural recovery, 64–67
elites, agrarian, 10–11, 118–19
Eurasian Economic Union (EEU), 111
Europe
    bans on food imports from, 102, 103–5
    sanctions, 101–2, 147–48
    seed imports from, 149–50
exports
    bartering for food in 1990's, 42–44
    Black Sea Grain Initiative agreement, 154–57
    of grain, 1, 65–67, 153–54
    grain export bans, 95–97, 148–49
    during pandemic, 134
    2030 Strategy Draft, 112

famines, 6–7, 22, 23–24
FAS (Anti-Monopoly Agency), 148–49
Federal Agency for Food Market Regulation, 72
Federal Tax Service (FNS), 138
Filtzer, Donald, 24
financial support for agriculture, 79–80
fixed food prices, 29, 137–40
food affordability crisis
    food production policies, 10–11
    government response, 135–40
    rise in prices, 2, 131–32, 134–35, 140
    seeds of, 15–16
food availability during pandemic, 135
food certificates, 142–44
food in politics
    from early states to War in Ukraine, 3–6
    in Russia and USSR, 6–9
    security and, 12–15
    seeds of crisis in Russia, 15–16
    self-sufficiency and exportation, 1
    understanding Russia through, 9–12
food packaging, 150–51
food policy as domain of *siloviki*, 109–10
Food Program (1982), 32, 33
food security. *See also* Food Security Doctrine
    in China, 166–67

    defined, 3, 86–87
    idea of legislating, 86–87
    as national security issue, 12–15
    during pandemic, 132–33, 134–35
    threats to use grain as a weapon, 155–56
Food Security Doctrine
    ban on food imports, 98–99
    comparison of drafts, 90–95
    creation of, 14
    food imports in, 91
    initiative to create, 89–90
    meaning and impact, 93–94
    nutritional independence in, 90, 92, 94–95
    overview, 85–86
    pandemic and, 15–16
    road to, 86–89
    social dimensions of food in, 91–92
    2020 version, 111–13
    2010 drought and, 95–97
    WTO accession, 97–98
food shortages
    during Brezhnev years, 28–32
    demise of USSR and, 37–41
    during Gorbachev years, 32–35
    individual responses to, 45–46
    during Khrushchev years, 26–28
    during Lenin years, 19–22
    1917 revolution and, 6–7, 19–21
    during pandemic, 132–33
    Putin's experience with, 13
    regional responses to, 41–45
    during Stalin years, 23–24
Food Supply Army, 21–22
food supply dictatorship, 21–22

Gaidar, Yegor
    agrarian reform program, 50
    debt negotiations, 40
    memories of food shortages, 37, 38
    Putin's export corruption scandal, 42
    shock therapy market reforms, 36–37, 39, 49
    subsidy reform, 53
garden plots, 45–46, 61
Gel'man, Vladimir, 79
Gerschenkron, Alexander, 4, 160–61
global problem of Russian and Ukrainian grain, 154–57

Global South
  grain war and, 155–56
  political role of food in, 5
Gorbachev, Mikhail
  Food Program, 32, 33
  food shortages during years of, 32–35
Gordeev, Aleksei
  Food Security Doctrine, 87–88, 90
  need for domestic production, 13, 63, 88–89
  role in grain boom, 67–70
  success of, 82–83
  support for agroholdings, 118, 119
Gracchus, Gaius, 4
grain
  Black Sea Grain Initiative agreement, 154–57
  crisis of 1998, 60–62
  decline in output in 1990s, 46
  early states and, 4
  economic drivers of recovery in, 64–67
  embargo on USSR, 31–32
  exports from Russia, 1, 8, 65–67, 153–54
  goals in Food Security Doctrine, 94–95
  Gordeev's role in boom, 67–70
  impact of 2010 drought on, 95–97
  impact of new approach to, 75–76
  imports by USSR, 24–25, 28, 30–31
  imports during 1990's, 40, 47
  infrastructure for, 74–75
  instruments of state support, 79–81
  liberalization of market, 53
  Putin's role in boom, 81–83
  return of state intervention, 70–73
  seed imports, 149–50
  shortages in USSR, 37–41
  state capitalism and, 13–14
  stolen after Ukraine invasion, 2, 154
  United Grain Company, 74–75
  Virgin Lands program, 25
  as weapon, 2, 154, 155–56
grain interventions, 71–73
grain war, 155–56
Great Grain Robbery, 30
Great Recession of 2007–2009, 88, 185n.15
Gustafson, Thane, 166

Hedberg, Masha, 104
Hitler, Adolf, 4, 7

humanitarian aid, 22, 40, 62

imports
  ban on food imports, 98–99, 103–9
  in Food Security Doctrine, 91
  Gordeev's criticism of need for, 88–89
  seeds, 149–50
  during transition to market economy, 40, 47
  by USSR, 28, 30–31
import substitution policies
  authoritarian regimes and, 160–62
  countersanctions, 103–9
  developmentalism, 207n.17
  seed imports, 149–50
  2030 Strategy Draft, 111–12
incomes, impact of pandemic on, 134
individual responses to shortages in 1990s, 45–46
instruments of state support for agriculture, 79–81
insurance, shipping, 153–54
Ioffe, Genrikh, 40–41
Italy, 103, 105, 107–8
Iushin, Sergei, 60, 80, 93–94, 117

John Deere Financial, 151–52

Khrushchev, food shortages during years of, 24–28
Kirov, Sergei, 23–24
Kissinger, Henry, 5
Konchalovsky, Andrei, 141
Koniaev, Nikolai, 40–41
KPRF (Communist Party of the Russian Federation), 86, 87–88, 143–44, 185n.14
Kristall sugar factory, 122
Kudrin, Aleksei, 138–39, 144
Kuznetsova, Polina, 106–7

Land Code, 65
Law on Turnover of Agricultural Land, 65
Lazzarini, Sergio, 13–14
Lenin, food shortages during years of, 6, 19–22
Lerman, Zvi, 116–17
Levada Center, 135, 143
Levin, Sergey, 74–75

liberalization of prices, 39–40
Liefert, Olga, 77
Liefert, William M., 77
Limagrain, 149–50
Linnik, Aleksandr, 116, 127–30
Linnik, Viktor, 108, 116, 127–30
Litvinov, Maxim, 22
loans, agricultural, 79–80, 122–23, 129
Lut, Oksana, 150

machinery, Western, 151–52
market economy, transition to
    debt negotiations, 40
    deregulation of prices, 39–40
    effects on agriculture, 46–47
    food shortages at beginning of, 37–41
    Gordeev's criticism of agricultural policies during, 68–70
    grain imports, 40, 47
    individual responses to shortages, 45–46
    overview, 36–37
    regional responses to shortages, 41–45
meat industry
    agroholdings, 116–17, 119
    drop in consumption in 1990's, 45
    goals in Food Security Doctrine, 94–95
    growth of, 66
    impact of WTO accession, 97–98
    import bans and, 103, 106
    Miratorg, 127–30
    shortages in USSR, 30
    state intervention in, 76–79
    2030 Strategy Draft, 111–12
Medvedev, Dmitry
    Food Security Doctrine, 14, 85, 90, 93–94
    "On the Strategy of National Security of the Russian Federation through or to 2020," 186n.26
    threats to use food as a weapon, 2, 155
Medvedev, Zhores, 58
Mel'nikov, Ivan, 143
Miller, Chris, 61
mini farms, 45–46
Miratorg, 108, 116, 127–30, 153
Mishustin, Mikhail, 137–38, 139–40
Moore, Barrington, 4, 160–61
Moshkovich, Vadim, 115–16, 123–27, 138

Mugabe, Robert, 5
Mulder, Nicholas, 103
Musacchio, Aldo, 13–14

Nabiullina, Elvira, 138–39
Napoleon, 4
National Mercantile Exchange (NAMEX), 72–73
National Rating Agency report, 112
national security, food supply and, 68, 163–64, 166
natural resources, bartering for food, 42–44
Navalny, Aleksei, 131, 135–36
Nazism, rise of, 4
Nechaev, Andrey, 39–40, 41, 51–52
Neduzhko, Andrey, 151
Nelson, Scott, 166
NEVZ (Budennyi Electric Locomotive Works), 26–28
New Economic Policy (NEP), 7, 22
Nikulin, Alexander M., 110
1917 revolution, 6, 19–21
1998 financial crisis, 60–62, 64–65
Novocherkassk Massacre
    discussion of, 26–28
    film about, 140–42
    overview, 7, 24–25
nutritional independence
    authoritarian regimes and, 160–62
    ban on food imports, 103–9
    countersanctions, 101–3
    failure to meet goals, 112–13
    food policy as domain of *siloviki*, 109–10
    in Food Security Doctrine, 86–88, 90, 91, 92, 94–95
    in Food Security Doctrine 2020, 111–13
    outlook for the future, 165–67
    overview, 79
    regime stability and, 99
    2030 Strategy Draft, 111–12
    understanding Russia through food, 162–65
    vulnerabilities in, 149–52
    WTO accession and, 97–98

Ocheretnaya, Putina, 37
October Revolution, 6, 19–21

240 INDEX

Ogloblina, Yulia, 143
oil prices, decline in, 106, 134
"On the Development of Agriculture" law of 2006, 77, 78
"On the Liberalization of Grain Market in Russia," 53, 70–71
"On the Procedure for Establishing Norms for the Free Transfer of Land Plots to Citizens," 51–52
"On the Strategy of National Security of the Russian Federation through or to 2020," 186n.26
open market, rise of. *See* market economy, transition to
overproduction of grain, 71–73, 75
Oxfam, 132–33

packaging for food, 150–51
panic buying, 148
Patrushev, Dmitry, 14–15, 109–10, 153–54, 158–59
Patrushev, Nikolai, 14–15, 109
PBS (Public Broadcasting Service), 154
perestroika, 7–8, 33–34
Podberezkin, Aleksei, 51
Poland, 105
political role of food. *See* food in politics
popular mobilization. *See* protests
prices of food. *See also* food affordability crisis
    after invasion of Ukraine, 148–49
    deflation, 152
    fixed, 29, 137–40
    government response during pandemic, 135–40
    impact of 2010 drought on, 95–97
    impact of Great Recession on, 88
    impact of pandemic on, 131–32, 134–35, 140
    imported, 68
    price caps, 2, 16, 137–39, 140
    protests linked to, 5–6
    during transition to market economy, 40–41
private farming
    attempts to reform agriculture, 50–53
    failure of reforms, 56–58
    overview, 49

    persistence of Soviet farms, 58–60
    political backlash against, 53–56
procurement interventions, 71–73
Prokopenko, Aleksandra, 153
Prosecutor General investigations, 137–38
protests. *See also* Novocherkassk Massacre
    in 2020–2021, 135
    demise of USSR, 35
    lack of, 15, 41
    1917 revolution, 19–21
Public Broadcasting Service (PBS), 154
Putin, Vladimir
    annexation of Crimea, 98–99, 101
    ban on food imports, 103–9
    crisis of 1998 and, 62
    export scandal in St. Petersburg, 42–44
    grain export bans, 95–97
    opposing perspectives on, 83, 162
    personal experience with food shortages, 13
    policies in food production, 10–11
    prioritization of domestic food market, 149
    reaction to impact of Great Recession, 88–89
    rejection of food certificates, 144
    response to rising prices during pandemic, 135–37
    role in grain boom, 81–83
    thanking adversaries for sanctions, 1
    transition to dictatorship, 160–61

rationing, 31, 32, 34–35
regime stability, importance of food for, 82–83, 93–94, 137–41, 162
regional responses to shortages in 1990s, 41–45
Revolution of Dignity, Ukraine, 98–99, 101
RIA Novosti, 2
Romanov Empire, downfall of, 6, 19–21
Rome, grain distribution in, 4
Rosagroleasing Company, 13–14, 80, 81
Rousseau, Jean-Jacques, 4
ruble, devaluation of, 60–62, 64–65, 88, 134, 185n.15
Rusagro, 115–16, 123–27, 151–52

Russian Agricultural Bank
  (*Rosselkhozbank*), 13–14, 70, 80, 126
"Russia's Food Supply: Problems
  and Solutions' Mechanisms"
  (Gordeev), 68
*Russia's Food Supply: Problems of Theory
  and Practice* (Gordeev), 68
Rutskoi, Aleksandr, 50–52, 54
Rylko, Dmitry, 119–20
Ryzhkov, Nikolay, 34

Sal'ye commission, 43–44
sanctions
  after invasion of Ukraine, 147–52
  countersanctions, 101–3
  food import ban as response to, 98–99,
    102, 103–9
  food policy as domain of
    siloviki, 109–10
  Food Security Doctrine 2020, 111–13
  grain embargo on USSR, 31–32
  limited effectiveness of, 103
  overview, 7, 101
  Putin's thanking nations for, 1
Sberbank, 125, 126
SBS Agro Bank, 79–80
Scott, James, 4
seed imports, 149–50
self-sufficiency in agriculture
  authoritarian regimes and, 160–62
  food affordability crisis linked to, 15–16
  food security and, 86–87
  Food Security Doctrine, 14, 91, 94–95
  growth in, 1, 3, 8
  as national security issue, 13
  outlook for the future, 165–67
  overview, 10–11
  pandemic predictions, 133
  understanding Russia through
    food, 162–65
Seliunin, Vasilii, 176n.19
Sen, Amartya, 5, 47–48
Serova, Evgenia, 55, 64–65, 86–87
Shagaida, Natalya, 116–17
shipping companies, 153–54
shock therapy market reforms, 36–
  37, 39, 49
siloviki, food policy as domain of, 109–10

Skynnik, Elena, 81
Skynnik, Elena, 93
smuggling of Ukrainian grain, 154
Sobchak, Anatoly, 27–28
Sobyanin, Sergey, 103
social contract, 29, 35, 201n.64
social mobilizations. *See* protests
*Social Origins of Dictatorship and
  Democracy* (Moore), 4, 160–61
social problems in agriculture, 57, 59
Society and Democracy in Germany
  (Gerschenkron), 160–61
Solnechnye Produkty, 126
Solzhenitsyn, Aleksandr, 27
sovereign democracy, 82–83
Stalin, food shortages during years of,
  7, 23–24
Starikov, Ivan, 51–52
state agricultural policy, 78
state capitalism, 13–14, 84, 145
state intervention in agriculture
  attempts to reform, 50–53
  collectivization policy, 23–24
  grain export bans, 95–97
  instruments of state support, 79–81
  livestock sector, 76–79
  during pandemic, 132, 135–40
  return to in 2000's, 70–73
storage of grain, 73, 74–75
St. Petersburg, Russia, 41, 42–44
"Strategy for the Development of the Food
  and Food Processing Industry of the
  Russian Federation until 2020," 94
subsidies
  Agrocomplex and, 123
  during Brezhnev's reign, 29–30
  Miratorg and, 129
  persistence of Soviet farms, 58–59
  reform of Soviet-era, 53
  Rusagro and, 126
subsidized loans, 80, 122–23, 129
subsistence agriculture, 45–46
suburban garden plots, 45–46
Sutyrin, Sergey F., 97–98

Taubman, William, 26
Taylor, Brian, 83, 163
Tetra Pak, 150–51

Thomson, Henry, 9–10
Tkachev, Aleksandr, 109, 115, 120–23
Trotsky, Leon, 21–22
Trotsuk, Irina, 110
Turkey, 154–55, 188n.3
2007–2009 Great Recession, 88
2010 drought, 95–97
2020 Food Security Doctrine, 111–13
2030 Strategy Draft, 111–12, 114

Ukraine, War in. *See* War in Ukraine
United Grain Company (UGC), 72, 74–75, 153
United States
 American Relief Administration, 22
 exports of grain to USSR, 28, 30–31
 food relief in 1998, 62
 Food Security Act, 89–90
 grain embargo on USSR, 31–32
 Jackson-Vanik amendment to Trade Act, 97
urban bias, 5, 9–10
Ushachev, Ivan, 90
Usmanov, Alisher, 141
USSR, political role of food in
 during Brezhnev years, 28–32
 during Gorbachev years, 32–35
 during Khrushchev years, 24–28
 during Lenin years, 19–22
 meat production in, 77
 1917 revolution, 23–24
 overview, 6–9
 during Stalin years, 23–24
 urban bias in, 10
Uzun, Vasily, 116–17

Valdai Discussion Club, 1
Virgin Lands program, 25

Volchkova, Natal'ia, 106–7
Volodin, Vyacheslav, 166

Wallace, Jeremy, 9
War Communism, 21–22
war crimes, 154
War in Ukraine (2022)
 agroholdings expansion into Ukraine, 157–58
 Black Sea Grain Initiative agreement, 154–57
 domestic food market and, 152
 grain exports and, 153–54
 grain stolen after, 2, 154
 impact on Russian food market, 148–52
 overview, 3–6, 147
 sanctions, 147–48, 153
 seed imports after, 149–50
weapon, food as, 2, 154, 155–56
Wegren, Stephen K., 33, 51–52, 110
Wengle, Susanne, 99, 118
Western agricultural machinery, 151–52
wheat. *See* grain
World Trade Organization (WTO), 91, 97–98, 111
World War I, 19–21
World War II, 7, 24

Yeltsin, Boris. *See also* agrarian reforms
 deregulation of prices, 39–40
 "On the Liberalization of Grain Market in Russia," 53, 70–71
 praise for food policies, 54
 surprise at seeing U.S. grocery stores, 34

Zhirinovsky, Vladimir, 138, 143
Zhukov, Iurii, 29
Zlochevskii, Arkadii, 60, 62, 69, 82